D1600974

America's Weather Warriors

America's

Weather Warriors

1814-1985

CHARLES C. BATES

and

JOHN F. FULLER

Texas A&M University Press
COLLEGE STATION

Copyright © 1986 by Charles C. Bates and John F. Fuller

Library of Congress Cataloging-in-Publication Data
Bates, Charles C. (Charles Carpenter), 1918–
 America's weather warriors, 1814–1985.

 Bibliography: p.
 Includes index.
 1. Meteorology, Military—United States—History—
19th century. 2. Meteorology, Military—United States—
History—20th century. I. Fuller, John F. (John
Frederick), 1935– II. Title.
UG467.B38 1986 355.34'32 85–40746
ISBN 0-89096-240-5

Manufactured in the United States of America
First edition

Contents

Illustrations

WC-130
WB-47E
WB-57F
WC-135B
Sgt. Alice Hill
Sgt. Vickiann Esposito
Vice Adm. A. D. Struble and AGC Joseph Zaffino
Col. William S. Barney
Sgt. Michael Connell, Vietnam, 1968
Capt. Thomas E. Taylor and T. Sgt. Robert L. Smith
Col. John W. Collens III and Col. Edwin E. Carmell
DMSP readout site VI, Tan Son Nhut, Vietnam
General Lavelle with Brigadier General Best and Colonel Newhouse
Commando weathermen in training, 1964
Naval Oceanography Command detachment, USS *New Jersey*
Capt. Donald G. Buchanan
Command Master Chief Amos R. Fields
Brig. Gen. Albert J. Kaehn
Brig. Gen. George E. Chapman
Navy environmental facilities, Monterrey, California

FIGURES

MAPS

$\mathcal{T}_{ables}$

Foreword

Nearly a half century ago I was serving as supply officer of the 4th Observation Squadron based at Luke Field, Hawaii. This was the height of the depression, and we could fly only four hours per month; I was thoroughly bored. Then I noticed on the bulletin board that volunteers were being sought for "meteorology school." Someone behind me muttered, "It has something to do with weather." It sounded far better than counting pillows and bed sheets. So I signed up. When the time came in 1937 to attend the "met course" at the California Institute of Technology, it was, for me, the beginning of two decades in military meteorology—and a period of which I enjoyed every minute.

My weather tours provided repeated opportunities to use a blend of technical and flying skills. It proved possible to work with some of the greatest meteorologists ever, including Jacob Bjerknes. I had the good fortune to serve as staff weather officer to the famed General of the Army Omar N. Bradley and, indirectly, to the even more famous General of the Army Douglas MacArthur during some interesting and very turbulent times.

World War II brought a veritable explosion in the military usefulness of meteorology. The basis for much of this was a unique university training program for new weather officers fostered and implemented by such farseeing professors as Carl-Gustav Rossby, Horace R. Byers, Henry G. Houghton, Joseph Kaplan, Sverre Petterssen, Athelstan F. Spilhaus, and their associates. Of equal importance were the money and resources made available as the nation's leaders and scientists rose to the challenge of global war. Military meteorology went on to play a major role in winning World War II while advancing the basic science and its applicability. Luckily, the wartime impetus carried over into peacetime. Much of the fine new talent fostered by this war effort went on to dominate the U.S. meteorological profession, which has made huge strides in the better use of weather knowledge for mankind as a whole.

How this took place has gone largely unheralded. In fact, most members of the learned callings, including earth scientists, are oblivious to the role military meteorology played—and still plays—in our technological society. Similarly, although most military commanders are aware of the importance of good weather advice in the planning and execution of strategic and tactical warfare, most military histories skip far too quickly over the weather factor. To be sure, air force practice called for weather units to prepare unit histories from time to time. But these manuscripts, though useful, tend to be mere chronicles of dry facts and organizational changes.

During mid-1982, this gap in the literature was discussed during a luncheon I hosted in honor of octagenarian Col. Arthur F. Merewether, dean of the Air Weather Service. "Merry" had been the service's second chief (1940–42), as well as the twentieth president of the American Meteorological Society (1954–55). Two other longtime military weathermen were present, Cols. Richard Gill and Robert Bundgaard, as well as one of my military oceanographers from the Normandy invasion—Lt. Col. Charles C. Bates. We decried the lack of any comprehensive account of military meteorology and wondered what could be done.

The loudest griper was the junior officer present. So I challenged Bates to take corrective action. As a good soldier, he did so. For reinforcement, he obtained the off-hours services of the graduate historian and jet fighter jockey, Capt. John F. Fuller, the present historian of the Air Weather Service. The team of Bates and Fuller proved to be a good one. As the senior member, Bates served with seven different U.S. weather squadrons, as well as the British navy, in major combat theaters of World War II. Fuller, as a member of the post–World War II generation, supplemented and complemented Bates's experiences by providing insights and data sources derived from his work on Air Weather Service history during the past eighteen years.

While perusing their account of military meteorology, I was repeatedly struck by the way weather brought about or nullified military victory, and by the bravery and skill of meteorologists in uniform. The names of note are many—Matthew F. Maury, the founder of modern oceanography; Albert James Myer, the creator of the army weather service; Adolphus W. Greely, recipient of the congressional Medal of Honor at the age of ninety; Robert A. Millikan, the first American to win the Nobel Prize; Francis W. Reichelderfer, who directed both the national civilian and naval weather services; Robert M. Losey, the first U.S. officer killed by enemy action during World War II; and Richard E. Ellsworth, Jr., who built up America's largest weather squadron, only to crash fatally a few years later while leading a low-level practice bomber attack intentionally through foul weather over Newfoundland. Of equally gripping interest were the weather factors involved in a multitude of air, sea, and ground battles extending from the trench warfare of World War I to the battles of World War II, Korea, and Vietnam—and even in the aborted Iranian hostage rescue attempt of 1980.

This book fills an important gap in the literature. I endorse it enthusiastically not only to those interested in an unusual aspect of science but also to military commanders at all levels who wish to use weather as an ally rather than to face it as a foe.

THOMAS S. MOORMAN
Lt. General, USAF (Retired)

P*reface*

History is replete with entries chronicling weather's capricious effects on war, warriors, and weapons. Some of the most famous generals—Hannibal, Genghis Khan, and Eisenhower, for example—used a basic knowledge of weather and climate to attain major victories. Other leaders, such as Xerxes of Persia, Kublai Khan, and Philip II of Spain, had supposedly invincible armadas wrecked by unforeseen storms. Because weather can truly be a life-or-death matter on the field of battle, meteorologists have repeatedly been asked to contribute their skills to the art of warfare.

This holds true particularly in the United States, where separate meteorological observation networks were created by the army and the navy over 125 years ago. After the Civil War, the Army Signal Service built and operated the nation's first full-fledged weather service, which led to the formation of the civilian U.S. Weather Bureau in 1891. Military meteorology reappeared during World War I but between world wars dwindled to a residual level. As a consequence of World War II the U.S. Army and Navy, with the aid of allied military forces, created a world weather network of the first order. Then followed two regional wars fraught with meteorological considerations and change, both technical and social. As a result, since 1940 twenty-five of the successive thirty-four presidents of the American Meteorological Society have served in the military sometime during their professional careers. On the other hand, the saga of the intertwining of a major science with the military arts is poorly documented in a world overflowing with books. A search of library holdings reveals a dearth of literature filed under the category "meteorology—military." To be sure, there is a sizable "gray" literature developed by historians and specialists of the several military services, as well as a number of informative graduate theses. But none are readily available to the reading public, and no author ever before pieced together the complete story of the weather warriors.

To remedy that lack, the authors prepared this overview of meteorologists in uniform. Our story ranges over 170 years, five armed services, four major wars, and the intricate interaction among the civil and military weather services, the U.S. Congress, and the meteorological services of friendly powers. The account is personalized and stresses human interplay, for technical literature already documents the scientific advances made to date. To provide extra information on the human side, we have used copious notes. Thus, certain readers may prefer to read the main theme of the book straight through and then turn back to scan the supplementary information. Moreover, to keep the book to a marketable size, we exercised much judgment about what should—and should not—be covered and in how much detail. Unfortunately certain omissions took place during this streamlining process. On that score we apologize, as we do for any factual errors that may have crept in. But we believe the basic goal has been met— the assembly of an account delineating what a unique aspect of applied science has meant to our nation over nearly two centuries.

Acknowledgments

First and foremost, this book is dedicated to our immediate loved ones, Pauline Bates and the Fuller siblings—Judy and Howard—for their willingness to tolerate the toil and turmoil that book preparation injects into family affairs.

Many helped with personal interviews and provided extensive material from personal or official files. These persons included Col. Robert C. Bundgaard, Col. George E. Chapman, Capt. William D. Duthie, Rear Adm. Sir John Fleming, Dr. Robert D. Fletcher, Col. Richard M. Gill, Capt. George J. Haltiner, Comdr. Donald E. Hinsman, Capt. Willard S. Houston, Jr., Capt. Ronald E. Hughes, Comdr. C. B. Ihli, Capt. William W. Kellogg, Col. Arthur F. Merewether, Professor Walter H. Munk, Capt. Harry E. Nicholson, Maj. Norman A. Riley, Maj. Samuel B. Solot, Comdr. Zemo Tarnowski, and Lt. Warren C. Thompson.

Valuable documentation—file material, photographs, obscure articles, and personal recollections—was kindly provided by the following: AGC Richard D. Ackerman, Maj. Robert M. Allan, Jr., Frances D. Ashley, Lt. Col. James Beck, Neil H. Benfer, CWO Ray Boylan, Maj. Reid A. Bryson, Professor Horace R. Byers, Lt. Robert D. Case, John H. Conover, Lt. Comdr. Walter J. Cook, Capt. George P. Cressman, Howard F. Crombie, Capt. Arthur A. Cumberledge, Anne Roan Drummond, AGCM Amos R. Fields, Lt. Comdr. R. J. Fitzsimmons, Capt. John P. Fleet, Col. Joseph O. Fletcher, Capt. William J. Francis, Comdr. Thomas V. Fredian, Maj. Lester Gaynor, Capt. J. Leon Gilchrist, Col. Alexander R. Gordon, Capt. Lawrence Grabham, Lt. Col. Henry H. Harrison, William E. Hart, Capt. Katherine J. Hinman, Lt. Comdr. Lawrence Hogben, Jack M. Hubbard, Patrick Hughes, David S. Johnson, Capt. Virgil J. Johnson, Col. Oliver K. Jones, Capt. J. E. Koehr, Rear Adm. William J. Kotsch, Peter E. Kraght, Lt. Col. Irving P. Krick, Professor Helmut E. Landsberg, Maj. Dale F. Leipper, Margaret A. Le Mone, Capt. Gilbert MacDougall, Dr. Patrick D.

McTaggart-Cowan, Dr. Jerome Namias, Professor Harold D. Orville and Professor Richard E. Orville, AGCM Ronald W. Palmer, Henry Rado, Capt. Daniel Rex, Lt. Comdr. Peter H. Ranelli, Capt. Johnnie M. Sears, Dr. Joanne Simpson, Saul Singer, Comdr. Margaret C. Smith, Dr. Athelstan F. Spilhaus, YCM Johnnie Stephens, Prof. Aylmer H. Thompson, Comdr. Florence W. van Straten, Maj. John E. Wallace, Frances L. Whedon, Capt. Robert M. White, Comdr. James W. Winchester, Capt. Paul M. Wolff, Comdr. Francis R. Wooldridge, and Lt. Gen. Donald N. Yates.

In addition to providing extensive background material, several persons reviewed parts of the text to ensure accuracy: Comdr. Roswell F. Barratt, Dr. Albert P. Crary, Charles W. Dickens, Col. Dale J. Flinders, William A. Jenner, Maj. Archie M. Kahan, Brig. Gen. Leo A. Kiley, Rear Adm. Denys W. Knoll, Capt. Wilbert M. Lockhart, Lt. Col. David M. Ludlum, Comdr. Frederick K. Martin, Lt. Gen. Thomas S. Moorman, the late Comdr. Francis W. Reichelderfer, Capt. Richard C. Steere, Rear Adm. Hubert E. Strange, Col. Philip D. Thompson, Capt. Connelly R. Ward, AGC Joseph Zaffino, and Col. Leonard E. Zapinski.

Several historians and archivists have been most accommodating: D. C. Allard and Stanley Kalkus (Naval Historical Center), Dr. Jo Anna Kessler (History of Aviation Collection, University of Texas at Dallas), Alison Kerr (Los Alamos National Laboratory), Ruth P. Liebowitz (Air Force Geophysics Laboratory), Elaine M. Pospishil (U.S. Army Communications Command), Charles A. Ravenstein (Albert F. Simpson Historical Research Center, U.S. Air Force), Rebecca Robbins and Paul J. Scheips (U.S. Army Center of Military History), William B. Strong, Jr. (U.S. Army Communications— Electronics Command and Fort Monmouth), Peter Suthard (National Air and Space Museum), and Grover Walker (Naval Air Museum).

We are particularly grateful to the following copyright holders for permission to quote excerpts, which are also appropriately referenced in the text: Col. Jacksel M. Broughton, USAF (Ret.), for quotes from his *Thud Ridge*, 1969; Doubleday—*Crusade in Europe*, by Dwight D. Eisenhower, 1948; *Mission with LeMay: My Story*, by Curtis LeMay and MacKinlay Kantor, 1965; and *A Soldier Reports*, by William C. Westmoreland, 1976; Harcourt Brace Jovanovich, Inc.—*Operation Deepfreeze*, by George J. Dufek, 1957; Harper & Row, Publishers, Inc.—*Global Mission*, by Henry H. Arnold, 1949; Holt, Rinehart and Winston—*A Rumor of War*, by Philip Caputo, 1977; Houghton Mifflin Company—*Hinge of Fate*, 1950, and *Closing the Ring*, 1951 (volumes 4 and 5 of *The Second World War*) by Winston S. Churchill, and *The Patton Papers* by Martin Blumenson, 1974; Little, Brown and Company—*Prime Time, The Life of Edward R. Murrow*, by Alexander Kendrick, and *American Caesar: Douglas MacArthur, 1880– 1964*, by William Manchester, 1978; Mrs. Wilma Miles—*A Different Kind of War*, by Milton E. Miles, 1967; William Morris Agency—*A Soldier's Story*, by Omar H. Bradley, 1951; Harold Ober, Agent—*Now It Can Be Told*, by Leslie R. Groves, 1962; Oxford University Press—*Sun Tsu—The Art of War*, translated by Samuel B. Griffith, 1963, and Simon & Schuster—*A General's Life*, by Omar N. Bradley and Clay Blair, 1983. In addition, the New York Academy of Sciences and the American Meteorological Society kindly allowed us to reproduce tables, diagrams, quotes, and photographs for which they hold the copyrights.

Finally, we appreciate the efforts of William B. Shedd who edited an early draft to make certain that laypeople would find the text readable. Professor Aylmer Harry Thompson of the Department of Meteorology of Texas A&M University (and a retired colonel in the U.S. Air Force Reserve) also reviewed the draft and provided cogent comments of great value.

Abbreviations and Acronyms

AAF	Army Air Forces
AFB	Air Force Base
AFCRC	Air Force Cambridge Research Center
AFCRL	Air Force Cambridge Research Laboratory
AFGWC	Air Force Global Weather Central
AMS	American Meteorological Society
ARVN	Army of the Republic of Vietnam (South Vietnam
ATC	Air Transport Command
AWS	Air Weather Service
DMSP	Defense Meteorological Satellite Program
ESSA	Environmental Science Services Administration
FEAF	Far East Air Forces
FY	fiscal year
GHQ	general headquarters
GPO	Government Printing Office

JTF	Joint Task Force
MS	manuscript
MAC	Military Airlift Command
MATS	Military Air Transport Service
mb	millibar (pressure level in the atmosphere; 700 mb occurs at a height of approximately 10,000 feet; 500 mb, approximately 18,000 feet)
MIT	Massachusetts Institute of Technology
NAS	Naval Air Station
NASA	National Aeronautics and Space Administration
NOAA	National Oceanic and Atmospheric Administration
ONR	Office of Naval Research
RAF	Royal Air Force
RG	record group, National Archives
SAC	Strategic Air Command
TAC	Tactical Air Command
TF	Task Force
TIROS	Television and Infrared Observational Satellite
USA	United States Army
USAF	United States Air Force
USAAF	United States Army Air Forces
USCG	United States Coast Guard

USN	United States Navy
USS	United States Ship
VFR	visual flight rules

GUIDE TO ARMY, AIR FORCE, AND MARINE CORPS RANKS

Gen.	General (0-10 rank, four stars; colloquially, refers to any one of five levels of general officer)
Lt. Gen.	Lieutenant General (0-9 rank, three stars)
Maj. Gen.	Major General (0-8 rank, two stars)
Brig. Gen.	Brigadier General (0-7 rank, one star)
Col.	Colonel (0-6 rank)
Lt. Col.	Lieutenant Colonel (0-5 rank)
Maj.	Major (0-4 rank)
Capt.	Captain (0-3 rank)
1st Lt.	First Lieutenant (0-2 rank)
2nd Lt.	Second Lieutenant (0-1 rank)
CWO	Chief Warrant Officer
WO	Warrant Officer
M. Sgt.	Master Sergeant
T. Sgt.	Technical Sergeant
S. Sgt.	Staff Sergeant
Sgt.	Sergeant
Cpl.	Corporal
A1c.	Airman, 1st class (2nd- and 3rd-class ranks also exist)

Bvt.	Brevet (term indicating honorary rank without the pay of that rank)

GUIDE TO NAVY AND COAST GUARD RANKS

Adm.	Admiral (0-10 rank, four stars)
Vice Adm.	Vice Admiral (0-9 rank, three stars)
Rear Adm.	Rear Admiral (upper half—0-8 rank; lower half—0-7 rank; two stars)
Capt.	Captain (0-6 rank)
Comdr.	Commander (0-5 rank)
Lt. Comdr.	Lieutenant Commander (0-4 rank)
Lt.	Lieutenant (0-3 rank)
Lt. (jg.)	Lieutenant (junior grade) (0-2 rank)
Ens.	Ensign (0-1 rank)
CPO	Chief Petty Officer
LPO	Leading Petty Officer
AGCM	Command Master Chief Aerographer's Mate
AGCS	Senior Chief Aerographer's Mate
AGC, CAerM	Chief Aerographer's Mate
AEROG, AerM, AG	Aerographer's Mate (exists as 3rd, 2nd, and 1st class)

America's Weather Warriors

Chapter 1
Military Weather Programs in the 1800s

Meteorological science in the United States was conceived and brought forth by the Army Medical Department. It was nurtured in the then unknown West as in the East, and it gained strength year by year.
— Maj. Charles Smart, USA, to the Third International Meteorological Congress, 1893

Man has been subjected to weather and climate, good and bad, ever since his primitive forefathers began to think and walk. Two millennia ago, Aristotle wrote *Meteorologica*, the first systematic treatise on this subject. After Aristotle there was a long hiatus in meteorological science until the early seventeenth century. That is not to imply weather and climate had little impact on mankind during that interval. Between the seventh and tenth centuries a mild "climatic optimum" fostered the initial settlement of Iceland and Greenland, but there followed an unusually stormy era during the eleventh to fifteenth centuries that adversely affected food supply and ocean shipping routes. On the frequent fields of battle, leaders time and time again were also frustrated by severe cold, adverse winds, and intolerable storms.[1]

In 1607 Galileo developed the thermometer, followed soon by Torricelli's invention of the barometer in 1653. By that time European outposts dotted the eastern coast of North America. During 1644–45, at Swede's Fort near today's Wilmington, Delaware, the Reverend John Campanius kept the continent's first written weather record. Nearly another century went by, however, before another systematic observer, Dr. John Lining of Charleston, South Carolina, began making the first instrumental weather observations in 1738. Then, between 1772 and 1777, Thomas Jefferson, at Monticello, Virginia, teamed with James Madison, a cleric in Williamsburg some 120 miles away, to conduct the first known series of simultaneous but distantly separated meteorological measurements. That astute natural philosopher and politician Benjamin Franklin, using a similar correspondence method, had deduced as early as 1747 that a September hurricane in 1743 had moved northeastward from Virginia to Cape Sable, Nova Scotia, along what he perceived to be a typical storm track.[2]

THE ARMY SURGEON GENERAL

The first known instruction for armed forces of the United States to observe weather phenomena regularly came in 1802. As president, Jefferson instructed army captain Meriwether Lewis to make weather observations along with other duties during his expedition with William Clark to the Pacific Coast and back between 1804 and 1806.[3] However, it was not until May 2, 1814, during the War of 1812, that Physician and Surgeon General of the Army James Tilton directed his surgeons to record the weather regularly. Nonetheless, because of the press of other duties, few formal weather records were ever taken.

In 1816 Congress created the office of the surgeon general of the army, and the new appointee, Joseph Lovell, quickly ordered all hospital, post, and regimental surgeons "to keep a diary of the weather, and to note everything of importance relative to the medical topography of his station, the climate, diseases prevalent in the vicinity."[4] In justifying this rule to Secretary of War John C. Calhoun, Lovell commented, "The influence of weather and climate upon diseases, especially epidemic, is perfectly well known. . . . To this end, every surgeon should be furnished with a good thermometer, and in addition to a diary of the weather, should note everything . . . that may tend to discover the causes of diseases, the promotion of health, and the improvement of medical sciences." At that time, the impact of weather on a soldier's health received far more attention than it does today, but as late as World War I, the military suffered more deaths in wartime from nonbattle causes (primarily disease) than from combat.[5]

By 1825, eighteen military posts sent in climatic records. Medical officers participating in the program were particularly proud that weather observations began simultaneously with the establishment of a new cantonment, even during campaigns. By 1853, ninety-seven reporting points extended coast to coast and from the Mexican to the Canadian borders. Within this army grid several states independently set up weather observation programs of their own: New York in 1825, Pennsylvania in 1837, Ohio in 1842, and Massachusetts in 1849.[6]

In 1849 the brilliant electromagnetician Joseph Henry, secretary of the three-year-old Smithsonian Institution, started a far more elaborate and precise weather network. His system used the new Morse telegraph to report to Washington, D.C., daily instead of every three months, as did the army system, which was designed to advance medical, not natural, science. In fact, the army confessed at the time that its goal was only to be a major collector of weather information for climatic analysis. As a consequence, it intentionally left to others the study of massive amounts of accumulated raw weather data that could be used, it was hoped, to develop finite laws of nature that would lead to accurate weather forecasting.[7]

Fortunately, there was no shortage of such students of the atmosphere. As early as 1831 William G. Redfield, founder of the influential American Association for the Advancement of Science seventeen years later, postulated that storms, instead of being straight-line gales, were revolving whirlwinds of great size. Soon after that, James P. Espy, an articulate teacher of mathematics at Philadelphia's Franklin Institute, argued instead that a cyclonic storm was a system of inflowing winds, not necessarily radial, directed obliquely into a low-pressure axis. Aggressive, a good salesman, and a frequent public speaker, Espy, known as the "Storm King," proceeded to Washington in 1842 to demand that Congress divert the James Smithson bequest of $508,000 into the formation of a national weather service, with himself, of course, as its head. When that proposal failed, powerful congressional friends had Espy appointed "meteorologist to the U.S. government" and placed on the army surgeon general's rolls between 1842 and 1847 as a "clerk," with the sizable annual salary of $2,000.[8]

After a year in that post Espy turned in his *First Report on Meteorology* to the surgeon general. That document was a careful analysis of the weather in the eastern United States for January–March, 1843. Illustrated with beautifully engraved charts, his report observed that storms customarily began west of the army's weather network and moved easterly, like a north-south "line of battle," with a velocity that carried them from the Mississippi to the Connecticut river in approximately twenty-four hours. Espy concluded: "It is highly desirable to surround storms and keep them constantly in view from their beginning to their end. . . . May not some of them ever reach the shores of Europe?" To find out, he proposed that France and England be asked to join the United States in a project in which mariners would conduct widespread simultaneous measurements in the North Atlantic Ocean. Parochial army circles did not favor the idea, however, so Espy turned his attention to the more receptive navy.[9]

THE U.S. NAVY HYDROGRAPHIC OFFICE

As early as 1838 navy secretary James K. Paulding requested the eight-year-old Depot of Charts and Instruments to begin meteorological observations every three hours around the clock.[10] Four years later, while reviewing the depot's weather interests, the House of Representatives Committee on Naval Affairs commented:

> Meteorology. To be a good judge of the weather is considered an important qualification for a seaman; the safety of a ship and her crew may depend on the promptness and accuracy of his judgment. . . . If [Professor Espy's theory of storms] is correct, the day is not distant when we shall be able, by means of a barometer and windvanes, to calculate the precise point where a storm is raging. Navigators will thus be enabled to steer clear of it, and take advantage of the favorable winds blowing in its outer edge.[11]

In July of the same year Lt. Matthew F. Maury, upon taking command of the depot, began his own revolution in maritime meteorology. For some time he had been aware of the lack of organized knowledge about wind, current, and weather patterns along the main arteries of ocean commerce. Thus, totally at the mercy of the weather, shipmasters sailed strictly "by guess and by God." What was needed, he wrote, was a wind and current chart that "proposes nothing less than to blaze a way through the winds of the sea by which the navigator might find the best paths at all seasons."[12]

Initially, Maury attacked the problem by poring over a large collection of dusty naval ship logs destined for the scrap bin. To supplement that information, he appealed to American shipmasters during 1842 to send in additional meteorological and oceanographic observations. Surprisingly, they did not see fit to do so. Maury persevered. By combining the old naval data with new information coming in from the fleet, he was able to issue charts showing optimal sailing tracks for the North Atlantic by late 1847 and for parts of the South Atlantic and North Pacific during 1849.[13] The first test of Maury's charts came early in 1848 when they were used by the barque *W. H. D. C. Wright* during her cruise from Chesapeake Bay to Rio de Janeiro and back. Southbound, she took 38 days; returning, she took 37 days. A typical one-way passage was 55 days. Similarly, ships that normally took 180 days to sail from New York to San Francisco found that they could cut the trip to about 133 days. Then in 1851, the clipper *Flying Cloud* made the outbound trip in 89 days. Such savings in sea time were not only a boon to the seasick passengers but also of great economic value to the operators and owners of the sail-powered merchantmen still dominating the high seas at the time (steam-powered vessels did not yet achieve great ranges).

Such successes gave Maury the long-sought cooperation from the U.S. Merchant Marine, and by late 1851 more than a thousand ships had turned in meteorological logs of his design. To digest these, he soon had a staff of about twenty lieutenants and passed midshipmen (today's ensigns) supplemented by two civilian professors.[14] By 1860 this team turned out a six-part global series of track, trade wind, pilot, thermal, whale, and storm and rain charts supplemented by eight volumes of sailing directions containing elaborate articles on maritime meteorology. In the early 1850s the world's merchant marine was estimated to be saving upwards of $15 million per year, and the press soon gave Maury the informal title of "Pathfinder of the Seas." In fact, New York City businessmen went so far in 1853 as to give him a set of silver plate and a purse of $5,000.

Maury's greatest reward, however, was the opportunity to convene the world's first maritime conference in Brussels, Belgium, during August and September, 1853. His initial hope was to hold an international gathering that would develop standardized meteorological observations for land and for sea. But in his opening remarks he admitted, "The object of our meeting, then, gentlemen, is to agree upon a uniform mode of making nautical and meterological observations on board vessels of war."[15] Ultimately, the conference agreed on two observing formats, one for naval vessels and one (in abbreviated form) for merchant vessels. Maury noted that, although war vessels turned in much better weather observations, merchantmen were still needed in the program because they could provide more and better distributed measurements. On behalf of the U.S. Navy he also extended an invitation for all ships' captains, regardless of flag flown, to participate in this global observation program, a practice that, once started, continued with some fits and starts until the late 1940s. Within a couple of years, international exchange of standardized weather reports from land stations also caught on.

In 1855 Maury published one of the all-time best-selling scientific books for laymen: *The Physical Geography of the Sea and Its Meteorology*. It went through fifteen editions in the United States and twenty-two in Great Britain. For all of these efforts, gold medals and honors from twelve countries were bestowed on Maury, and he was elected to forty-five learned societies, twenty of them foreign. Notwithstanding these accolades, Maury suffered considerable criticism from his more mathematically oriented contemporaries—particularly from Alexander Dallas Bache, great-grandson of Benjamin Franklin and longtime superintendent (1843–67) of the U.S. Coast Survey, and from Maury's military superiors, even though he was promoted to the rank of commander in 1858.[16]

With the outbreak of the Civil War in 1861 Maury left what had become known as the Hydrographical Office and joined the Confederate navy with the rank of commander. His former command continued its interest in maritime meteorology, however, and in 1866 issued *The Way to Avoid the Center of Our Violent Gales*. Three years later came *The Barometer, Thermometer, Hydrometer and Atmospheric Appearances at Sea and on Land as Aids in Foretelling Weather*. Despite such publications and the issuance of an upgraded series of pilot charts in 1876, the staff of the Hydrographical Office's Division of Meteorology dwindled to two officers and a civilian laborer by

1885, at which time fewer than 200 merchant marine vessels continued to turn in cooperative nautical reports.

This situation changed for the better in 1886 when the troubled Army Signal Corps was directed to transfer all marine meteorological efforts to the naval Hydrographic Office. This made available 500 daily weather reports from the North Atlantic Ocean alone, such reports being filed as soon as merchantmen touched port in the United States. In March, 1888, the office began regular preparation of a daily synoptic chart of the North Atlantic, for such a plot was useful in both technical studies and in updating the new edition of highly touted pilot charts used as "teasers" to encourage marine observers to turn in hydrographic as well as meteorological and oceanographic data. This project proved highly successful; by 1895 there were 3,118 observers on the Hydrographic Office's rolls; most of them were foreign, and they cooperated so that they would receive free pilot charts.[17] However, the divisional staff, consisting of one officer, four "nautical experts," a stenographer, and a messenger, could not keep up with this data flow.

To solve the problem, the new hydrographer, Comdr. Charles P. Sigsbee, suggested in his annual report for 1895 that the new system for "electrical counting and averaging" of census data patented by Herman Hollerith six years earlier be used to stem the tide of raw weather data engulfing his bureau. In 1897 Hydrographic Office Publication 113, *The Treatment of Marine Meteorological Data, with Special Reference to the Work of the United States Hydrographic Office*, described a method for placing each daily set of weather observations on a single punched card, permitting the data to be recalled and used for either synoptic or climatological purposes. This is the first known instance of machine-processed meteorological data.

Despite the technical alertness of the Hydrographic Office, when the Spanish-American War broke out a year later, the navy and President William McKinley relied on an agricultural agency, the U.S. Weather Bureau, to issue hurricane warnings. In fact, McKinley advised the bureau's chief, Willis Moore, that he feared these tropical storms more than he feared the Spanish fleet. Radio was still not available, so the best the navy could do was to station a fast cruiser at Key West, Florida, ready to dash to blockading fleet units off Cuba if the Weather Bureau advised that a hurricane threatened.

THE U.S. ARMY CORPS OF ENGINEERS

During 1858 Capt. George G. Meade of the Corps of Topographical Engineers (renamed the Corps of Engineers in 1863) organized a team of meteorological and hydrographic observers as part of the "Survey of the

Northern and Northwestern Lakes"—the Great Lakes. Reporting by mail to Detroit, this network noted such conventional measurements as wind, cloud cover, temperature, precipitation, evaporation, barometric pressure, and lake level. As early as 1862 the survey superintendent, Col. W. F. Raynolds, called to his superiors' attention the observation that most lake storms moved west to east. Hence, he wrote, "By aid of the magnetic telegraph, the approach of storms could be foretold and notice given for the benefit of commerce."[18] Nothing tangible came from that proposal. Then, in 1876, the system was melded into the much larger Army Signal Service meteorological network. Left for posterity were 13 feet of musty records at the National Archives.[19]

THE U.S. ARMY SIGNAL CORPS

The U.S. Army's third try at operating a major meteorological program lasted only from 1870 to 1891. Yet it had enduring effects. Out of this effort came not only the civilian-operated national weather service of 1891 (the U.S. Weather Bureau) but also the concepts and the manpower needed for resurrecting the army's and navy's in-house weather services when World War I required them a quarter of a century later. As a by-product, the army also ended up in 1891 with a greatly expanded Signal Corps, capable sixteen years later of initiating an Aviation Section, the forerunner of today's U.S. Air Force.

How the army came to create and operate the first nationwide weather service for all the citizens is a complicated and dramatic story. For three decades (1838–69) a variety of individuals and groups attempted to interest Congress in supporting an integrated, nationwide weather observation program. Foremost among such attempts was that by the Smithsonian Institution, a meteorological network operator since 1849.[20] There, in 1856, Institution visitors could view a plot of daily weather conditions portrayed by pieces of appropriately colored cards hanging from pins inserted into a map of the United States east of the Mississippi River. As late as 1865, Joseph Henry, the Institution's secretary, regularly pleaded in his annual report to Congress that there should be an integrated weather system capable of "predicting the approach of storms and giving the ships of our Atlantic Coast due warning of the probability of danger." Finally, on September 1, 1869, the new director of the Cincinnati Astronomical Observatory, Professor Cleveland Abbe, started a three-month experiment. Funded by the local Chamber of Commerce, his test involved the operation of a midwestern weather observing network, the issuance of a daily bulletin, and, on September 22, Abbe's first publicly published daily weather probabilities.

Abbe was unsuccessful in expanding this initiative to the Great Lakes area because of his inability to solicit funds and technical cooperation from the Chicago Board of Trade. Disappointed, his friend Increase A. Lapham, a Milwaukee civil engineer who had tried to start a Wisconsin state weather service nine years earlier, sent a memorial on December 8, 1869, to Congressman Helbert E. Paine. Attached to the memorial was a *Milwaukee Sentinel* article of the same date listing 1,914 vessels already lost at sea on the Great Lakes that year, primarily because of bad weather. To counteract these losses, Lapham suggested that the Chicago Academy of Science form a meteorological department funded by those benefiting from it the most. Paine proved to be no ordinary politician. At Western Reserve College he had been a student of Professor Elias Loomis, and he was well versed in Loomis's research on storm structure, which correctly anticipated Bjerknes's polar front theory eighty years later.[21] With Lapham's suggestion in hand, Paine wrote and introduced congressional legislation proposing that a federal agency such as the Smithsonian be authorized to operate an experimental weather service.

On December 16, 1869, Paine's bill was given to the House Committee on Commerce. Immediately upon its publication, Paine received a visit, with permission of the secretary of war, from a highly excited forty-one-year-old Col. Albert J. Myer, the army's chief signal officer.[22] Needing peacetime work to keep his shaky, minuscule Signal Service in being, Myer had sold the secretary on the idea that collection and diffusion of weather information by the federal government could be done more reliably and cheaply if assigned to a military rather than a civilian agency. Paine accepted this concept and quickly amended bill H.R. 602 to direct the secretary of war to operate such a weather service. Events moved swiftly. By January 26, 1870, the congressman had received favorable comments from Surgeon General Barnes of the Army Medical Department, the Smithsonian's Secretary Henry, and Professor Loomis, among others. As Paine had been a major general of the Wisconsin Volunteers, his fellow Civil War veterans who dominated Congress were not about to let him down. His bill was converted to a joint resolution, passed by the House on February 2 and the Senate on February 5, and signed by President Ulysses S. Grant on February 9, just sixty-three days after Lapham had mailed in his memorial.[23]

Nineteen days later Secretary William W. Belknap assigned the much coveted responsibility for establishing a national weather service to Myer and his Army Signal Service and Military Telegraph. However, the secretary continued the stipulation that all of the service's officers, except Myer, had to be on temporary detail from other army units, subject to recall if needed. Myer also had another difficulty to overcome: neither he nor his troops knew anything about meteorology. To overcome this problem, he immediately questioned the nation's leading meteorologists about how he should proceed. He then started formal meteorological training at the Signal Service School in decrepit, muddy Fort Whipple, Virginia, on the outskirts of Washington.

The next step was the hiring of two civilian experts: George C. Maynard as "Electrician" and Increase Lapham, no less, as "Assistant to the Chief Signal Officer." Myer personally hired Lapham while in Chicago (which was to be Lapham's duty station), and on the same day (November 8, 1870) Lapham issued the service's first storm warning for the Great Lakes.[24]

Myer's meteorological budget grew rapidly, as did the number of army weather stations.[25] After being on the job only six weeks, Lapham advised that he could spend but three days a week in Chicago, and by the following May he was off the payroll. To fill the critical need for a nationally known forecaster, Myer showed genius and courage. Although the famed Cleveland Abbe had publicly criticized the concept of a national weather service run along military lines, Myer persuaded the professor to leave Cincinnati and become the chief signal officer's "Assistant" (read "Chief Forecaster and Scientist"). Duty would start on January 3, 1871, at a pay level of $3,000 per year.

Once in place, the Myer-Abbe team worked remarkably well.[26] On February 19, 1871, Abbe issued Washington's first "Weather Synoptic and Probabilities." Maynard, too, lost little time in being useful, and within the year, his "cascade" system permitted the transmission of all key weather reports from across the nation to Washington in approximately thirty minutes. For a while, however, the Western Union Telegraph Company proved hard to deal with, even refusing to process weather messages during March, 1871.

Despite the normal difficulties of getting a new technical service started, Congress appreciated the progress that the service made. On June 10, 1872, Congress expanded the army's responsibility to include the entire nation by providing "for such additional stations, reports and signals as may be found necessary for the benefit of Agricultural and Commercial Interests." This is what Myer had hoped for all along; from the very first he had named his weather component the Division of Telegrams and Reports for the Benefit of Commerce. By 1873 the division was preparing an average of thirty-five weather bulletins and sixty weather maps daily. A special farmers' bulletin was quickly prepared from each midnight weather forecast (except that from Saturday night). Then it was telegraphed to nineteen Signal Service printing stations in key cities, printed, and rushed by early morning mail to 6,042 rural post offices, where the postmasters were required to keep a log of time of forecast receipt and display. Warnings of cold waves and approaches of storms were disseminated by flying signal flags from thousands of coastal points and major governmental buildings. In Ohio such flags were even flown from moving express trains.[27]

Additional environmental services were added during the 1870s. These included river level reports, frost warnings, hurricane alerts based on reports from subsidized weather stations in the West Indies, marine meteorology, the journal called the *Monthly Weather Review*, and the establishment of local liaison groups giving feedback on quality of the service. Supplementing these were in-house instrument development, international data exchanges (Canada's started in 1871), and supporting research, including upper-air studies involving cloud photography, mountain stations on Pikes Peak and Mount Washington, and special balloon flights by the aeronaut Professor Samuel A. King.[28]

Much of the success in building up such an all-encompassing weather service in ten years came from Colonel Myer and his wife, Kate, who was independently wealthy. Starting in 1878, they entertained Washington society extensively in a mansion located on the present site of the Army and Navy Club. A *Hartford Courant* reporter covering a diplomatic corps reception given by President and Mrs. Rutherford B. Hayes wrote that he had not met "the weather . . . but had met the weather's wife and found her very charming."[29] It was particularly pleasant news when Secretary of War Alexander Ramsey on February 24, 1880, upgraded the Signal Service to the Signal Corps and designated Myer a brevet brigadier general. But his happy state of affairs proved short-lived, for Myer, now popularly known as Old Probabilities, died six months later.

His replacement, Brig. Gen. William B. Hazen, was also a Civil War veteran who had friends in Congress. Whereas Myer ran a "loose ship" and stressed public service, Hazen was both a strict disciplinarian and an aggressive sponsor of scientific research and publication by both his military and expanded civilian staff. In mid-1881 the euphoria ended. The longtime disbursing officer of the Corps, Capt. Henry W. Howgate, was caught embezzling, perhaps as much as $60,000 a year for the previous four years. Not only was Howgate sent to prison but Congress also in retaliation reduced the corps' annual appropriation of $375,000 approximately by the amount that had been embezzled each year.

Hazen recruited actively in high schools and colleges for potential "observer-sergeants" and also arranged for two highly qualified sergeants to be commissioned each year as "weather officers," despite indignant protests from the regular officer corps. Yet in 1884 he stubbornly refused to enlist W. Hallett Green, the first Negro graduate of the City College of New York, which caused trouble with the new secretary of war, Robert Todd Lincoln, son of the president, who favored the enlistment. Hazen continued to tangle with Lincoln over the twice-aborted annual resupply missions to the Signal Corps meteorological and magnetic research expedition of 1881–84 on Lady Franklin Bay, Ellesmere Island, as part of the International Polar Year. After setting a record for penetrating farthest north (latitude 83°24′N), the party under 1st Lt. Adolphus W. Greely ran out of food when resupply ships never appeared. Eventually seven of twenty-five men survived the ordeal, one man having been shot dead because of pilfering.[30] Finally, Hazen's outspoken protests about the botched supply operation earned him a court-martial and a presidential reprimand for criticizing his secretary.

By that time, the Signal Corps was spending nearly $1 million a year to operate a network of 132 weather stations, only 7 of which were directed by civilians. Once the new secretary of war, William C. Endicott, was at his desk during 1885, the famed chief of staff Gen. Philip H. Sheridan convinced him that the army could ill afford to fund and man such a strongly civilian-oriented technical service. The question of whether the government should have a "Department of Science" had come up, too. Sheridan had already testified to the joint House-Senate commission investigating the matter (also known as the Allison commission after its chairman, Senator W. E. Allison): "The signal detachment . . . are no more soldiers than the men at the Smithsonian Institution. They are making scientific observations of the weather of great interest to navigation and to the country at large. *But what does a soldier care about the weather! Whether good or bad, he must take it as it comes*" (italics added).[31]

In early 1886 Secretary Endicott ordered termination of the Signal Corps "Study Room," where Professor Abbe directed an applied research team and a gradual elimination of the Signal School at Fort Myer (the former Fort Whipple) the following year. In mid-1886 the Allison commission's final report included this statement: "The Signal Service is now a Weather Bureau with a corps of men performing this civil service while they are enlisted in the Army. . . . The Army gets no benefit from this Signal Corps, and places no reliance upon it for any military service." The commission also found that Hazen had turned the corps into a "uniformed police force" that spent as much time monitoring each other (daily performance reports were required) as on reporting the weather.[32] In the midst of this constant uproar, Hazen died suddenly on January 16, 1887.

His replacement proved to be Captain Greely, the intrepid polar explorer. Upon being detailed to the Signal Corps from the 5th Cavalry Regiment in 1873, Greely had been one of the first five weather officer forecasters in the Corps. Before his polar adventure he had directed the building of 2,000 miles of military telegraph lines in West Texas and the Dakota Territory during 1876–79.[33] Although impetuous, he chose not to fight the long-simmering congressional belief that the national weather service should be in civilian, not military, hands. So by an act of October 1, 1890, Congress directed the Signal Corps to transfer all its meteorological activities (including buildings, coastal telegraph lines, equipment, and manpower) to a weather bureau to be created in the Department of Agriculture the following July 1.

With this functional transfer, the Signal Corps budget for meteorology fell from $753,000 in fiscal year 1890–91 to $32,000 in the ensuing year. However, the chief signal officer remained responsible for "the necessary meteorological instruments for use on target ranges and other military uses." This responsibility was largely window trimming, for it amounted only to supplying the ranges with sling psychrometers, compensated aneroid barometers, and automatic anemometers. The same equipment also went to coast artillery units. Only in Alaska did the meteorological tradition of the corps linger. There the Weather Bureau often tied into the army's rapidly expanding telegraph network and sometimes asked sergeants' wives to be weather observers in the more isolated outposts.

Chapter 2
The Rebirth of Military Meteorology (1900–1919)

There is no more interesting illustration of the application of new scientific methods to warfare than is furnished by the development in meteorology during the Great War.

—Lt. Col. Robert A. Millikan, Signal Corps, USA
(Nobel Laureate in Physics, 1923)

THE PREWAR STATE OF THE ART

During the early 1900s the U.S. Weather Bureau monopolized the field of meteorology. Most of its people were trained on the job; only two universities—Johns Hopkins and Harvard—offered course work in the field. However, the bureau hired externally when necessary. For example, in 1900, the year Marconi received his basic radio patent, the Weather Bureau hired "special agent" Professor Reginald A. Fessenden, the country's most prolific inventor, next to Thomas A. Edison. Fessenden's assignment: to develop a weather radio system. By year's end he was transmitting useful signals to vessels hundreds of miles to sea. In 1902 the bureau began acquiring powerful wireless stations for this purpose. One was on Long Island, not far from a navy transmitter; eventually, a hue and cry arose about duplication of services.

In response President Theodore Roosevelt created an interdepartmental board (Brigadier General Greely was one of its members) on June 24, 1904, to regulate federal use of wireless telegraphy. Boards moved quickly in that era. Thirty-five days later, Roosevelt issued an executive order requiring the Weather Bureau to turn over to the navy all coastwise wireless telegraph apparatus. In return, the bureau furnished to the navy and to other parts of the public service "such meteorological data as it or they may desire at no cost to them."[1] Moreover, neither the Hydrographic Office nor any other naval entity was to request funds for making ocean forecasts. Because of this dictate, "Hydro's" Division of Marine Meteorology was abolished on December 1, 1904, and its records sent to the Weather Bureau.

The bureau's first chief, Mark W. Harrington, commented as early as 1893 that "the exploration of the upper air is the immediate requirement for the satisfactory advance of meteorology," but this was easier said than done.[2] Besides observing sites on towers and mountain tops, meteorologists occasionally used such aerological probes as multiple kites in tandem, manned balloons, tethered balloons, and free balloons. Workable meteorographs for measuring air temperature and pressure were carried aloft by free balloons as early as 1893 in France and by Weather Bureau kites during 1898.

In 1914 this field work was centralized at Drexel, Nebraska, not far from the Army Balloon School in the city of Omaha, Nebraska. The bureau's Aerological Division consisted of ten people—six at Drexel under Bertram J. Sherry, and four in Washington under the division chief, Dr. William R. Blair. The equipment was quite modest: two kite reels; a dozen Marvin-type meteorographs, commonly defective in one way or another; twenty-five kites of varying sizes; a supply of pilot balloons for measuring winds aloft (pibals); and six theodolites, only two of which had the Blair modification, which permitted the field of view to remain horizontal no matter what the elevation of the sighting tube.[3] The technical capabilities of the team were somewhat better. For example, between July 9 and 22, 1914, twenty sensor-equipped balloons were released for studying high-level diurnal variations, and all but one of the instrument packages were retrieved. Tracking was accomplished by using a pair of theodolites 3.2 miles apart. Normally, good measurements were obtained up to at least 56,000 feet, and one release achieved the height of 102,300 feet.

THE GREAT WAR

When the Germans swept across the plains of Flanders in August, 1914, nearly reaching Paris, America's political and military leaders doubted that aviation could play a meaningful role in warfare. To be sure, the army had experimented with manned balloons off and on since the Civil War. In July, 1908, the Signal Corps purchased a nonrigid dirigible. A month later it also bought a "military aircraft" from the Wright brothers. Following a civil demonstration of a ship-to-shore flight in 1910, the navy began buying Curtiss "hydroaeroplanes" in 1911. Even so, there was little military enthusiasm for this new observational technique: 12 of the first 48 Army pilots lost their lives in aircraft accidents. By early 1915 the United

States had only 50 of the 2,400 qualified pilots in the world, as well as but a score of military aircraft, compared with France's 1,200.

To obtain a better scientific and technical understanding of the major unresolved problems pertaining to flight, Congress authorized a National Advisory Committee for Aeronautics (NACA) as a rider on the Naval Appropriation Act of March 3, 1915. Chaired by Brig. Gen. George P. Scriven, the chief signal officer, the twelve-man committee was authorized to spend $5,000 a year for experimentation and clerical expenses. According to the group's first summary report, October 30, 1915, undoubtedly with the wishes of its Weather Bureau member Professor Charles F. Marvin, "The Weather Bureau is well equipped for the determination of the problems of the atmosphere in relation to aeronautics."[4] All that was lacking was the standard Washington requirement: more money!

In practice the situation was more complex than Marvin would admit. During the preceding December, Harvard's Robert DeCourcy Ward, the initial American professor of climatology, published the first of nineteen articles during the next five years delineating "the weather factor in the Great War."[5] Based on press and other reports, Ward's write-ups convincingly described how new facets of modern warfare demanded close-in meteorological support. The most important needs were vastly improved ballistic wind data for antiaircraft gunners, for long-range artillerymen firing at unseen targets, and for gas warfare; the enhancement of sound ranging to locate hidden enemy guns; and support of aircraft not only in reconnaissance but also in the newer modes of bombing, artillery fire spotting, and providing defensive cover to friendly aircraft. Such tactical support was subordinate to the overriding, strategic issue of how to schedule major offensives to avoid being bogged down by "General Mud" in rainy spells. Ward did not find it surprising that by mid-1915 the British, French, and German armies had formed their own military weather services to provide up-to-the-minute weather observations and forecasts for the field of battle.[6]

THE REBIRTH OF THE SIGNAL CORPS WEATHER SERVICE

President Woodrow Wilson was reelected in November, 1916, using the slogan "He kept us out of war!" By the time of his inauguration the following March, that promise looked very doubtful. Yet, with no money, NACA did nothing to get a military meteorology effort under way. In contrast, using donations from outside sources, the newly formed National Research Council (NRC) of the elitist National Academy of Sciences set out to be the dominant scientific center for meeting the military's wartime needs. NRC's dynamic leader, Dr. George Ellery Hale, an astronomer, had persuaded the University of Chicago's noted molecular physicist, Dr. Robert A. Millikan, to come east and work on the problem of submarine detection, as well as to direct what would become the NRC Division of Physics, Mathematics, Astronomy and Geophysics. By then, Germany's submarine blockade was so effective that French and British leaders believed their countries could not last another six months unless the course of the sea war was reversed.

After Russia's czarist government succumbed, President Wilson asked Congress to declare war on April 6, 1917. By June, after much debate, America's leaders decided to field a self-contained army in France rather than to detail individual units as subordinate components of existing French and British armies. Secretary of War Newton D. Baker had laid plans earlier that year to expand vastly the Aviation Section of the Signal Corps by bringing in Brig. Gen. George O. Squier to be chief signal officer. Squier probably held the only earned Ph.D. degree in the U.S. Army, having obtained one at Johns Hopkins while assigned to nearby Fort McHenry. He was well known and an enthusiastic supporter of military aviation. Although the army spent only $600,000 on aviation between 1909 and 1915, Squier learned in late June 1917, that he might be spending a $650-million appropriation to build 10,000 aircraft. In addition, he needed to set up special scientific services such as sound ranging and meteorology.

To explore his options, Squier gave a luncheon at the Willard Hotel on June 29 for the new NACA chairman, Dr. Charles D. Walcott of the Smithsonian, and Dr. Hale and Dr. Millikan of the NRC. After some arm twisting, Squier persuaded Millikan to enter the army as a major and form the Science and Research Division of the Signal Corps. Squier's bait was that Millikan could then feed Signal Corps problems and funds directly to the NRC for solution and recommendations. Among Major Millikan's first assignments was a directive from Squier to plan and implement an "Army Meteorological and Aerological Service."[7] By then, such a service was needed not only to respond to an urgent cablegram from the American Expeditionary Forces (AEF) chief signal officer, who asked for officers with certain scientific specialties, including meteorology, but also to meet the known domestic needs of the Aviation Section, the Gas Warfare Service, the Ordnance Proving Grounds, the Field Artillery, and the Coast Artillery (the latter not only manned coastal defense but operated antiaircraft guns).[8]

Because Millikan remained deeply involved in many NRC projects, including the all-important antisubmarine task, he very much needed full-time meteorological staff support. On July 16, 1917, he recommended five highly qualified men for Signal Corps commissions, all of whom were immediately approved. Three were Weather Bureau men: Blair, the aerologist who had earned his Ph.D. under Millikan at Chicago; Sherry, Blair's field specialist, and Edward H. Bowie, a supervisory forecaster in the Washington office. From the academic community came Professor Henry G. Gale, a Millikan colleague at Chicago, and Dr. Alan T. Waterman, whose doctoral degree had been awarded by Princeton just the year before. Blair, Bowie, and Gale, like Millikan, became majors; Sherry and Waterman were made first lieutenants.[9]

The leadership problem solved, the next task was to determine the type and scope of weather service overseas. An ad hoc planning group of Majors Millikan, Blair, and Bowie, plus the Weather Bureau's Professor Marvin, exchanged cablegrams with the AEF on this subject and decided that the initial need in France was for 21 officers and 156 enlisted men. Brigadier General Squier also charged the group not only to determine domestic military weather needs but also to estimate the manpower needed "to undertake for the first time in the history of the world the problems of mapping the upper-air currents over the United States, the Atlantic, and western Europe in aid of aviation, and particularly with reference to trans-Atlantic flight." These last two demands indicated a need for another 15 officers and 200 enlisted men. For manpower, Marvin agreed that Millikan could draw heavily on the Weather Bureau's staff of 600 persons. In addition, Marvin offered to give the first 150 Army weathermen, in lots of two to ten men assigned to a score of bureau field stations, on-the-job training.[10] The bureau would also provide the meteorological gear needed to start up the army service.

The refined Millikan-Blair plan called for a three-part weather service—foreign operations, domestic operations, and aerological studies—of 27 officers and 475 enlisted men. The NRC reviewed the plan on August 3, 1917, as did the NACA shortly thereafter, both with positive results. Having paid proper obeisance to the scientific community, Squier ordered the Signal Corps Meteorological and Aerological Service into being during late August, 1917, with Millikan in command. This action gave Millikan his third urgent, contemporaneous responsibility, for he still retained his NRC post. Fortunately, he was a workhorse and capable of delegating.[11] Blair took responsibility for the European operation; Sherry, soon to be captain, took over domestic operations and aerological research.

IMPLEMENTATION OF THE MILLIKAN-BLAIR PLAN

To meet increasingly urgent demands from the AEF for at least minimal meteorological support, Majors Blair and Bowie left for France during September, 1917. Settling in at the Bureau Centrale Météorologique in Paris early the next month, Bowie began issuing weather forecasts similar to the kind he had made in Washington. Valid for the following twenty-four hours, such predictions covered sky condition, possible precipitation, temperature, and expected winds. A typical forecast read: "Cloudy tonight; probably showers Friday; not much change in temperature; gentle wind, mostly southwest."[12]

Simultaneously, Blair laid the groundwork for the 300-plus meteorological troops expected to arrive in England and France during early 1918. Visiting the British and French military weather services, he found them smooth-running operations that held the respect and support of their clients. Using these services as a guide, he completed arrangements in short order, particularly those needed for the critical exchange of telegraphic weather messages in the international weather code between the three services. One Blair idea was quickly shot down, however—the recommendation that the AEF weather service should be a unit of the army's burgeoning Air Service.[13]

Stateside, Sherry and his alter ego, Waterman, were deeply involved in recruitment. It was already agreed between Millikan's office, NRC, and the General Staff's Committee on Education and Special Training that the meteorological service would be an elite corps. Even its privates should have meteorological experience or college training in engineering, mathematics, or the physical sciences. Officer appointees came largely from the Weather Bureau, the academic community, and other components of the armed services in which an officer was not being used to his full scientific potential. More than 125 of the enlisted men came from the Weather Bureau; the threat of a draft call did wonders to encourage volunteers. Filling the remaining 375 enlisted slots was more difficult. On hand was a pile of letters from technically qualified people eager to be officers but not privates (the pay for privates was $17.80 per month plus keep). However, many other well-qualified men preferred to be privates in the army's weather service than doughboys in the trenches, so the authorized number of recruits was reached well ahead of schedule.

By the spring of 1918, 200 military weathermen finished their training at Weather Bureau field stations and entered the system. For example, the first nine graduates had been ordered to Fort Omaha's balloon school as early as late November, 1917. There they opened the army's first full-fledged military weather station of the twentieth century. After this first rush, the decision was made to standardize training and alleviate the bureau's work load by sending additional prospective weathermen to a formal school.[14]

Not until May, 1918, did a 315-man detachment arrive at the Texas Agricultural and Mechanical College (Texas A&M), a school as military as West Point, to be converted into army weather observers. The day's work started at sunrise for the 32nd Service Company of the Signal Corps. Besides two hours of daily military drill, the trainees faced a full curriculum of classroom and outdoor laboratory work provided by a top-notch instructional staff. Because the best textbook, Davis's *Elementary Meteorology*, was twenty-four years old, Dr. Charles F. Brooks of Harvard's Blue Hill Observatory substituted a series of forty-two detailed lectures.[15] It was such a talented class that staff and students soon developed a method of single theodolite observation of pilot balloon ascents (pibals) to replace complex double theodolite tracking, thereby simplifying balloon work on the western front.

By the time the Texas A&M class graduated in early September, 1918, much had happened in the United States and in Europe. On May 24, Millikan, by then a lieutenant colonel, removed his Signal Corps insignia and replaced them with the wings of the new Air Service, becoming responsible for the physical science side of aircraft production.[16] He also remained in charge of the army's weather service. By late August this service consisted of thirty-seven domestic military weather stations, of which twenty-six had upper-air capability. Observations were made in the metric system, then converted to whatever units the customers requested. Except for the Washington staff of twenty-five, the largest weather unit was the group of twenty-two men at the Aberdeen Proving Ground, Maryland. It provided aerological data for the improvement of long-range firing tables. In addition to making hundreds of pibals, the Aberdeen detachment arranged for more than 350 meteorological aircraft ascents to altitudes that normally reached 10,000 feet.[17]

With Squier's and Millikan's backing, good progress was made in charting and forecasting upper-air currents. Three prime users existed: the fledgling army air mail service between May and August, 1918, when it was turned over to the Post Office Department; researchers interested in postwar flights by commercial aviation across the North Atlantic Ocean; and psychological warfare specialists. In late 1917, Lieutenant Sherry had pointed out to the third group that the malnourished, restive common folk of Germany and the Austro-Hungarian Empire could easily be subjected to torrents of propaganda leaflets dropped from pilot balloons. Although the powers-that-be agreed that European winds above 10,000 feet blew west to east most of the time, they also maintained that balloons of this type could not travel much more than a hundred miles from launch because hydrogen leaked so rapidly through the rubber envelope.

Professor S. R. Williams (Amherst College), W. J. Lester, and Sergeant Redman, working as a team, quickly devised a much improved sealant for the envelope and a simplified ballast control.[18] During the week of October 3, 1918, they ran a test from Omaha, using sixty modified balloons programmed for an initial altitude of 15,000 feet and a final flight altitude of 25,000 feet before terminal descent. Thirty-four of these experimental vehicles were promptly recovered, some as close as Iowa and two as far away as New York and Virginia (960 miles from the starting point). Because each balloon could carry several hundred leaflets but cost no more than three dollars, Sherry's suggestion was clearly validated. The Military Intelligence Service placed a large order for such devices, an action quickly canceled by the signing of the armistice on November 11, 1918.

But the war still had to be won or lost along the western front. Major Blair had spent much of the winter of 1917 – 18 familiarizing himself with the battle terrain and the vagaries of French weather, ordering and scrounging meteorological gear, and determining the AEF's weather needs. Finally, during March and April, 1918, the first of his 300-man contingent began arriving in groups of 50 at Langres. Only small quantities of meteorological equipment, mainly French, were on hand, and American combat forces were still dispersed among British and French commands. Blair therefore spent the time until early May checking out his troops on French weather instruments and explaining how to support field forces. By then, requests were trickling in for meteorological stations, and on May 9 the first purposeful American weather reading was taken at a flying field near Ourches (Meurthe et Moselle) for the First Army Corps observational group. [19]

By the early summer of 1918 nearly a million American troops were in France, eager to end the war to end all wars. Weather detachments first moved into the forward combat zone on July 18 with the First Army Corps during the major counterattack at Chateau-Thierry. From an observation balloon position, the weather unit provided ballistic wind and weather data for corps artillery and to aviation. On July 27, the Fourth Army Corps meteorological detachment near Royameux (Meurthe et Moselle) started supplying ballistic wind data for all trajectories every four hours, night and day, over the next 109 days. The same unit, moving up with its corps prior to the St. Mihiel drive of September 12, began to make weather observations within 4 to 6 miles of front-line trenches. At one time, German shells dropped within 100 feet of the weather station. [20]

It had long been obvious that Bowie's generalized forecasts out of Paris were of little aid. The master forecast center therefore moved 165 miles east, to Blair's headquarters at Colombey-les-Belles near Nancy. By August 16, using two teams of five forecasters each and four daily maps, the center was issuing weather forecasts every twelve hours to the First Army fighting along the Lorraine sector. In early November, all artillery units, as well as the Air Service, were receiving every two hours current air temperature, air density, and wind direction and velocity from the surface to 16,600 feet (see Appendix A). A squall warning service was also provided, to announce the approach of high winds.

The army weather service in France ultimately consisted of the master station ("Nemo"), six detachments stationed with army corps headquarters along the battle front, and sixteen noncombatant units (normally commanded by noncommissioned officers) located throughout France at ports of entry, supply depots, and training centers. Customers were pleased with their weather information. The chief signal officer's annual report of 1919 concluded "that practically all bombing and a great deal of the artillery, gas, and other operations of the First and Second Armies were based on the weather forecasts issued by the Meteorological Section of the Signal Corps." Brigadier General Mitchell, not given to flattery, reported separately that the forecasts were indispensable to Air Service operations. Certainly the AEF Meteorological Section was well satisfied; a unit history claims that its organization was "the most complete . . . of its kind in the world" and that its forecasts had been "better than those issued by any meteorological service, military or civil."[21]

This was the most temporary of situations. Upon the signing of the armistice, meteorologists outdid most others in lining up homeward-bound transport. By Thanksgiving Day fully half the section was aboard outbound shipping. Stateside, it was equally bad, for almost everyone's enlistment was just for the "emergency." Lieutenant Colonel Millikan departed on December 31, 1918, to be immediately replaced by Lt. Col. John C. Moore. However, Squier did not want to see his fifteen-month-old weather service disappear. He immediately canvassed major army commands for peacetime needs for weather information and received some heartening replies. Coast Artillery needed thirty-five weather detachments, the Air Service ten, Field Artillery four, and Ordnance Corps two—a total of fifty-one units.

Meeting this demand would not be easy, for on April 11, 1919, the Signal Corps Meteorological Section was down to eleven officers and forty-nine enlisted men, enough to meet a fifth of the identified need.[22] After fruitlessly trying to obtain men from other parts of the army, Squier solved his immediate problem by dropping the Coast Artillery request, suggesting that it make its own ballistic wind measurements. This permitted spreading his eleven weather detachments among remaining claimants, with the Air Service getting the lion's share.

REAPPEARANCE OF NAVAL METEOROLOGICAL
CAPABILITY

Once World War I broke out, the navy's air arm was among the first U.S. military forces to be operational in France. During November, 1917, Capt. H. I. Cone, officer in charge of Naval Forces, Europe, cabled the Navy Department, urgently requesting qualified officers to interpret weather reports pouring into the French coastal air stations that had been turned over for naval antisubmarine patrols.[23] President Roosevelt had wiped out the navy's meteorological capability thirteen years earlier; now, in 1917, the Signal Corps had largely preempted assistance by the Weather Bureau.

Capt. N. E. Irwin, director of Naval Aviation Operations, relayed Cone's request to Lt. E. H. McKittrick, commander of the naval air detachment at the NACA-inspired ground school in military aeronautics at the Massachusetts Institute of Technology. Unfamiliar with the Boston area, McKittrick asked Roswell F. Barratt, one of his students who had a degree (architecture) from MIT, where meteorology was taught in the area. Harvard came to mind. A week later, the two trudged up an icy path to meet Alexander G. McAdie, director of the university's Blue Hill Meteorological Observatory.[24]

Although courteous, Professor McAdie was reluctant to start a teaching program. Yet he had volunteered his observatory's services to the war effort. He finally agreed to take eight of McKittrick's students for six weeks' instruction beginning December 3, 1917. His main stipulation was that it be a course in "aerography," not "meteorology": "The distinction between meteorology and aerography may not ineptly be illustrated by saying that the former is a study of the atmosphere from the standpoint of the automobilist while the latter is from the viewpoint of the aviator."[25] McAdie also demanded that the course be taught at the postgraduate level, even though his students would carry the humble rank of seaman second class, with a pay rate of $20.90 per month.

In addition to Barratt, the navy's first class in aerology consisted of Joseph B. Anderson (formerly a college physics instructor), Clarence N. Keyser, J. Clement Boyd, Archibald S. MacDonald, Walter F. Prien, and William S. Vanderbilt. Even before commissioning, Barratt was conferring with the U.S. Naval Observatory about equipment needs.[26] Responsible for procuring, issuing, and repairing the navy's weather instruments, the agency retained the function well into World War II. Acquisition was going to be difficult. The army had already borrowed heavily from the Weather Bureau and also contracted most of the production of the two leading domestic manufacturers, Taylor Instrument Company and Julian P. Friez.

During the week of January 20, 1918, Barratt was called to the office of the acting secretary of the navy, Franklin D. Roosevelt, who had been expediting Barratt's equipment requests.[27] Stepping inside, Barratt saw McAdie. Noting the mystification on their faces, Roosevelt said to the lowly ensign, "Well, you asked us to get the professor!" Barratt had earlier commented to Lt. John H. Towers (the navy's third aviator) that it would be a shame for a group of raw aerologists to show up in England and France without some recognized name, such as McAdie. Towers had passed this on to Roosevelt, who followed through, as a good Harvard man, by inviting Professor McAdie to review the navy's future course in aerography. During the chat Roosevelt offered McAdie a naval commission to get the field effort under way. But McAdie, who was fifty-five, demurred; it was at this point that Roosevelt had suddenly called for Ensign Barratt.

The teacher and his student were sent outside to discuss the problem privately. McAdie finally promised to join if it meant his spending only thirty days overseas. Roosevelt agreed, and the resulting paper work moved quickly. On January 25 the supervisor of the Naval Air Reserve Force requested that McAdie be enrolled as a lieutenant commander and posted to the aviation desk in the Office of the Chief of Naval Operations to set up a "Naval Aerological Organization." His actual enrollment date of February 1, 1918, can thus be considered the formal beginning of the modern naval weather service.[28]

Even before McAdie was sworn in, Captain Irwin had set a goal of manning each coastal aerographic station with two officers and six quartermasters (Class A, aerographic) so that such a unit could provide winds-aloft measurements every two hours when needed, particularly at blimp bases. Thus, as early as January 1918, Lt. William F. ("Cyclone Bill") Reed, Jr., on leave of absence from the Weather Bureau, was offering aerological training to quartermaster strikers and to officer candidates at the Pelham Bay Park, Long Island, quartermaster school. Now that the navy's goal was to train sixty aerographic officers as quickly as possible, McAdie also agreed, though reluctantly, to continue the Blue Hill training program.[29]

While waiting overseas transport in February and March, 1918, McAdie and his first graduates wrote *A Manual of Aerography for the Unites States Navy* and worked out with the Naval Observatory a standardized aerological equipment list for naval air stations. Then on April 16, McAdie, eight junior officers, and fifteen quartermasters finally left to organize an American aerogaphy service at French and Irish stations. In London the famed Sir Napier Shaw, director of the Meteorological Office, and Rear Admiral Parry, the Hydrographer Royal, welcomed them graciously. Sir Napier arranged for the Royal Meteorological Society to elect several of them as society fellows and gave them access to his "Forecast Room," where they could learn how forecasts of British weather could be made primarily from cloud analysis (there were no ship reports to the west of the British Isles because of radio silence). Rear Admiral Parry also offered to lend twenty sets of aerological instruments for station use.[30]

Mid-May found McAdie and Barratt in Paris, where Dr. A. Angot, director of the Bureau Centrale Météorologique, and the U.S. Army's Major Bowie helped get the long-awaited U.S. Navy aerological service under way. However, within a month, McAdie took off for Blue Hill, leaving Barratt, now a lieutenant (junior grade) in charge of eighteen aerographic stations in France and Ensign McDonald in charge of five stations in Ireland.[31] By the war's end, two other aerographic units were in Italy. All told, twenty-two aerological officers went to Europe. They usually issued weather forecasts that covered short periods—six, twelve, and twenty-four hours—with special emphasis on visibility (fog and haze), cloud height (if low), precipitation, and wind patterns, particularly any local winds that compelled the men to place blimps and seaplanes in hangars.

In the "Zone of the Interior," Ens. E. B. Buck performed yeoman service on the Washington scene, advising the director of naval aviation operations where to post domestic aerological units and how to man them. As of November, 1918, seven of these units existed—Key West, Miami, and Pensacola (all in Florida), Chatham (Cape Cod), Rockaway Inlet (Long Island), Anacostia (District of Columbia), and San Diego (California), as well as two in Nova Scotia (Halifax and North Sydney).

As early as 1915 the navy had installed wind direction and velocity sensors at each end of the speed course at NAS Pensacola. However, the first aerologist, Lieutenant Reed, did not report in until April, 1918, from Pelham Bay Park. On May 4, by flying seaward of Pensacola in an R-6 aircraft, Reed made the Navy's first recorded weather reconnaissance flight.[32] On June 19, 1918, he then started a regular series of pibals to provide upper wind velocity and direction data for navigational training flights. These were soon supplemented by using the cantankerous kite balloon *Nurse* to suspend a Robinson anemometer and wind register at altitudes of 425 feet, 2,375 feet, and 2,700 feet. Eventually this procedure was simplified by taking six soundings per day to an altitude of 1,000 feet. Additional upper air data were also acquired by lashing an aerograph to the wing struts of an N-9 aircraft.

As soon as the fighting in Europe ended, most of the navy's aerographic personnel wanted out. At its peak, the aerographic section had 53 aerologists (all reservists) and 200 enlisted men. By October, 1919, the count stood at 5 officers and 3 enlisted men. Still, the secretary of the navy's annual report for 1919 noted that "the war has shown the importance of security and dispensing reliable meteorological data to ships and stations concerned with aeronautical work." Nevertheless, in late 1919 the aerographic section was transferred from aviation and placed in an auxiliary support division of the Bureau of Navigation, which also included sections pertaining to photography and messenger pigeons.[33] At the urging of the Weather Bureau, President Wilson had also ordered the convening on September 22, 1919, of an interdepartmental board on meteorology to determine what role, if any, military weather services should play during peacetime. But before all this happened, the dwindling aerographic section was given one last major task—to provide comprehensive weather information for the first mass aircraft flight from the United States to England.

TRANS-ATLANTIC FLIGHT OF THE NANCIES

Although the end of World War I found the U.S. Navy operating more than a thousand seaplanes, most were of French and British manufacture. To overcome that embarrassment, Rear Adm. David W. Taylor, chief of the Bureau of Construction and Repair, ordered that work begin in September, 1917, to build a flying boat capable of nonstop flight across the Atlantic Ocean. The first test flight of this huge wood-and-canvas seaplane came thirteen months later. Costing just $30,000, this class of Navy-Curtiss aircraft (there were four of them, nicknamed Nancies) used four 400-horsepower Liberty engines and a wingspan of 125 feet to lift as much as 24,600 pounds. Normal cruising speed was 72 knots loaded.

Orders issued in February, 1919, activated NC Seaplane Division 1 under the command of aerography's earlier friend and now a commander, Towers. As a consolation prize to senior naval aviators kept on domestic desk and instructional duty during the recent hostilities, navy secretary Josephus Daniels, a noted squasher of naval initiatives, surprised everyone by authorizing the division to conduct a mass flight, with intermediate stops, from Rockaway Inlet to Plymouth, England, as soon as feasible. The real reason for this rush was the British hope of making the first trans-Atlantic flight; they were readying no less than seven aircraft to win the *Daily Mail's* £10,000 prize for such a crossing.[34]

Obviously, there was no time to waste. However, because McAdie was nowhere in sight at the Navy Department, Towers asked Barratt, just back from England, to plan a supporting meteorological observation network. To aid the operation, Secretary Daniels authorized the navy to deploy a "bridge of ships" (forty-nine destroyers placed at intervals of 50 nautical miles) between Trepassey Bay, Newfoundland, and Plymouth via Ponta Delgada (the Azores) and Lisbon (Portugal). To aid navigation, each ship would "make smoke" during daylight whenever a Nancy was heard. At night, star shells would be fired at 5-minute intervals and searchlights would be trained on smoke trails to indicate wind direction.

The all-important weather information would come from several sources. The British Meteorological Office kindly offered to radio European weather collectives to the U.S. Weather Bureau in Washington, as well as to the command post aboard the seaplane tender USS *Aroostook* in Trepassey Bay, beginning May 1, 1919. To fill regional gaps in surface weather observations normally provided by cooperating merchant vessels, three battleships (USS *Utah, Texas,* and *Arkansas*) were spotted north of the track-line and two battleships (USS *Wyoming* and *Florida*) to the south. Quartermasters (aerographic) and meteorological equipment were also aboard ten of the in-line destroyers to provide observations every six hours. Finally, assigned seaplane tenders carried forecasters as follows: USS *Baltimore* in Halifax harbor—Lieutenant Commander McAdie; USS *Aroostook* in Trepassey Bay—Lieutenant Barratt, assisted by Willis R. Gregg of the Weather Bureau; USS *Melville* at Ponta Delgada—Lt. J. B. Anderson; and USS *Shawmut* at Lisbon—Ens. Francis W. Reichelderfer.

Three Nancies (NC-1, NC-3, and NC-4) arrived one by one in Trepassey Bay by May 15, the NC-4 aircraft having flown only five hours when she left Rockaway Inlet. To ensure takeoff, the planes needed moderate surface winds. Aloft, they needed a tail wind component of 10 knots, minimal cloud cover permitting celestial navigation and easy spotting of destroyer numbers, and wave heights of less than 10 feet should an aircraft abort and have to taxi to shelter. At noon on May 16, Gregg advised, "All in all, I believe that the conditions are as nearly favorable as they are likely to be for some time."[35] Barratt similarly informed Towers that weather and sea conditions looked favorable to him. And at midafternoon, Bowie's forecast out of Weather Bureau, Washington, indicated the same.

All three seaplanes got under way at 6:00 P.M. Lt. Comdr. Albert C. ("Putty") Read, in NC-4, trusting Barratt's wind forecast, took 660 pounds less fuel on board than did Commander Towers in NC-3 and Lt. Comdr. N. L. Bellinger in NC-1.[36] They planned to stay in formation, but Read's plane kept outrunning the other two. After making landfall on the westernmost Azores island, NC-4 finally landed alongside the USS *Columbia* in Horta Harbor in the midst of fog banks, 15 hours, 13 minutes, and 1,380 nautical miles out of Trepassey Bay. But with an active warm front lying south of the flight path, the two slower aircraft met increasingly bad weather and thickening fog. NC-1 finally sat down in heavy seas 160 miles northwest of Fayal Island and sank three days later. NC-3 also force landed in heavy seas. By a combination of drifting and taxiing, and despite damage to the plane, the crew made it safely to Ponta Delgada 42 miles away to end their part of the mission. On May 27, NC-4 was off and away to Lisbon; three days later she flew on to Plymouth. Elapsed flying time for the entire route proved to be 53 hours, 58 minutes, spread over twenty-three days. The return to the United States for a heroes' welcome was by ship, however, for aircrew and for aircraft.

Because of intense international interest in the epochal flight, Gregg's meteorological summary of this event appeared in the *Monthly Weather Bulletin* just a month later. As he saw it, four key lessons had been learned: (1) marine barometers on ships needed improvement because it was impossible to calculate surface pressure gradients for wind values accurately; (2) upper-air observations from pilot balloon ascents at sea were very useful in flight planning; (3) radio equipment in aircraft still suffered from a lack of range and static suppression; and (4) if having fixed weather station vessels at sea for aiding trans-Atlantic flights was not feasible, a much larger network of cooperating merchant and naval vessels was needed for regularly transmitting accurate weather observations to shore.[37] Just the same, although Gregg's suggestions were valid and the North Atlantic had now been crossed by air, two more decades went by before passenger flight schedules were advertised and maintained across such a stormy sea.

Chapter 3
The Advent of Modern Weather Forecasting (1920–1939)

Take a large, almost round, rotating sphere 8000 miles in diameter. Surround it with a murky viscous atmosphere of gases mixed with water vapor. Tilt it back and forth with respect to a source of heat and light. Freeze it at the ends and toast it in the middle. Fill most of its surface with liquid that constantly feeds vapor into that atmosphere. . . . Then try to predict the conditions of that atmosphere over one small area 50 miles square for a period of one to three days in advance.

—Agenda for the Raytheon Company
weather radar symposium (January, 1963)

THE NORWEGIAN SCHOOL OF METEOROLOGY

Between 1915 and 1919, the horsepower of aircraft engines increased fourfold, vastly increasing speed, range, altitude, and payload. But the art of navigating aircraft saw little change. Altimeters and compasses remained inaccurate and sluggish, as did tilt meters, so flying during the 1920s was mostly visual and by the seat-of-the-pants. Pilots preferred to fly at 3,000 feet or less and verify their position by such checkpoints as railroads, rivers, and cities, particularly if the city names were painted on roofs or water towers. Before taking off, a pilot would gaze at the weather around him. If he liked it, he took off. He then kept going until clouds enveloped him. At that point he could fly back to an open airport or find an open field to sit down in until the weather cleared. Even the relatively skilled U.S. Aerial Mail Service had 75 percent of its forced landings induced by weather along the Washington–New York–Chicago–Omaha route.[1]

Nevertheless, the Weather Bureau could not provide better meteorological support to aviation until it could overcome the technical lag caused by lack of funds. President Wilson's interdepartmental board on military meteorology in early 1920 had already decided that (1) the U.S. Weather Bureau would continue as the primary agency for collecting and disseminating meteorological data and information; (2) the army and navy would maintain skeletal weather organizations that could, after a quick recruiting effort, man military facilities as necessary, particularly those far removed from the Weather Bureau's central offices and in specific need of unique meteorological advice; (3) the three weather organizations would exchange data and reports in such a way as to enhance efficiency and avoid duplication.[2]

Unfortunately for the military, the bureau's thinking as the national weather service was that forecasting was basically empirical, extrapolative, and two-dimensional. Thus, in 1916, when the agency asked its best forecasters to document their techniques, the consensus of the review board was "that the only road to successful forecasting lies in the patient and consistent study of the daily weather maps." This meant that a person could rise to the rank of forecaster from the very bottom simply by being diligent, and some did.[3]

Placing weather forecasting on a rational, three-dimensional basis was largely the work of a small, talented group of Scandinavians working at the Bergen Museum's newly formed Geophysical Institute in Norway. With the spread of World War I, Norway was unable to supply its all-important farming and fishing communities with weather forecasts because of impoundment of weather data by the warring powers. To remedy this situation the government brought back Norway's leading hydrodynamicist, Professor Vilhelm Bjerknes, from the University of Leipzig (Germany) and asked him and the museum to see what could be done using a grant of 100,000 kroner, starting in 1917. Three students (H. Solberg, Tor Bergeron, and Bjerknes's son, Jacob) were set to analyzing weather data from a tight station network covering southern Norway supplemented by data from frequent pilot balloon ascents.[4]

Two years later young Bjerknes postulated an extra-tropical cyclone model wherein warm, cold, and occluded fronts existed as sloping interfaces between sharply differing air masses (see Fig. 1).[5] The term *front* was derived from the phrase "battle front," then very much on the minds of everyone. As Bjerknes saw it, a nearly continuous conflict occurred on a circumpolar basis between warm, moist air masses (typically from the south or west) and cold, dry air masses (largely from the north or the east).[6] To start such a battle, one air mass or the other would thrust into the other's domain, the cold air underrunning and the warm air overriding. Then somewhere on this sloping interface, a tiny ripple would form and, steered by prevailing westerly winds aloft, move with an eastward component. If atmospheric conditions were just right, this wavelet could grow during the next few days into a huge storm vortex capable of modifying the air column

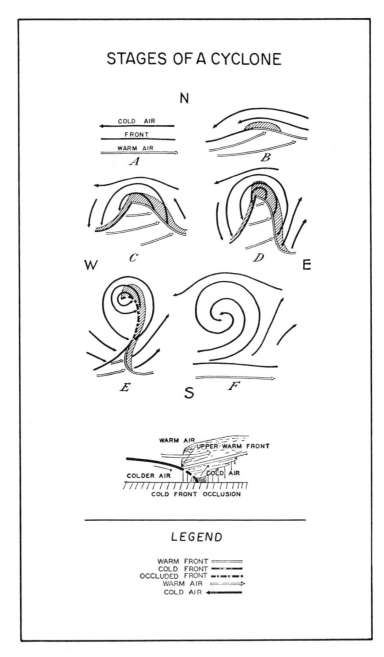

Fig. 1. *Above*: ground plan of an extra-tropical cyclone's life cycle; *below*: vertical cross-section of cold front occlusion. (From U.S. War Department, *Weather Manual for Pilots*, TM 1-230)

up to the base of the stratosphere. Gradually the contrasting air masses would lose their identity in such a low pressure area, and the consequent "occluded" storm center would drift away to the northeast to slowly refill. By then, the "polar front" would have been restored, waiting for the contrast in air masses to become so great once again that the entire cyclone cycle would repeat itself.

Noted British wartime meteorologists such as David Brunt, Ernest Gold, and C. K. M. Douglas accepted this "air mass analysis" concept early on. In contrast, the U.S. Weather Bureau under instrument-oriented Marvin clung rigidly to its intuitive extrapolation of the movement of pressure centers and squall lines, rather than drawing fronts and predicting their movement on the basis of mathematical considerations.[7] Consequently, it was quite natural for Americans to emphasize the provision of better current weather information to aviators, rather than better forecasts.

In 1922 the Army Air Service started a "Model Airway" between Norfolk, Virginia, and New York City via Washington, and from Washington to Dayton, Ohio, home of the service's flight test facility. The airway not only had a string of light beacons such that the next one was always in sight (assuming good visibility) but also a radio beam system by which a pilot could tell whether he was drifting off the airway. As a prime participant, the chief signal officer added extra weather stations along the airway route and ensured "that pilots flying regularly over this route be kept advised of weather conditions along the airway, particularly of storms and fog."[8]

Four years later the new Air Commerce Act required the Department of Agriculture to provide an improved service of "weather reports, forecasts, warnings, and advices for the safety and efficiency of air navigation."[9] Also during 1926, a twenty-seven-year-old meteorologist, Carl-Gustav Rossby, arrived at the Weather Bureau via a research fellowship of the Swedish-American Foundation. Rossby, who could be either a first-class theoretician or a promoter par excellence, was assigned a desk in a dingy, remote corner of the library, where his "Norwegian theories" would not annoy senior officials. But Rossby was not easily disposed of. In July, 1927, the Daniel Guggenheim Fund for the Promotion of Aeronautics established the Committee on Aeronautical Meteorology. At the urging of the navy's aerological desk officer, Lt. Francis W. ("Reich") Reichelderfer, the committee selected Rossby to be its chairman.[10] Then, in December of that year, Rossby moonlighted a weather forecast for the nation's new hero, Col. Charles A. Lindbergh, to use in a 27-hour nonstop flight from Bolling Field, District of Columbia, to Mexico City. Marvin, in a fit of pique, soon withdrew the bureau's welcome mat for the aggressive Swede.

The spring of 1928 found Rossby in California, using Guggenheim funds to extend the Weather Bureau's fledgling airways weather reporting service south from Oakland to Los Angeles. By talking and partying with pilots of the Fokker trimotors of the Western Air Express, which were not equipped with radios, Carl-Gustav discovered that aviators could fly this foggy, mountainous route safely only if there were many more weather reports than the standard airways service provided. Before Rossby and his summer aide, twenty-two-year-old Horace R. Byers, got through, they had arranged for thirty subordinate observing stations to supplement the bureau's basic four.[11]

Although nine years had gone by since the Bergen school published frontal and air mass analysis concepts, no U.S. college yet taught the technique. Moreover, both the army and the Weather Bureau trained their forecasters in-house. Over in the navy, Reichelderfer did not like this approach and finally cajoled MIT into offering a full year's meteorological curriculum as of September, 1928, with Rossby as lead instructor. Consequently, in a little more than two years after coming to America, Rossby, still not thirty years of age, went from being an ignored research fellow to founding meteorological education at the nation's leading school of technology.

MIT's West Coast competitor, the California Institute of Technology (Cal Tech), had also prospered under the postwar leadership of Millikan. Cal Tech, too, lacked a meteorological curriculum; how this gap was filled is also relevant. Once Rossby departed the Los Angeles area, Western Air Express hired as its staff meteorologist the twenty-year-old Joseph J. George, a physicist just out of the University of California at Los Angeles. Two years later, Byers, as one of Rossby's first MIT graduate students, suggested to his musician brother-in-law, Irving P. Krick, that he should look into meteorology, as music was not paying well.[12] Krick chose Cal Tech, where he learned meteorology from the world-famous seismologist Dr. Beno Gutenberg, who had been a German army meteorologist during World War I, as well as from observing Weather Bureau methods at its downtown Los Angeles office.

By 1932 Krick knew enough weather forecasting to seek a job at Western Air Express. George was on vacation, so Krick saw the chief pilot, Jimmy James. James gave Krick the job of "baggage slinger" at Burbank Airport, but with the option of talking to pilots about basing their flight plans on "Norwegian-style" weather maps. Krick proved to be an excellent salesman (and still is), and Western's pilots quickly took to this new style of weather presentation. Thus, when George came back, he not only had to add Krick to his staff but also had to draw frontal lines on the weather briefing charts.

Meanwhile, Krick continued working on his master's degree in meteorology at Cal Tech. Then, after learning that the navy had lost a large new dirigible, the USS *Akron*, in a thunderstorm off New Jersey on April 4, 1933, he advised the noted Dr. Theodore von Karman, chairman of Cal

Tech's Guggenheim Aeronautical Laboratory, that the deadly situation could have been forecast.[13] Armed with this information, von Karman approached Millikan, the chairman of Cal Tech's Executive Council, about setting up a graduate curriculum in meteorology. Reflecting on his own challenging years in military meteorology, Millikan agreed. By September, 1933, Cal Tech had a department of meteorology with Krick as chairman and the world-famous von Karman and Gutenberg as lecturers in boundary-layer and upper-atmospheric phenomena, respectively.

Although MIT and Cal Tech were offering the very latest in meteorological thinking, Marvin at the Weather Bureau remained indifferent. In fact, his hands were full just keeping the national weather service afloat; cuts by President Roosevelt made it necessary to dismiss nearly 500 employees out of 1,600 and to reduce the budget from $4.5 million in FY 1932 to $3.8 million in FY 1934. On top of this, the Great Plains were experiencing a persistent, severe drought that began in 1930 and now had created a dust bowl. At the urging of the scientific community, FDR created during July, 1933, a Scientific Advisory Board, chaired by Dr. Millikan, to assess the Weather Bureau. Two other members of the five-man board were also from academia—Dr. Karl T. Compton, MIT president, and Johns Hopkins's Isaiah Bowman, a geographer and chairman of the National Research Council. It was a stacked deck, and the seventy-four-year-old Marvin soon retired.

Taking over at M Street was the aeronautical meteorologist Willis Gregg, who had supported the Nancies' flight fifteen years before. Thus, it was no surprise that the bureau's annual report for FY 1934 cited "a need for a broader and more open-minded viewpoint regarding the utilization . . . of what is known as 'air mass.'" Things began to change. Yet Gregg's annual report for FY 1938 reflected a note of puzzlement: "It was formerly supposed that a more comprehensive knowledge of weather proccesses and more complete information regarding them would both clarify and simplify the problem of weather forecasting. In actuality, although the problem has been clarified, it has not only failed to become simpler, it has become many times more complex—yet for that reason far more interesting." Then, on September 15, 1938, Gregg died suddenly of a heart attack.

The Millikan Committee again went into action and radiogrammed the unsuspecting Commander Reichelderfer, now executive officer of the battleship USS *Utah*, that Millikan wanted to see him immediately on his arrival in port. Reichelderfer agreed to take the helm of the Weather Bureau, even if it meant a cut in pay.[14] He also could bring Rossby in to serve as assistant chief for research and education. The switchover came on December 15, 1938. Thus, in just thirteen years, two young proponents of the Bergen way of thinking had taken over the old-line, die-hard Weather Bureau!

STABILIZING THE NAVY'S AEROLOGICAL PROGRAM

To reaffirm the interdepartmental board's finding on the role of military meteorology, the secretary of agriculture wrote his navy counterpart on January 14, 1920: "It is fully recognized that certain meteorological work and observations must of necessity be conducted by the Navy in connection with its operations at base stations and on vessels at sea, but such work does not involve duplication of effort."[15] With national policy thus established, Lt. Comdr. R. M. Griffin, as head of the Aviation-Navigation and Photographic Division within the Bureau of Navigation, encouraged reservist Lieutenant (jg) Keyser to push along with determining the needs and goals of the aerology branch.[16] The goals Keyser worked out were to place an aerological unit at each of the dozen air stations of the navy and the Marine Corps, plus on the carrier USS *Wright* and the seaplane tenders USS *Shawmut* (Atlantic Fleet) and USS *Aroostook* (Pacific Fleet). To train the requisite manpower, a four-month meteorological course had been started for officers and ratings at Pensacola on November 1, 1919; it was followed by a two-month postgraduate course in weather forecasting for the five officers at the Weather Bureau's Washington office.

Navy aerology continued to have a shaky existence. Its main customer, the fleet air arm, had no single spokesman within the Navy Department. The situation was rectified by the formation of the Bureau of Aeronautics on September 1, 1921, with Rear Adm. William A. Moffett as bureau chief. Moreover, the bureau's organization chart provided for operating, training, personnel, and aerology sections within the all-important Flight Division.[17] Aerology's return to the world of aviation did not, however, guarantee personnel stability; simultaneous cuts in the associated officer corps reduced manpower levels from thousands to a few hundred.

Keyser failed his conversion exam to regular navy status, so he resigned in early 1922 to sell real estate. Reed filled in on an acting basis, but he, too, could not convert because of age limitations. Fortunately, Lieutenant Reichelderfer at Hampton Roads passed his conversion exam, so in June, 1922, he took over the aerology desk. His task was clear-cut: "to build up the entire naval meteorological organization—personnel, selection of stations, instruments, operations, analysis and forecasting methods."[18]

Some progress had been made; for a time the aerological service numbered fifteen officers and twenty-three enlisted men, with six men in training. By mid-1921 nine field units were taking regular, twice-daily pibal soundings and transmitting the data via telegraphic code to "Weather Bureau, Washington." The Weather Bureau sent back selected surface reports and generalized twenty-four-hour weather forecasts, including flying conditions, to cooperating military units and to navy radio stations in Arlington, Virginia; North Chicago, Illinois; Point Isabel, Texas; Key

West, Florida; and Puerto Rico (Cayey and San Juan, June to November only) for wireless transmission to ships at sea. Plans also called for Radio San Francisco to do the same for the Pacific area the following year.[19]

Upon taking over, Reichelderfer was eager to improve weather forecasting. At the height of the Billy Mitchell airpower-seapower controversy a year before, Reichelderfer had been flying his own forecast for bombing runs against the former German battleship *Ostfriesland* on July 18, 1921. During his squadron's return to Hampton Roads, the aircraft had to penetrate a line squall so severe that some pilots landed on the beach to avoid crashing. Reichelderfer's "busted" (inaccurate) forecast was based on the classical Abercromby storm model of 1885, which contained no discontinuity surfaces. But he knew of the Bjerknes cyclone model from his reading, so he began using frontal analysis for his own weather charts, thereby establishing a largely unheralded technical first in American meteorology.

By 1923 Reichelderfer had a manpower problem. Although Pensacola regularly turned out weather observers, they were still designated "Quartermaster-Aviation" and continually drifted out of the program. Late that year, he was able to have the rate of "Aerographer" established, the number of annual classes for the rating increased to three, and the training shifted to Anacostia. So that seniority in the program could be built up, the navy accepted any background provided a man was trainable and reliable.[20] By 1925 it became possible for practically all field units to be run by chief petty officers.

Solving the aerological officer problem was far more difficult. In-house training failed to motivate graduates to stay in the speciality.[21] Senior line officers considered themselves competent weather forecasters (after all, you only needed to keep track of the barometer) and thought poorly of any promising young officer who wished to specialize in "weather guessing." It became necessary to draft officers for aerological training. Yet, by 1925, only two aerologists were on duty: Reichelderfer at the bureau desk and Lt. Joseph B. Anderson, a lighter-than-air flight specialist, at the sole dirigible base, NAS Lakehurst, New Jersey.

By then, the zealous Brigadier General Mitchell had made remarkable progress in convincing the nation that it needed a national air force; the incompetence of army and naval aerial spectaculars helped make his case. One of these got underway on August 31, 1925, when two of the navy's new long-range, twin-engine seaplanes (PN9-1 and PN9-3) left San Francisco on a nonstop flight of approximately 2,100 nautical miles to Pearl Harbor, Hawaii. Five hours out, PN9-3, with engine trouble, ditched at sea during darkness. Twenty hours later, PN9-1 ran out of fuel 420 miles short of Oahu. Despite a string of guard ships, the aircraft dropped out of sight and was presumed lost.[22] Then, a day after the PN9-1's highly publicized disappearance, the navy's first domestically built rigid dirigible, the USS *Shenan-*

doah, left Lakehurst en route to the Air Service Balloon and Airship School at Scott Field, Illinois, for a swing over midwestern country fairs. Unfortunately, she also crashed in a predawn line squall on September 3, killing fourteen crew members.

Mitchell immediately renewed his accusations, which led to his court-martial. President Coolidge empaneled a special board chaired by Dwight W. Morrow of J. P. Morgan and Company to investigate the issue of military aviation and determine the future role of commercial aviation. After hearing ninety-nine witnesses and reviewing hundreds of submissions, the board recommended in late 1925 that each military service operate greatly enhanced air arms. One of the lesser recommendations was that "greater attention to be given to the study of weather" in both civil and military agencies.

The Morrow board's recommendation permitted Reichelderfer to raise once again with the Bureau of Navigation (which also acted as a bureau of personnel) the issue of improving the professional training of aerologists. This time, he found the new desk officer for postgraduate training, Capt. W. D. Puleston, highly enthusiastic about starting a sophisticated course for eight officers on July 1, 1926. The first year would be at Annapolis and the second year "at a yet-to-be selected university which offers the best course on weather." Puleston quickly delivered eight volunteers, most of whom had six or more years of sea duty. But Reichelderfer could not come up with a suitable second-year university. Finally, Harvard's militarily oriented climatologist, Henry DeCourcy Ward, agreed, with MIT's help, to take the initial class.[23] But future classes were to be handled entirely by MIT. This arrangement overcame the bottleneck, and by 1934 the navy carried twenty-four aerologists on its rolls, a number shrinking to eighteen by 1940.

In large part, this shrinkage came from the attitudes of such navy leaders as Rear Adm. Ernest J. King who, as chief of the Bureau of Aeronautics, testified on May 30, 1933, before the joint congressional committee on dirigible disasters: "Insofar as there is any prospect of there being a corps of aerological officers, there is none whatsoever at the present. If they want to continue to be naval officers, they will have to do some work aside from aerology. If you keep a man in aerology, or in airships, or in the heavier-than-air line, he cannot get to be head of the [naval] service."

AEROLOGICAL ACTIVITIES BETWEEN THE WORLD WARS

Between 1920 and 1940 the Aerology Section continuously sponsored technique and instrument development but its success was typically modest

Table 1. Naval Contributions to Aerological Technology (1920–1936)

Year of First Mention	Initiative
1920	Development of gore kite balloons to lift aerographs designed and built by U.S. Naval Observatory.
1922	Improvement of marine theodolite for measuring balloon ascents at sea
1923	Mounting of anemometers on 600-foot tower at Radio, Va.
1924	Improvement of aerological plotting board and instrument mast.
1925	Investigation of long-range weather forecasting; beginning of daily aerographic flights to height of 10,000 feet during April, to 15,000 feet the following February, at NAS Anacostia.
1926	Transmission of weather maps by "radio television" to USS *Kittery* and USS *Trenton*.
1927	Building of recorder to use with radio goniometers provided by Robert Watson-Watt of British Air Ministry in a radio static direction finder network.
1928	Sponsorship of technical studies of aircraft icing, fog dispersal, fog forecasting, and improvements in upper-air observations while at sea.
1929	Utilization of temperature-entropy diagrams; development of device to warn dirigibles of dangerous electrical conditions.
1932	Initiation of aerological flights at Guantanamo Bay, Cuba, to more accurately compute ballistic densities.
1935	Beginning of development of buoy-mounted automatic weather station (first device available during 1939).
1936	Support of U.S. Bureau of Standards development of radio-meteorograph, with first marine installation during 1938 aboard USS *California*.

SOURCES: Annual reports of the Secretary of the Navy (1920–1936).

because of limited funding and the intractability of the assigned problem. For example, it took seven years (1921–28) to develop an improved shipboard balloon theodolite. Some of the more interesting efforts are listed in Table 1. The period was also highlighted by the pressing need for aerological officers to continue to sell their skills to aviators and, far more difficult, to interest the "gun club" (i.e., battleship admirals or those about to be). C. G. Andrus, a specialist in upper-air measurements for the Weather Bureau, cogently describes the situation during 1921: "The attitude of aeronauts toward guidance by a trained aerologist is not always one of amenability. Aviators, in balloons and in planes, are often of a type characteristically daring and aggressive; they enjoy to a degree the obstacles presented by difficult weather. Some airmen instinctively feel that meteorological advice deprives flying of some of its sporting chances and of its gameness, and consistently will not avail themselves of the assistance of the aerologist."[24]

Despite Andrus's words, most lighter-than-air operators sought aerological advice. During the 1920s the public still was deeply interested in the national and international balloon races held each summer. Both navy and army teams participated; they covered distances up to 1,200 miles in eighteen to sixty hours, if severe weather or approaching coastline did not abort the flight.[25] However, more serious was the possibility of using rigid dirigibles as long-distance scouts for the battle fleet. Rear Admiral Moffett and Lt. Comdr. Charles E. Rosendahl often pointed out that the huge airships USS *Akron* and USS *Macon* were capable of carrying their own fleet of five short-range scouting aircraft and could cruise nonstop at 50 knots up to 8,100 nautical miles. During the heyday of the concept, the navy was authorized to procure and field-test five rigid dirigibles 600 feet or more in length, like Germany's Zeppelins.

As might be expected, airships were weather sensitive. They could be walked into or out of their hangars (a process called docking) if the surface wind velocity was 5 mph or less.[26] Outside mooring to masts could be done only when surface wind velocities were below 30 mph. When the ships were so moored, a close guard had to be kept on the streaming direction. A sudden wind shift, such as onset of a sea breeze at Lakehurst, could actually stand an airship on her nose, as happened to the USS *Los Angeles*. While aloft, the airship was affected by the weight of rain, snow, or ice on the external skin; by strong headwinds that might actually drive the ship backward; and by diurnal heating and cooling of the internal gasbags, which changed the airship's lifting capacity. However, the greatest problem was created when the airship encountered severe atmospheric turbulence associated with line squalls (cold fronts) or isolated summer thunderstorms.

Overcoming these meteorological hazards was the task of the airship commander and his assigned aerologist. As early as 1921 Comdr. Louis H. Maxfield, while commander of the precommissioning detachment for the ZR-2, wrote his superiors from Howden, England, describing how British meteorologists directly involved themselves with airship operations. It was a practice that the U.S. Navy should duplicate, he said, rather than relying on generalized forecasts from the Weather Bureau.[27] He went so far as to propose to the president of the Naval War College that a meteorological expert be assigned to the next fleet war games.

The response of the Navy Department was positive. An aerological facility was assigned on September 4, 1923, to the Naval Airship Construction and Experimental Station at Lakehurst. Unfortunately for airship enthusiasts, between 1921 and 1934 four of the navy's monsters of the air crashed with loss of life because of structural problems, severe weather conditions, or both. Each accident was investigated in depth. Dirigible advocates vowed to do better each time. However, advocates of fixed-wing aircraft like the New York *Daily News* were quick to counterclaim that for the price of a fleet dirigible such as the USS *Akron* one could buy seventy-six pursuit planes at $20,000 each and seventy-six bombers at $50,000 each. Yet such heroes as Lindbergh and Brigadier General Mitchell testified to the Congress during 1933 that development of the rigid dirigible should continue both for commercial and for military purposes; Mitchell went so far as to state that future airships had the potential "to sink anything on the top of the water or under the water." But Rear Adm. King, speaking as chief of the Bureau of Aeronautics, maintained at the same hearings: "the backbone of the Navy today is the battleship . . . it can stand up and take it and you have nothing else that can. . . . I see no prospects of airplanes alone displacing surface ships."[28]

Both enlisted and officer weather specialists found airship duty exacting and exciting. During the catastrophic flight of the USS *Shenandoah*, Lieutenant Anderson ended up astride the dangling keel walkway when the control car tore away. He was pulled to safety by a line passed from above. And when the USS *Akron* crashed off Barnegat Inlet, New Jersey, the ship's aerologist, Lt. Herbert M. Westcoat, and two chief aerographers, Earl P. Hackett and Leon D. W. Liles, lost their lives. Investigating boards for both crashes, after hearing the testimony from naval and Weather Bureau specialists, concluded, as they had for the *Shenandoah's* flight: "The commanding officer was entirely justified in starting the flight at the time chosen, as the weather maps and reports indicated nothing which would have rendered it unsafe or inadvisable."[29] Both boards did recommend a more extensive meteorological service. The *Akron's* board specifically suggested that four general weather maps per diem be issued by the United States Weather Bureau instead of two as at present.[30]

Aerologists posted to the Pacific area fared somewhat better than those on the East Coast. Lt. Comdr. Wilbert M. ("Red") Lockhart proved to be the best of the navy forecasters for the Pacific Ocean. An Annapolis graduate (1917), he saw duty on gunboats, destroyers, light cruisers, and battleships before starting the third postgraduate aerology course in mid-1928.[31] Upon graduation from MIT, he replaced Maguire at the aerology desk of the Bureau of Aeronautics. In looking for ways of being useful, he recalculated the fleet's just completed long-range, first-salvo results by utilizing nearby NAS San Diego winds measured up to heights of 30,000 feet rather than by the conventional practice of using surface-wind values. Lockhart's adjustments caused the first salvos to fall within 50 yards of the target, much closer than the more typical and unsatisfactory 100 to 200 yards. With these data, he convinced the Bureau of Ordnance to direct force commanders thereafter to use true ballistic winds and densities, supplied courtesy of the nearest aerological station.[32]

In early 1933 orders came to implement one of Lockhart's recommenda-tions—a weather survey of the far north Pacific Ocean. With the assign-ment came the impressive title "Commander, Bering Sea Aerological Expe-dition." He set up weather stations on Kanaga and St. Paul islands during April and May, 1933. He then spent the next eleven months at the Dutch Harbor naval radio station, creating the first indepth, twice-daily North Pacific weather analyses with the help of two exemplary aides, Chief Aer-ographer Jack Shirley and Aerographer's Mate 3rd class Kimberly.[33]

By the fall of 1934 Lockhart had become communications officer on the battleship USS *Pennsylvania*, with additional and subordinated duty as aerological officer to the Commander in Chief of the U.S. Fleet (CIN-CUS)—there being but one fleet in those days. Lockhart discovered that the fleet, because of limitations on fuel costs, exercised at sea only three to four days a month. Moreover, the exercise planners did not take weather's va-garies into account. Yet occasional, extremely gusty Santa Ana winds of autumn and winter could affect the operational area, causing low clouds and severe haze. With the fleet operating by a rigid exercise plan formulated far ahead, sometimes only three or four of the thirty-five scheduled exer-cises could take place because of the Santa Ana winds. Fortunately, Adm. Joseph N. Reeves listened to Lockhart's suggestion, and the next monthly exercise schedule carried the notation: "Zero hour of exercise beginning will be upon signal from CINCUS." Because of the careful aerological advice, the results surprised everyone; the fleet completed thirty-four of thirty-five scheduled exercises. As a consequence, the minuscule aerological service was gaining the confidence of most top naval commanders.

AN ARMY STEPCHILD

Three years after the armistice Army Regulation (AR) 105-210 of November 12, 1921, finally delineated the peacetime role of the Signal Corps Meteorological Service. For the next fifteen years command echelons carried on a debate concerning the scope and type of weather service to be provided, particularly to the assertive and often rebellious Army Air Ser-vice. Throughout this entire postwar period, the Signal Corps never had more than eleven weather officers at a time. Even so, the number of army weather stations grew from eleven to a peak of forty-one, a good example of emphasis on quantity, not quality.

During this evolutionary period the basic goal of the five major generals who served as chief signal officer (starting with Squier, who had reinstituted the army's meteorological service) was to retain and preserve the army's communication function during a time of great austerity, rapid tech-nological change, and shifting military priorities. As might be expected, the meteorological desk within the Office of the Chief Signal Officer moved from time to time. In 1921 the meteorological section was one of four—the others being pigeon, photo, and commercial—within the special services division. Two years later, the meteorological section became part of the Intelligence Division, where it stayed until 1929, when it became a division in its own right.

Technical leadership and direction of the Signal Corps weather function during the 1920s and 1930s rested heavily on four World War I volunteer weathermen—Blair, Thiessen, Sherry and McNeal, all of whom converted to regular army status. Meteorological training was centralized at Camp Vail, New Jersey, for observers as well as for enlisted and officer forecasters. To anyone familiar with the "old army" between the wars, it comes as no surprise that the intellectual attributes of the initial observer trainees were not too high. Of the first forty-three students who took the five-month advanced course, only seventeen had grades of 75 or better, thereby earning diplomas; the others received certificates of attendance. In the best Signal Corps–Weather Bureau tradition, the army weather stations remained primarily observation and information dissemination points; the Weather Bureau provided most of the forecasting expertise. However, Lieutenant Thiessen recalled that army pilots by 1924 were no longer satisfied with generalized forecasts that might simply read as follows: "The weather will be partly cloudy and warm over New England and east of the Appalachian Mountains . . . and cloudy with general rains in the region of the Great Lakes." Nevertheless, the chief signal officer's prime interest lay in expanding and improving the airways network and adding weather observation stations, either Weather Bureau or army. During 1924 Blair did get to serve, however, as the advance weather observer-forecaster for the Army Air Service round-the-world flyers slowly working their way westward along the Aleutian Island chain.[34]

During the 1920s the army, like the navy, placed considerable emphasis on manned balloons. For a time, balloon flights were even a requirement for receiving one's wings for piloting heavier-than-air aircraft. As 2nd Lt. Don McNeal wrote in the *Monthly Weather Bulletin* for June, 1920, penetrating a thunderstorm meant a "balloon flight crowded with interesting observations and experiences." Dr. C. Leroy Meisinger (the brightest of the Texas A&M military meteorology graduates) and a fellow balloon pilot Lt. James T. Neely tested this concept to the ultimate on June 2, 1924. Weather Bureau employee Meisinger and his military teammate were completing the last of ten free balloon flights for studying air motion at different levels within cyclonic disturbances. When they left on this flight from the Air Service Balloon and Airship School at Scott Field, weather conditions looked satisfactory. Near midnight, lightning hit the hydrogen-filled gasbag, and both plunged to their deaths. Capt. William E. Kepner, who taught meteorology at the balloon school, lived to tell of a hair-raising trip through a strong cold front while piloting the damaged army blimp RS-1 en route from San Antonio, Texas, to Scott Field on October 16, 1928.[35]

Until the mid-1930s the army General Staff emphasized the creation of a defensive air force capable of giving close air support to ground combat forces, plus protecting the nation's land borders; the navy held the sole responsibility (which it jealously guarded) for stopping attacks from the sea. Thus, during aerial maneuvers held in New England in 1931 not far from the Canadian border, hundreds of army aircraft participated from throughout the country. The Signal Corps weather service worked out well during this much-publicized two-week test of defense plans. The chief signal officer's report for that year noted that its meteorological arm was the "most capable ever available to a military organization," and that the exercise demonstrated that the "training of personnel and methods used in military meteorology are essentially correct."

Nevertheless, some were still dissatisfied with the state of the art in weather forecasting. Lieutenant Commander Reichelderfer, for example, did not know why the weather charts he drew at Lakehurst differed so much from those drawn at MIT. So he spent half of 1931 visiting the Bergen group—J. Bjerknes, Tor Bergeron, Hans Solberg, and Sverre Petterssen—to determine the cause. His comprehensive report on the Norwegian forecasting method was marked "Restricted" before being filed in Washington because it was not yet in final form. But the classification generated the rumor that the "Reichelderfer Papers" contained information that the Air Corps and the Weather Bureau lacked. Inevitably, a copy was bootlegged outside the navy, and soon hundreds were avidly reading his report to learn what Reichelderfer had found.

The quality of weather predictions for army aviation remained marginal because the best Weather Bureau forecasters remained in downtown district offices and never met their flying clientele face-to-face. It seemed that army aircraft always crashed because of bad weather. For instance, after participating in an impressive flyover of the Chicago World's Fair on September 9, 1933, Maj. John G. Cogan tried to bring his seven-plane squadron of Douglas observation aircraft back to base at Mitchel Field, Long Island, the same night. Unfortunately, a pea soup fog rolled in on the sea breeze that afternoon. In the ensuing confusion, three of the aircrews (including Cogan and another pilot, 1st Lt. Julius K. Lacey) bailed out, their aircraft crashing willy-nilly in an inhabited area. Only two pilots, one of whom was 1st Lt. Arthur F. Merewether, were skilled or lucky enough to land as planned in the darkness.[36]

Responding to the series of accidents, Professor Jerome Hunsaker, chairman of MIT's department of aeronautical engineering (wherein resided meteorology), soon visited Brig. Gen. Oscar Westover, deputy chief of the

Air Corps. Hunsaker, a Naval Academy graduate with years of extensive experience, noted bluntly: "General, your pilots need some weather training. You are having too many crashes and losing too many pilots. Now we at MIT have a problem, too. We don't have a suitable aircraft for taking really good APOBs [airplane weather observations]. Let's make a deal. We at MIT will teach your men meteorology for free if you'll send along an Army airplane with them."[37] This seemed fair enough, so Westover agreed.

Looking at the roster of army pilots scheduled for further ground school, the Air Corps personnel desk spotted "Merewether, Arthur F., 1/Lt." Not only was the name appropriate, but the pilot was also at blind flying school (a course that had just opened at Langley Field) and would soon be capable of safely penetrating cloud cover. In December, 1933, Merewether enrolled at MIT.[38] This meant getting up at 5:00 A.M. each day to take the early morning APOB in some of the century's worst Boston weather and also carrying a full load of graduate courses. Obviously, if MIT had an Air Corps meteorological student, Cal Tech must have one, too; Merewether's Cal Tech counterpart was 1st Lt. Robert M. Losey.

Then, out of the blue on February 5, 1934, President Roosevelt announced that, to resolve a contractual dispute with the commercial airlines, the Army Air Corps two weeks later would begin flying all of the nation's air mail. This twelve-week task proved to be an operational disaster. Blind flying was still new, and the army's open-cockpit combat aircraft had neither turn-or-bank nor artificial horizon indicators. Despite a rapid installation program at the Middletown, Pennsylvania, air depot, the indicators ended up being mounted too low on the instrument panel. Improper equipment, pilot inexperience, extremely bad weather, and inadequate ground support caused the mail to get through on schedule only one-third of the time.[39] Worse, ten army pilots died in crashes during the first three weeks of the mission.

This fiasco placed a tremendous crimp in the continuing campaign of the Air Corps for increased military emphasis on air, rather than land, power. Aviation enthusiasts, of course, preferred to blame the deficiency in air mail service on unusually bad weather. To sort out the facts, President Roosevelt formed a board on April 17, 1934, under Newton D. Baker, who, as secretary of war in World War I, had dealt before with ebullient Air Corps claims and demands. After hearing 105 witnesses and studying some 500 written statements submitted by Air Corps officers, many of whom thought the Baker board was stacked in favor of the army's high command, the group made recommendations that astounded many. The board strongly urged unity of command, as well as the immediate creation of a centralized Air Corps combat arm that would be called the General Headquarters Air Force. The unpleasant proviso was that this new force commander, who would control much of the army's combat aviation, should report directly to the General Staff. This, of course, would leave the chief of air corps with supply and manpower functions.[40]

A lesser recommendation overcame the long-held intransigence of the Signal Corps toward giving the army's weather service higher priority in manpower, technology, and equipment, particularly with respect to its sister service, the Air Corps. Baker suggested that the chief signal officer create three new meteorological companies (in addition to three already in place) with the sole mission of supporting the Air Corps "mobile striking force."[41] But upon becoming chief signal officer in January, 1935, Maj. Gen. James B. Allison made it clear he would not be another General Hazen who allowed the tail (i.e., the minor weather role) to wag the dog, namely, the army's continuing priority need for speedy, accurate, and reliable communications both in peace and in war. From Allison's point of view, even though the weather component made up only 5 percent of his command, additional personnel billets for any extra weather units would have to come from resources outside the Signal Corps.

After five months on the job Allison launched his campaign for additional manpower with a letter to the adjutant general. This action started a two-year donnybrook involving many command levels. Eventually, Allison's letter acquired thirteen endorsements. Many were contradictory because the Air Corps did not want the weather mission unless additional people and dollars came with it. Halfway through the hard-fought maneuvers, the Air Corps even agreed to having the Agriculture Department's Weather Bureau provide basic services by placing civilian forecasters in a lead role at twenty-eight military airfields. This idea was quickly shot down from two sides. The Bureau of the Budget objected because, with cheap in-house labor, the army could perform the service for half what the Weather Bureau would charge. Gen. Malin Craig, the army's chief of staff, likewise objected to having highly paid civilians doing the same job alongside professional soldiers. The man in khaki would be certain to become discontent, a fact of life that Hazen had discovered the hard way in the 1880s.

The addition of thirteen endorsements to a military proposal before action is taken now seems puerile. But it was the Great Depression. No immediate military threat loomed, and there seemed to be time for the supercilious games that peacetime staffs tend to play. Finally, after sixteen months of bickering, army assistant chief of staff Maj. Gen. John H. Hughes advised the Air Corps that, as the prime user of a technical service such as weather, they should be the prime provider. This cut the Gordian knot. Within a month the Air Corps proposed a method for doing so. Craig's office quickly concurred, and the historic spin-off from Signal Corps to Air Corps sponsorship took place on July 1, 1937, under these guidelines: (1) Weather service would be provided by the Army Air Corps to itself and to ground forces at the division level or higher. (2) Weather services required by army services other than the Air Corps would be provided by themselves. (3) The chief signal officer would maintain responsibility for development, storage, and issuance of meteorological supplies and for meteorological communications. (4) Signal Corps officers in the regular army and with a weather specialty could apply for temporary Air Corps duty but would have to become rated pilots for permanent integration. (5) Signal Corps enlisted meteorological personnel could transfer to Air Corps without loss in grade, and future training of such personnel for weather observing and forecasting duty would be an Air Corps responsibility.[42]

With all the necessary paperwork in order, 6 officers and 180 enlisted men of the Signal Corps joined 16 rated officers (pilots or navigators) and some 100 enlisted men of the Air Corps. Of the Signal Corps officers, only Capt. Don NcNeal, who had been a weather instructor sergeant at Texas A&M in 1918, shifted over permanently. The forty-six-year-old McNeal then became dean of the fledgling Air Corps weather service and director of its training program, a role he maintained throughout World War II.

THE EMBRYONIC AIR CORPS WEATHER SERVICE

1st Lt. Robert M. Losey happened to be manning the weather desk for the chief of Air Corps, General Westover, when meteorology became a full-fledged aviation function. Westover's staff was small, so Losey had direct access to the chief, and decisions about how the new service should be organized took little time.[43] The final plan called for three domestic weather regions under a regional control officer in each case, with operational areas roughly coinciding with those of the three General Headquarters Air Force wings. Supplementing these was the General Headquarters staff weather officer at Langley Field, plus independent weather stations for bases overseas. By 1939 the organizational structure diagrammed in the manner shown in Fig. 2. Overall, the three weather squadrons assigned to the three weather regions operated forty-two installations of varying complexity. These field units could be anything from a simple airways observer facility to a major base weather station (at least two officers and fifteen enlisted men). The primitive Alaskan Territory did not rate a single weather detachment. But the more pleasant climes of Panama, Hawaii, Puerto Rico, and the Philippine Islands merited a total of nine weather units.

Whereas the Signal Corps concept rigidly required each meteorological company to have exactly the same table of organization and equipment, the Air Corps gained flexibility by recognizing that weather regions had varying needs. For example, the 1st Weather Region, although it covered the western half of the nation, needed only six major base weather stations. In contrast, the 3rd Weather Region, in the center of the continent, needed not

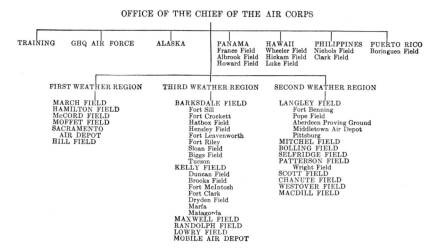

Fig. 2. Organization of the Air Corps Weather Service, 1939. (U.S. War Department, *Weather Manual for Pilots*, TM 1-230)

only the same number of base weather stations but also sixteen smaller weather units for observational and training purposes.[44] In late 1939 Losey validated his service's requirements at 40 weather officers. On hand were 30 officers (and 388 enlisted men), double what the Signal Corps had been using two years before.

By now the Air Corps had been receiving B-17 heavy bombers for the past three years. Consequently, its airpower enthusiasts watched with great interest what effect bombing raids would have on military and civilian targets in Spain, Ethiopia, and China. When Russia invaded Finland in November, 1939, Lieutenant Losey saw a way of breaking away from desk duty. His opposite number in postgraduate weather training, First Lieutenant Merewether, was then getting over a bout of arthritis at nearby Walter Reed Hospital. Losey proposed to Gen. Henry H. ("Hap") Arnold, the new Air Corps chief, that the aviators needed someone in Finland to observe the "Winter War"—namely, Losey. Arnold agreed but only if Losey could come up with an immediate replacement. "That's easy," Losey replied, "I've got just the man—Merewether's over at Walter Reed!" Within two hours Losey's orders were cut for Finland, and Merewether took over the Weather Station, Training and Operations Division, at headquarters on January 18, 1940.[45]

Chapter 4
World War II—The Home Front

Each war brings new weapons, new methods of transportation, and new instruments of communication. Warfare, in all these phases, is affected by weather, and sooner or later makes new demands on the meteorologist, necessitating a change in methods of observations, communication, and forecasting in the war theaters.

—U.S. Weather Bureau Record of War
Administration (1948)

GETTING ORGANIZED

After Nazi Germany invaded Poland on September 1, 1939, American military leaders were more than ever convinced that the United States would eventually end up in combat with the Axis powers and Japan. The only questions were when, where, and how. In the interim, America's military power required an explosive buildup.

Fortunately, the meteorologists in the army's and navy's weather services had tremendous stamina. As the Air Corps Weather Section chief, First Lieutenant Merewether had a supporting staff of two—a civilian and a secretary. In the adjoining Navy Department building, Lieutenant Commander Lockhart, as officer in charge of the aerological section within the Bureau of Aeronautics flight division, had a staff of three—Lt. Thomas Rafferty, a yeoman, and an aerographer's mate who, after preparing a daily weather forecast, posted it on the hallway door. Merewether's and Lockhart's worries were many. What kind of field organizations would be needed when war came? Where could they find enough trained manpower for such units? How should they be equipped? In developing preliminary answers, they regularly worked past midnight in the steamy, nonairconditioned summer days of 1940 and on into the cooler months.

Lockhart's biggest worry was how the naval weather service could transmit and receive weather data once the fleet observed wartime radio silence.

The issue was spotlighted in September, 1939, when, by chance, he spotted his friend John Patterson, director of the Canadian Weather Service, in a U.S. Weather Bureau hallway. Patterson said that he was there to inform Commander Reichelderfer that Canada was ceasing weather broadcasts in the "clear." In addition, the Canadian weather reports regularly transmitted by landline to Weather Bureau, Washington, would be encoded and for Weather Bureau internal use only. On the spot, Lockhart convinced Patterson that such internal usage could be extended to the U.S. Navy and Army Air Corps provided the data were handled confidentially and all further transmissions were in military code. What Patterson did not know was that the U.S. Navy had no workable method for doing such transmission on a high-volume basis.[1]

The task of solving that problem was assigned in November, 1939, to a special weather unit formed at NAS Anacostia, District of Columbia, under Comdr. J. B. Anderson, assisted by AGC J. W. Reams. The eventual solution was to feed all acquirable weather reports into a central point, where a team of the best forecasters available would analyze the data and redistribute the end products (forecasts and "canned," i.e., numerically encoded, weather charts) by encrypted wireless and teletype messages. As Lockhart maintained, such a key facility with its supporting communications could be logically termed a "weather central."

By early 1940 two weather centrals were operating in the Washington, D.C., area—the navy's at NAS Anacostia and the Air Corps' (labeled the Research Center) at adjoining Bolling Field. Later on, with the outbreak of war, these centrals were shifted adjacent to the Weather Bureau's forecasting center to save manpower and avoid duplication. In the meantime the navy was able to establish its first Pacific area weather central at San Francisco in October, 1940. Lockhart took that command and arranged for his Bureau of Aeronautics replacement to be an MIT classmate, the "balloonatic," Lt. Cdr. Howard T. ("Shorty") Orville. As a consolation prize for assuming headquarters duty, Orville was designated an aeronautical engineering duty officer (aerology), the second such officer in the navy (Lockhart was the first).

In the Munitions Building, Merewether also made solid progress. Within two months starting in December, 1941, he activated four new weather squadrons (5th, 6th, 7th and 8th). By then, he had a military assistant, 2nd Lt. James W. Osmun, handling equipment matters with the Signal Corps. At Bolling Field, the Air Corps Research Center was directed by a former geologist, Capt. Don Z. Zimmerman; it was regularly providing forecasts for the South Atlantic air ferry route, as well as special weather studies upon demand. Although the center could issue forty-eight-hour forecasts, chief of the Air Corps General Arnold wanted weather predictions ten days ahead at least as good as those being generated by Professor Franz Baur at the German Institute for Long Range Weather Forecasting.

Moreover, from his days at March Field, California, Arnold remembered that his friend Krick had said that he could reliably predict weather situations a month ahead.[2] Arnold summoned Merewether: "What are you doing about long-range weather forecasting?" "General, I've got a good man, 1st Lt. Moorman, studying it at MIT." "But why not at Cal Tech?" "Because there's no course on it there!" "Well, you call Krick and if he does have such a course, let him name four of his previous Air Force graduates and send them out there for that course!" Merewether immediately phoned Krick, who created a course on the spot. Soon the men Krick selected (Captain Zimmerman and 1st Lts. Harold L. Smith, Milton W. Arnold, and John B. Ackerman) were en route to Pasadena. By autumn they were back at Bolling, enabling the first Air Corps thirty-day weather forecast to be issued on October 20, 1941. Unfortunately, little forecast skill was evident. Even so, by March, 1942, weather projections based on Krick's improved map-typing techniques were sent regularly to major Air Corps weather facilities.[3]

Backed strongly by Secretary of Commerce Jesse Jones, his new departmental boss, Commander Reichelderfer called a meeting on July 26, 1940, to discuss how the three Washington-based weather organizations could work together more closely. The chief topics on the agenda were research proposals (particularly for long-range weather forecasting), allocation of trained manpower to civil and military weather functions, and the recruiting and training of additional weather observers and forecasters.[4]

Six months later the war scare was far enough along for the group to constitute itself formally as the Interdepartmental Committee on Meteorological Defense Plans as of January 21, 1941. By midyear the title was simplified to Defense Meteorological Committee. After President Roosevelt designated the Weather Bureau a "war agency" by Executive Order 8991 on December 26, 1941, the group's letterhead changed to read "Joint Meteorological Committee." The group began handling Joint Chiefs of Staff weather matters. Then in February, 1942, the domestic committee was supplemented by the Combined Meteorological Committee staffed with personnel from Great Britain, Canada, Australia, South Africa, New Zealand, and the United States. The U.S. group was to handle weather issues for the Combined Chiefs of Staff, particularly the vexatious problem of standardizing weather codes, as well to develop the initial aspects of weather annexes for upcoming amphibious invasion plans.[5]

One of the most useful products of all these committee meetings was the Weather Bureau's Historical Northern Hemisphere Weather Map Series, which was started in October, 1941.[6] Initially, the series ran only from January, 1929, through June, 1939, but, in 1943, the years as far back as 1899 were added. Each of these daily charts contained about 600 weather observations. Preparing a year's maps meant locating, adjusting, and spotting more than 200,000 entries from many sources whose quality differed widely. Pressure gradually built for having the full forty-year map series available for weather typing purposes. By late 1943 more than 1,000 persons were involved in the project, including sixty army weather officers and meteorological staff members at Cal Tech, UCLA, and New York University.

TRAINING EN MASSE

In the spring of 1940 France and the Low Countries unexpectedly fell to Hilter's forces; in response, on May 16, President Roosevelt announced that the United States should quickly build 50,000 military aircraft, nearly a hundredfold increase in aviation personnel and facilities. If there were to be enough instructors for the new pilots in training, Captain Merewether had to do something quickly. By existing law, the only untapped pool of military personnel with college backgrounds available to him were washed-out aviation cadets. He also needed a place where meteorologists could be trained. MIT came to mind. Merewether flew a biplane to Nob Hill, Vermont, landed in a field, and hitchhiked into town to convince Professor Sverre Petterssen that MIT should set up a crash ninety-day course for forty washed-out cadets and Weather Bureau fellowship students funded by the Civil Aeronautics Administration.

Petterssen quickly agreed. But as graduation day neared in September, 1940, Merewether and his cadets had a major problem. Air Corps headquarters was not about to grant officer's commissions to ninety-day wonders when cadet counterparts still in flight training had to go a full nine months before pinning on gold bars. Despite considerable hue and cry, the weather cadet graduates remained cadets for nearly another year, many of them serving at base weather stations. However, others sought and accepted direct naval reserve officer commissions.[7]

Even before the ninety-day-wonder program flopped, Merewether was arranging a nine-month aviation cadet training program providing rigorous postgraduate training at the nation's five meteorological schools. The arrangements, as worked out with Reichelderfer, called for speeding up the formation of full-scale meteorological courses at UCLA and the University of Chicago (the latter to be headed by Rossby, with Horace Byers once again his lead assistant). In addition, Rossby would chair a new and powerful University Meteorological Committee. Krick's national influence was to be modified to some extent by posting the great Norwegian meteorologist, Jacob Bjerknes, as the top instructor for the UCLA curriculum. More or less simultaneously, many of America's young scientists and mathematicians faced a choice: being drafted into the infantry at $21 per month or volunteering to be a meteorology aviation cadet at $75 per month and undergoing nearly a year of postgraduate training at some of the nation's best universities. Many opted for the second choice.[8]

In early 1942 Merewether left the Washington maelstrom. His replacement, Don Zimmerman, was then advised by Brig. Gen. Harold M. McClelland, director of AAF Technical Services, that the AAF ought to have approximately 5,000 weather officers by January, 1944, and twice that number early the next year.[9] The existing university weather cadet program could not meet such a demand. So the Technical Training Command started a vast but short-lived AAF Weather Training Center at Grand Rapids, Michigan, in early 1943. By late March of that year, 1,473 cadets, operating under West Point discipline, were drawing practice weather maps in the municipal auditorium. The following month, enlisted observer and forecaster courses were also started at Grand Rapids. The center's combined enrollment peaked in the neighborhood of 3,600 before it was rapidly phased out in late 1943 because of a gross overestimate of training requirements.

Even further back in the manpower pipeline were another 3,000 premeteorology students attending college in uniform on twenty additional campuses. But the big buildup came to a halt after Maj. Gen. Barney M. Giles of the Air Staff insisted during May, 1943, that the AAF would easily have enough weather officers to meet foreseeable needs through 1944. Thus, the last large cadet training group started classes on October 4, 1943. Moreover, Giles was right; at graduation the following June, almost all the 1,800 new weather officers were assigned to other duties.

In contrast to the AAF program, which trained 6,200 weather cadets before commissioning, the naval program for training 1,800 aerological officers commissioned the young men and women first. They went then to a seven-week "charm school" to learn how to be officers before studying alongside the AAF weather cadets or attending the weather course at the Naval Postgraduate School, Annapolis, Maryland.[10]

But no matter the color of the uniform, the budding military meteorologists found the training rigorous. At the universities half of the lead instructors were recently emigrated from Europe, so the students first had to learn how to interpret what was being said. Much of the teaching was highly theoretical. Thus, A. Raymond Gordon, who eventually became a reserve AWS colonel, recalls his first lecture in thermodynamics from Chicago's Michael Ference:

> Immediately we were in over our heads, completely befuddled by his notation and esoteric nomenclature. After the class, seventy guys still in civilian clothes stood around as if shell-shocked, each with his own personal thoughts as to how he would fare in the infantry. Two or three days went by before someone took a consensus and turned up the fact that, with the exception of one or two,

the entire group was getting as little from Ference's lectures as if he were delivering them in Swahili. After a delegation passed on this information to the scholarly professor, he lowered his sights considerably and gave the course at, what to him, must have seemed like the kindergarten level.[11]

The Army Air Corps achieved an equally rapid expansion of its training program for enlisted personnel. On April 11, 1940, the forecaster school at Wright Field was combined with the observer school brought from Scott Field to form a comprehensive "Weather School," still under Captain McNeal, at Chanute Field, considered by many the Siberia of the Air Corps because of its location on the bleak Illinois prairie. The ten-week observer course emphasized practical studies; the twenty-two-week forecaster curriculum was one of the most difficult in the technical program of the Air Corps. In the latter course students not only prepared weather maps and predictions but also attended lectures on calculus, vector analysis, and radiation. At its peak, Chanute graduated 150 to 200 weather observers every two weeks, plus approximately 300 enlisted forecasters every three months.[12]

By May, 1942, women were needed to free men to fight. However, the army's initial try at putting women in uniform was far from a happy one. Females, no matter how skilled, had to be auxiliaries—hence the name, Women's Auxiliary Army Corps (WAAC). Most were assigned to office or chauffeuring duties on a base during the day, then returned at night to the post's WAAC company housing area for supervision by a female officer acting as a housemother. In mid-1943 the situation began to improve. No longer auxiliaries, females were made part of the army and served in the Women's Army Corps (WAC). By this time, the AAF Weather Service had requisitioned 500 WAACs and advised domestic squadron commanders that contingents of eight WAACs (seven weather observers and a clerk) per post company could be assigned to local post or base weather stations stateside. To assist in this program, a WAAC officer was assigned to Weather Wing headquarters, and in May, 1943, the first weather women began appearing at army weather stations. All told, 242 WACs performed weather duty during World War II. None, by the way, were designated "colored."

Unfortunately, army rules initially prohibited women from receiving specialized training prior to permanent field assignment. Thus the first WAC contingent at the 16th Weather Squadron at Great Falls, Montana, consisted of former waitresses reclassified as "potential weather observers."[13] Nevertheless, in the spring of 1944, 3rd Weather Squadron commander Lt. Col. Oscar A. Heinlein established the first all-WAC weather observing station at Kelly Field, Texas. Fourteen of the squadron's thirty-seven WAC observers were assigned to Kelly, and by August, 1944, Heinlein had formed two more all-WAC observing units—at Bergstrom Field, Texas, and at Carlsbad Army Air Field, New Mexico. During that same August a former Bergstrom weather observer, 2nd Lt. Roberta R. Price, was also assigned to squadron headquarters to serve as the assistant adjutant and personnel officer, a WAC first at the squadron level. [14]

Although the female observers did a good job of chart maintenance, map spotting, and record filing, Heinlein decided in late 1944 to break up his all-WAC observing sections. In periods of extremely severe weather, the 3rd Weather Squadron reported, "WAC observers do not seem to be as stable as weather observers should be." However, the squadron noted that assigning one male observer per shift stabilized the situation. WAC observers also suffered an old problem—coordination of weather station duties with extra duties frequently assigned by their local WAC detachment commander.

One attempt was made during 1944 to upgrade WAC enlisted observers to forecaster status. Ten WACs were added to the sixty males assigned to Chanute's April class for enlisted forecasters. Five WACs graduated the following September—Sgt. Lois McFetridge and Cpl. Jean Smith (assigned to Kelly), Sgt. Jeanette Thom and Cpl. Sarah Applebaum (assigned to Bergstrom), and Sgt. Dorothy Woodward (assigned to Carlsbad). At the end of the year Heinlein reported that the accuracy of McFetridge's and Smith's forecasts were on a par with those prepared by males. However, because of the surplus of male forecasters, this WAC training program was not repeated.

Weather squadrons overseas sometimes had WACs assigned as clerical workers after May, 1943. Most were enlisted, but one WAC officer, 1st Lt. Doris J. Witherspoon, is known to have served as a weather equipment specialist in the Pacific theater west of Hawaii. Although very few WACs ever saw the inside of an aircraft, the Women Airforce Service Pilots (WASP) did, logging more than 60 million noncombat miles as they ferried all types of aircraft, including the latest fighters. In addition, between November, 1943, and December, 1944 (when the WASPs were disbanded), fifteen of their pilots were assigned to the AAF Weather Service to ferry personnel on administrative and inspection trips. [15]

From a woman's viewpoint, the navy offered a far more hospitable environment. Even initially, the navy used professional women truly as professionals, granting them reserve rather than auxiliary status. In 1942, at Commander Orville's urging, twenty-five female scientists and mathematicians were chosen for aerological duty. After attending the first formal indoctrination class at the Reserve Midshipmen's School (Women's Reserve) in Northampton, Massachusetts, they joined meteorological classes at MIT. To rate selection, the women had to hold a master's degree or higher. Following graduation in September, 1943, most of these WAVES (Women Accepted for Volunteer Emergency Service) were assigned as forecasters to the navy's rapidly growing complex of domestic air stations. However, Florence van Straten, who held a Ph.D. in chemistry, was posted to Orville's office to assist in preparing operational analyses based on war diaries and battle reports, which would advise the fleet how best to use weather information. [16]

Naval policy also permitted young women to be sent early on to enlisted weather training. For example, sixty-five had graduated as aerographer's mate (3rd class) from the school at Lakehurst NAS by June 30, 1943, a number that grew into the low hundreds by the war's end. Women saw duty at such nonstateside outposts as Pearl Harbor and Argentia, Newfoundland. [17]

Before World War II policy in both the Air Corps and the navy held that blacks were not acceptable in those services, except as steward's mates in the navy. Finally, political pressure required the air force in 1941 to activate two all-black fighter outfits (the 99th and 100th Pursuit Squadrons under the parent 322d Fighter Group) at Tuskegee Institute, the famed Negro college in Alabama. On March 21, 1942, a "Colored" (military orders of that era distinguished between "Colored" and "Caucasian" units and men) weather detachment was established at Tuskegee. A few days later, 1st Lt. Wallace P. Reed, a graduate of MIT's Class II, arrived to become detachment commander. It was the first and only all-black weather unit in the Air Corps. Because of War Department policy, all enlisted weathermen at Tuskegee, forecasters as well as observers, had to be trained in-house at the base weather station, even taking their qualification tests there. [18]

Black weather officers were another matter. Because the official line was that blacks lacked suitable technical backgrounds for qualification as pilots or in scientific fields such as meteorology, the black quota for meteorology aviation cadets was just seven as late as November, 1942, which Judge William Hastie specifically protested when he resigned the following January from his post as civilian aide on Negro affairs to the secretary of war. Meanwhile, Reed continued to command the Tuskegee weather detachment until the war's end; as of June, 1945, his command consisted of sixteen enlisted men and four officers, all black. [19]

Although the Air Corps weather service lagged in utilizing women, it was well ahead of the navy in training military oceanographers. A month after the Pearl Harbor attack the service formed an oceanography unit under the reservist Capt. Harry R. Seiwell. At the time, the world's leading physical oceanographer, Professor Harald U. Sverdrup, had been designated a naval security risk because close relatives lived in occupied Norway. Although Sverdrup was still director of the famed Scripps Institution of Oceanography, little was going on there, and he wished to help where he could. Seiwell was quick to provide funds and support personnel for attacking a number of problems, including the construction of drift charts to be used by airmen downed in the Pacific Ocean. But his biggest project was the development of the quantitative method for predicting sea, swell, and surf conditions for amphibious assaults. Walter Munk, a former army ski trooper, had tried to do this for the North African invasion while working for Seiwell during late 1942. The Sverdrup-Munk technique was not ready, however, until May, 1943, when eight AAF weather officers arrived at Scripps to evaluate the method.[20] The results were excellent. A second AAF group of officer trainees quickly followed, but by then the Joint Meteorological Committee had ordained that the Air Corps oceanographic effort must be turned over to the navy. Eventually, by mid-1945, the navy sent seven groups of aerological officers to Scripps for training in oceanographic forecasting. However, none of these students ever surmised that this new field would expand so steadily that, in 1977, the Naval Weather Service would disappear, melded into the Naval Oceanography Command.

The World War II weather training program was highly successful. Once initial shortages were overcome, the AAF and the navy had an adequate supply of weather specialists, both officers and enlisted men. At the time of the initial Japanese attack, the Air Corps included 400 weather officers and 2,000 enlisted weathermen. By early 1945, when 1,008 weather detachments were operating in fifty-eight countries, the units were manned by 4,500 officers and 14,800 enlisted personnel.[21] In the navy the growth rate was even greater: at the beginning of the war, there were only 90 aerologists and 600 aerographic ratings; by the end of hostilities, those numbers had grown to 1,318 and 5,000, respectively.[22]

EQUIPPING THE MILITARY WEATHER SERVICES

Throughout World War II, because of compromises made in 1937, the AAF's growing weather service had to rely on the priorities and good graces of the tradition-bound Army Signal Corps for all research and development, procurement, and supply of weather equipment. Until relief on October 1, 1944, the definitive Army Regulation 94-150 also required the Signal Corps to install and perform major maintenance on all weather and weather communications gear, thereby creating a split command that gave rise to continual vexation. Because weather played such a small role in the chief signal officer's empire, the informal pillar of bureaucratic strength regarding that command's meteorological responsibilities from February, 1942, on became Mrs. Frances L. Whedon, a new civilian employee. Meteorological section chiefs came and went rapidly, but Whedon stayed; finally, in 1947, she formally assumed the role herself.[23] Invaluable to her operation was the Air Corps meteorological liaison officer to the Signal Corps, Lt. Col. Marcellus Duffy, who coordinated his service's needs both for weather communications and for weather instruments.

Duffy had marked difficulty in prying modern weather instruments out of the stodgy Signal Corps laboratory complex at Fort Monmouth, a situation made even worse during 1943 by an unusually sharp cutback in the laboratory's civilian weather staff. In desperation, Duffy and his assistant, the now Capt. Spilhaus, came up with their own facilitation scheme. Spilhaus (better known as "Spilly") began visiting overseas commands wearing the star insignia of Arnold's personal staff.[24] Then, in his own persuasive style, Spilhaus suggested that the field commanders send urgent messages to the Signal Corps for specific equipment still caught in red tape. Because combat command requests for new hardware were sacrosanct, the meteorological laboratory at Eatontown (renamed the Watson Laboratory in 1945) would promptly complete and ship the desired equipment.[25]

Despite the heavy bureaucracy, Eatontown and the rest of the Fort Monmouth complex turned out seventy-five new or improved items of meteorological equipment during World War II.[26] Of special value were mobile weather stations for the AWS, rawinsonde gear for the field artillery, an all-weather Rawin method of tracking radiosonde balloons using radio-direction finders (SCR-658), and the comparable but far better method using radar (SCR-584), which came along a year later, in 1945. Eatontown also reinvented (but with improvements) the fifteen-year-old British–U.S. Navy sferics technique of tracking thunderstorms by using a three-station radio-fixing system (AN/GRD-1) tuned to lightning discharges—a method that worked for frontal zones but not for tropical cyclones. The AAF Weather Service also developed numerous innovations in applied meteorology (see Table 2 for those of special note).

Turning to the navy, one finds its meteorological supply system to be as simple as the army's was complex. Once the Bureau of Aeronautic's aerological section completed an allowance list for a certain type of field unit, this equipment package was promptly converted into a mass purchase request by the Naval Observatory's aviation office.[27] Following delivery, this gear was then stored at the Philadelphia Navy Yard, to be distributed as needed. As the scope of the war grew, subordinate supply pools were created during 1943 at such distant locations as Alameda, California; Dutch Harbor, Alaska; Noumea, New Caledonia; Brisbane, Queensland; and on the island of Trinidad.

On August 18, 1943, the navy's aerological function was large enough to be broken into two organizational components. Captain Orville took most of his Bureau of Aeronautics staff to form a new desk in the Office of the Deputy Chief of Naval Operations (Air), to run the Naval Weather Service. Left behind in the Bureau of Aeronautics was the aerographer's mate J. A. Shirley, now an up-from-the ranks "mustang" lieutenant, who commanded the Aerological Equipment Section in the Aircraft Maintenance Branch. Mustangs tended to play it safe, so the navy did not see a flood of new weather instruments during the war years. Some of the more interesting

Table 2. Army Air Force Contributions to
Meteorological Technology (1942–1945)

Date	Initiative
June, 1942	Land-line test transmission of facsimile weather charts (Washington, D.C., to Presque Isle, Me.).
August, 1942	Activation of 1st Weather Reconnaissance Squadron (Test) at Patterson Field, Ohio, using modified B-25 bombers. *
Spring, 1943	Radiosonde transmitters/receivers deployed to field units.
September, 1943	Harbor and air defense radars adjacent to Panama Canal used by 6th Weather Squadron for weather surveillance; designated weather analogs transmitted by teletype to selected commands to assist in forecasting beyond 72 hours in advance.
July, 1944	AAF B-17s begin regular long-range hurricane reconnaissance in the Caribbean and Gulf of Mexico.
February, 1945	B-29s of the 655th Bombardment Squadron, Heavy, begin weather reconnaissance flights over Japan.

* Also see George E. Forsythe, "War-Time Developments in Aircraft Weather Reconnaissance," *American Meteorological Society Bulletin* 27, no. 4 (1946): 160–63.

items that did appear (the year of introduction is shown in parentheses) were an automatic weather station using expendable parachute (1942); a radar pulse repeater for Rawin soundings (1942); the propeller-type Aerovane® (1944); a microseismic detector network for hurricane tracking (1944); pressure pattern flying using John Bellamy's concept (1944); and "kytoons," combining the characteristics of balloons and kites (1945).[28]

THE INFRASTRUCTURE OF AEROLOGY

So that the navy's weather service would be acceptable to wartime commanders afloat, seagoing units were compact and self-contained. In return, the Chief of Naval Operations agreed during early 1942 to place aerological detachments aboard all combatant vessels larger than destroyers, a decision that meant that 300 such detachments would be needed. In January of the same year President Roosevelt approved a program for 27,500 naval aircraft, thereby vastly expanding the number of naval air stations as well. To support all this, the number of aerological units increased from 50 in June, 1940, to 124 in December, 1941, and to 406 units a year later. An all-time peak of 1,587 weather detachments was reached on August 1, 1945.

Many of these units consisted of just a single weather observer posted to a scouting submarine in the far Pacific Ocean or aboard a Coast Guard weather trawler operating off Greenland or Iceland. Aircraft carriers, aircraft tenders, and amphibious command ships, however, typically rated a comprehensive unit comprising an aerologist, a chief aerographer's mate, and ten to fifteen rated or nonrated enlisted men.[29] Of the various seagoing junior officer billets, that of carrier weather officer was among the worst (Appendix B). Hours were long and responsibility heavy. Appreciation, if any, was hard to find. The weather guesser's life was further tangled by his often having to work for three masters—the ship's commanding officer, the flag officer aboard as strike force commander, and the ship's operations officer, who wrote the weather officer's fitness report.

Less exciting but far easier duty was found ashore at what eventually proved to be a score of fleet weather centrals. A work force of a central could number as high as twenty-two officers and sixty enlisted personnel, particularly if associated communications and encrypting/decrypting loads were heavy. The Joint Hurricane Weather Central founded in Miami, Florida, during June, 1943, in conjunction with the AAF Weather Service and the Weather Bureau, offered particularly favorable duty.

Initially, the two navy aerologists and ten enlisted men posted to Miami had it easy, for the 1943 Atlantic hurricane season was a very light one. The 1944 season, however, was among the worst on record. Advisories and warnings were issued on ten tropical disturbances, four of which reached full hurricane intensity. The hurricane of September 8–16, 1944, was fully as intense as the one of six years before that had killed or injured 1,100 persons along the Atlantic seaboard. Fortunately, the Joint Meteorological Committee had, as of February 15, 1944, approved a formal plan for regular hurricane hunting/tracking flights by AWS reconnaissance aircraft and upon request, by naval aviation units. The plan worked well, for despite wartime radio silence of ships in the initial path of the storm, aircrews were able to detect and track the storm center five days before it made landfall.[30] As a consequence, 145 navy, Marine Corps, and Coast Guard aviation and shore bases had ample time to implement storm bills, thereby adequately protecting the 12,765 aircraft assigned to those bases.[31]

Before long-range weather reconnaissance aircraft were available, the navy and its affiliated force, the Coast Guard (jocularly known as the Hooligan Navy), had to assign weather station vessels to fill critical gaps in ocean coverage. President Roosevelt had started this practice on January 25, 1940, when he ordered the Coast Guard to inaugurate an Atlantic Weather Patrol. By war's end, sixteen North Atlantic points above 15° north latitude were continuously monitored, eleven by the Coast Guard and five by the British navy. Weather equipment, including pibal, rawin, and radiosonde gear, plus observational personnel, were supplied to eighteen Coast Guard ships by the U.S. Weather Bureau, while the U.S. Navy took up the slack for the other eight Coast Guard cutters. This practice was in stark contrast to that in the Pacific region: there, only one cutter served on weather duty; the U.S. Navy substituted its own motley assembly of forty-one ships, including three yachts.[32]

THE AAF WEATHER SERVICE SETTLES IN

Administrative turmoil. That simple phrase explained the evolution of the AAF meteorological service infrastructure between March, 1942, and July, 1945. During that forty-month interval the role of weather service chief had seven different titles. Despite the upheaval, all of these triple-skilled individuals (they were West Pointers, pilots, graduate meteorologists) with one or more of these designations went on to become general officers, an impossible thing to do in the navy system. In fact, of the fifty senior Air Corps weather officers on June 1, 1942, twenty-two achieved ranks ranging from brigadier general to general. Much of that success was due to the individuals themselves. However, it also paid to be on hand when the army's aviation arm expanded from 1,700 to 250,000 officers during a six-year period.[33] Paralleling this expansion was an increase from eight weather squadrons as of Pearl Harbor day to twenty-nine weather squadrons during November, 1945.

Nineteen of these squadrons controlled weather detachments outside the continental United States. Assignments overseas came frequently, often without special preparation of either the individual or his unit.[34] Unit travel by sea was particularly uncomfortable for enlisted men. For example, when the 21st Weather Squadron shipped from New York for England in July, 1943, its complement of some 100 officers and 300 enlisted personnel were aboard the former Grace Line cruise ship *Santa Elena*. Although the ship was designed to carry 300 passengers in comfort, 5,000 military men were aboard. The enlisted personnel were "hot-bunked" in racks mounted six high in the ship's holds; they endured long outside queues to eat from mess kits. In vivid contrast, officers shared twin cabins and ate at tables covered by dining cloths and were served by deft Italian waiters.[35] But whether one went by ship or aircraft, worldwide dispersal was relatively swift. Thus, author Bates's seventy-man cadet class was graduated in May, 1943. Sixteen months later, known overseas postings were China—ten; India—nine; Brazil—four; northwestern Canada—three; western Pacific—three; Aleutians—two; England—two; Newfoundland—one; and Greenland—one.[36]

Domestically, the most critical wartime weather forecasting project that the AAF Weather Service dealt with was carried out in extreme secrecy. In 1942 meteorological cadets at the University of Chicago were debating what was going on in the out-of-bounds Metallurgy Laboratory just below their map practice room in the Physics Building. In 1945 the facility's experimental findings with atomic chain reactions needed to be verified by Test Trinity on the remote salt flats of Alamogordo, New Mexico. Trinity's director, Dr. Kenneth T. Bainbridge, and his boss, the legendary Dr. J. Robert Oppenheimer (a former Cal Tech faculty member), obviously needed someone to head the meteorology section of the experiment.[37] Wishing to have someone they could select and control, in March 1945 they temporarily hired a Cal Tech civilian meteorologist rather than take potluck with the military. Their choice was Jack M. Hubbard, a physicist who had taken a master's degree under Krick during 1941 before doing airline work in South America and serving as an AAF civilian research meteorologist.[38]

Hubbard had little time to organize his group: the world's first atomic explosion was scheduled just four months later. His fourteen-man team was extremely low in rank. Even so, the unit was further subdivided into four subsections (radar and rawins, pilot balloons, radiosonde, and base weather and records), supplemented by a meteorologically instrumented C-45 flown by 1st Lt. Raymond Stockton.[39] The overall task was twofold: provide local weather forecasts to ensure safe on-site conditions for firing the nuclear device and determine that the resultant atomic fallout would come down in a sparsely inhabited part of the desert. The annual climatic singularity of the region arrived on schedule, as Hubbard had feared. The dry and terrifically hot days of June gave way to surges of moisture from the south. Consequently, violent thunderstorms with frequent lightning would form in afternoon hours and continue throughout the night before dying out in early morning. Nevertheless, on Friday night July 13 the experimental device was atop the detonation tower, a ready-made lightning rod if there ever was one. President Truman was particularly eager for the shot to take place. He could use it in negotiations with Premier Stalin at the Potsdam (Berlin) conference, slated to open the following Monday. Because the monitoring equipment needed darkness, the preferred shot time became Sunday night. But Hubbard was forecasting afternoon and evening thunderstorms for the next two days.[40]

By then, Hubbard was receiving help from another Krick associate, Col. Benjamin G. Holzman, whom Hubbard had been authorized to invite to the test along with the AAF Weather Service chief, Col. Donald Yates. For technical backup Holzman had Maj. John A. Wallace specifically assigned to the AAF Weather Central in the Pentagon for providing surface and upper-air forecasts to ultra-high levels for all New Mexico. Holzman would then call daily, from a pay phone, for Wallace's input. From Wallace's point of view, this arrangement was very unsatisfactory. One day, he finally said, "Look, Ben, New Mexico is one hell of a large area. If you tell me where you are, I am sure I can do a much better job of preparing the forecasts." Holzman replied, "This is a super-secret operation. But when I call tomorrow, I'll call you collect; you listen to the operator tell you where the call is coming from." It worked. So despite the tightest security, Hubbard had the benefit of using both his own local team and that of the master weather central almost half a continent away.[41]

Sunday evening arrived with monsoonal weather—a light drizzle and lightning in the distance. With zero hour but seven hours away, the upper winds would carry the radioactive plume directly over Amarillo, Texas. At midnight the light rain was continuing. Mist wafted past the shot tower. Maj. Gen. Leslie Groves, director of the Manhattan Project, and Dr. Oppenheimer tensely conferred, decided to blame the weathermen, and ordered the test delayed until just before dawn.[42] At 2:00 A.M. a full-fledged thunderstorm swept through the area. Fortunately, it did not burn out the complex test wiring. By 4:00 A.M. the rain stopped. At 4:45 A.M. Hubbard presented his final prediction: "Winds aloft very light, variable to 40,000, surface calm. Inversion about 17,000 feet. Conditions holding for next two hours. Sky now broken, becoming scattered." Neither Amarillo nor any other large town appeared in danger of fallout. The shot took place forty-five minutes later, and the world has never been the same.

*C*hapter 5
World War II—Defeat of Hitler and Mussolini

A storm is neither a friend nor an enemy; it cannot be controlled, praised, or punished; but it must not come unannounced. The forecaster must not let himself be taken off guard. . . . . The science, challenge, and the excitement that stem from a feeling of purpose and usefulness, become great riches when one gets a task to forecast for a decisive and important operation that has been fully explained. Then, one has become a member of a team; one exchanges science (and sometimes wisdom); one asks and one answers; and one feels that the team is a oneness and, because of that, it must win the victory.

—Sverre Petterssen's diary the night of the
RAF raid against the battleship *von Turpitz*

TRANSPORT ROUTES TO EUROPE, AFRICA, AND THE MIDDLE EAST

Over the North Atlantic   President Roosevelt publicly formalized the "Keep Britain Afloat" campaign by signing the Lend-Lease Act on March 11, 1941. From then on, the Joint Chiefs of Staff gave highest priority to moving badly needed supplies eastward. But stating the need to do so was far easier than making it happen, for German submarines were sinking the ships and supplies faster than new ships could be built. Consequently, establishing air routes to the United Kingdom, Africa, and the Middle East in the shortest time possible was an absolute necessity. Fortunately, useful real estate existed. In early April, 1941, the United States agreed to defend Greenland—and, three months later, Iceland. Moreover, the Canadians and the British had been experimenting since November with flying twin-engined Lockheed Hudson patrol aircraft over the North Atlantic in formation from Gander Lake, a new, remote air field in eastern Newfoundland.

Only the lead aircraft in each flight carried a navigator. Still, of the first three flights of twenty-eight Hudsons, twenty-five made it, thanks to perceptive weather forecasts supplied by "Pat McFog" (Patrick McTaggart-Cowan), Gander's weather specialist.[1] During 1940 these were the only military crossings except for one British PBY (Catalina) supplemented by scheduled weekly flights of Pan American Airways passenger flying boats between Botwood, Newfoundland, and Foynes, Ireland.

The Army Air Corps formed its own Ferrying Command on May 29, 1941; six weeks later an American manned flight route for wheeled aircraft was declared operational to Great Britain via Gander. Air Corps weather detachments were already in Greenland and Iceland, and on August 13, 1941, the 8th Weather Squadron was activated, with headquarters on the American side of Gander.[2] Under the leadership of Capt. Clark L. Hosmer, the squadron hastily began creating a network of weather facilities stretching across a fourth of the globe north of 40° north latitude. The polar front wended its way through the region, causing some of the stormiest, foggiest, and iciest weather in the northern hemisphere.[3] Three main air routes cut across the area, plus an extra southerly route via Bermuda should tail winds be unusually favorable. The far northern route extended along the great circle from the West Coast aircraft factories to Scotland via Hudson Bay, Baffin Land, central Greenland, and Iceland. Although this path had been touted as north of the zone of bad frontal weather, the weather problems proved worse than along the route a few hundred miles to the south. This second route was the one favored by thousands of combat cargo, fighter, and twin-engined bomber aircraft during the 1942–44 buildup: short hops from Maine to Newfoundland or central Labrador, continuing by southern Greenland and Iceland to the United Kingdom. Four-engined aircraft could also take that route or, winds permitting, cross the North Atlantic in one leap from Newfoundland to Scotland.

To minimize the weather factor, by late 1944 the 8th Weather Squadron operated twenty-six base weather stations, plus an extra twenty observing units that extended from the Azores to Hudson Bay and from Bermuda to Baffin Land. Manning the network were 125 officers and 600 enlisted men, frequently living in hellholes where delivery of supplies and mail typically came during bitter winter nights at intervals of many weeks. Before leaving for these northern points, the famed polar explorer Vilhajalmur Stefansson warned the men, "Don't eat polar bear livers!" But the biggest worry these men had was how to facilitate the massive movement of aircraft eastward.[4]

Because all weather observations had to be encoded before radio transmission, no matter how critical the situation, these reports would come in four or more hours later than if they had not been encrypted. And whenever the northern lights were acting up, the transmissions would be garbled beyond retrieval or be blacked-out entirely. Forecasting for the two major air bases in western Greenland—Narsarssuak and Sondrestrom Fjord—was particularly hair-raising. Both strips lay in long fjords against the ice cap and were subject to violent downslope (*foehn*) winds. Moreover, the surrounding mountainous terrain was unforgiving, so there were no instrument approaches. In fact, the minimum ceiling for landing at Narsarssuak was 8,000 feet. But one way or another, the flights went through, as in early 1942, when the entire Eighth Air Force passed by in Operation Bolero en route to new combat bases in England.

Germany, too, used a number of sites in eastern Greenland as far north as 77° north latitude for advance weather outposts. On September 13, 1941, the United States committed one of its first acts of war against Germany when the cutter *Northland* of the Coast Guard's Greenland Patrol seized the German-controlled weather trawler *Buskoe* off southeast Greenland. In addition to its many other duties, which included weather reporting and the transport of 8th Weather Squadron personnel, the patrol continued searching for and eliminating German coastal weather stations, a task not fully completed until October, 1944.[5]

The Sea Route   No matter how bad things were on land, they were always worse at sea. As the war progressed, the Coast Guard Atlantic Weather Patrol continued to build. By May, 1945, twenty-six such frigates were based at Argentia, Newfoundland. Once on station, these ships filed weather reports every three to four hours, twenty-one days at a time from a 10-mile square. Then the rotating station schedule permitted brief port calls (interspersed with occupying new stations) at Bermuda, Greenland, Iceland, and Boston before the ships had to return to Argentia and start a new duty cycle. Because the posting of four-man teams of civilian weather observers aboard a combat ship in a war zone also created problems, 125 Weather Bureau employees agreed to convert to chief aerographer's mates in the Coast Guard Temporary Reserve—except for a few who, having better academic backgrounds, rated officer commissions.

The hazards of such duty cannot be understated. In the first half of 1942 German submarines were achieving a kill ratio of 40 to 1 against Allied shipping. When the weather ship *Muskeget* was reported missing at her station 450 miles south of Cape Farewell, Greenland, on September 9, 1942, her relief ship, the *Monomoy*, reported at least twenty U-boats within striking distance of where the *Muskeget* had gone down with all hands (117 officers and men plus 4 civilian observers). Three months later the weather trawler *Natsek* also disappeared with all hands, probably having capsized because of heavy topside icing.[6]

Initially, to win this Battle of the Atlantic, the Allies relied on large, slow-moving merchant convoys supplemented by long-range air patrols of the Royal Air Force Coastal Command, Royal Canadian Air Force, U.S.

Navy and Coast Guard, and, until 1943, the U.S. Army Air Force. Dependent on visual sightings until early 1943 when short-wave airborne radar came in, the patrols ranged as far as 500 miles from land and attacked the U-boats on the surface while they were charging batteries or repositioning themselves. Aerial patrols of this type needed all weather support they could get. In the case of USN Patrol Squadron 73 flying Catalinas out of Reykjavik, the fleet air base was known informally as Camp Kwitcherbelliakin, for many of the sailors who manned it had been given the option of staying in a Stateside brig or going to Iceland. Here the aerological office operated round the clock using a staff of one lieutenant commander, two ensigns, and seven to ten third- and second-class aerographer's mates.[7] Weather observing was nearly as challenging as forecasting, for a continuous hourly log (Monthly Aerological Record, or MAR) had to be maintained by inking in a complex system of tiny circles. It was a full-time job. During just one eight-hour MAR watch, eleven types of precipitation could be logged, as steady rain, rain showers, drizzle, snow, showers of snow pellets, and so forth followed one another.

But even more challenging duty fell to the lot of one posted as an aerologist in early 1943 to one of the new "baby flattops" of the USS *Bay* class. Eventually, sixty-seven small escort carriers (CVEs) were built on merchant hulls of as little as 12,000 tons displacement. Unfortunately, their first sea assignments were winter convoy duty, even though it was known that convoy commodores sought the worst possible weather in order to suppress submarine attacks. As a consequence, the first three homeward-bound crossings made by the CVE never launched an aircraft because of impossible sea conditions. However, with better weather and the overruling of Adm. Ernest J. King's conviction that convoying was the only answer to the submarine threat, CVEs began to be used in hunter-killer teams consisting of a CVE and a couple of destroyers. Such teams could pin down and wait out suspected undersea targets until they could move in for the kill. These, plus the advent of airborne radar, reversed the Battle of the Atlantic with startling results, and in May, 1943, one-third of the U-boats at sea were sunk.[8]

To Africa and Beyond   While all this was going on in the stormy North Atlantic, ATC was busy establishing a year-round route: Puerto Rico—Trinidad—British Guiana—Brazil (Belem and Natal)—Ascension Island—Accra, Ghana—Khartoum, Sudan—and Cairo, plus an extension to Teheran and Karachi. In early 1942, before the route was in, travelers could fly (daylight hours only) by Pan American Airways Clipper seaplane as far as Lagos, Nigeria, although it took nine days to do so. To speed things up, the route was militarized. Consequently, when the 9th Weather Squadron was organized in late July, 1942, it inherited twenty-one detachments already in place (courtesy of the 4th and 6th Weather Squadrons) between West Palm Beach, Florida, and Natal, Brazil.[9]

To continue weather coverage eastward, the 19th Weather Squadron was formed in June and dispatched the following month to Accra, in the hump of Africa. Then late in the year, after the control of northwest Africa passed to the Allies, the loop was finally closed: passenger and cargo aircraft in the United Kingdom could return to the United States during winter months by flying south to Casablanca and Dakar-Accra before turning west and flying the South Atlantic ferry route in reverse. But it was not until the autumn of 1943 that the Portuguese permitted open use of their Lajes airstrip on Terceira Island, the Azores, thereby providing the much-needed direct air route from Washington, D.C., to Africa and the Middle East.[10]

In 1940 the British had opened up a trans-Africa air ferry route to get military aircraft to the Middle East. Then, in 1941, Pan American Airways had further improved the route as it flew aircraft and critical supplies from the United States to Basra, Iraq, and to Teheran for transfer to the Russians under the Lend-Lease program. But the route was still primitive in June, 1942, when nine weather officers and sixty enlisted personnel of the 19th Weather Squadron began providing services between Accra and Cairo, a responsibility that extended all the way to India by year's end. In early 1943 the squadron established a weather central at Cairo and took on an even higher priority mission: supporting Ninth Air Force bomber and fighter operations in the central and eastern Mediterranean region.[11]

From mid-1943 until the war's end, the 19th also supported the Persian Corridor, a network of roads and railroads from the Persian Gulf through Iran over which the Allies funneled supplies to Russia. Summers were relentlessly and excessively hot; the formal U.S. Army history labels such weather "that unappreciated hobgoblin of the Persian Corridor."[12] In the region between Ahwaz and the Persian Gulf, summer temperatures rarely fell below 100° F and the average noontime temperature in the shade fluctuated between 120° F and 140° F. All the weather squadron's detachments in Iran (Hamadan, Sultanabad, Dorud, Andimeshk, and Abadan) were observation-only, except in Teheran; that detachment furnished round-the-clock observing and forecasting services. In addition, Teheran and Abadan conducted radiosonde ascents. Each Iranian unit hooked into a weather teletype network capable of placing hourly weather reports into all receiving stations within eighteen minutes of the observation hour. Unfortunately those weather reports evidently fell by the wayside, for they were not part of the climatic records available to the AWS when it failed to predict the suspended dust that contributed so dramatically to the ill-fated attempt to rescue American hostages from Teheran in April, 1980.[13]

Meteorologists assigned to tropical weather squadrons and fleet weather centrals faced an anomalous situation until late 1943. They were required to forecast a unique type of weather for which none were trained! Fortunately, weather along the southern ferry route was reasonably benign (primarily convectional, although some stratus and fog might occur). Two features, however, were worth charting and avoiding: tropical cyclones (called hurricanes if wind speeds exceeded 64 knots) and the poorly understood Intertropical Convergence Zone (ITC, or the "equatorial front"), which intermittently snaked its way around the globe between 5° south latitude and 14° north latitude. Winds aloft were characteristically not a major problem, although Byers and McDowell coyly noted: "Occasionally the easterlies on the Brazil to Ascension track are so strong as to make the island out of the range of some types of aircraft." To overcome this lack of knowledge, the University of Chicago, with the aid of the 9th Weather Squadron, opened the Institute of Tropical Meteorology in October, 1943, at Rio Piedras, Puerto Rico.[14] At long last, one could be formally instructed in such esoteric phenomena as easterly waves, polar troughs, shear lines, triple-point cyclonic centers, and ITC perturbations.

In retrospect, it is clear that the air ferry routes to the United Kingdom, Africa, and the Middle East accomplished much, no matter whether the weather was tropical or extratropical. All told, some 50,000 combat aircraft were flown directly to these war theaters with relatively few losses attributable to weather, thanks to devoted and elaborate meteorological support. This heavy work load continued even past the war's end; in June, 1945, for example, the AAF Goose Bay weather detachment cleared 1,118 flights (including 789 tactical and 259 cargo aircraft) in one thirty-day period.[15]

OPERATION TORCH (NOVEMBER, 1942)

On July 25, 1942, Roosevelt cabled British Prime Minister Churchill that American forces would join those of the British Empire and the Free French in capturing North Africa later that year. Maj. Gen. Dwight D. ("Ike") Eisenhower learned the next day that he would be the supreme Allied commander, and firm planning for Operation Torch began on July 31. Except for landings in faraway Guadalcanal the following week, Torch would be the first major U.S. amphibious operation in forty-five years. On September 8, Ike set November 8, 1942, D day with simultaneous landings at three locations: in the Mediterranean, near Algiers (33,000 men); at Oran (39,000 troops); and along open Atlantic beaches north and south of Casablanca (35,000 troops).[16] Because most of the fighting at Oran and Casablanca would involve Anglophobe Vichy French troops, American assault troops would make up nearly 80 percent of the total. The catch here was that most of the U.S. soldiers and their equipment would have to depart directly and surreptitiously from Stateside. In addition, landing across the open beaches would be tricky, for French engineering data used to build the Casablanca breakwater suggested that high ocean swells and surf might prohibit safely beaching landing craft on four of five days during a typical November.[17] Moreover, the coast was notorious for mountainous swells observed to rise from relatively calm seas without any local warning and to cause hours of violent surf during fair weather. On November 8 the tide would be ebbing, so beached landing craft would have to retract promptly to avoid being stranded until the next high tide.

The Atlantic landings were to be led by R. Adm. Henry K. Hewitt and Maj. Gen. George S. Patton. Soon Hewitt recommended that the landings be delayed for a week. That idea was dismissed. Increased moonlight would make surprise less likely, and the climatic odds suggested that there would be less favorable weather. In any event, Roosevelt had already signaled Churchill on September 3 that "bad surf on the Atlantic beaches is a calculated risk," emphasizing need to get on with the operation. As Eisenhower later wrote: "Meteorological reports indicated that a steady deterioration of weather was to be anticipated, beginning in the early fall; naturally, therefore, time became of the essence," and "everything was done to launch the attack at the earliest possible date."[18]

Hewitt and Patton, using analyses prepared by Lt. Cdr. Richard C. Steere, decided they needed three days of ocean swells with heights below 8 feet accompanied by clear skies for effective air support. Hewitt chose to depend upon Steere's embarked aerological unit (two aerologists, six aerographer's mates, and five radiomen) for the requisite weather and wave forecasts, backed up by the navy weather central located with the Weather Bureau in Washington, D.C.[19] Patton, under way as a guest aboard Hewitt's flagship, the USS *Augusta*, also wanted long-range weather and surf forecasts from AAF Weather Central's team of Washington specialists directed by the newly promoted Major Krick.[20] To counterbalance Krick's long-range forecasts, which Patton wanted up to three weeks before the event, Lt. Cdr. Denys W. Knoll had the Weather Bureau complex adjoining the fleet weather central supply him with biweekly five-day forecasts; Knoll then converted them to swell and surf forecasts for transmission to the USS *Augusta* via Captain Orville's office in the Pentagon.[21]

Hewitt's armada of 107 ships sortied from Norfolk during the week of October 23; the Mediterranean assault forces left England on October 22 and 26. Housed in the sail maker's shop aboard the *Augusta*, Steere's aerological team issued regular forecasts for forty-eight hours ahead supplemented by the special Knoll forecasts after October 31 (D − 8, or 8 days before D day). Steere's radiomen intercepted not only Washington and London forecasts but also those from Gibraltar, where Krick had arranged for 1st Lt. Kenneth A. Willard to fly regularly with RAF Hudsons on antisubmarine patrol in order to observe wave conditions far offshore.[22] Initially, the Western Naval Task Force had a smooth passage, but as day D − 2 (November 6) appeared, Steere noted a weak cold front approaching the assault area slowly from the west, with probable passage late on D day. Fortunately, the ocean swell situation looked good: vigorous storms along the polar front were moving northeastward into the Icelandic area and could not generate surf higher than six feet on the beaches. To Steere, it looked like a "go" situation.

Others were not so sure. Writing General Marshall on November 6, Patton mentioned a forecast of "fair to bad surf conditions" for the eighth (D day), with worsening weather after that. However, he ended hopefully, "The forecasts have been relatively inaccurate." Eisenhower, who had arrived in Gibraltar from England aboard a flight of three B-17s on D − 3, also wrote: "I tentatively decided" late on the seventh that "unless [weather] conditions should improve, to divert the [Hewitt] expedition into Gibraltar." Eisenhower's worry may have stemmed from an AAF Weather Central message that arrived on the USS *Augusta* near midnight on D − 2, an hour after Steere had advised the two on-board staffs that offshore winds would help reduce the sea and swell on D − 1. The alarming message, out of the blue as far as Steere was concerned, read: "Outlook for landing operations very poor through 11th of Nov. with peak swell about 15 feet on 8th of Nov. CMA Good conditions late 12th or 13th until the 16th."[23]

Steere found Hewitt trying to get some sleep on a cot in the flag bridge and advised him of the adverse forecast but also pointed out that the two of them could see the ocean surface off Morocco but that the message senders could not. Inasmuch as there was no evidence of incipient swell, Hewitt, after asking a few questions, merely said, "Thank you, Steere. Let's discuss the situation tomorrow." During the next day, Hewitt was so at ease that he needed only two weather briefings to reassure himself that the landing should go as planned.[24]

Late on D − 1, waves off Morocco did begin to subside. Early on D day, sea conditions were relatively calm (breakers 2 to 4 feet), with fair to hazy skies. Even so, because of inexperienced boat crews, a guide boat out of position, and a rocky coast, 64 percent of the 370 landing craft used at the Fedala beachhead were damaged in the breaker zone.[25] The respite in surf conditions proved short-lived, for waves began kicking up again that afternoon. On the next two days, heavy surf damaged many more landing craft as well, although skies remained clear. In retrospect, November 8 proved to be the best day of the month for invading Morocco. If carried off four or five days earlier, high ocean swells and local bad weather would have hampered both amphibious and air support. If the invasion had come a week later, the long spell of clear skies would have favored fierce counterattacks by the German air force against the dispersed task force ships.[26]

CAPTURING NORTHWEST AFRICA

Sixteen days after Eisenhower decided when North Africa would be invaded, America's first mobile weather squadron—the 12th—was activated at Camp Griffiss, England, on September 24, 1942. Its task was simple—support the new Twelfth Air Force under the command of Brig. Gen. James H. Doolittle. With just six weeks to prepare his weather squadron for the invasion, Lt. Col. Joseph A. Miller, Jr., could not even inspect all his detachments: some would be coming directly from the States; others, drawn from the 18th Weather Squadron, would embark at Bristow, England, as Miller himself did on October 22.[27]

On D day (November 8) Miller landed 18 miles from Oran. Four days later he had his headquarters operational at Tafaraoui Airport, Algeria. By then the weather squadron had had its first fatality; 1st Lt. James W. Pflueger drowned during the initial landing at Vedella when his landing craft capsized within 150 feet of shore. As might be anticipated, confusion was common during the outfit's shake down during the first month. Nevertheless, the squadron's first weather forecast was issued at Tafaraoui on November 22. Two filler groups also arrived—one from the States and one from England—at the turn of the year, bringing the squadron's total strength to 495 officers and men, enough to operate a dozen widely scattered weather stations.

The squadron's first major forecast for a bombing mission came on November 22. It verified nicely. But two days later a second mission was foiled because target weather was worse than forecast. This bad weather was, unfortunately, a harbinger. "Now came the rainy season," wrote Churchill concerning late November: "It poured" and "our improvised airfields became quagmires." Ike labeled the "bottomless mud" a "major problem," one that was to "plague us throughout the bitter winter."[28]

All of Algeria finally fell, and in January, 1943, the Allies took the offensive in Tunisia. As the front moved east, so did the weather squadron, maintaining stations within 40 to 50 miles of the battlefront. When Field Marshal Erwin Rommel's famed Afrika Korps counterattacked and broke through at Kasserine Pass in mid-February, 1943, the Germans overran Thelepte, where the squadron had a weather station, and drove to within 10 miles of another station at Tebessa. After the Germans retreated, weathermen under 1st Lt. David M. Ludlum quickly reoccupied their Thelepte site, only to find that the Germans had blown up their extensive underground home. Even so, Thelepte became an important forecasting unit for not only Allied fighter and bomber units, but also for nearby artillery batteries, to which it supplied ballistic wind data.[29]

Fortunately, Tunisia became a trap into which Germany poured men and supplies, so when the collapse came, 349,206 German and Italian troops

Above left: Lt. Matthew Fontaine Maury, "Pathfinder of the Seas" (*National Archives*). *Above right*: Col. Albert James Meyer, founder of the U.S. Army Signal Service (*National Archives*). *Below left*: Sgt. Alexander McAdie as Signal Service weather observer in 1882. *Below right*: 1st Lt. Adolphus W. Greely, pioneer in military weather forecasting (*National Archives*).

WAR DEPARTMENT WEATHER MAP.

SIGNAL SERVICE U. S. A.

DIVISION OF TELEGRAMS AND REPORTS FOR THE BENEFIT OF COMMERCE.

Washington, Wednesday, November 1, 1871—7.35 A. M.

PUBLISHED BY ORDER OF THE SECRETARY OF WAR.

REFERENCES.

○ CLEAR   ⓇRAIN

🚩 FAIR   ⓈSNOW

● CLOUDY   ⟶ Arrow flies with wind.

First figures show state of Thermometer.
Middle line figures show state of Barometer.
Last figures show Velocity of wind in miles per hour.
Absence of arrow indicates calm.

SYNOPSIS FOR THE PAST TWENTY-FOUR HOURS.

The barometer has risen from the Middle and East Atlantic coasts to the valleys of the Ohio and Tennessee, with rain from Virginia to Lake Erie and eastward. An area of high barometer has moved from Missouri over Lakes Huron and westward, with brisk northerly winds on Lake Michigan and southwesterly winds on the lower lakes, and cooler northwest weather. Northerly winds clear and cold weather now prevail on Lake Erie. Northwesterly winds probably now prevail west of Michigan and Illinois.

PROBABILITIES.

The area of lowest pressure will probably pass eastward down the St. Lawrence valley, with falling barometer on Ontario, veering to northwest and diminishing force. New England, and with increasing winds and cloudy weather on the lower lakes. Northwest weather on the upper lakes. Fresh northwest winds on Lake Erie; rising barometer and cold weather extend from the southwest and Illinois northerly winds, with cloudy weather, continue from the Gulf.

Cautionary signal is ordered for to-day at Oswego.

CUBA

ST. DOMINGO

Above left: Comdr. Roswell F. Barratt, director of the navy's World War I weather program in France (*courtesy R. F. Barratt*). *Above right*: Maj. William R. Blair, commander of the army's European weather effort in World War I (*USA Signal Corps*). *Below*: U.S. Army weather forecast center at Colombey-les-Belles, France, in December, 1918 (*USA Signal Corps*).

Above left: Dr. Robert A. Millikan, director of the army's World War I weather program (*USA Signal Corps*). *Above right*: Map-spotting telegraphic weather reports in France during 1918 (*USA Signal Corps*). *Below*: NC-4 seaplane, the first aircraft to make a trans-Atlantic flight (*National Air and Space Museum*).

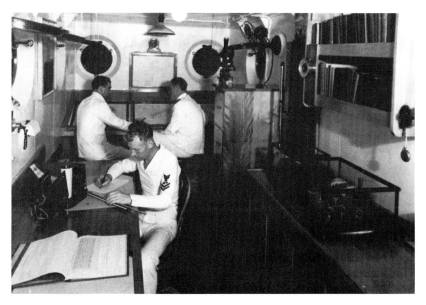

Above left: Capt. Randolph P. Williams before his stratospheric balloon flight in April, 1935 (*USA*). *Above right*: Fatal balloon ascent of 1st Lt. J. Neely and Dr. C. L. Meisinger on June 2, 1924 (*courtesy Capt. Frank Clark, USAF, Ret.*). *Below*: USS *Wright*'s aerology shack, 1930. Visible equipment includes theodolite, barometers, pen registers, climatic log, and aerograph (*USN*).

Above: Lakehurst NAS Primary Aerographer's School, Class 16, 1939; Instructors (*front row, l. to r.*): T. Sgt. L. S. Maddy, Lt. Howard T. Orville, and AGC F. A. Bardot. Graduating at the bottom of his class was Zemo C. Tarnowski (*top row, fourth from left*), a war hero five years later (*USN*). *Below*: Army weather unit on maneuvers near the Pee Dee River, North Carolina, during December, 1927 (*USA Signal Corps*).

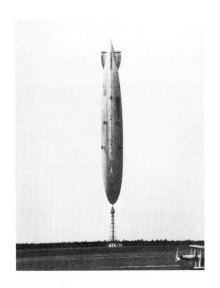 

Above left: USS *Los Angeles* at Lakehurst NAS in an unanticipated sea breeze on August 25, 1927 (*USN*). *Above right*: Capt. Wilber Lockhart, USN, creator of the term *weather central* (*courtesy W. Lockhart*). *Below*: Maj. Don McNeal lecturing U.S. Army Air Corps weather technicians about 1939 (*USAAC*).

Above left: 1st Lt. A. F. Merewether before APOB flight in early 1934 (*courtesy A. F. Merewether*). *Above right*: Capt. Don Zimmerman and 1st Lt. T. S. Moorman, Jr., inspect their new publication, TM 1-230 (*USAAC*). *Below*: American Airlines weather forecasters of 1935; *clockwise from lower right*: Irving Krick, C. R. Smith (company president), Earl Ward, David Garrow, Dr. George Taylor, Curtis Rockefeller, Benjamin Holzman, Lester Barnes, and D. Portman (*American Airlines*).

Above: University of Chicago meteorological graduates of November, 1942; *front row, l. to r.*: Prof. Oliver R. Wulf; Captain Starbuck, USAAF; Prof. Carl-Gustav Rossby; and Prof. Horace R. Byers (*courtesy R. A. Bryson*). *Below left*: Capt. Robert Losey with U.S. Minister Florence J. Harriman in Norway during early 1940. *Below right*: Lt. Gen. Carl Spaatz awarding the Legion of Merit to Col. Donald Yates during late 1944 (*USAAF*).

Above left: Maj. David Ludlum and S. Sgt. Philip Craig in Rome during June, 1944 (*courtesy D. M. Ludlum*). *Above right*: Cpl. Paula Eberstadt (*left*) and Cpl. Evelyn Barclay about to make a pibal run in 1944 at Minter Field, Bakersfield, California (*USAAF*). *Below left*: Athelstan F. Spilhaus, the USAAF's most charismatic weather officer during World War II (*courtesy A. F. Spilhaus*). *Below right*: Frances L. Whedon, chief of the meteorological section, Office of the Chief Signal Officer, 1947–56 (*USA*).

Above left: Dr. Sverre Petterssen, noted academician, who made many critical World War II weather forecasts (*USAF*). *Above right*: Capt. Richard Steere, key naval forecaster for Operations Torch and Husky (*USN*). *Below left*: Rear Adm. Sir John Fleming, KBE, DSC, RN, senior naval weather advisor for Operation Overlord (*courtesy J. Fleming*). *Below right*: Group Capt. John M. Stagg, RAF, senior weather advisor for Operation Overlord (*courtesy Copyright Section, Her Majesty's Stationery Office*).

Above: USAAF meteorologists posted to Scripps Institution of Oceanography during July, 1943; *left to right*: H. G. Venn, J. C. Crowell, G. W. Timpson, ————, C. C. Bates, R. S. Klepper, Prof. Harald U. Sverdrup, C. J. Burke, ————, ————, Y. Dawson, D. F. Leipper, and B. E. Olson (*University of California*). *Below*: AAF Weather Service WASP pilots assigned as of November, 1943; *front row, l. to r.*: Margaret M. Isbill, Virginia M. Hope, Yvonne C. Ashcraft, Dorothy I. McLean, and Babette J. DeMoe; *back row*: Hazel L. Doll, Neva L. Calderwood, Eunice M. Barratt, Dorothy C. Fowler, and Jane L. Page (*USAAF*).

Above left: AGC Zemo Tarnowski, commander of American troops in two Japanese prison camps (*USN*). *Above right*: Rear Adm. Denys K. Knoll, the only aerological officer to become Oceanographer of the Navy (*USN*). *Below left*: Brig. Gen. Kenneth C. Spengler, AWS reservist who became first executive director of the American Meteorological Society, 1946– (*USAF*). *Below right*: Lt. Col. Leon M. Rottman, leader of "Rottman's Rugged Rangers" during the invasion of Leyte Island (*USAF*).

Above: Col. A. F. Merewether, Col. A. W. Throgmorton, Col. H. H. Bassett, and Col. T. S. Moorman, Jr., in war-torn Wiesbaden, Germany, during 1945 (*USAAF*). *Below*: USAAF weather personnel at Amchitka Island fighter strip in January, 1943; *left to right*: Sgt. C. B. Block, S. Sgt. C. E. Pickett, Sgt. F. A. Dodge, S. Sgt. B. T. Plumlee, and WO William C. Norquist (*USAAF*).

Above: 10th Weather Squadron Headquarters personnel at Barrackpore, India, in early 1945; *top, l. to r.*: Caldwell, Benifield, Crawford, Dillow, Colonel Ellsworth, Lieutenant Colonel George, Wagner, Albaugh, Mr. Dunn, Dr. Fletcher, and Vick; *bottom*: Hums, Montgomery, Lewis, Porter, Rado, Polard, Ellis, and Martin (*USAAF*). *Below*: Wind reading by AerM/lc Robert Sizemore at Shanpa, Inner Mongolia, during late 1944 (*USN*).

Above: B-25D aircraft (*USAAF*). *Below*: WB-29 aircraft with nuclear "bug catcher" atop fuselage (*USAF*).

had been killed or taken prisoner. Yet the Mediterranean Sea was still not open for uninterrupted transit from Gibraltar to Suez. Foreseeing the problem, the Combined Chiefs of Staff had advised Eisenhower as far back as January that "an attack against Sicily will be launched in 1943 with the target date as the period of the favorable July moon."[30]

THE INVASION OF SICILY

In theory, undertaking an amphibious operation in the central Mediterranean during the height of summer should have been about as free of weather concerns as anyone could hope for. But Murphy's Law is a very real phenomenon in the "weather game"—if the unusual can happen, it probably will, at the most inconvenient time. Even Churchill, the strongest proponent of attacking the "soft underbelly of Europe," worried about invading Sicily: "This was the greatest amphibious operation so far attempted in history but all depended on the weather."[31] The assault, called Operation Husky, would be by two armies simultaneously: the newly formed Seventh Army under Patton, and the British Eighth Army, which had already fought all the way west from Egypt under Lt. Gen. Sir Bernard L. Montgomery. Eisenhower, wearing a fourth star by then, was supreme commander of the 478,000 men in these armies, as well as two naval task forces, one under the newly promoted Vice Admiral Hewitt and the other under Vice Adm. Sir Bertram Ramsay of the Royal Navy. This armada of more than 2,200 ships and landing craft was the largest yet assembled for an amphibious assault.[32]

Eisenhower and his planners wanted as much tactical surprise as possible. Several conditions had to be met. There had to be a waxing moon because troop carrier pilots needed some moonlight for finding assigned drop zones for the paratroops aboard. On the other hand, the naval fleet needed total darkness to cover its approach to Sicily. For D day, which was set for July 10, the boat operators wanted choppy water inshore to make their bobbing craft harder to hit. On the airside, the bombers needed several days of good weather in advance of the operation for preparatory air strikes against Italy and Sicily, as well as clearing skies once the beachheads were established.[33]

AAF Weather Service personnel, both at home (Asheville, North Carolina) and within the deployed 12th Weather Squadron, worked around the clock to generate necessary climatic analyses and updated forecasts. On the navy side, a special aerological unit under Commander Steere studied the assault area, issued forecasts for practice assaults, and conducted research in swell and surf forecasting, including refinement of the Steere surf reporting code.[34]

"As history now knows, that forecast was perfect," cabled Col. William O.

(Oscar) Senter, the second in command at the AAF Weather Service, a month after the invasion, when he visited Sicily. In fact, he added, "the weather for the invasion of Sicily was made to order."[35] However, in the minds of most British and American paratroopers, as well as U.S. naval personnel, Senter's declaration assumed far too much. What happened was more like the following.

On July 9 (D − 1), western Europe was under the influence of a polar maritime air mass flowing from the northwest. A secondary cold front extending from Sardinia across Italy to a 1,008-mb low in northwest Yugoslavia also moved southeastward, tightening the pressure gradient. During the frontal passage across Sicily, about 7:00 P.M., the invasion force, then in midchannel between Tunisia and Sicily, was experiencing northwest winds with gusts to 37 knots and waves 12 feet high. The landing craft, poor seagoers at best, were having a bad time, and most aboard them became violently seasick.

As might be expected, the meteorologists were being grilled on all sides. "How long will the storm last?" Patton demanded of his embarked weather officer. "It will calm down by D day!" "It had better!" threatened the army's "Old Blood and Guts."[36] On Hewitt's flagship (USS *Monrovia*), Commander Steere thought the strong winds would taper off and that as the landing forces got closer to the beachheads, the lee effect should take over.[37] At Eisenhower's headquarters in Tunis, the desireability of a twenty-four-hour postponement came under discussion. But after Ike conferred with British meteorologists attached to his naval deputy, Admiral of the Fleet Sir Andrew B. Cunningham, it appeared that the gale should abate, and Churchill was advised: "Weather not favorable but operation proceeding."[38]

The initial big test of the weather forecast came about midnight when the U.S. 82nd Airborne Division made its first large-scale drop in combat. Under the command of Col. James M. Gavin, one of its reinforced regimental combat teams parachuted three hours ahead of the main American landings to take the Ponte Olivo airport and important high ground nearby. After being briefed by 12th Weather Squadron forecasters, 226 AAF C-47s with the paratroopers aboard left Tunisia at sunset on D − 1. The low-flying pilots found that the quarter moon gave little light. Salt spray from the tossing sea coated their windshields, and night formation lights were already intentionally dim. This, combined with surface winds of 27 knots and insufficient practice in night flying with unfamiliar V patterns, shattered formation discipline. Planes straggled, and the mass flight missed its checkpoint at Malta. Then navigational difficulties along a complicated track between Malta and Sicily, plus the continuing strong winds, caused extra delay, requiring the planes to approach their drop zones in nearly complete darkness. Thus, aircrews could not pick out final checkpoints. Smoke from earlier Allied bombing further obscured drop zones. The results? Gavin's 3,405 parachutists were widely scattered over a 50-mile area of southeastern Sicily. It nearly doomed further American airborne efforts in the war.[39] The 1,600 British paratroopers who arrived in gliders fared little better. Towed mostly by AAF C-47s, 133 gliders were released, but only 54 landed in Sicily. Of those, just 12 were in or near the assigned drop zone. The rest tragically went into the sea, taking the troops to the bottom.[40]

By 1:00 A.M. on D day, north-northwest winds were already as low as 7 knots off Gela, the center of the American landing beach area. At sunrise, the surf at Gela, although to a height of 2 to 6 feet, was sweeping down the beach, causing many landing craft to broach and thus be difficult to retract. But by then army Rangers were ashore as an organized unit. Surrounding the town, they caught the Italian command staff in bed and had 600 prisoners by daybreak. However, 18 miles away at Scoglitti, the easternmost tip of the American assault area, conditions were not so good. A 10-to-16-knot northwesterly wind blew directly on to the beach, and the swell offshore remained 10 to 12 feet high. The attack transports were finding it difficult to offload nauseated troops, supplies, and vehicles into pitching landing craft, and the craft themselves found it equally difficult to penetrate the heavy surf rolling over the outer bars before hitting the beach itself. Boat formations were understandably irregular, and landings in an assault wave were far from simultaneous. By noon of D + 1, the broaching problem was so bad that only 66 of an original 175 LCVPs—landing craft (vehicles and personnel)—and LCMs—landing craft (medium)—remained operational in the Scoglitti area.[41]

In compensation, the storm caused the defenders to let down their guard. Axis intelligence officers had repeatedly warned their superiors that the weather of early July would be propitious for amphibious landings. Allied convoys had also been spotted off Malta as early as D − 4. But the moon was past full phase, and Italian meteorologists and naval officers advised that the weather was too adverse for a beach landing. As Sir Andrew noted in a dispatch, "the effect [was] of making the weary Italians, who had been alert for many nights, turn thankfully in their beds saying 'tonight at any rate they can't come,' BUT THEY CAME!"[42]

Equipped with a jeep, radio, and basic weather gear, a 12th Weather Squadron mobile weather unit was aboard one of the early LSTs headed for a landing point five miles east of Gela. That proved impossible because of enemy air attack. A short while later, a sister LST was hit by a bomb amidships, detonating ammunition, land mines and gasoline aboard. To aid survivors, the bow of the first LST was turned into the burning ship. Weather team members, led by Capt. Howard J. Simpson, displayed exceptional bravery during the rescue effort. Not only Simpson but also two of his men, T. Sgt. Leslie G. Nuhn and S. Sgt. James F. Graham, received Silver Star medals.[43] Additional dive bomber attacks held up the weather team's landing until the following morning, when they dug in a quarter of a mile from the beach. Then, because of sharp German counterattacks on the Gela plain, they took two more days to reach their objective—the airport at Point Olivo. Finally, four days after D day, Simpson's unit was in limited operation, distributing weather forecasts despite frequent air raids against the three AAF fighter squadrons using the air field.

By the following day, July 15, the Allies held an unbroken front across all of southeastern Sicily. A month and a day later American and British patrols simultaneously entered Messina, Sicily's largest city and but a short ferry ride to the Italian mainland.[44] While all this progress was being made, the weather was typically clear. Heat therefore became the main weather problem, as temperatures climbed as high as 100° F. Even "desert rats" of the British Eighth Army complained that the furnacelike heat of the North African desert never seemed quite as hot as that of Sicily, where the humidity was higher.

PROBLEMS IN SOUTHERN ITALY (SEPTEMBER, 1943 – MARCH, 1944)

For a change, the amphibious assault to reoccupy southern Italy (Operation Avalanche) took place in good weather. The area lay under the influence of a weak ridge of high pressure in a quasi-stationary air mass when first the British and then the Americans successively invaded south to north on September 3 and September 9. Again, Commander Steere was the on-scene aerologist for Vice Admiral Hewitt as the U.S. Fifth Army hit the heavily defended beaches along the Gulf of Salerno 40 miles southeast of Naples. Until that highly useful port fell on October 1, Steere found only one occasion to put out a local storm warning for squalls and thunderstorms.[45] On September 22, the forecast verified as an occluded frontal situation, reinforced by local mountainous terrain, generated winds with gusts up to 80 knots near Salerno itself. Despite Steere's advance notice, thirty of the larger landing craft (LCTs or larger) and sixty-four of the smaller landing craft (LCMs and LCVPs, primarily) broached and stranded. Even worse, vital unloading operations were virtually halted for two days.

On October 1 British forces captured Foggia's airfield complex near the Adriatic coast and across from Naples. Now, American heavy bombers could fly north from Foggia across the Alps to German and Austrian targets, to the east and Balkan targets, and west to aid the tactical air forces in isolating German forces from Rome and the Po Valley. By late December, two AAF groups, each consisting of heavy bombers, medium bombers, and fighters, were operating out of the Foggia district. Even so, the 12th Weather Squadron headquarters still remained across the Mediterranean in

Algeria. Consequently, Colonel Miller developed span-of-control problems: his units were not only in Italy but scattered over North Africa, Sicily, and Corsica as well. The squadron was at one-half strength, and the general technical proficiency of those assigned was below par. All this affected service during a time when persistent heavy rains kept falling and men and vehicles were continually mired in mud.

For Miller, things really hit the fan when Professor Rossby showed up in late January, 1944, to conduct an in-depth technical inspection as the expert consultant to Secretary of War Henry L. Stimson on weather matters. Soon Rossby charged that Miller and Maj. Gordon B. Weir, station commander for Bari, Italy (a unit being upgraded into a joint Anglo-American weather central to support Headquarters, Fifteenth Air Force, and comparable RAF commands), were too poorly versed in basic meteorology for the vital positions they held. With the pending shift of the Mediterranean air war from prime emphasis on short-range tactical warfare to long-range strategic bombing, Rossby feared that the methods Miller had used so successfully to support tactical air operations in North Africa and Italy would no longer work. In Rossby's damning statement, Miller was not "sufficiently familiar with either basic meteorology or recent advances in this field to set standards for his men and to organize a precision-type forecast organization."[46] Rossby then recommended that Miller and Weir be removed, although he softened the blow by pointing out that Miller was "an outstanding soldier and enthusiastic officer" and should be posted to a weather reconnaissance squadron, where he could use his skills as a B-25 pilot.

Well aware of the weather squadron's deficiencies before Rossby spent five weeks spotlighting them, the AAF Weather Service leadership (which, if any culpability was involved, shared in it as much or more than Miller did) ignored the dynamic Swede's suggestions and did not (in fact, could not) dismiss Miller.[47] However, the leadership did dispatch Dr. Jacob Bjerknes of UCLA (who was then in England) and Vincent J. Oliver, the best synoptic meteorologist in Rossby's department in Chicago, to Italy for upgrading the squadron's technical skills by on-site visits and pertinent technical lectures.

By that time Eisenhower was in England, and Gen. Sir Henry Maitland Wilson was Supreme Commander, Allied Forces, Mediterranean. His armies bogged down before they reached Cassino, Italy (the direct route to Rome), because of near-perfect German defenses and continuing severe winter weather. To overcome this, the high command called for a surprise amphibious landing at Anzio to cut lines of communication in the German rear, and, they hoped, to capture Rome as well. Operation Shingle would utilize the VI Corps, comprising both British and American troops. Although not a maximum operation, it was still large, involving 110,000 men and 5,200 vehicles landed deep within German-held territory by a fleet of 354 vessels during midwinter. Despite unfavorable climatic odds,

Allied planners asked the meteorologists to provide three or four January days with clear skies and calm seas.

As a Britisher, Sir Henry wanted his top weatherman to come from the British Meteorological Office (BMO). This proved to be Col. Sverre Petterssen, now of the Norwegian Air Force and loaned to the BMO. On January 14, 1944, Petterssen arrived to do the invasion forecast at the 12th Weather Squadron's advanced headquarters (complete with interim weather central) in the Royal Vesuvius Observatory, halfway up the volcano's slope. Accompanying him was Wing Commander Meade, RAF. Although Petterssen spent most of his time at the observatory, he briefly visited the Bari weather central where he, too, became critical of Major Weir's technical competency. But it was on Mount Vesuvius, where he kept two map-plotters busy full time preparing upper-air maps while he lectured the assembled staff on his upper-air theories, that Petterssen made the challenging Anzio forecast.[48]

Petterssen saw a potential weather window within the week, so U.S. VI Corps troops boarded ships at Naples on January 21 for the 90-mile trip up the coast. Anzio weather on D day, January 22, was as forecast, and the initial troops went ashore unopposed. "The day was sunny and warm," a paratrooper remarked later, "making it very hard to believe that a war was going on, and that we were in the middle of it."[49] But despite tactical surprise, the corps commander, Lt. Gen. John P. Lucas, chose caution and eventually was relieved of command as Anzio stagnated into a three-month stalemate.[50]

On Anzio's eve, while Petterssen was dining with 12th Weather Squadron officers at the plush Albergo (Hotel) Eremo adjacent to headquarters, two of the squadron's observers were already aboard ship sweating it out with the rest of the assault force. Less than four hours after crossing the beach on D day, S. Sgt. Clifford H. Wolf and S. Sgt. Alfred W. Hunt were on the air with weather observations needed for close air support. During that first week Wolf counted forty-six German fighter attacks, including one that gave him a concussion when a bomb landed 50 feet away.[51]

A long three weeks later, an eleven-man mobile weather team arrived on February 15 to end Wolf's and Hunt's pressure-packed vigil. Commanded by Italian-speaking Capt. Valde V. J. Moncada, the team included an enlisted station chief and forecaster, a chief observer (S. Sgt. David W. Fogo), and three radio operators. By February 19, the team provided twenty-four-hour observing and forecasting services to some two dozen beachhead customers, including corps headquarters and those of the U.S. 3rd Division and 1st Armored Division. Later on, the Anzio weather team also acquired one of the Scripps-trained wave forecasters to work with naval authorities, for everything coming and going had to be by sea. So important was the over-the-beach flow of supplies that the perceptive newspaper columnist Ernie

Pyle commented that a day of bad weather "harmed us" more than a month of German shelling.[52]

Survival at Anzio meant going underground. The weather team's choice in this matter was a small cave once used as a wine cellar. Even so, on March 28, its entrance took a direct hit from a German 170-mm shell coming from a railroad gun unaffectionately referred to as Whistling Willy. The explosion killed Staff Sergeant Fogo and wounded another observer. Following a brief tribute by fellow team members, Fogo was buried at Anzio in the very terrain he was helping to defend, thereby adding another cross to what eventually became the largest American military cemetery in Italy.

OPERATION LUDLUM

Despite Anzio, the wretched weather, rugged terrain, and stubborn German resistance kept the Allies stalled well into February, 1944, along an east-west line 70 miles southeast of Rome. To start moving again toward the Eternal City required a major attack on the battlefront's west side, a task assigned to the U.S. Fifth Army, now under Lt. Gen. Mark W. Clark. Spearheading the attack was the New Zealand Corps (two divisions with over 15,000 vehicles) commanded by Gen. Bernard C. Freyberg. Freyberg, as well as Generals Clark and Arnold, thought that the offensive should be prefaced by an all-out bombing attack against the town of Cassino. Lt. Gen. Ira C. Eaker, whose bombers of the Mediterranean Allied Air Forces would be used, remained somewhat dubious. He failed to see how Freyberg's forces could use an air attack to advantage. The incessant rain had forced local streams out of their banks, washing away most bridges and turning floodplains into a quagmire incapable of supporting foot troops, much less heavy armor. But Eaker was overruled.[53]

Eaker's aircraft were to begin the assault any time after February 24. However, Freyberg demanded a forecast of three consecutive days without rain as a prerequisite. Such weather would provide Eaker's pilots good visibility and Freyberg's tankers drier ground.[54] In contrast to the Anzio forecast a month before, the responsibility for the "go or no-go" weather prediction fell to a young meteorologist of the wartime generation, Capt. David M. Ludlum—Clark's staff weather officer and a veteran of the North African and Sicilian campaigns. His assignment was especially difficult. When the weather was good on one side of Italy, it was typically poor on the other because of the mountain-chain effect. For example, if it was open at Cassino, where the bomber pilots wanted clear skies to 14,000 feet, there could well be zero visibility at such home fields as Foggia (rain), Naples (fog), and Sardinia (low clouds).

For three frustrating weeks foul weather prevailed. Even so, pressure built to launch the initial air attack, code-named Operation Ludlum and the only World War II operation to be named after its weatherman.[55] By early March, Clark urged Freyberg and Eaker to attack without ideal weather. At 5:00 P.M. on March 14 Ludlum finally issued a "go-ahead" forecast with the proviso of canceling by midnight should conditions change (Appendix C). At 8:30 the next morning, wave after wave of B-17s, B-24s, B-25s, and B-26s began roaring over the German-held side of Cassino in the greatest massed air attack in direct support of ground forces to that date. By noon, 2.5 kilotons of bombs had been dropped, an amount five and a half times that dropped by B-17s and B-26s on the illustrious Abbey of Monte Cassino a month before. Then came the Allies' heaviest artillery barrage of the developing war, with some 85,000 shells hitting the assault area.

Unfortunately for Ludlum, Cassino's weather began clouding up in the afternoon, canceling other planned bomber strikes. As the New Zealand infantry finally advanced, their supporting tanks were halted by debris. By dusk, very heavy rains began and continued through the night. Bomb craters and cellars became small lakes; together with the spongy ground, they completely stopped armored vehicles. Moreover, the German paratroopers who still infested the ruins put up a tenacious defense. By dawn it was clear that tanks could not move through Cassino for at least thirty-six hours. Then followed six days of inconclusive probes against the German positions. Finally, on March 23, Allied commanders, their troops exhausted, called off the offensive after losing 2,000 men.[56]

In analyzing the failure at Cassino, Allied air and ground commanders exchanged criticisms. Air commanders claimed that the ground forces were too late with too little after the March 15 bombing, for the New Zealanders had only seventeen casualties the first day. But the ground commanders maintained that they had been led by air power advocates to expect too much. All agreed, however, on two points—the German paratroopers were too tough, and the rains reappeared much sooner than forecast.[57] But the war was far from over, and with better weather conditions during May, the Allies reached Rome on June 4, 1944.

TITO'S PARTISANS

After North Africa fell, the U.S. Ninth Air Force cooperated with the RAFs Middle East Air Command to keep pressure on Hitler's forces in the Balkans and eastern Europe. One of the better ways of doing this was to ensure that the Germans occupying Yugoslavia did not liquidate Marshal Josip Broz Tito's pesky partisans. As the fighting intensified, the need for supplies airdropped by British and AAF C-47s became urgent. But aircrews often found, after making the long trip (usually at night) across the Adriatic Sea from Brindisi, Italy, that they were unable to off-load this badly needed war materiel. For example, during February and March, 1944, 62 of the 186 C-47 missions could not drop or land supplies because of adverse weather, and another 97 missions were scrubbed before takeoff.

To overcome the weather factor, the Cairo-based 19th Weather Squadron trained eleven officers and sixteen enlisted men to work behind the lines with Tito's guerillas and provide simultaneously on-the-spot meteorological information for future cargo operations. The risky operation began the night of March 14, 1944, when two enlisted weather observers and a supporting radio operator parachuted into the mountains of Slovenia. With them went weapons (including submachine guns and side arms), a radio, supplies, and weather gear. The latter packets included mercury and aneroid barometers, rain gauge, hand-held anemometer, sling psychrometer, barograph, theodolite, pibal balloons, hydrogen generator, plotting board, and conversion tables. Once the team linked up with the partisans, the gear was taken to a base camp by oxen-drawn sleds and carts, this being the sole means of transport. Ten days later, the three-man team was on air with ciphered weather transmissions four times daily.

On May 14, 1st Lt. Robert J. Schraeder, a forecaster, also parachuted in to join the team. Shortly after his arrival the Germans launched a new offensive and, at one point with the enemy but two miles away, the weather team cached its equipment and fled. Conditions continued to be far from ideal. Security, rather than geography or meteorological considerations, determined where and when the observations could be made. Observations were taken with weapons at the ready and nearby, and only when the weathermen were accompanied by an armed patrol. The weathermen themselves were often tapped for guard duty and patrols, day and night. One of their first observation sites was near Draja. Perhaps coincidentally, the village was wiped out by a dozen German Stuka dive bombers launched from an airfield ten minutes away by air. Fortunately, the team received no injuries. But because attacks and ambushes were a way of life, they were forced to move continually, often at night, over rough mountain trails.

Finally, on August 6, the weather unit was ordered out of Yugoslavia. The last weather observation was transmitted a week later. Then their departure was delayed: a German attack cut the road to the landing strip, and the partisan escorts decided that it was too dangerous to proceed. Thus, it was September 3, 1944, before the weathermen were airlifted from Slovenia.[58]

STRATEGIC BOMBARDMENT IN EUROPE (1942–1945)

In its official account of World War II the AAF pointed out that weather conditions "were to provide one of the greatest obstacles to daylight precision bombing" and proved to be the AAF's "worst opponent." Similarly,

General Arnold, writing about strategic bombardment in Europe, stated: "We faced the fact that weather in that theater, especially in the daytime, would remain as constant an enemy as the Germans."[59] As early as March, 1942, Major General Eaker, while commander of the Eighth Air Force, acknowledged that fact when he requested prompt dispatch of AWS meteorologists to England "to begin the study of this beastly weather."[60]

Zimmerman's response was to assign the tenth-ranking meteorologist in the Air Corps, Lt. Col. Anthony Mustoe, as staff weather officer, Eighth Air Force, and regional control officer, 18th Weather Region (an area comprising the British Isles). Having had to go by sea, Mustoe finally arrived in June. Another ten weeks passed, however, before his troops (forty-four in all) arrived and could begin a course in British weather codes at Station Pinetree (phonetic symbol for Eighth Air Force and 18th Weather Squadron headquarters). Within fifteen months the squadron numbered more than a thousand personnel and was operating eighty-seven detachments over a land area a little less than Colorado's.

Despite the plenitude of meteorological reports from the island complex, plus top-secret intercepts (Manx) of German weather reports for the continent, forecasting grew more difficult during 1943.[61] The RAF unarmed weather flights could no longer penetrate critical but heavily defended areas, so weaponed AAF B-17s started transporting RAF weather observers over the requisite routes. Meanwhile, Lt. Col. Murray O. Jones, plus eight subordinate officers and three enlisted men of the 18th Weather Squadron, were trained as aerial weather observers and machine gunners at the RAF Air-Met School near Bovingdon, England.[62]

In June, 1944, the effort became the all-American 8th Weather Reconnaissance Squadron (Heavy) (Provisional), although that designation was dropped and others substituted, such as the 308th Reconnaissance Squadron (Heavy). The first aircraft were B-17s with British meteorological sensors attached to the pitot tubes. But by September, 1944, B-24s with roomy nose turret areas made into joint navigator–weather observer compartments replaced the B-17s. Although not categorized as weather reconnaissance bombers (WBs), those special aircraft provided the only scheduled flights from late 1944 to early 1946 that acquired detailed upper-air data over the Atlantic Ocean between southwest England, Greenland, and the Azores.[63]

In addition to regional weather, the Ninth Air Force needed real-time weather information over likely targets and routes to and from. This requirement was met by duos of P-51s commanded by Maj. Maxwell W. Rowan, formerly assistant staff weather officer to the Ninth Air Force. Although his operation started on January 2, 1944, the unit did not become the 9th Weather Reconnaissance Squadron (Provisional) until five months later. All weather observations were strictly visual and immediately radioed back in the clear. It was a busy outfit, for the squadron logged 1,362 sorties, flying combat missions every day but two, between June 5 and December 14, 1944. Lt. Gen. Carl A. ("Tooey") Spaatz estimated that between June and August, 1944, Rowan's unit saved $30 million in aircraft fuel costs alone.

Another long-term effort to improve weather coverage over the Eurasian land mass also bore fruit in mid-1944. As far back as mid-1941, at the time of the Lord Beaverbrook–Ambassador Harriman Lend-Lease mission to Moscow, British and American officials had urged the Soviet Union to exchange synoptic weather data with the United Kingdom and the United States. Consequently, though grudgingly, the Russians agreed to exchange data involving fifteen Siberian weather stations between Khabarovsk and the fleet weather central in San Francisco.[64] Then, in July, 1942, Lt. Col. Donald Yates and Lt. Col. James F. Thompson of Headquarters, AAF Weather Service, worked in Moscow with Gen. Yevgeniy K. Federov, director of the Soviet Hydrometeorological Service, to improve the agreements for the exchange of weather information, codes, and communications. A three-man Soviet mission, led by their naval service's Capt. Constantine F. Speranski, made a reciprocal visit to the United States during early 1943 with Colonels Yates and Moorman serving as hosts. The Russians liked what they saw. During the visit there was a vast improvement in quantity and quality of the Russian data. Speranski promised to speak to Federov about maintaining this condition, but Russian weather reports again became sporadic after the mission returned to Russia. However, the visit did result in an increase to thirty stations in the Khabarovsk–San Francisco exchange.

As the opening of the western front neared, Federov finally agreed with Capt. Denys Knoll, USN, and Col. Lewis L. Mundell, USAAF, on May 27, 1944, to exchange data from 100 weather stations on each side. This action came none too soon. On June 2, 1944, heavy bomber groups of the AAF began a three-month stint of bombing deep inside Germany before landing inside guarded fences in the Soviet Ukraine. Then, after being refueled and rearmed, the bombers would carry out another bombing sortie during the long flight to home bases in Italy and England. To provide direct weather support in the field, the 18th Weather Squadron placed five officers and nine enlisted men inside Russia, a practice that proved to be of very short duration.

Ploesti (August 1, 1943)   Nearly 40 percent of Germany's petroleum supply came from the Ploesti oil fields of Romania and the nearby oil refineries. Within a month after the Pearl Harbor attack, U.S. air planners were studying the feasibility of bombing Ploesti. However, serious planning had to wait until the wipeout of German forces in Tunisia during 1943 freed the Ninth Air Force. In the final plan 177 B-24 bombers were to come in over the heavily defended targets at low altitude (500 feet). A 2,400-mile trip, it would be the farthest distant raid of the war up to that point.[65]

The advance climatic studies by the 19th Weather Squadron took on extra importance. Strong headwinds could not be tolerated, either going or returning, if the B-24s were to make it back. Because of the range, fighters could not provide total escort coverage, so en route cloud cover was needed. And over Ploesti, the B-24s needed clear skies and southerly winds—the latter so that after the aircraft dropped their incendiary bombs on first approach, the wind would spread the fires over the rest of the complex. By studying daily weather maps of the preceding forty years, AAF meteorologists learned that the desired conditions were most likely to occur in March or August. March was too soon, so August became the weather window. As forecast, weather conditions proved to be nearly ideal along the route on August 1, 1943, and the raid was launched.

En route to Ploesti the formation met generally clear weather, but there were enough towering cumulus clouds to destroy flight discipline. Consequently, the lead group reached Ploesti somewhat ahead of the others, thus alerting the defenses. The Ploesti weather was also clear (as forecast), and it became something like a turkey shoot. Although 42 percent of Ploesti's refining capability was knocked out, 54 of the B-24s were lost, as were 532 airmen.[66]

Schweinfurt (October 14, 1943)   In June, 1943, the long-promised round-the-clock Allied strategic bombing campaign got under way in earnest—the RAF hit urban areas at night, and the U.S. Eighth Air Force struck selected targets by day. In the latter case, the priority targets were factories and installations critical to keeping the Luftwaffe operational. Of particular interest were the Schweinfurt ball-bearing plants, for they produced half of all the scarce bearings manufactured in Germany—the bearings that kept the country's mechanized might in motion. Lieutenant General Eaker and his British-based subordinate commander, Lieutenant General Spaatz, knew weather to be the most serious limitation on their daylight bombing campaign. No amount of aircrew skill or fortitude could put bombs on targets that were invisible from flight altitude; tactics for bombing through cloud using on-board radar were, at that stage, unproven. Cloud-free targets were a must. The Americans knew it; so did the Germans.

Four major air strikes to the heart of occupied Europe in mid-October, 1943, marked a turning point in the daylight bombing campaign. The fourth and final strike was against Schweinfurt on October 14—the first raid on these ball-bearing plants in two months. Two hundred ninety-one B-17s departed bases in England with P-47 fighter escort. But when fuel considerations forced the P-47s to turn back, the bombers met wave after wave of German fighters all the way into and away from Schweinfurt. The air battle was truly epic. German weathermen had correctly forecast that Schweinfurt would be the only area in their country having weather favoring daylight bombing. Consequently, their fighters were massed so as to inflict on the Eighth Air Force the highest percentage of losses yet suffered—some sixty B-17s destroyed and seventeen others heavily damaged.

Strategically, the October 14, 1943, raid was the most important of sixteen raids against the Schweinfurt plants. It caused the most damage and the greatest interference with production, so much so, in fact, that it led to a reorganization of the ball-bearing industry. On the other hand, it caused only a temporary production setback, and four months later the Eighth Air Force was told to hit Schweinfurt again. The air battle also demonstrated that for the time being, the Eighth had lost air superiority over the German heartland, an edge that could not be regained until long-range fighter escorts were available. Accordingly, the Eighth Air Force made no additional deep penetrations during any clear weather over Germany for the rest of 1943. And it is fortunate that they did not plan to do so, for the weather turned bad.

Operation Argument—The Big Week (February 19–25, 1944)   As 1943 wound down, Eighth Air Force officials anxiously awaited a spell of clear weather that would permit a concentrated series of strikes against the sources of German air power. Drafted in November, 1943, the plan (code-named Argument) called for coordinated, massive air attacks against a dozen factories, mostly in the Leipzig area, producing fighter aircraft or their components. Argument's minimal requirement for success was three consecutive days of clear weather over most of central Europe, plus weather at the home bases in East Anglia and southern Italy suitable for safe takeoffs, landings, and assembly in formation. Ideally, Argument needed a week of overall good weather, not a very common phenomenon during fall and winter months, when severe storms somewhere between London and Berlin could be expected on an average of one every three days.[67]

The prime responsibility for mounting Argument fell to the United States Strategic Air Forces in Europe (USSTAF) established on January 1, 1944, under Spaatz's command. For Argument, USSTAF controlled the Eighth, Ninth, and Fifteenth Air Forces. Responsible for each day's air strikes was Spaatz's deputy for operations, Maj. Gen. Frederick L. Anderson, Jr. During January, Argument was scheduled repeatedly—every time, in fact, early weather reports offered a glimmer of hope. But each time, deteriorating weather forced a cancellation. By early February destruction of German fighter production was so urgently needed that Spaatz and Anderson were willing to take more than ordinary risks to complete the task, including losses when staging in adverse weather. Consequently, Argument was ordered to be completed by March 1, 1944.

With USSTAF's activation, Spaatz needed a central coordinating weather unit in his headquarters to consolidate (and override, if necessary) the weather opinions put out by harried meteorologists at the bomber commands.[68] A request for such a meteorological central was sent in early January, 1944, from Spaatz to General Arnold via no less than Lieutenant Colonel Krick, a visitor to the theater. Arnold agreed to the plan. But when Rossby learned that Krick might get the top appointment, the Swede went into action. When the USSTAF Office of the Director of Weather Services was activated on February 12, 1944, its head was the deputy director of weather at Headquarters, AAF—Col. Donald N. Yates.[69] A no-nonsense West Pointer, Yates had been a Krick student just five years before.

Even as Yates took over, the weather situation improved. On February 17 Krick briefed Spaatz that, according to weather analogs, a prolonged period of visual bombing weather would begin about February 20. Before that, February weather over Europe had been dominated by two extensive high-pressure areas, one centered over the Baltic and one just west of Ireland. However, if the Baltic high should move east, as predicted by the Yates team, wind speeds over Germany would increase and break up the persistent low cloud cover that had held on day after day. Accordingly, Spaatz ordered tentative launch preparations. As time wore on, the more seasoned forecasters of the 18th and 21st Weather Squadrons (supporting the Eighth and Ninth Air Forces, respectively) remained pessimistic despite long, wrangling telephone conferences about the weather pattern. Even so, the day before the proposed launch date, the USSTAF team issued a forecast calling for clouds over Germany to break into four-tenths coverage or less by noon on February 20.

During the night of February 19–20 the RAF bombed Leipzig through solid overcast. The prospects of visual bombing a half-day later seemed remote. Moreover, severe icing conditions had been encountered along the route, a condition that could badly hamper escorting fighter aircraft. But Spaatz was willing to launch without fighter protection. Then, early on February 20, a reconnaissance aircraft returning from northeast of Leipzig reported breaks in the undercast. Anderson therefore declared Argument a "go" and set the time over target for noon that day. The employed force would be the largest in AAF history to that date—sixteen combat wings (more than a thousand bombers). In addition, all available AAF fighter escorts (seventeen groups), plus sixteen RAF fighter squadrons, were deployed in close support.

During East Anglia's near-dawn hours heavy clouds hung over many of the bases, and snow sprinkled some of the runways. However, the ascending bombers broke through the cloud deck at 7,000 feet and began the two-hour task of assembling in mass formation prior to turning seaward. The North Sea undercast was solid except for occasional breaks. Above, the sky was cloudless. As the bombers moved over the continent the undercast began to break, and by the time the planes reached Leipzig and related targets, the ground could be seen. Most of the B-17s and B-24s got their bombs away with good results. That mission became the first of six days of intensive, high-level bombing labeled the Big Week; the weather stayed generally favorable, with the exception of February 22–23, through February 25.

How big was Big Week and what were its implications? It was certainly a maximum effort. The AAF flew 3,800 bomber sorties and 3,600 fighter sorties. Almost 10,000 tons of bombs were dropped—a number roughly equal to that dropped during the Eighth Air Force's first year of operation in England. In addition, some 2,300 RAF sorties, chiefly at night, dropped another 9,200 tons of bombs. Losses were heavy: the AAF lost 226 heavy bombers and 28 fighters (approximately 2,600 airmen killed, wounded, or missing), and the RAF lost 157 bombers. But the cost to the opposing Luftwaffe was also appalling—600 fighters. Although the Allies could quickly replace their aircraft and air crews, the Luftwaffe began to falter.[70]

By the end of the month it was evident that the Luftwaffe no longer controlled European skies. The London correspondent for *Time* reported that favorable weather during Big Week was "probably as significant historically as the famous wind which once scattered the ships of the Spanish Armada." And Eisenhower, less than four months later, could reassure his troops on the morning of the Normandy invasion that "if you see fighting aircraft over you, they will be ours!"

U.S. Strategic Bombing Survey   As the war drew to a close Roosevelt ordered implementation of a U.S. Strategic Bombing Survey. Its roster of officers read like a who's who, including such luminaries as George W. Ball, John Kenneth Galbraith, and Paul H. Nitze. The study utilized more than 1,100 people and eventually published some two hundred authoritative reports. One of these analyzed AAF Weather Service support and weather factors relative to bombing operations in Europe.[71]

From the amassed statistics it was determined that, because of weather and weather forecasting, only 55 percent of the Eighth Air Force's monthly potential could be utilized. Target weather forecasts by the 18th Weather Squadron between June, 1943, and April, 1945, were verified at an overall accuracy of 58 percent. Twenty-four-hour forecasts of home base and route weather were verified at 75 percent, and forecasts of eighteen hours or less, at 87 percent.

How did the senior air commanders rate their forecasting support? "Weather is the essence of successful air operations," wrote Arnold; and Spaatz resolved that "in military air operations weather is the first step in planning and the final determining factor in execution of any mission." Thirty-five years later Eaker emphasized that the quality of weather support was of "major importance"—the cutting edge of air power's sword. "In general, and especially in bomber operations out of England, the Allied weather service was superior" to that of German service, Eaker concluded.[72]

Spaatz's deputy in 1942, Maj. Gen. Haywood S. Hansell, Jr., labeled weather "a greater hazard and obstacle than the German Air Force" and adjudged the weather forecasting during the winter of 1944 "unreliable" and "inaccurate." And James H. Doolittle, who assumed command of the Eighth Air Force in 1944, started off on the wrong foot by recalling two missions because the weather service forecast that home bases in England would be fogged in when the planes returned. "Both times the forecasts were capricious," he wrote, "and I was left, as the bombers returned in bright sunshine, with egg on my face."[73] His boss, Spaatz, sarcastically remarked, "Doolittle, it looks like you don't have the guts to command a large air force." Doolittle further recalled, "One of the most serious problems was finding the weather on the Continent very different from what the meteorologist had predicted," a situation rectified in part by having "air scout" fighters fly ahead of the bomber stream to confirm weather conditions over the targets.

OPERATION OVERLORD—ASSAULT ON NORMANDY (JUNE 6, 1944)

Looking back, it is difficult to imagine how the time and place of the world's largest amphibious invasion came as a complete surprise to the German high command. Yet, by judicious interpretation of a highly complex weather pattern, Allied meteorologists produced one of the most momentous forecasts of all time.[74]

To launch Operation Neptune, the initial assault phase of the attack against northwest Europe (Operation Overlord), the Allies planned to use 3,601 assault craft backed up by 300 warships. These were to land six reinforced infantry divisions (three American, two British, and one Canadian) along a 50-mile stretch of Normandy coastline during D day, following the drop of a British and two U.S. airborne divisions. Then, in the next two weeks, an additional 625,000 troops and nearly 100,000 support vehicles would move across the beaches, weather permitting (see Map 1).[75]

General Eisenhower, as the Supreme Allied Commander, stated the problem.

> We wanted to cross the Channel with our convoys at night so that darkness would conceal the strength and direction of our several attacks. We wanted a moon for our airborne assaults. We needed approximately forty minutes of daylight preceding the ground assault to complete our bombing and preparatory bombardment. We had to attack on a relatively low tide because of

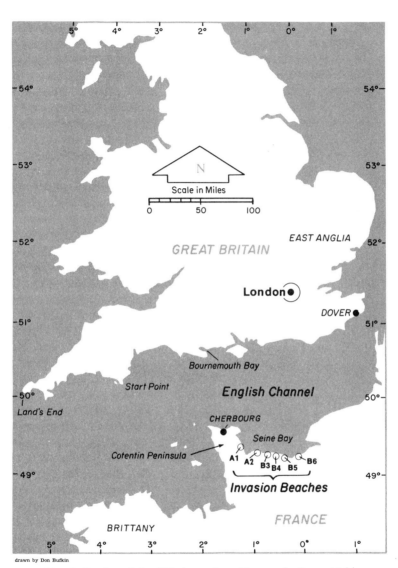

Map 1. Region of the Allied assault on Normandy, June, 1944.

beach obstacles which had to be removed while uncovered. These principal factors dictated the general period; but the selection of the actual day would depend upon weather forecasts. . . . If none of the three days (which we had chosen) should prove satisfactory from the standpoint of weather, consequences would ensue that were almost terrifying to contemplate. Secrecy would be lost. . . . A wait of at least fourteen days, possibly twenty-eight, would be necessary—a sort of suspended animation involving more than 2,000,000 men![76]

To carry this reasoning further, Allied and German planners believed that such a huge invasion force had to capture and operate a major permanent seaport within a few days of the initial attack or it would fail because of inadequate supplies.

Selection of Eisenhower's personal meteorological support team was a touchy matter. In November, 1943, two months before Ike arrived in England, the British Air Ministry's Meteorological Office posted a dour, hesitant civilian, Dr. J. M. Stagg, to the slot of Senior Weather Adviser, Supreme Allied Commander. Stagg's earlier specialties had been earth magnetism, solar radiation, and administration. At appointment time he just happened to be in London, serving as weather service manager for the British army. When the Royal Navy learned that Sir Nelson Johnson had assigned Stagg to the top weather post for what would be basically a seaborne assault, the news was unwelcome. The senior service expected the choice to be someone highly experienced in forecasting Britain's tricky weather.

U.S. Army officials in England were equally displeased, for it meant that their weatherman, Colonel Yates, would be deputy to a civilian. In fact, they felt so strongly that Ike's chief of staff, Gen. Bedell Smith, got into the act along with the vice chief of the British Air Staff and Air Chief Marshal Sir Arthur Tedder, the deputy commander of the Supreme Headquarters, Allied Expeditionary Force (SHAEF). As late as March 29, 1944 (less than six weeks before the hoped-for D day), SHAEF posted orders placing Yates in charge of its meteorological section, with Dr. Stagg as chief adviser. This action prompted the Air Ministry to spend the extra money to frock Stagg as an RAF group captain, making him equivalent in rank to Yates. As a result, a new SHAEF order placed Stagg back on top, effective April 18.

Eisenhower's personal headquarters, then at Bushey Park near London, had to be reasonably mobile and so did not have space for an associated weather central. Instead, Stagg and Yates set up the organizational pattern shown in Fig. 3. Therefore, only Stagg and Yates (with Stagg's assistant, Squadron Leader George D. Robinson of the RAF) were at SHAEF, ready to brief Ike and his staff as needed. Supporting these two briefers were three weather centrals—the USSTAF central (within walking distance), which Yates also commanded; the RAF's central (civilian operated) in suburban

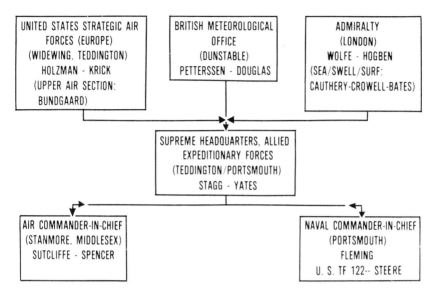

Fig. 3. Organizational diagram of forecasting weather for Operation Overlord.

Dunstable; and the Royal Navy's central two floors underground in downtown London.

That consortium began practice forecasts once a day during late April for the assault areas. Its three sets of clients were SHAEF (Stagg and Yates), the Allied fleet's chief meteorological officer (Instructor Comdr. John Fleming, RN), and the chief meteorological officer for the Allied Expeditionary Air Force (AEAF), Col. Norman C. Spencer, Jr., USAAF, and his British alternate, Dr. R. C. Sutcliffe. By using scrambled telephone links and a duo team of forecasters on forty-eight-hour rotation, each weather central took a five-day turn at opening the daily map discussion. Once the discussion moderator—either Stagg or Yates—achieved a degree of agreement among the centers about how the weather pattern would evolve, the drill was repeated for the subordinate elements: wind, cloud, visibility, rainfall, and confidence factor. As soon as the wind forecast was agreed upon, the Admiralty's Swell Forecast Section (which had been listening in) would generate sea, swell, and surf forecasts to be read back to interested participants at the end of the weather conference.[77]

The personalities of these daily (twice daily as D day neared) conference participants varied widely. Of the six working forecasters, the dean was Dunstable's C. K. M. Douglas, a World War I pilot, who had been predicting British weather since 1918. Although diffident, Douglas had total recall of unique weather situations even decades before, an analog approach that Krick could not rebut without consulting forecasters in Washington, D.C. Douglas's alternate, Colonel Petterssen, loved to argue endlessly with his fellow academic, Lieutenant Colonel Krick, at Widewing. Krick's counterpart, Lieutenant Colonel Holzman, as a civilian based at Gander, Newfoundland, had spent a winter (1941–42) forecasting North Atlantic weather. As far as Stagg was concerned, his team's lightweights (and he never met them face-to-face) were the Admiralty forecasters, Instructor Lt. Geoffrey Wolfe and his alternate, Instructor Lt. Lawrence Hogben, a Rhodes Scholar from New Zealand.[78]

May, 1944, proved to be a very favorable weather period for undertaking the invasion. Unfortunately, D day had been slipped a month because of a shortage of landing craft and the inability of the tactical air forces to complete knocking out all German airfields within 120 miles of the assault area. This moved D day ahead to June 5. Then Ike decided to move south and use Admiral Sir Bertram Ramsay's headquarters for the Allied Naval Commander-in-Chief of the Expeditionary Force (ANCXF) (Southwick House) at Portsmouth for the final decision-making sessions before the invasion. So on D − 8 (May 28) Stagg and Yates unexpectedly superimposed themselves on Commander Fleming's tiny facility housed in half of a Nissen hut, not far from the mansion. The crowding was so unbearable that Stagg found it difficult to get to the weather charts and resolve in his own mind the sharply different views advanced by the centers at Widewing and Dunstable. Then Stagg became further incensed at Fleming (an issue Fleming learned twenty-seven years later) when Fleming was found to be briefing Ramsay informally before the admiral entered the top-level briefing sessions.[79]

Yates reported later that despite such irritations and tensions Eisenhower's weather briefing sessions took place as follows:

> At periodic intervals each day Stagg and I reported to the Supreme Commander who in every case had assembled his Deputy, Chief of Staff, the Commander in Chief of Army, Navy, and Air and their deputies, and his G-3. During these briefings, Admiral Ramsay . . . had present his meteorological officer for personal advice. No other meteorologists were present. The normal procedure was for Stagg to present with appropriate aids an analysis of the synoptic situation and then in general terms present the forecast for the period in question. I followed with more specific information on the impact of the forecast on the operations of the strategic and tactical units of the Air Force, troop carriers, paratroop units, and, if any, the impact upon the Army operations. Admiral Ramsay's Met officer usually volunteered information on the operational implications of the sea and swell portions of the forecast. We were then queried at length by all members of the group. The briefings to the Supreme Commander usually lasted from thirty minutes to an hour.[80]

Unfortunately, the invasion-perfect, stable weather patterns of May no longer existed. Instead, by D − 4 (Thursday), the day on which naval forces

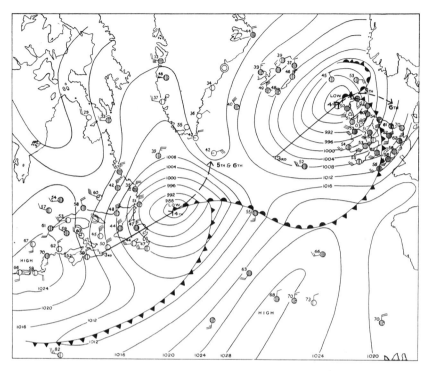

Map 2. Surface weather map for the evening of June 4, 1944. Arrows into low centers indicate movement of the past twenty-four hours, while dashed lines show subsequent movement. (Courtesy Dr. Lawrence Hogben)

in remote western Scotland had to begin leaving port, the weather map looked as if it were April. A pronounced polar front, complete with rapidly developing, eastward-moving storm centers, extended from south of the Aleutian Islands and across half the globe well into Europe. The most likely storm track lay over or just to the north of the British Isles—which location could make a great difference. To the south, the Azores summer high-pressure area featured an unusually high central value of 1,030 mb and extended a major lobe northeastward over southern Ireland and Brittany (see Map 2).

Eisenhower requested that the critical twice-daily weather briefings (4:15 A.M. and 9:30 P.M.) begin on Friday morning (D − 3). Unfortunately, the state of the art did not permit any of the three weather centrals to be convincing as to what the future would hold for the next five days. Widewing was optimistic, favoring the dominance of high pressure from the Azores lobe over the area of interest. Dunstable was pessimistic, believing that Scotland would soon see several fast-moving lows that would adversely affect English Channel weather. The Admiralty equivocated but thought the situation would be borderline on D day. By Saturday night all three weather centrals were pessimistic. Again, at the early Sunday briefing (D − 1) Stagg was still, as Ramsay's chief of staff had previously noted, "six foot two of Stagg and six foot one of gloom." Stagg's prediction was for a strong cold frontal passage with gale winds during Sunday night or early Monday (the proposed D day), so Ike ordered a twenty-four-hour postponement and recall of combat forces.[81]

But what next? Would there be a sizable high-pressure ridge behind the front, giving invasion weather on Tuesday and lasting into Wednesday? In two hard-fought map discussions later on Sunday, Widewing argued yes, Dunstable was again pessimistic, and the Admiralty thought it worth a chance. Stagg and Yates went with the majority vote. Following Stagg's presentation that night at 9:30 P.M. Ike asked his commanders in chief for their views. Fleming recalls how it went: "First, Admiral Ramsay said he was prepared to resume the operation—he had no misgivings at all. Then General Montgomery said he was ready to go as long as the Navy could get him there. Air Chief Marshall Leigh Mallory was, however, by no means happy and stated that in some ways conditions would be borderline, if not worse. Finally, Eisenhower, after having considered all the pros and cons, closed the conference and launched the invasion with these simple words: 'OK! Let's go!'"[82]

As Stagg and Yates returned to their tent, it was blowing hard and raining. One remarked to the other what a paradox it was that in less than a day Overlord had been postponed when the weather was calm and then remounted during rain and gale winds. It was definitely a storm to remember: as its center moved across the Scottish Shetlands during the night of June 4−5, barometric pressure fell to 977 mb at Wick, the lowest June atmospheric pressure of the century in the British Isles to that date.

Dawn of D day on June 6 found the assault beaches cloud-covered and windy but approachable. By then, and despite many problems during the drops of parachutists and gliders, the airborne troops were making progress, particularly in the British sector near Caen. But Leigh-Mallory's fears came true as 329 B-24 Liberators swept in over Omaha Beach to drop 13,000 bombs on coastal defenses just behind the sea cliffs. Solid undercast extended to 18,000 feet so the aircraft formations delayed their drops by several seconds, causing many of the bombs to drop as much as three miles inland. And although the landing craft at Omaha and Utah beaches were handling the moderate sea and surf reasonably well, specially modified "amphibious tanks" with canvas skirts were sinking with such regularity that only five of thirty-two such armored vehicles reached shore safely. But as forecast, cloud cover improved as the day wore on, and by the next afternoon surf heights were as low as one foot.

What SHAEF did not know at the time was that their fine tuning of the weather situation had caught the German high command totally off guard. After a long series of tiring May alerts, the chief of the German Weather Service, Lieutenant General Richard Habermehl, advised that the upcoming unsettled weather of June 4–6 made conditions unfavorable for an Allied invasion. The naval experts agreed, believing that a successful landing required five consecutive days of favorable weather.[83] Consequently, no invasion alert was issued for the night of June 5–6, 1944.

Instead, Fld. Mar. Erwin Rommel was in Germany seeing Hitler about the disposition of tanks and helping his wife celebrate her birthday. Col. Gen. Friedrich Dollmann, the Seventh Army commander directly in charge of defending Normandy and Brittany, had divisional commanders Hellmich, von Schlieben, and Falley at Rennes on June 5 for a two-day map exercise that was to start the next day. Even the commander of the 21st Panzer Division in Normandy had chosen to visit the Paris nightclubs on the evening of June 5. What these German officers did not know was that their in-baskets on the morning of D − 1 (June 5) held a far more ominous weather forecast. This prediction, prepared by von Rundstedt's chief meteorologist, Dr. Müller, at 5:00 A.M. provided a map analysis and thirty-six-hour weather forecast remarkably similar to the one just generated by Stagg's team across the Channel (Appendix D). Müller's, too, was calling for clearing skies and diminishing winds on June 6 after the frontal passage. In fact, his "outlook for enemy attacks" for the night of June 5–6 reads, "clouds will clear from the west, and conditions for attacks will be more favorable."

With hindsight, Stagg commented that post–World War II improvements in weather forecasting would not have markedly improved the D day weather forecasts. On the other hand, despite initial scepticism and lack of discussion discipline, three weather centrals had been better than one. Yates believed the opposite: "This was a most cumbersome operation, and one which I would never recommend for future use. Just give me one center with a mixture of experts where I can knock their heads together." But if just one central had been used, the haunting question remains—would crowd psychology have taken over and allowed the most persuasive person to dominate? Then, if such a meteorologist had been badly wrong, as one of the operation's forecasters noted later, "disaster would have smitten us!"[84]

NORMANDY AND BEYOND

Colonel Moorman and his 21st Weather Squadron supported the initial Normandy assault phase, which lasted until D + 24 (July 1, 1944), in four ways. First, two volunteer observers jumped with the 82nd and 101st

Airborne Divisions at 1:00 A.M., five hours before the infantry crossed the beaches. Second, weather observers were included in air support parties that landed behind the beaches with glider units or waded across the strand with assault troops. Typically comprising eight men, a half-track, and a radio-equipped jeep, each party guided close-support air strikes while the attached weather observer advised incoming fighter pilots on target weather and transmitted hourly weather reports to the command ships offshore. Third, observer specialists were assigned to air coordination units attached to each airborne and ground force division headquarters, some proving more useful than others. Fourth, fourteen van-mounted, mobile forecasting detachments plus associated radio trucks were assigned to all corps head-quarters and above.[85]

By D + 12 the Allies had moved some 629,000 troops, 95,000 vehicles, and 228,000 tons of supplies onto the restricted beachhead. To break out, however, the high command needed a guaranteed off-loading rate of 30,000 troops and 30,000 tons of supplies daily. This required, it was thought, the construction of artificial harbors off American and British beaches (Mulberry A and B, respectively). To form the requisite breakwaters would take thirty-one massive concrete caissons per Mulberry, with each caisson taking at least forty-eight hours to tow across the English Channel. Tows began as early as D + 3. However, the final major tow needed a hundred tugs and could wait for a period of guaranteed good weather. Because the breakwater concept was British, Admiral Ramsay would give the final signal for the trek. Upon being advised by Commander Fleming that the three-day period after June 17 looked unusually favorable, Ramsay ordered the caissons under way.

Fleming's forecast (identical to those of Widewing and Dunstable) called for a strong Azores high-pressure area of 1,030 mb to extend eastward over southern England from just west of Ireland, thereby giving light channel winds. What no one foresaw was that a weak cyclone lying over southern France and Spain would intensify in place, somewhat like a summer "heat low." This deepening coincided with a slight pressure buildup over southern England to create a tight pressure gradient that, by the next day, was causing unannounced gale-force winds directly down 120 miles of the English Channel. At the far end of this fetch was the oncoming convoy of Phoenix caissons, plus thousands of Allied landing craft off-loading troops and supplies close inshore. The upshot was chaos on the beachhead between 9:00 A.M. on June 19 and 3:00 P.M. on June 22. Off the highly exposed Omaha strand, Phoenixes had to be scuttled or beached.[86] Inshore, two Loebnitz piers, opened to truck traffic three days before, were twisted beyond repair by the surf. Jammed-up landing craft, with inadequate holding tackle and inexperienced crews, suffered 700 vessel casualties, some as large as LSTs. Soon the beach was so cluttered with wreckage that resupply was difficult even when the surf died down. Frontline troops were beginning to get down to their last crates of hand grenades, so a C-47 airlift had to be instituted to bring in more ammunition.

The media were quick to call this worrisome incident starting on D + 13 the Great Storm. In practice, Commander Steere, offshore in the flagship USS *Augusta*, reported no peak gusts exceeding 32 knots. Even so, the unanticipated wind pattern struck fear into forecasters' hearts. Later, Stagg passed Eisenhower a note, pointing out that June, 1944, had had the worst June weather of the past twenty years and that their alternative D day would have ended in a howling gale. By now, doubly lucky Eisenhower could send the memorandum back with a longhand note: "Thanks, and thank the gods of war that we went when we did!"[87]

The long-desired port of Cherbourg fell on D + 23 (June 29). However, one of Hitler's secret weapons—the pressure, or "oyster," mine, plus severe harbor demolition, kept the daily unloading rate in the port below 8,500 tons until mid-August, a rate that the open beaches at Omaha and Utah had reached on D + 7. Bates learned during a July inspection trip to the beachhead that despite this heavy dependence on acquiring military supplies through open roadsteads, neither the navy nor the army had used the detailed wave forecasts. The missing link appeared to be a lack of correlation between off-loading rate and wave height.[88] Once Bates developed the relationship, Colonel Moorman met with Maj. Gen. C. R. Moore, the theater's chief engineer and the person responsible for managing the army's unloading operation. They agreed that the army "amphibs" should have a beachhead weather station.

By mid-September, Detachment YK, which had two Scripps-trained oceanographers, 1st Lt. Donald W. Pritchard and 1st Lt. Robert O. Reid, was on Omaha Beach. The detachment soon proved so skillful at predicting how the environment would control pending off-loading operations that the engineer beach commander kept operations going full tilt until early November rather than shutting down in late September, as originally planned. In the meantime, the Germans tied up thousands of troops, thinking that such seaports as Lorient, Dieppe, and Le Havre must be kept out of Allied control at all costs.[89]

Once the beachhead buildup was complete, the Allied armies began breaking out of Normandy on July 25 (D + 49). Within eight days Patton's armor was on the loose, first toward Brittany, then toward the Rhine River itself. Detachment YD, as part of the XX Corps, participated, by a series of seventeen moves, in what was reputed to be one of the fastest sustained marches in history: the corps covered 600 miles from St. Jacques to Verdun by September 25, 1944. By now, Hitler's forces were in deep trouble, for the Allied forces had landed during perfect weather in southern France (Operation Anvil) starting on August 15, 1944. But as the Allies' supply lines lengthened, their pursuit of the Germans across France and Belgium ground to a halt in the shadows of Germany's "Westwall"—the ominous Siegfried line in the south and the Rhine River in the north.

OPERATION MARKET-GARDEN: THE AIRBORNE INVASION OF HOLLAND

By September, 1944, SHAEF's planners had considered more than a dozen ways to deploy the First Allied Airborne Army (FAAA), only to see each scenario overtaken by events. Then, on September 10, Eisenhower approved Montgomery's bold plan to turn the Germans' northern flank. Three airborne divisions would be dropped behind the enemy's lines, clearing a 60-mile-long corridor from Holland's southern border to Arnhem. The British Second Army would next turn the flank at Arnhem for a direct thrust into the German heartland. Key to the plan, code-named Market (airborne assault)-Garden (ground offensive), was capturing five bridges intact, particularly the massive Rhine River bridge at Arnhem.[90]

Market-Garden became the largest airborne endeavor of any war. The ambitious plan called for 35,000 troops and supporting gear to be airlifted from England on three consecutive days. The FAAA (U.S. 82nd and 101st Airborne and the British 1st Airborne Divisions) came under the command of Lt. Gen. Lewis H. Brereton. More than 20,000 men, 500 vehicles, 330 artillery pieces, and 590 tons of equipment were scheduled for first-day delivery. Using twenty-four American and British air bases, some 4,700 Allied aircraft would be deployed on D day (the largest number ever used in a single airborne assault), including bombers to soften German positions, fighters for escort and flak suppression, troop carriers (2,000 of them, mostly C-47s), and gliders (approximately 600). Just to get the troop carriers and gliders off the ground on D day took more than two hours.

The final selection of D day depended upon the weather forecast, a joint responsibility. In this instance, the FAAA's costaff weather officers were Mr. Jacobs, a civilian and senior meteorological officer of the RAF's 38th Group, and Lt. Col. Richard J. Kent of the 21st Weather Squadron. They directed a combined meteorological section at FAAA headquarters. To generate consensus forecasts for Brereton and his staff, formal and informal conferences were held daily between major RAF and U.S. weather forecasting centers in England. Each afternoon at 4:30, Kent and Jacobs issued the official four-day forecast—prepared to a large degree beyond the forty-eight-hour period—by using Krick's map-typing technique. Twenty-four-hour outlooks were issued eighteen hours beforehand, followed four hours later by the official twenty-four-hour forecast (amended every two hours if necessary). Weather coverage was far better than three months before. Not only were additional Russian data coming in but numerous 21st Weather Squadron units were reporting regularly from the continent. Thrice-daily weather reconnaissance flights were also timed so that their reports fed into the FAAA weather unit at eight, six, and four hours before each day's planning meeting.

Operational weather criteria were quite specific. The route to Holland had to have good visibility and no turbulence because the towed gliders would be in close formation and often needed to land close together. Thus, one might carry an antitank gun, a second glider the gun's prime mover, and the third, ammunition and gun crew. Over the assault area, the paratroopers wanted a minimum of 1,000-foot ceilings, 1-mile visibility, and surface winds of 25 miles per hour or less; the glider pilots needed at least 1,500-foot ceilings and 1.5 miles of visibility. With North Sea weather being notoriously fickle, even in early autumn, Brereton wanted a guaranteed three days of combat weather. Thus, what the staff meteorologist wished for was a stagnant high-pressure area over the area of operations.

On Saturday, September 16, Kent and Jacobs briefed Brereton and his staff at 4:30 P.M. that marginally favorable weather appeared forthcoming over the next four days. A high-pressure system from the southwest would be over Belgium on Sunday. Fair weather with few clouds and gentle winds should prevail until Wednesday. Fog was likely on and after Monday but only at dawn and early morning. Two and a half hours later, Brereton gave the go-ahead signal for laying a strip of airborne troops to the north along the road leading to Arnhem on the following day.[91]

Two hours before Sunday's launch Kent and Jacobs issued their final operational forecast at 8:00 A.M., calling for generally favorable weather. The forecast held for that day, and the vast air armada, assembled in immense triple columns some tens of miles across and a hundred miles long, swept out over the North Sea. The Germans were surprised at first, and, with accurate air drops, most of the day's key objectives were taken, although with heavy casualties. Among those jumping with the 101st Airborne was Sgt. John F. Motylewski of the 21st Weather Squadron, who sent back on-site weather reports whenever possible until the division was relieved a few days later.

Weather problems developed on Monday (D + 1), September 18, and on all but one day for a week thereafter—most were caught by the twenty-four-hour operational forecasts, some not. Fog at home bases delayed drops in Holland that Monday, putting Market-Garden behind schedule at a time when German resistance toughened. Because of the unfavorable weather, few reinforcements and supplies reached Holland on Tuesday and Wednesday while the 1st Airborne Division was suffering serious losses in the attempt to capture the Arnhem bridge. An airlift of a Polish brigade to Arnhem, canceled on Wednesday, was then attempted Thursday. But, because of wretched weather (troop-carrier pilots took off in near-zero visibility), only 1,000 of the 1,500-man brigade were dropped. The Poles were too few and too late, especially after extremely poor weather on Friday scrubbed all scheduled missions. Weather on Saturday was favorable, but resupplying the British and Poles at Arnhem was especially difficult because of the small defensive perimeter they held. Bad weather once again halted all troop-carrier missions on Sunday, the day the Germans broke through the Allied corridor in Holland at midpoint and put a stranglehold on Market-Garden.

Weather the next day, Monday, September 25, restricted airlift operations. But by then it mattered little. When the Germans had blocked the main road midway in the Allied salient and moved tanks up to cut off the British troops trapped north of the Rhine in Arnhem, Montgomery ordered them withdrawn south of the river, thereby abandoning Market-Garden's primary objective.

Ironically, the weather that played a key part in the defeat of the British 1st Airborne Division saved them in the end from annihilation. On the night of September 25–26, under cover of gale-force winds and rain and under the noses of unsuspecting Germans, about 2,400 British and Polish troops swam or were ferried across the Rhine to the south bank and safety. The division's courageous stand cost more than 75 percent of its 10,000 men. In a tribute to the unit, the 1st Airborne designation was dropped from the British army's roster. Thus ended in failure the great airborne venture. It cost dearly. One-third of 35,000 men were lost in nine days. Of 11,853 casualties, 9,333 were either killed or missing. In fact, this casualty total approximated the number of Allied casualties lost in Normandy during June.

"The attack began well and unquestionably would have been successful except for the intervention of bad weather," Eisenhower wrote later: "this [weather] prevented the adequate reinforcement of the northern spearhead and resulted finally in the decimation of the British airborne division."[92] After the debacle General Arnold dispatched officers to Europe to conduct a postmortem. Their report picked out several areas for criticism. One was the weather factor, which had not been looked at close enough during planning, with grave consequences. For example, weather had reduced fighter aircraft effectiveness and accomplished what the Luftwaffe could not—furnish protective cover for German troops. Weather had also impaired airlift operations and upset Market-Garden's delicate timetable. Even Montgomery, who asserted that Market-Garden was 90% successful (because all objectives but the Arnhem bridge were achieved), conceded that the single most important preclusion to total success was the weather.

As part of the extensive Market-Garden critique, Kent and Jacobs were directed by theater authorities and the AAF Weather Service to review the weather support role. They concluded that long-range forecasting for the FAAA's operational thresholds was difficult because of the weather phenomena in the area of operations and that the weather experienced did not match seasonal averages and, except for September 19, it was as forecast; in short, "there were no inadequacies in the weather service." The FAAA later acknowledged, too, that although the weather had been poor, it was no worse than expected and forecasts were satisfactory.

WINDING DOWN THE WAR (DECEMBER, 1944–MAY 1945)

Although the war was not going well for Hitler by late 1944, he still believed that weather might help stave off disaster in the west. His hope was to assemble and then strike under the cover of bad weather with twenty-four divisions through the lightly defended Ardennes forest area near the junction of Belgium, France, and Luxembourg. Once past the forests, his panzers would sweep south of Antwerp and reach the North Sea, meanwhile encircling much of the Allied army. To do all this would take at least ten days of bad weather capable of grounding Allied airpower. His meteorologists spotted such a condition in late November. But that interval had to be passed by because the necessary logistical support could not be completely marshaled, although the bad weather that began in mid-November did mask the German effort to concentrate their military forces.

When the Ardennes offensive came on December 16, it was a stunning surprise to the Allies. For the first seven days of the Battle of the Bulge, inclement weather critically limited the help that friendly air power could render to the outnumbered defenders. Eisenhower stated afterward: "As long as the weather kept our planes on the ground, it would be an ally of the enemy worth many divisions."[93] Because Allied aircraft could not fly close support during the first week, Hitler's weather criterion had been met. Still, it was not an unmixed blessing, for the alternating rains, snows, and thaws muddied roads and hampered the movement of German armor. When a five-day period of good weather finally set in on December 23, friendly air power quickly helped break the back of the last major German attack on the western front.

In an analysis five months later, the captured General Field Marshal von Rundstedt noted: "Weather is a weapon the German Army used with success, particularly in the Ardennes offensive. . . . This Battle of the Bulge, as you call it, might have changed the entire course of the war, had it not been for the fact that the United States [Army] Air Force so quickly took advantage of the break in the weather." It was ironic, whether divine providence or sheer coincidence, that on December 23, General Patton, whose Third

Army had been directed to help relieve pressure on the Bulge, and whose armor had been slowed by the same weather, summoned his chaplain to compose a prayer for distribution to his troops: "Almighty and most merciful Father, we humbly beseech Thee, of Thy great goodness, to restrain these immoderate rains with which we had to contend. . . . Grant us fair weather for Battle."[94]

The counterattack to destroy the Ardennes salient came on January 3, 1945. But the van of Allied armor had hardly passed through the infantry before bad weather again began to take effect. Fog was so pervasive that not a single tactical aircraft supported the attack at any time during the day. In fact, the pattern changed little over the next fortnight. Only once in two weeks did visibility permit tactical aircraft to operate all day long, and on only two other days did fighter-bombers get airborne. For the entire month of January, Eighth Air Force strategic bombers were totally down eleven days because of bad weather; tactical aircraft of the Ninth Air Force (day fighters, fighter-bombers, and medium bombers) could not operate for thirteen of the thirty-one days. Thus, their assigned weathermen were far from popular people as long as the forecasts called only for more bad weather.

Better weather gradually returned by March, 1945. By now, the 21st Weather Squadron was supplying specialized services in the fields of artillery ballistics, soil trafficability, flood prediction, and smoke-laying, as well as continuing in the bread-and-butter business of aiding air attacks. And by Victory-in-Europe (V-E) Day on May 7, the squadron had achieved its peak historical strength of 266 officers and 1,014 enlisted men. Moorman and his mobile weather squadron performed admirably under the stress of battle, at the cost of only nine fatalities—four from combat and five from field accidents. General Eisenhower, too, had had his fill of bad European weather. As early as July 20, 1944, in the presence of General Bradley, he had muttered: "When I die, they ought to hold my body for a rainy day and then bury me out in the middle of a storm. This damned weather is going to be the death of me yet."[95]

Chapter 6
World War II—Defeat of Japan

*This generation of Americans can still remember the black days of 1942.
. . . In those hours Germany and Japan came so close to complete
domination of the world that we do not yet realize how thin the thread of
Allied survival had been stretched.*

—General George C. Marshall, USA

PEARL HARBOR AND THE METEOROLOGICAL AFTERMATH

On December 1, 1941, the Army Air Corps Detachment, Weather, Hawaii, at Hickam Field, was upgraded to the 7th Air Corps Squadron, Weather (Regional Control). Five nights later, T. Sgt. Daniel A. Dyer had the duty of drawing the midnight weather map. He sketched in an extensive storm system to the northwest of the Hawaiian Islands. What he did not know, nor did his higher command, was that a Japanese strike force was hiding in that bad weather, about to launch a postdawn attack against Hickam. Shortly, Dyer and four other enlisted Air Corps weathermen, while dashing to battle stations, were killed by an 800-pound Japanese bomb.[1]

After the attack, the U.S. Weather Bureau and the military immediately ordered all weather transmissions to and from Hawaii encoded. The work load jumped tenfold with no immediate increase in personnel. As a result, the Honolulu-based units of the U.S. Weather Bureau, the Air Corps, Hawaiian Airlines, and Pan American Airways joined forces with the navy's weather central on Ford Island in the center of the huge Pearl Harbor base complex. This central, then just five months old, began with a staff of four officers and twenty-five sailors, plus access to the powerful radio transmitter, NPM, for sending storm warnings. By early 1942 the facility had become the world's largest weather central.[2]

In the field, naval radiosonde units were operating at Palmyra and Wake islands, supplemented to the west by conventional surface weather stations at Johnston and Midway atolls plus Agana, Guam. As the Japanese empire rapidly spread east and south, Wake and Guam were soon captured.[3] Emphasis was then placed on creating a series of new weather stations along the Hawaii—New Zealand—Australia air route. This resulted in naval units at Canton Island, Bora Bora (Samoa), Suva (Fiji Islands), Noumea (New Caledonia), and Auckland (New Zealand), supplemented by a Marine Corps weather unit at Wallis Island and 7th Weather Squadron detachments at Christmas Island, Baker Island (just south of the Japanese-held Gilbert Islands), and Espiritu Santo (New Hebrides) (see Map 3).

Before Wake Island fell on December 23 the Air Corps was bold and desperate enough to stage aircraft from Hickam Field to Wake and then, by using forecasts of winds up to 30,000 feet, to fly completely across the Japanese mandated islands to the Australian air base at Port Moresby, New Guinea. After Wake was captured, the joint weather central at Ford Island still had to route long-range flights safely through the largely unknown equatorial front to the southwest of Hawaii. As this worked out, such aircraft departed before the early morning forecast was completed. Once completed, the forecast was radioed to the aircraft en route. If the forecast was satisfactory, the pilot continued; if not, he returned.

The importance of good navigation and wind forecasts for safe island hopping was underscored by a tragic incident involving Capt. Edward V. Rickenbacker, America's leading ace in World War I and founder of Eastern Airlines. Following his arrival by air from San Francisco at Honolulu on the morning of October 20, 1942, Rickenbacker was to proceed on a secret War Department mission to General MacArthur's headquarters in New Guinea. By 10:30 P.M., after a day of inspecting AAF units in the area, Rickenbacker was ready to leave by B-17. Capt. John ("Jack") M. Feeley, a 7th Weather Squadron forecaster at Hickam, briefed Rickenbacker's pilot, Maj. William T. Cherry, Jr., to expect high-scattered clouds and headwinds on the ten-hour leg to Canton Island. On takeoff roll, the B-17 blew a tire. Cherry ground-looped the plane to keep from going into the bay, and the octant fell to the floor in the violent maneuver. The navigator, 2nd Lt. John J. DeAngelis, who had made more flights (nine) across the Pacific than any other Air Transport Command navigator, took the octant with him aboard a second B-17 that Cherry got off the ground shortly after midnight. After the estimated time of arrival for Canton passed about nine and one-half hours later without sight of the island, DeAngelis decided his octant was out of calibration. The star shots he had taken that night, and sun lines he had shot that morning, together with drift meter readings, had given him erroneous readings suggesting a slight tailwind instead of a headwind. Cherry immediately decided to home in on Canton's radio, only to discover that the plane's radio compass and loop antenna were inoperative, making

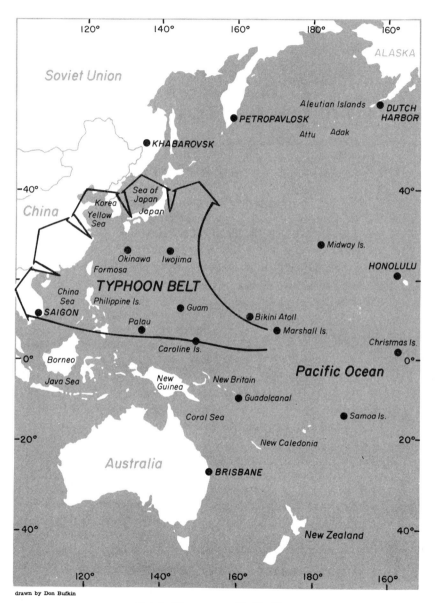

Map 3. The western Pacific Ocean.

drawn by Don Bufkin

radio navigation and dead reckoning impossible (there was no pelorus or astrocompass aboard). Unable to obtain help through radio contact with Canton and Palmyra Island, and running out of gas, Cherry put the B-17 down on the ocean. There followed three harrowing weeks aboard rubber rafts in shark-infested waters and a death before the men were rescued.

AAF chief General Hap Arnold ordered a full-scale investigation. "The basic cause was purely and simply a failure of the crew to properly check their equipment . . . before departure," Arnold was advised; weather service together with communications and Air Transport Command procedures were identified as "weak spots." In a confidential report to the secretary of war, Rickenbacker lashed out at Arnold's ferrying operations in the South Pacific (lack of control and discipline among air and ground crews, improperly trained aircrews, in particular navigators, and so on) but made no mention of weather service. However, in books he later published, Rickenbacker criticized Feeley's forecast, saying it called for headwinds of 10 mph that were much less than those actually encountered. But Cherry, interrogated less than a month after his rescue, confirmed that headwinds were as forecast and that the tailwind factor they navigated by resulted from a damaged octant. "Weather," Cherry testified, "did not affect the navigation at all." Nevertheless, officers up and down the chain of command, among them Feeley, were relieved following the Rickenbacker episode. Feeley was returned to the mainland in an injustice to the weather service.[4]

Notwithstanding the Rickenbacker incident, pilots were urged to report weather as they flew. To assist, the weather central developed the first exclusive aircraft weather reporting and forecast code—the SAP-1. Thousands of requests came in for this terse code, not only from army and navy units but also from Pan American Airways and from the Royal Australian Air Force, which was taking delivery of many Lend-Lease aircraft. All this effort, plus compiling special climatic studies and distributing aerological gear, created an acute shortage of meteorological personnel. Solving this problem proved simple. With the backing of Adm. Chester Nimitz, commander in chief, Pacific Fleet, fifty seamen were taken from in-port ships and trained at a special school run by the central for third-class aerographer's mates.

Because of the great distances in the southwest Pacific region (4,500 nautical miles from Hawaii to Australia), the operating area of the 7th Weather Region was reduced as quickly as possible. On April 22, 1942, the 15th Weather Squadron was activated at Townsville, Australia, to provide meteorological support, particularly to Maj. Gen. George C. Kenney's newly formed Fifth Air Force based at Brisbane. The following November, the newly formed 17th Weather Squadron, soon to be based at Noumea, assumed responsibility for weather detachments in Guadalcanal and islands farther east. Although most of these stations were pestilence ridden (filariasis affected nearly 10 percent of the enlisted men) and dangerous (four weathermen died in combat), one of its stations—Aitutaki in the Cook Islands—was truly a South Sea island paradise.[5]

BATAAN AND CORREGIDOR

Leaving American air and sea power at Hawaii twisted and burning, the Japanese quickly turned to the Philippines. After being grounded temporarily by a dense fog on Formosa, the Japanese planes attacked the American bases by air during late morning (Filipino time) of the same day. Most of the new B-17s of the Air Corps, as well as many of their fighter escorts (P-40Es), were caught refueling at Clark Field and were destroyed.[6] Simultaneously, a force of 110 Japanese naval bombers demolished the Cavite naval base on the southern side of Manila Bay. As these buildings were largely wooden, the facility rapidly burned to the ground, including the Asiatic Fleet's weather central.

During the ensuing invasion by Japanese forces, some fifteen weathermen of the 5th Weather Squadron, headquartered at Nichols Field on Manila's outskirts, were among the last-ditch defenders of the Bataan Peninsula and the island of Corregidor. The squadron commander escaped to the south; two of his sergeants, T. Sgt. Johnnie Crews and S. Sgt. Joseph Schoebert, joined Filipino guerilla groups and fought in the jungles for the next three years. Most were killed or taken prisoner; 1st Lt. James E. Cooke evidently died in a prisoner-of-war camp.[7]

At the time of the air attack the Cavite weather central was staffed by three officers; eight aerographer's mates, or strikers; a senior radioman; and nine Filipino radiomen of the Insular Force. The unit commander, thirty-four-year-old Lt. Denys W. Knoll, was an MIT weather graduate with additional duty as staff aerological officer to the Asiatic Fleet. Knoll had been transmitting his Far East weather data back to Ford Island in code as early as three months before the attack because one of his section leaders, AerM1c. Harry Cook had developed a method for decrypting Japanese weather reports radioed from their mandated islands.[8]

Once Cavite was destroyed, Knoll's group shifted operations to the Manila Observatory, operated by Father Charles E. Depperman, S.J., on the grounds of Ateneo University. When Manila was declared an open city on Christmas Day, the fleet weather central finally moved to fortified Corregidor Island at the mouth of Manila Bay. Despite the continuing need to help man beach defenses, the aerological team kept up its Japanese radio intercepts and continued to send out two canned weather maps per day to Hawaii, long after Gen. Douglas MacArthur had departed by submarine for Australia on March 11, 1942. Then during the night before the island's surrender on May 5 and 6, Knoll, too, along with eleven other officers and thirteen nurses, was ordered out, by special order of President Roosevelt, on the submarine USS *Spearfish*.[9]

In about a week the Japanese came searching among the navy prisoners for a "Chief Flying Meteorologist Tarnowski." Their goal was to learn how the Americans had been drawing weather maps that incorporated Japanese weather data. After three days of interrogation, including twice being led out for execution by a busy firing squad, Zemo Tarnowski, aerographer's mate 1st class, finally satisfied the Japanese general in charge and reverted to being a conventional prisoner of war. But once this amazing twenty-three-year-old reached Japan, his fellow inmates dragooned him into serving as camp commander on behalf of the prisoners in not one, but two, Japanese prison camps—Umeda Bunsho and Tsuruga, both on Honshu Island. The duty was far from pleasant: he was punished along with any of his men for stealing rice or other supplies, acts that occurred many times.[10]

THE DOOLITTLE RAID

Within four months of the attack on Pearl Harbor the Joint Chiefs of Staff approved an audacious raid against four Japanese cities—Tokyo, Yokohama, Kobe, and Nagoya. There would be two payoffs: the Japanese would see the need to keep forces to defend the home islands, and American morale would improve once the United States began to counterattack. As planned by the pioneer of blind-flying, Dr. (now Brig. Gen.) James H. Doolittle, twelve AAF B-25 bombers would take off from the carrier USS *Hornet* after she had steamed as close as she dared to Honshu during bad weather. Having dropped the bombs, the aircraft would proceed to a friendly airfield near Chuchow, China.[11]

A navy climatological study suggested that the raid take place between April 15 and May 15, 1942, with the carrier task force running west along the 40th parallel and just south of the polar front. An additional weather requirement was to sneak the USS *Hornet* out of San Francisco harbor during fog so that no one would know which way she was going with all the outsized B-25s on her flight deck. Two other weather controls also had to be met. The task force under R. Adm. William F. ("Bull") Halsey needed to refuel at sea just before the strike so that the ships could retire at full speed immediately after the launch. Wind speed over the carrier deck had to be 40 or more knots if the heavy land-based bombers were to get airborne in such a short space.[12]

Weather conditions were favorable on April 2, so the task force left fogbound San Francisco unnoticed. Running west, the *Hornet* had a miserable voyage for her crew and AAF passengers, but beautiful weather for hiding the mission. Almost every day was stormy. Then, for a short period on April 17, approximately one thousand nautical miles from Tokyo, the weather was reasonably calm, suitable for refueling from the accompanying oiler. During an ensuing cold frontal passage with gale winds, the raiders slipped undetected through the outer line of Japanese picket vessels. But luck ran out about dawn, when additional patrols were spotted and one Japanese vessel had to be sunk by gunfire.

Despite the lack of weather reports from the enemy-held territory to the west, the task force aerologist felt enough encouraged by the cold front to advise that the situation looked favorable.[13] The target areas should be clear with scattered clouds, and there would probably be tail winds on the last leg of the route because of high pressure centered over Japan. Despite a heaving sea, the first B-25 launched at 8:20 A.M. while the carrier steamed within 650 nautical miles of Tokyo.

Target weather was clear, as forecast. But then trouble set in.[14] A second storm center had formed over the China Sea. Although the storm's wind pattern gave tail winds, the cyclonic disturbance also caused dense low clouds, rain, and fog to shroud the mountainous east China coast. It was dark by then, fuel was low, and Chuchow lacked navigational aids. One after another, the tired B-25 crews bailed out or crash-landed wherever they could. Several died or were executed by the Japanese, but the rest, including Doolittle, returned to the United States for a hero's welcome.

CORAL SEA

Despite Doolittle's dramatic raid, the order of battle in April, 1942, favored the Japanese rather than the American navy. By then, the Japanese perimeter south of the equator ran from Indonesia to New Guinea to the Solomon Islands. The next logical Japanese step before invading Australia was to conquer the key Australian base at Port Moresby, New Guinea. To combat this initiative before it started, the commander in chief of the Pacific Fleet introduced two carrier task forces (TF-17 with the USS *York-town* and TF-18 with the USS *Lexington*) into the Coral Sea just northeast of Queensland. As the two carriers rendezvoused there May 1, the weather was dominated by a moderate cold front that had moved northeastward from Queensland and stagnated in typical fashion, largely along 10° south latitude—the Japanese perimeter already described.[15]

By May 4 the *Yorktown* was refueled and had steamed north into a band of poor weather (stratocumulus, cumulus, and cumulonimbus clouds with patches of limited visibility from showers and rain squalls) caused by the stagnant front. After a 7:00 A.M. launch, *Yorktown's* aircraft broke out of the heavy cloud cover 20 nautical miles away from the target—Tulagi Harbor, well inside the Solomon Islands. The result: total surprise and the sinking of two destroyers, a cargo ship, and four gunboats. Then on May 7 the two U.S. carriers, still launching despite moderately poor weather, had their aircraft fly back through the far worse frontal weather to attack an enemy carrier force ferreting them in return. Again, when the pilots broke into the clear and spotted Japanese warships, they achieved tactical surprise and the quick destruction of the small carrier *Shoho* and a cruiser. As it grew dark, a couple of Japanese aircraft even tried to land on the *Yorktown*, not knowing that they had the wrong carrier at a time when the task forces were probably within fifty miles of each other.

During the night, TF-17 and TF-18 steamed south-southeastward, leaving the protective cover of the frontal zone and entering the relatively clear skies of the southeast trade winds. Now the tables turned. Two big Japanese carriers, *Shokaku* and *Ziukaku*, were in the bad weather zone, and their enemy was in the clear. Contending scout aircraft saw each other at about the same time, so opposing launches were simultaneous. Lt. Comdr. Hubert E. Strange, the aerologist on the *Yorktown*, urged his pilots to stay below the cloud deck so that they could fly visually all the way to the *Ziukaku*.[16] They did, and damaged her badly.

Unfortunately, the *Lexington's* pilots used different tactics and could not locate the *Shokaku*. Meanwhile, Japanese aircraft attacked the U.S. carriers in the clear. The overall result: the *Lexington* was sunk; the *Yorktown* was damaged, and both sides were willing to call it a stalemate. But the key lesson was that the Battle of the Coral Sea proved to be a major naval engagement during which ten surface ships were sunk without their ever firing guns at one another. It added a new meaning to the old nautical term "having the weather gauge," for cloud cover and visibility were now more important than the wind field when launching air attacks without using electronics as the dominant means of detection.[17]

MIDWAY ATOLL

Although World War II had many large-scale naval air battles, the most important was the one that determined who should control Midway Atoll and its two tiny islands of about a thousand acres. As the furthest northwestern tip of the Hawaiian Island chain, Midway was the control point for access to Hawaii from the west. After the Battle of the Coral Sea, Adm. Isoroku Yamamoto believed the time had come to occupy this unsinkable outpost. By then, the status of the five large U.S. carriers was as follows: the *Lexington* was sunk, the *Yorktown* was damaged, the *Saratoga* was in the shipyard at Bremerton, Washington, and the last two carriers, the *Enterprise* and the *Hornet*, were apparently somewhere in the South Pacific.

To execute his plan Yamamoto was assigned Japan's most powerful fleet in history—an armada of over one hundred warships, including eight carriers and eleven battleships, plus transport and supply vessels for the final amphibious assault on the atoll. Moreover, he had enough warships to run a diversionary thrust against Dutch Harbor (in the Aleutians) a day before the main strike. And finally, to guarantee tactical surprise, his strike forces would use the cover of easterly storms, as had the task force that had so successfully attacked Pearl Harbor.[18]

What he did not know was that the Pacific Fleet command, via decrypted Japanese radio traffic, knew of his plan.[19] The remnants of TF-17, including the patched-up *Yorktown*, were quickly brought back from Australia, reinforced with cruisers and additional destroyers, and stationed northeast of Midway, as was a second carrier task force, TF-16, built around the *Hornet* and *Enterprise*. For the latter part of May and the first two days of June, a large high-pressure area centered northeast of the atoll kept cold fronts away. On June 3, the 2:30 A.M. weather map drawn at Pearl Harbor's joint weather central showed a weak storm center some 650 nautical miles northwest of the atoll. A weak cold front extended south and southwest from the cyclonic low as well. It suggested that a likely time for the potential Japanese attack would be near dawn on June 4.

At 9:04 A.M. on June 3 patrol planes spotted Japanese cargo and troop ships bearing 247° at a distance of 470 nautical miles in the comparatively good weather of the warm sector south of the storm center. Long-range AAF B-17 daylight attacks were launched to combat the threat. But the puzzling question remained—exactly where were the Japanese carriers and battleships? In fact, the main enemy battle force had been steaming within the intensifying storm system all through the day on June 3 and the night of June 3–4. But the storm center moved faster than the ships, and at sunrise on June 4, a navy Catalina patrol spotted two enemy carriers through a break in the clouds behind a rain squall. Almost simultaneously, a second Catalina spotted a large formation of Japanese fighters and bombers on their way to strike the atoll. U.S. carrier planes began counterstrikes at 9:28 A.M., some effective and some ineffective. But by day's end, four large Japanese carriers were sunk, at the cost of just the *Yorktown*.[20]

Because the Japanese carrier force was within the modified polar air mass behind the front, visibility and cloud cover within scattered showers were unrestricted during one of the great air battles of all time. However, the pilots needed to adjust to the wind shift associated with the front, so Strange advised his pilots to watch for a change in direction of the whitecaps. Other U.S. carrier flight units apparently did not do this, as their attack formations were far more ragged than those from the *Yorktown*. Once daylight broke on June 5 the air battle was renewed against straggling Japanese cruisers and destroyers until the targets retreated westward into the low ceilings and poor visibility of an approaching storm.

ALASKA—WAR IN MISERABLE WEATHER

As of early 1940 the Alaskan Territory had only 72,000 inhabitants, roughly half of whom were aboriginal natives. The year before, the navy had begun building its first operating bases (Sitka, Kodiak, and Dutch Harbor) for the defense of a rugged coastline spanning 57° of longitude. The weather along the 1,050 miles of the Aleutian Island chain was so bad that Adm. Ernie King acknowledged the area to be one of the world's most rugged war theaters. The most western of these bases, Dutch Harbor, was so subject to williwaws (unforseen gusts of wind with speeds of 100 knots) that the navy chose Kodiak, just off the Alaskan mainland, as its main Alaskan base. There, by October, 1941, a fleet weather central was operating under Comdr. H. S. Hutchinson, who also coordinated aerological affairs throughout the Alaskan sector.[21]

The equivalent unit in the Army Air Corps was the Air Corps Detachment, Weather, Alaska, activated on January 11, 1941, at Ladd Field near Fairbanks. Following the Pearl Harbor attack, the unit became the 11th Weather Squadron under Lt. Col. Wilson H. Neal; three decades later the squadron would become the oldest Air Force unit continuously serving in Alaska. One of the squadron's earliest forecasting efforts was to aid Russian pilots flying Lend-Lease aircraft without deicers across Alaska to Anadyr in Siberia. Russian-speaking weather forecasters were posted for that purpose to Fairbanks, Galena, and Nome. In addition to coping with the language problem, forecasters had to guarantee visual flight rules weather to the numerous P-39 and P-40 fighters making the trip. Nome was particularly troublesome during the long polar summer days. Here, the strip could easily go (and often did) from clear to zero-zero in a matter of minutes should the bank of persistent, low-lying sea stratus offshore suddenly move landward in front of a weak sea breeze.

Another problem was forecasting icing conditions, as heavily loaded C-47s, the supply workhorses of the vast roadless region, typically flew at altitudes of 7,000 to 10,000 feet in an area where mountains (e.g., Mount McKinley) on or near the flight paths were higher than 15,000 feet. Overall, these trips reported monthly icing occurrences per flight ranging from 6 percent (September) to more than 15 percent (February). Such conditions, when coupled with extreme cold, whiteouts, and poor navigational facilities, caused the Eleventh Air Force to lose seventy-two aircraft in the summer and fall of 1942; of these losses, only nine were attributable to enemy fire.[22]

Even before the shooting war came to Alaska, 1st Lt. Archie M. Kahan, a graduate of Cal Tech's first wartime class, was on his way to becoming Alaska's most noted (or notorious) weather forecaster. Soon after arriving at Elmendorf in March, 1942, Kahan was called to the base commander's office; he was directed to prepare a weather forecast, including precipitation, in detail for each day of the upcoming two weeks and to have it on the commander's desk by 5:00 that afternoon. The colonel (a command pilot and a West Pointer) had read of Krick's technique and assumed any Krick student could do as well. "A damnfool question deserved a damnfool answer," Kahan decided. So he took Krick's type-B north weather analog and assumed it would repeat through the fourteen-day period with unvarying regularity of prefrontal, frontal, and postfrontal weather on a three-day cycle. Apparently, Alaskan frontal waves at that time were moving through on just such a cycle. When Kahan's prediction for precipitation on the fourteenth day verified and the U.S. Weather Bureau's local twenty-four-hour forecast did not, his reputation was made.[23]

The Japanese navy's 2nd Mobile Force attacked Dutch Harbor on June 3, 1942, a feint related to the main attack on Midway Atoll. Damage was slight, but twenty-five Americans in the 5,000-man garrison were killed before the seventeen enemy aircraft disappeared into the prevailing mist. Next, the two enemy carriers tried an air strike against five U.S. destroyers but could not locate them in the dense fog. On the way back the Japanese planes were jumped by P-40s using forecasts from the six-man AAF weather detachment at the new Fort Glenn air base on the northern end of Umnak Island. Eight of the attackers were shot down, as were two of four enemy patrol seaplanes.

Despite visibility's being down to a mile, the Japanese made a second air attack on Dutch Harbor on June 4 before moving west. On June 6 their infantry took over undefended Kiska Island, where AerM William House had the misfortune of operating a ten-man weather detachment. The following day, another 1,200 troops went ashore at nearby Attu Island, the most western of the Aleutians. Three days later, a navy PBY aircraft observed that the Japanese had come to stay on American territory. To change that, AAF and navy aircraft began daily bombing of the two invasion areas through solid overcast (without noticeable results). To support that venture, new air bases were constructed along the island chain. The first of these, designed both for air and for ship operations, went in during September, 1942, on uninhabited Adak Island, 840 miles west of Kodiak. Although the airstrip was created by filling in a tidal flat, the joint army-navy weather central sat on the proverbial windy hill.[24]

Two meteorological processes gave the most trouble. The much touted and nearly incessant storm activity came from cyclonic storms rippling along the well-developed polar front lying south of the Aleutians, deepening until they merged into a semipermanent Gulf of Alaska low-pressure area. On the other hand, fog was more a local problem. Dense banks would form almost every day somewhere along the chain as warm, moist air from the south quickly cooled over the cold Bering Sea water encircling the islands. Such fog tended to be shallow and did not necessarily push northward over the higher ridges and central volcanic peaks. Thus, the lee side of individual islands, such as Adak, was often clear, particularly during diurnal afternoon warming of the land mass.

Forecasting for flights in and out of Adak was a tricky business. On January 18, 1943, the prediction called for thinning fog, so seven B-24s, five B-26s, and six AAF fighter escorts left Adak for an attack on Kiska Island 240 miles away. When the Adak fog did not thin, the planes were recalled. The faster aircraft squeaked in, but the slower B-24s were ordered on to Fort Glenn, two and one-half hours of flying time to the east. Two planes were never heard from again. Another crash-landed at Great Sitkin Island. One of the remaining four overshot when landing at Fort Glenn and piled into two parked fighters, destroying all three. The score for just one broken forecast: six friendly aircraft destroyed and no bombs dropped.[25]

To force an estimated 10,000 Japanese out of American territory, the Canadians and the Americans assembled more than 200,000 personnel. The initial strike on May 3, 1943, was to be against Attu, the farthest island. But alternating days of high seas and fog caused a week's delay. Then, during thick fog on the night of May 10, 500 Alaskan scouts made it ashore from submarines, and an assault ship was coached in by battleship radar. Visibility was still but a ship's length at 9:00 A.M., so thousands of assault troops in the second wave bobbed about for the next six hours before they went ashore—fog or no fog. The 2,379 Japanese retreated into the misty hills and put up a tremendous defense. Finally on May 30, when only twenty-eight Japanese were left alive, the battle ended. By then, 2,100 of the 11,000 Americans who had landed were sick and had trench foot; another 550 had been killed.

As far as American intelligence knew, Kiska held a far larger garrison than did Attu. The Allied armada, which formed in Dutch Harbor for the assault, included 3 battleships, 2 cruisers, 19 destroyers, 20 troop and cargo transports, and 114 LSTs; the vessels were to deliver 34,426 troops, 5,300 of whom were Canadians. In support were 24 heavy bombers, 44 medium bombers, 28 dive bombers, 12 patrol bombers, and 60 fighters. Then followed a period of intensive weather reporting by surface ships, aircraft, and a specially deployed submarine (with aerographer's mate on board), supplemented each noon by extensive weather map discussions at the Adak weather central. Finally, the forty-eight-hour forecast for Kiska predicted overcast with fog banks but with visibility generally 3 to 5 miles and ceilings of 500 to 1,000 feet.[26]

On August 15, 1943, the assault troops landed under weather conditions about as forecast. Rather than finding a battle on their hands, the troops found only four dogs awaiting their arrival! Atypically, all 5,183 Japanese had slipped away by surface ship during a 55-minute period eighteen days earlier. Even so, the infantry lost twenty-two men, mostly the result of firing at one another in the fog. Thus ended in low comedy the utterly miserable war for the Alaskan Territory.[27]

MACARTHUR'S "I SHALL RETURN!"

With the Japanese stalled at Midway Atoll and in the Aleutians during mid-1942, Admiral Nimitz and his counterpart, General MacArthur (now Supreme Allied Commander, Southwest Pacific) could finally take the offense in September by attacking Guadalcanal. To strengthen their hand, the Japanese decided to reinforce the base at Lae, New Guinea, with 7,000 troops who had moved through the Bismarck Sea from the northeast. On March 1, 1943, the convoy left Rabaul, New Guinea, under a canopy of low cloud, fog, and poor visibility. This equatorial front also created difficult flying conditions around the U.S. Fifth Air Force airstrip complex some 420 miles away, near Port Moresby. Japanese weathermen hoped the low cloud cover would last for five days, sufficient time for the eight troop ships to off-load and scuttle to safety. However, late on March 2, because of a bend in the equatorial front associated with a low-pressure area, the front cleared the area. Once the convoy was exposed, the Fifth Air Force had a field day, sinking half the transports plus four escorting destroyers.[28]

By mid-1943 MacArthur began planning to seize Lae in northeast New Guinea. This would be an amphibious assault by 10,000 troops at Lae proper, backed up by 1,700 paratroops jumping against Nadzab in the adjacent Markham River Valley. For the air drop, Lieutenant General Kenney wanted fog to cover western New Britain Island and the adjacent straits in order to keep Japanese aircraft away, but he wanted clear skies over his part of the operation. Australian and 15th Weather Squadron meteorologists disagreed in their forecasts: the Australian suggested September 3, 1943, as D day; the squadron spokesman urged September 5. Kenney decided "that neither one of them knew anything about weather, so I split the difference in the two forecasts, and told General MacArthur we would be ready to go on the morning of the 4th."[29] Upon hitting the beach, the invaders found no ground resistance. The eighty Japanese aircraft sent from Rabaul were delayed by the predicted fog, and the next day's parachute drop took place in clear weather, also as forecast.

In what became standard invasion procedure, the 15th Weather Squadron sent small teams ashore during the initial assault so that they could set up weather-observing sites once the beachhead was secure. The groundwork for this practice had been laid three months earlier when Capt. Ralph G. Suggs, a native of Waterproof, Louisiana, reported for duty as liaison officer to the Sixth Army advance command post at Milne Bay, New Guinea. An important part of his job was acquiring shipping space, equipment, and rations for the weather team included in each task force's D day assault echelon—although the 15th Weather Squadron's weather central with the Fifth Air Force at Port Moresby (moved forward to Nadzab eight months later) controlled team staging and movement. Such advance teams typically consisted of four to six men, divided evenly between observers and radiomen. They began to deploy during late June, 1943; by year's end, they could be found in contested spots such as Lae, Nadzab, and Finschhafen (New Guinea) and in Cape Gloucester (New Britain).[30]

Although weather information from such advanced teams was important, the weathermen also had to assist as riflemen in order to survive. Weathermen, however, were seriously deficient in combat training. So the AAF Weather Service in the States quickly formed a selected group of some fifty volunteers, officers and enlisted personnel, who secretly completed an intensive combat course at Kearns Field, Utah, during December, 1943. Within the 15th Weather Squadron these graduates became known as the JC-40 Group, renowned for physical fitness and mental ability, as well as for training in judo, swimming, weaponry, cryptography, and, last but not least, evasion and escape.

These specialists arrived in early 1944 to act as the nucleus of task-force weather teams. One of their first landings was at Biak Island with the 41st Infantry Division in late May, 1944. While naval units shelled Japanese defenses, the five-man weather team moved ashore with the initial assault. Because of stubborn enemy resistance, it was two days before they could set up their observing site—a scant fifty yards from the enemy. The weathermen got little sleep in their slit trenches because the Japanese yelled threats throughout the night.[31]

JC-40 weathermen also worked behind Japanese lines in the Philippines, assisting preparatory Allied air strikes before MacArthur's liberation of the islands, planned for the fall of 1944. In this case, the weathermen sailed from Australia aboard U.S. submarines—the lifeline of coast watchers, spotters, and guerillas throughout the southwest Pacific. The first of these guerilla weathermen departed from Darwin and, by May 10, 1944, six weather reporting stations (including one taking pibals) were operating on

Mindanao and the Samar Islands.[32] Five months later the number of guerilla weather units within the archipelago stood at thirty-nine, including five that had pibal and forecasting capabilities.

But a price was paid from time to time. In late September, 1944, the USS *Seawolf* left Brisbane on her fifteenth war patrol and under her third wartime skipper. Three days later she loaded soldiers and stores at Manus Island (Admiralty Group) destined for the Philippines. Among those boarding were two JC-40 Group observers, Sgt. Charles H. Hamill and Corp. Robert P. Herbig. On October 3 the submarine reported her last position, then was never heard from again. The evidence suggests that she was sunk with all hands (a crew of eighty-two plus seventeen army passengers) by her fellow countrymen off Samar's east coast after straying into an intensive hunt for a Japanese submarine that had just sunk an American destroyer.[33]

In mid-September, 1944, the Joint Chiefs of Staff ordered MacArthur to implement his much-publicized return by landing on Leyte Island two months earlier than planned. His 200,000 Sixth Army troops would be supported by carrier-based aircraft until air strips were available on Leyte for Fifth Air Force pilots. Facing only one Japanese division, MacArthur and Kenney were fully aware that "the chief hazard to Allied success at Leyte will be weather."[34] By that time the newly promoted Major Suggs was operating a full-fledged weather central on Owi Island adjacent to a Fifth Air Force advance command post. Suggs's meteorologists prepared climatic studies and long-range weather forecasts warning that the typhoon season had come (Leyte could expect at least one major tropical storm each month).

On October 16, 1944, an amphibious armada of 700 vessels, backed by more than 1,000 carrier-based aircraft, closed on the three small islands guarding Leyte Gulf's eastern approaches. High seas churned up by a typhoon passing north of Leyte Island a day later made it difficult to neutralize the enemy on the guard islands. Even so, on October 20, Mac-Arthur's much-photographed return to the Philippines took place in a quiet part of the beachhead under clear skies and in relatively calm seas.[35]

Among the unheralded troops who went ashore that day was a 15th Weather Squadron team of seven enlisted men led by 1st Lt. Lorin A. Hamel, who had led a similar team on the hotly contested Biak Island off northwestern New Guinea on May 27. Two days later the squadron's second unit came ashore under 1st Lt. Leon M. Rottman.[36] A short while later an element of Suggs's Owi weather central began to debark during an attack by four Japanese Zeros. The first native they saw ashore was a Filipino urchin purveying purloined American whiskey at nine dollars a bottle and bargain-basement coconut wine ("tuba") at two dollars a flask.

Suggs's weather central ceased operations at Owi on November 8 but opened for business five days later adjacent to an advance echelon of Fifth Air Force Headquarters at Burauen, Leyte Island. However, the Sixth Army's advance was slowed by new tropical storms (including two typhoons) that turned the few available dirt roads into seas of mud. Stubborn Japanese resistance included a parachute drop against the San Pablo airstrip less than a mile from Sugg's central. On December 6 approximately 200 Japanese severed the dirt road between San Pablo and Burauen, cutting off the central from the airstrip. Upon being issued carbines and ammunition, the meteorologists manned a perimeter around the central for the next two days. At one point, machine gun and rifle rounds were whistling through the weathermen's tents at cot level. Then a Japanese soldier crossed the defense line. Firing an American .30-caliber machine gun, he stitched a pattern from one end of the weather central to the other. Fortunately, some natives silenced the interloper with a bolo knife. After things finally calmed down, Rottman's unit dubbed itself "Rottman's Rugged Rangers," and the lieutenant grew fond of chiding complaining squadron replacements, "You should have been here when it was really rough."[37]

Leyte's fair weather lasted only a week after the landing. Then came the heavy rains, which turned central Leyte into a sty. During the first forty days ashore, 35 inches of rain fell at Dulag (Murphy's Law again, for the amount was twice the seasonal average). Most of the rain came in short tropical cloudbursts, but three typhoons brought rains of longer duration. There was even an earthquake. The water flooded camps and foxholes, the storms blew down tents, and the oppressively humid heat between rains made life miserable. Food spoiled rapidly. Much was made of MacArthur's relatively low casualty rates from enemy action. What happened to his troops' effective fighting strength because of poor physical health was a different story. Fevers of known and unknown origin were frequent, and incurable fungi grew under toenails and fingernails, as well as inside eyelids and in ear canals.

For combat purposes, Leyte became one huge bog. Airfield construction fell behind schedule, and the few Allied pilots who did get airborne found most of Leyte's spinal mountain range blanketed by dense clouds. Thus, even in the heat of battle, pilots had to husband enough fuel to go around or over the weather. Japanese convoys, by taking advantage of the storm surges that moved east to west, ran reinforcements to Leyte's west coast with considerable freedom from attack. The army engineers under Maj. Gen. Leif Sverdrup, Professor Sverdrup's younger brother, did the best they could. Yet, as Kenney's deputy for operations told him, "Mud is still mud no matter how much you push it around with a bulldozer." "Every night Kenney prayed for blue skies and every morning he was disappointed," wrote MacArthur's biographer, William Manchester. "Army engineers gloomily told him that it didn't much matter, the island's drainage was such that even the best steel runway matting would be washed away."[38] As a result, Leyte never became the air base that MacArthur and Kenney wanted.

On the other hand, Admiral Halsey's Third Fleet destroyed 2,000 Japanese aircraft in September, 1944. Halsey and MacArthur soon agreed that the navy could safely sealift the Sixth Army directly from Leyte to the Lingayen Gulf beaches, just 99 miles north-northwest of Manila. So at dawn on January 9, 1945, American troops went ashore, crossing the same beaches that the Japanese army had used to invade Luzon thirty-seven months before.

The Lingayen Gulf beaches offered the same advantages in 1945 as they had during 1941: mountain ranges offered protection from the northeast monsoon and shelter from sea, swell, and surf (except from the northwesterly quadrant). The forecasted excellent weather (scattered clouds, wind 10 knots or less, and visibility of about 6 miles in a slight haze) prevailed for the first day, and by nightfall 68,000 troops were ashore.[39] By midmorning on the second day, however, the surf reached heights of 6 to 8 feet as a small typhoon moved westward past the southern Philippines, and unloading stopped for the rest of the day. Unloading resumed on January 12. While waiting to disembark from an LST, 2nd Lt. Richard W. Beard, Jr., a forecaster with the newly activated 20th Weather Squadron, was killed when a kamikaze crashed his plane into the vessel. The overall attack went well, and on February 6 the 11th Airborne Division reached Nichols Field, the original home of the now totally dispersed 5th Weather Squadron.

Upon arriving in Manila, Lieutenant General Kenney chose to place FEAF headquarters at Fort McKinley, about twelve miles east of downtown. Most of the facility had burned to its foundations, but the spacious wooden quarters that had been Lt. Gen. Jonathan Wainwright's before the war still stood and became the temporary home of AAF weather officers working at the contiguous army-navy weather centrals just across the street. Built during June, 1945, the H-shaped structure provided working space for 224 specialists: 39 officers and 88 enlisted men of the FEAF weather central; 22 officers and 60 sailors of the Seventh Fleet weather central; and 1 officer and 14 men in the Army Airways Communication System unit.[40] In an adjacent Quonset structure Colonel Senter set up the FEAF Weather Group, initially composed of the 15th and 20th Weather Squadrons and scheduled to include the newly formed 27th and 28th (Mobile) Weather Squadrons when they arrived to assist in the final assault on the Japanese home islands.

ISLAND HOPPING

While the U.S. Sixth Army worked its way northward from Guadalcanal and New Guinea to Manila, the Marine Corps, with extensive navy and army support, cleared Japanese garrisons from myriad Pacific islands lying east of Formosa and the Philippines. To avoid the poor weather of the intertropical front, the overall strategy called for an attack on the Gilbert Islands (Operation Galvanic) just north of the equator in late 1943, followed by an attack on the Marshalls (Operation Flintlock) in early 1944.[41] The first of these major assaults came against Tarawa Atoll on November 20, 1943. The hydrographic information was none too good, and the initial waves of Higgins assault boats grounded on coral heads far out on the beach flat. As a result, hundreds of marines were killed by a hail of fire as they waded ponderously to the beach.

To avoid similar problems in the future, the 3rd Amphibious Force established a unique team, the Hydrographic and Special Beach Observers. The four members, all graduates of the Scripps military oceanography course, were Comdr. Oliver D. Finnigan (force aerologist) and three naval reserve ensigns—William M. Johnson, Donald D. Murphy, and Warren C. Thompson. In August, 1944, they accompanied the 3rd Amphibious Force when it undertook to seize some southern Palau Islands that would provide airfields for the upcoming invasion of Leyte.[42]

Well before dawn on September 15, Thompson and a co-observer, Lt. Comdr. G. H. Heyen, Royal Australian Navy (Reserve), were airborne, waiting for enough light to check Peleliu's beaches. Three passes were made as low as 20 feet over each potential assault beach to determine sea and swell direction, width of surf zone, and breaker height, period, and type. Breaker heights all appeared to be less than 2 feet. Dropping their findings to the flagship, they loitered to watch the assault. When a nearby U.S. plane went down in flames, their pilot decided it was time to back off from the beach.[43]

Johnson and Murphy conducted comparable surf observation flights over the beaches at Leyte the following month. For the Lingayen Gulf assault, the duo also prepared wave refraction diagrams that alerted beachmasters as to where wave divergence would lower raging surf by as much as 70 percent. Such information was of course extremely helpful and permitted the continued unloading of critical cargo on D + 1 when the rest of the wide strand was impassable.

The team's next work area was heavily defended Iwo Jima, the halfway point between the XXI Bomber Command bases in the Marianas Islands and their targets in Japan. Starting on February 16, 1945 (D − 3), Johnson and Murphy made presunrise reef and surf observation flights on the west side of the volcanic island while Thompson did the same on the east side. Uncharacteristically for winter, oceanographic conditions at H hour proved excellent. On D + 2 their luck began to run out. While they were aboard the escort (jeep) carrier *Bismarck Sea*, getting ready to sail on a fast carrier strike against Okinawa, the ship was sunk by a Japanese bomber.[44]

After rescue, they flew beach reconnaissance against Okinawa (the assault was scheduled for April Fool's Day). Then on the sunny afternoon of March 29 Thompson's new carrier, the *Wake Island*, took hits from two kamikaze aircraft, although the ship remained afloat. Eventually the work got done, and on Navy Day in the fall of 1945, Vice Adm. T. S. Wilkinson, commander of the 3rd Amphibious Force, awarded his trio of flying aerologists Air Medals plus gold stars for "making observations that were of great importance to amphibious commanders in making decisions as to the feasibility of using designated beaches."[45]

ANOTHER ENEMY — TYPHOONS

As the Allied forces began to operate intensively near the Philippine Islands during October, 1944, they expected some severe tropical storms, even typhoons. However, there were far more than expected. Although a typhoon had hampered the landings at Leyte in October, the full danger of such killer storms began to be fully appreciated when Admiral Halsey and his aerological-navigation officer, Comdr. George F. Kosco, misjudged the intensity and location of a typhoon approaching the Third Fleet on December 17, 1944. Halsey was thinking more about refueling and reinitiating air strikes against Luzon on December 19 than about dodging what he took to be a tropical storm—until too late to do much about it. The result: three destroyers capsized, with the loss of 778 officers and men; 146 combat aircraft smashed; and serious damage to carriers, cruisers, and smaller vessels. Following a court of inquiry, Nimitz noted in a fleet letter that "it was the greatest loss that we have taken in the Pacific without compensatory return since the First Battle of Savo" in January, 1942.[46]

On June 4–5, 1945, Halsey and Kosco repeated this grievous error by navigating the Third Fleet through the center of another intense typhoon whose diameter was slightly more than 100 miles. The "big boys" of the forty-eight-ship task force—the carriers and the cruisers—suffered the most damage. The carrier *Hornet*, whose forward flight deck was caved in, had, in fact, suffered more damage than she had while sinking more than a million tons of Japanese shipping. Seventy-six aircraft had also been destroyed. Nimitz was incensed, and his second court of inquiry into "Halsey's typhoons" recommended that Halsey be relieved of his command. After the furor subsided, President Truman promoted the national hero to five-star rank because of his famed pursuit of the enemy, dating back to the Doolittle raid against Tokyo.

Halsey, to be sure, had been urging scheduled weather reconnaissance flights since the first inquiry into his actions, but the concept was turned down as being of too low a priority for patrol aircraft. Responding to a further inquiry about why his destroyers had capsized, Halsey wrote: "I also wish to state unequivocally that in both the December, 1944, and the June, 1945, typhoons the weather warning service did not provide the accurate and timely information necessary to enable me to take timely evasive action. For that inadequacy I can not accept responsibility."[47]

Fortunately, the AAF introduced specially equipped B-24 weather reconnaissance aircraft into the western Pacific. The 655th Bombardment Squadron, Heavy (forerunner of today's 55th Weather Reconnaissance Squadron), began operations from Guam in January, 1945, under the command of Lt. Col. Nicholas H. Chavasse and flew its first meteorological mission on February 3. By April the squadron consisted of three flights—A at Guam to fly weather missions in support of Twentieth Air Force B-29 raids against Japan, B at Iwo Jima to help the VII Fighter Command, and C at Okinawa to assist elements of the Twentieth Air Force. To cover the region, twenty-one B-24s and twenty-five flight crews were required, each mission carrying a specially trained weather officer. By the time the squadron returned Stateside in 1946, it had flown more than 5,000 hours on 508 missions. Although the war was over, one of the unit's busiest months was September, 1945, when the squadron located and tracked nine typhoons just as the Allies were occupying the remnants of Japan's defeated empire.[48]

Before early 1945 the Pearl Harbor weather central was the naval focal point for issuing forecasts and storm warnings, including typhoons in the central and western Pacific region. Located some 3,500 nautical miles from what was then the main area of combat, the central under Captain Lockhart worked at a severe disadvantage.[49] Weather data came in slowly because of coding and transmission priority delays; also, ships and airborne aircraft maintained strict radio silence while in transit or on patrol. One deadly consequence was the central depicting Halsey's December typhoon 130 miles too far northeast and on a northwest trajectory (30° too far north) just before the debacle. Lockhart ended up in the doghouse, and the central established at Nimitz's advanced Pacific Fleet headquarters on Guam in May, 1945, was directed by the admiral's new fleet aerologist, Capt. Anthony Danis, a graduate of the navy's first aerology course at Harvard and MIT.

After Halsey's second typhoon fiasco early the next month, Danis's central added a typhoon-tracking unit manned by four aerologists and five enlisted men. But headaches gradually developed because Guam's forecast area overlapped by as much as twenty degrees the comparable areas assigned to fleet weather centrals at Manus Island, Chungking, Pearl Harbor, and Kodiak. The June fiasco also resulted in the institution of a coordinated typhoon weather reconnaissance program. On June 17, 1945, seven naval air bases from Eniwetok Atoll westward were ordered to have three aircraft each ready for weather reconnaissance flights as needed by the fleet command in Guam.

Such aircraft were typically PB4Ys (Privateers, the high-tail version of the B-24), but a few were Catalinas, and three at Peleliu were PVs. Because aircraft drift could not be measured at night, the sorties were mostly daylight ones. Thus, new morning fixes on storm centers did not arrive in Guam until about 11:00 A.M., long after Nimitz's morning briefing. Another problem was low observational quality; planes, pilots, and crews changed daily and operated without special weather instrumentation, although sometimes aerologists did go along as technical observers. Overall, by November 15, 1945, 836 naval weather reconnaissance missions had been flown, 347 of which concerned typhoons.[50] Only after hostilities had ceased did the navy catch up with AAF practice and commission during late 1945 two meteorological squadrons, VPM-1 and VPM-2, on the West Coast for Pacific deployment as "typhoon trackers."

THE CHINA-BURMA-INDIA THEATER

When war was declared against Japan, Col. Claire L. Chennault was brought back into the Army Air Corps with the rank of brigadier general and given command of the minuscule Fourteenth Air Force based in Kunming, China. However, the Japanese soon captured the Burma Road, the only land line the Allies had from the sea to Kunming and points farther inland. To keep Chennault's command supplied, as well as to engage in aerial combat over the hard-pressed Burma front, another new command, the Tenth Air Force, was established in New Delhi, India. To get fuel, bombs, and supplies to Chennault's forces meant 500 miles of flying from raw jungle air bases in northeast India (Assam province) to Kunming, over the Himalayas (the Hump), whose peaks extended to 15,000 feet.[51] During the wet monsoon (July–October), this route was bathed in low clouds plus torrential rains and featured some of the world's most violent thunderstorms, which reached upwards to 60,000 feet.

Lt. Col. Torgils G. Wold, as the staff weather officer for the Tenth Air Force, also became the control officer for the 10th Weather Region when it was activated on June 1, 1942. From Wold's first office, a converted bedroom in Delhi's Imperial Hotel, orders were issued to create six weather stations in the Assam Valley and one in faraway Kunming. Because Delhi was the end of a supply line that started half a world away, initial staffing was just forty-eight enlisted weathermen brought over by the Tenth Air Force and reassigned to Wold's command during August. No additional manpower was expected until early 1943, when a contingent training at Detrick Field, Maryland, was scheduled to arrive.

While they waited, Wold's weather squadron depended heavily upon the India Meteorological Department (IMD). Its able director-general, Dr. C. W. B. Normand, a Scot of great charm who had thirty years' experience in the Far East, was most cooperative, as was Krishna P. Rao, the IMD liaison officer in New Delhi. Yet by AAF standards, the IMD remained a primitive weather service, particularly in data transmission.[52] The RAF Meteorological Service in India, headed by Group Capt. W. H. Bigg, was equally limited and offered little help. The long-awaited Detrick cadre finally arrived—one officer, nine enlisted forecasters, forty observers, and one clerk, bringing the squadron's complement to nine officers and ninety-seven airmen as of January, 1943.

In the same month, at the Casablanca conference, the Combined Chiefs of Staff agreed with Roosevelt and Churchill that China must be kept in the war. That meant reopening the Burma Road by shifting from a defensive to an offensive war in the China-Burma-India (CBI) theater. Then in August it was decided to use the new B-29s (Super-Fortresses) to bomb throughout eastern Asia, even as far as Japan. Carolina weathermen being lectured on European weather were hastily placed aboard a troop train to San Pedro, California, where they began a seven-week voyage to India via the SS *George Washington*. But the key acquisition for the hard-pressed 10th Weather Squadron was a new commanding officer, Lt. Col. Richard E. Ellsworth, who flew in on August 24, 1943.

Ellsworth found an organization in disarray. Flinders wrote: "Rarely was he able to rely on his staff for the right answer to pressing problems. . . . Most of the pushing, the planning, and even the paperwork . . . was also done single-handedly by the colonel."[53] Yet the 10th Weather Region was vast. In a north-south direction, weather stations eventually ranged from Cocos Island, south-southwest of Sumatra (12° south latitude) to Urumchi (also known as Wulumuchi), China, well west of Outer Mongolia (44° north latitude). Distances were equally great going from west to east— from Jiwani, Baluchistan, on the Arabian Sea, to several stations in eastern China. Thus, Ellsworth's troops were asked to forecast a wide variety of meteorological conditions over some of the world's least-known areas and highest mountains. Moreover, they supported a bewildering variety of commands—the ATC and the XX Bomber Command, plus the Tenth and Fourteenth Air Forces; assorted ground combat forces (American, British, and Chinese); the RAF and the Royal Navy; and last but not least, the Southeast Asia Command, directed by Admiral Lord Louis Mountbatten, who resided in remote Kandy, Ceylon (now Sri Lanka).[54]

The thirty-two-year-old Ellsworth's approach to his staggering problems could be a case study in remote management. Although a West Pointer familiar with harsh military discipline, Ellsworth chose to be low-key, exhibiting loyalty and service downward as well as upward. He preferred self-starting weathermen and carefully used both carrots and sticks. As long as you got the job done and your customer was satisfied, he was on your side. His unique use of "Betsy," the squadron's C-47 with a Donald Duck caricature on its nose, tied it all together. In company with his chief pilot,

Maj. Harry M. ("Tex") Albaugh, Ellsworth and Betsy traversed the CBI, hauling personnel and equipment to set up outlying weather observer posts so remote that the natives had never seen a non-Asiatic person. At one point Betsy had logged more flights and carried more cargo over the Hump than any other "Gooney Bird," making it easy to understand why Ellsworth was accused of running "TWA," namely, the Tenth Weather Airlines.[55]

Within a month of his arrival, Ellsworth crossed swords directly with Chiang Kai-shek and the generalissimo's favorite airman, Chennault. With no weather reporting stations between Assam and Kunming, Ellsworth needed more weathermen in China. But Chennault and Chiang objected. The "balloon-blowers" would take up vital space on Hump aircraft; moreover, China would have to raise more rice to feed them because no food was transported over the Hump. As Chennault phrased it to Ellsworth: "You and communications [the AACS] want to put . . . [500] men into my area. I have found that I can operate a group and auxiliaries with . . . [125] men to the air group; thus you would rob me of four groups, and I don't intend to be robbed of the groups." But the official air force history notes that "weather remained the greatest single cause of fluctuations in the flow of air traffic between India and China." Ellsworth's plan finally prevailed.[56]

Besides conventional weather observing stations, three other data acquisition methods were commonplace. Because the pilot reporting system worked poorly, station forecasters in Assam took trips to Kunming and back on their own initiative, even though the unheated, unpressurized aircraft sometimes climbed to 25,000 feet over the Hump. Before the B-29 strikes against such famous cities as Mandalay, Rangoon, Bangkok, Saigon, and Singapore, the 2nd Weather Reconnaissance Squadron, under Lt. Col. James B. Baker, flew armed B-25s south and east over the Bay of Bengal and the Asiatic land mass (one mission on November 25, 1944, took the unit as far east as Hanoi). Mission flight tracks were normally specified by J. J. George, now a lieutenant colonel in charge of the India Weather Central on the campuslike grounds of 10th Weather Squadron headquarters at Barrackpore, just north of Calcutta.[57]

The unusual observational method was exemplified by 1st Lt. Charles Lewis. His small weather unit at Hailakandi, India, served the special forces—Col. Philip G. Cochran's Air Commandos (later popularized in Milton Caniff's cartoon strip *Terry and the Pirates*), Brig. Orde Wingate and his famed long-range penetration teams of British-led Chindits, and Brig. Gen. Frank D. Merrill's army "Marauders," who regularly hiked through and behind Japanese lines. Weather was critical in such operations; the commanders needed to know in advance when clear nights would permit landing gliders deep in enemy territory. To expand the weather coverage, three two-man teams moved into the Naga Hills, using opium-smoking, head-hunting Naga tribesmen as guides and baggage carriers.

Lewis also put in twenty hours of commando flying time so that he could learn firsthand the exact limits that weather imposed.[58]

As the B-29s would be arriving in less than a year, Ellsworth acquired approval for creating a weather central deep within China, at Hsingching, a grassy air strip not far from the major city of Ch'eng-tu. The first planeload of weathermen arrived on December 6, 1943. Six months later their rustic hostel was in the center of an important XX Bomber Command complex. The first bomber strike against Japan proper since 1942 came on June 15, 1944, as the B-29s left Hsingching for a twelve-hour run to their targets and back. To avoid having the B-29s caught on the ground in China by resilient Japanese air power, the world's most sophisticated bombers depended directly on predictions of favorable weather for the target areas.[59] The B-29s left from the bases at Kharagpur and Piardoba in India, refueled during the night at Hsingching, and made their bombing runs the next day. Return to India took place during that same day, thereby cheating the Japanese of any opportunity for a night attack.

Experience soon indicated that accurate weather forecasts for high-level bombing (30,000 feet) meant target destruction; a poor forecast meant an abort. Either way, every drop of aviation gasoline pumped aboard at Hsingching had to be airlifted over the Hump; the delivery rate was so slow that weeks of airlift were required just to provide enough fuel for one major B-29 raid. As the winter months set in, the Ch'eng-tu area was plagued week after week by solid stratus clouds. To make sure that the heavily loaded B-29s could safely climb through the clouds without icing up, the B-25s of Flight C, 2nd Weather Reconnaissance Squadron, led by Capt. Robert C. Kunz, tried it first. When the B-25s without deicers could do it, the B-29s were sent on their way.[60]

Several ploys were used for obtaining weather observations for the huge hostile area between Ch'eng-tu and Japan. Comdr. Denys Knoll, as a meteorological representative on the U.S. military mission to Moscow and then as an assistant naval attaché in Vladivostok, arranged for supposedly neutral Russia to send additional confidential weather messages from Khabarovsk, Siberia, to San Francisco, followed by further relay to Ch'eng-tu. Land reports also came in from 10th Weather Squadron units operating as far east as Kuei-lin and Foochow (the latter even had a sferics detector) and sporadically from the Chinese national weather service. Finally, when the B-29 raid was imminent, Lt. (jg) Mason O. Erwin, the U.S. Navy weather liaison officer, arranged for reports from submarines off China and Japan.

Still, such weather coverage did not satisfy the XX Bomber Command's demanding chief, Maj. Gen. Curtis E. LeMay. Why not use the Chinese Communist guerillas that infested the Japanese-held territory of northeastern China? At his direction, the secret Dixie Mission flew to Yen-an (the Chinese Communist capital, some 480 miles north of Chungking) on

August 7, 1944. There, they explained to Chairman Mao Tse-tung the requirement for a better method of rescuing B-29 pilots from areas he operated in. Then Major Dole explained the pressing need for better weather information from this contested region. Although Mao hated the generalissimo (who reciprocated the feeling), he was anxious to see his homeland rid of Japanese. So Dole received permission to start a modest radiosonde-rawin operation at Yen-an and to train Red guerillas to make simple weather observations. M. Sgt. William Cady, who spoke some Chinese, was posted to Yen-an, and gradually ninety guerilla units were equipped with meteorological kits and portable, hand-cranked generator-radio transmitter sets.[61]

Some of these Red teams operated as far east as the Shantung Peninsula, just across the Yellow Sea from Japan.[62] Generally speaking, that roving weather network was helpful. On some days a given unit might not broadcast because it was on the move to escape capture. And should U.S. policy begin to tilt too far away from Mao, his network would get balky. Even though LeMay and his bombers shifted in June, 1945, to the Mariana Islands, contrariness of the reporting system could be overcome, at least for the time being, by delivering additional medical items and other war supplies to Mao.

About the same time, Colonels Moorman and Ellsworth lent the U.S. component of the Admiralty's Swell Forecast Section in London to the Colombo, Ceylon, weather central, which was supporting the commander in chief of the British East Indies Fleet. The Royal Navy needed the entire section to provide surf forecasts for the invasion of Malaya's Kra Isthmus, which was projected for September 9, 1945, during the height of the southwest monsoon.[63] In preparation, the joint unit established a miniature wave observation network for the invasion of Rangoon (Operation Dracula) on May 3, 1945. Daily, B-25s of the 2nd Weather Reconnaissance Squadron flew low across the ocean south of Rangoon; T. Sgt. Ernest A. Lachner, oceanographic observer, was aboard to check for hazardous swell from the southern hemisphere. Then, just before D day, a tropical storm formed offshore. Although intense, it was but a hundred miles across and bothered neither the paratrooper drop on D − 1 nor the amphibious assault a day later.[64]

Following the collapse of Japan on August 15, 1945 (V-J Day), Lieutenant Colonel George, who had taken over from Ellsworth a month before, assigned weather liaison officers to the chief liberated airports throughout the Orient. First lieutenants drew this pleasant duty, including Flinders (Rangoon), Donald L. Perry (Singapore), James F. Church (Bangkok), James B. Norcross (Saigon), and George L. DeCoster (Hanoi). Even in 1945 DeCoster found it difficult to get decent weather data out of what became North Vietnam's capital. Somewhat more surprising was learning that the

Japanese were still operating a weather station at Phnom Penh, Cambodia, two months after the war's end.

AEROLOGISTS IN STRANGE PLACES — CHINA AND SIBERIA

It is a basic rule in the military: if something is vital to your operation, have it carried out by someone under your command if at all possible. Two months after the Pearl Harbor attack, Admiral King, as the navy's overall commander, called in an old China hand, Comdr. Milton E. Miles, and advised him: "You are to go to China and set up some bases as soon as you can. The main idea is to prepare the China coast in any way possible for U.S. Navy landings in three or four years. In the meantime, do whatever you can to help the Navy and heckle the Japanese."[65] In normal times one does not give a three-striper carte blanche to conduct wide-ranging military operations in the world's most populous nation.

Upon arriving in Chungking, the temporary capital of Nationalist China, Miles found that the Chinese embassy in Washington had arranged his access to Maj. Gen. Tai Li, director of the Bureau of Intelligence and Statistics—a combination of the U.S. Secret Service, the Federal Bureau of Investigation, and some of the Internal Revenue Service, but without the associated legal restraints. Li was totally loyal to Chiang Kai-shek and the generalissimo's haughty, American-educated spouse. Neither appreciated the frequent lectures on how to run the country that came from the commander of U.S. Forces in the China theater, no matter whether he be Lt. Gen. Joseph W. ("Vinegar Joe") Stilwell or his replacement, Lt. Gen. Albert C. Wedemeyer, both West Pointers. So Tai Li was told to use U.S. naval forces, supplies, and know-how to create a jointly run guerilla unit, the Sino-American Cooperative Organization (SACO), which would operate behind Japanese lines.[66] As Chiang later advised Miles (a vice admiral by then): "Two men in the same boat help each other."

Miles's highest priorities in China were to obtain radio-direction fixes on Japanese vessels, to plant magnetic mines in waters used by Japanese shipping, and to acquire weather observations for use by Pacific Fleet commands. The Joint Chiefs of Staff authorized only 150 tons of supplies per month and *no* aircraft for the SACO operation. For about a year after August, 1942, Miles had only two aerographer's mates assigned to his base camp, Happy Valley, just outside Chungking. About the same time that Ellsworth arrived in India, Comdr. I. F. ("By") Byerly arrived at Happy Valley to get serious aerological activities underway. Byerly's first effort was to create a corps of weather observers within Tai Li's guerilla forces. So that they could radio out information, the SACO group came up with an indigenous radio transmitter, using an umbrella for an antenna, simplified weather equipment that could be buried in a bag of rice, and a weather code (scarcely larger than a stamp) that could be swallowed if necessary. The first such weather class of 150 men was held near Lan-chou, not far from the Great Wall of China. The second class, near Hsifen in central China, consisted of 700 men.[67]

Four months later two more aerological officers appeared—Lt. (jg) John Mastenbrook and Ens. D. D. Harkness. By September 1944, the navy weather central at Chungking was on the air with four daily broadcasts of synoptic weather reports from both free and occupied China, plus pilot balloon and radiosonde reports from selected stations. In addition, there was a daily canned weather chart for continental Asia, and a forecast for China and several hundred miles offshore. This tiny navy central was the mouse that roared, for the AAF Weather Central farther inland near Ch'eng-tu had a staff of twenty-five officers and seventy-five enlisted men.[68]

The other navy meteorological installation on the Asian continent derived from a decision made by Premier Stalin in an apparently weak moment. At the Yalta meeting in February, 1945, the U.S. delegation pushed an AAF offer to establish, equip, and man thirty-seven weather stations in Siberia to help end the war against Japan. The Russians were glad to take the equipment, which began arriving in Murmansk during June, but demurred at hosting American weather observers. As a backup position in the following Potsdam conference of July, 1945, the Americans argued strongly for U.S. Navy weather centrals in Siberia instead. By then, Stalin wanted the United States to think favorably of the Soviet Union when the time came to slice up the Japanese empire. So General Anotov, chief of staff for the Red army, okayed weather centrals at Khabarovsk and Petropavlovsk.[69]

Although the war was over early the next month, the Soviet system had no quick method of canceling Anotov's approval. Thus, the U.S. Navy staff of eighteen officers and forty-two men led by Captain Arthur A. Cumberledge, plus aerological and radio equipment, were flown in by R5Ds to Khabarovsk via Alaska and Siberia during August 25–30, 1945. The Petropavlovsk contingent of eight officers and twenty-four men under Comdr. C. J. McGregor, who had to travel by sea via the USS *Bennett* (a destroyer) and the USS *Corl* (an amphibious assault ship), arrived slightly later, on September 6. The two navy weather centrals found highly primitive conditions and very inhospitable landlords. The first could be overcome by bringing in navy housing and equipment, but the second was insolvable. It quickly became obvious that the Russian liaison officers were more interested in monitoring what the Americans were doing than in aiding U.S. fleet operations. Russian women introduced into the two camps as housekeeping aides proved to be intelligence operatives. Finally, Anotov had the top-level policy guideline reversed, and the naval weather centrals were asked to leave Siberia by December 15, 1945. Even departure was inefficient, though, and the Khabarovsk central staff did not leave the Soviet Union until January 3, 1946.

ENDING THE PACIFIC WAR

On August 6, 1945, aerologists of the Amphibious Forces, U.S. Pacific Fleet, were meeting aboard a flagship in Manila Bay with the AAF's surf forecasters, Capt. John C. Crowell and Capt. Charles C. Bates, about the final assaults on the Japanese home islands—Operation Olympic against Kyushu (November) and Operation Coronet against Honshu (March). But the session did not get beyond the first cup of coffee before the public address system reported that an atomic bomb had been dropped on Hiroshima.

Japan's demise had been in the making for some time. Using new bases in the Mariana Islands, the XXI Bomber Command launched its first high-level raid in November, 1944, against Tokyo. For the raid, the 73rd Bombardment Wing launched 111 B-29s, but dropouts and an extensive undercast allowed only 35 bombers to drop loads visually and with but slight damage. According to later analysis, one problem was that the B-29s were pushed by a tail wind of 120 knots, thus creating a true ground speed of about 400 knots and introducing unforseen bombsight errors.[70]

During the second high-level attack three days later the winds near Mount Fujiyama seemed even worse. Upon turning and running downwind, the lead bomber made 522 knots over the ground, some 120 knots faster than in the first raid.[71] Thus was discovered the subpolar jet stream, a high-altitude, high-velocity thread of air embedded in the broad flow of the prevailing westerlies. The aviators also contended with a very well developed polar front that could, because of very cold Siberian air flowing over the warm Kuroshio Current (Japan's Gulf Stream), cause tremendous clouds and even thunderstorms along the flight path.

Those two raids were precursors of events to come. Weather soon proved here, as elsewhere, to be the most serious obstacle to high-altitude precision daylight bombing of Japan. Outbound aircraft could not hold formation for mutual defense at altitude, fuel usage was outrageously high in the fierce winds, and tactics used did not provide the desired accuracy.[72]

After the XXI Bomber Command's new boss, LeMay, had studied the situation, he ordered a switch in bombing tactics. Rather than clinging to longtime doctrine, he had the B-29s make individual, low-level (5,000 to 15,000 feet) night attacks with incendiary bombs against Japanese urban areas. Because of a skillful mix of climatological studies, extensive aerial reconnaissance, Russian weather data relayed from San Francisco, and meteorological prognoses, the bombing results were spectacular. The most notable raid destroyed much of Tokyo by means of an induced fire storm (at the cost of 100,000 lives) during the night of March 9, 1945.[73]

Fire storms, one of man's most hideous inventions, could be triggered only under the most favorable meteorological conditions if conventional weapons were used. That situation changed with the successful nuclear detonation at Alamogordo on July 16, 1945. It was hoped that this weapon would force the emperor to sue for peace before the Allies suffered a half-million casualties along the beaches of Japan. Two nuclear devices—Fat Man and Little Boy—were rushed to Tinian Island in the Marianas. The War Department, in a letter dated July 25, 1945, directed Lieutenant General Spaatz, as commander of the U.S. Army Strategic Air Forces, Guam, to drop the "first special bomb as soon as weather will permit visual bombing after or about 3 August 1945." With only two bombs available, visual bombing was specified: the drops had to be exactly on target.[74]

Spaatz delegated to LeMay, now his chief of staff, the job of deciding when the weather would permit the world's most important aerial mission.[75] The critical forecast was prepared on Guam by the AAF Weather Central, which even Spaatz saw fit to visit on August 2. The central's ranking staff weather officer was Maj. Robert J. Shafer; technical assistance was provided in part by the University of Chicago's very practical John C. Bellamy, who was still on the island researching the wind problem. Initially, it looked as if Little Boy could be dropped on August 4 against the primary target, Hiroshima. But LeMay scrubbed the mission because of unfavorable target weather. On August 5 the forecast called for favorable weather the next day, so a launch was ordered.

Once aloft, Col. Paul W. Tibbets, piloting the B-29 *Enola Gay*, was under instructions to select the final target based on reports from three weather B-29s that were preceding him over primary, secondary, and tertiary targets; he was to return if all three were covered by clouds. A few hours later Tibbets received the Hiroshima report verifying the forecast: two-tenths cloud cover at lower, middle, and 15,000-foot altitudes. That weather report, as the official air force account reads, "sealed the city's doom." The weather proved so perfect that the detonation, scheduled for 8:15 A.M., actually occurred just forty-five seconds after that.[76]

Three days later, on August 9, Nagasaki's fate was determined by a different kind of meteorological quirk. Although two weather planes reported visual conditions at Kokura, the primary target, the bomb-laden B-29 was delayed fifty-five minutes at the rendezvous point off Japan. Upon arriving over Kokura, the crew found that dense haze and smoke made the visual drop impossible, even though they made three passes over the target. So Maj. Charles W. Sweeney flew on to Nagasaki. He found eight-tenths cloud cover below, but it improved to five-tenths during the last twenty seconds of the approach to the target. This improvement permitted release of the bomb visually at the end of what had started out as a radar-guided bomb run because fuel was low. Consequently, the bomb went off over Nagasaki's industrial area rather than above the city proper, thereby saving thousands of lives. Japan sued for peace the next day.[77]

Chapter 7
Reversion to Peacetime
(1945–1950)

The eye of a hurricane is an excellent place to
reflect upon the puniness of man and his works.
If an adequate definition of humility is ever written,
it's likely to be done in the eye of a hurricane.
—Edward R. Murrow[1]

DEMOBILIZATION

Once V-J Day arrived, the rush was on to get out of uniform. The rapidity of the process was evident from the rate at which the AAF's military on-board count dropped: V-J Day—2,253,000; December, 1945—888,769, and December, 1946—341,421. As General Arnold told his command, "Get down to rock bottom!" The AWS demobilization mirrored that of the rest of the military: V-J Day—17,800 persons manning 312 domestic and 546 foreign stations, followed by a mid-1946 postwar low of 4,209 persons in 279 detachments. The more points a weatherman had in total service, time overseas, and combat awards, the sooner he was released, leaving the inexperienced newcomers to run the operation as best they could (see Fig. 4).[2]

It became impossible to operate a satisfactory weather service at many key points around the world, particularly along the still very active air ferry routes. On March 19, 1946, the commander of the ATC North Atlantic Wing, Haywood Hansell, Jr., who had reverted to brigadier general, wrote: "If the requirement for discharge is lowered to 42 months' service as of 31 October, only ten forecasters will be left in the entire [8th Weather] Squadron. It is apparent that the North Atlantic Weather Service will then be required to curtail forecasting activities at most of the major air bases. . . .

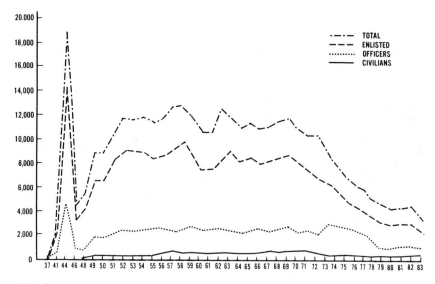

Fig. 4. Air Weather Service personnel assigned as of 30 June (1937–1980). (Courtesy Air Weather Service)

If the weather service breaks down, it may bottleneck the entire North Atlantic operation."[3] Hansell offered several options. New trainees could be sent overseas immediately; experienced weather officers at foreign bases could be asked to stay as paid civilians; local talent could be hired, or U.S. airlines could be requested to assign civilians who had been military forecasters to critical air bases. An amalgam of all these alternatives was eventually tried with a modicum of success (Project Hypo), and the weather squadron, along with its sister units, muddled through.

Meanwhile, Col. Donald Yates, the AWS commander, was thinking far ahead. He once observed, "I'm tired of consultants. In the next war, we're going to have our own damned Ph.D.'s already in uniform!" So Yates wrote to promising young officers, requesting that they apply for permanent military commissions. To entice them, he noted: "Plans for the post-war Weather Service provide for the annual assignment of outstanding officers to leading universities for further education in meteorology including the opportunity for acquiring Master and Doctor degrees."[4]

In those days the king makers of the American meteorological profession numbered five—Professors Rossby and Houghton (the outgoing and incoming presidents of the AMS); Commander Reichelderfer, the Weather Bureau chief; and Colonel Yates and Captain Orville, who headed military weather units. They were in complete agreement that a special effort had to be made to retain in meteorology a sizable fraction of the six thousand weather officers then being demobilized. The bureau would take some, academia a few. But the big hope was that industrial and agricultural meteorology could be expanded. To that end, Rossby persuaded his peers to convert the AMS from a low-cost, low-key scientific society into an articulate, highly visible professional association. Within nine months the society had permanent housing on Boston's Beacon Hill, initially at 5 Joy Street; even more important, Lt. Col. Kenneth C. Spengler had become the organization's talented executive secretary, a post he still holds.[5]

Despite Rossby's hopes for an expansion of industrial meteorology, most industries found that they could obtain their weather information free from the Weather Bureau. Nevertheless, a few demobilized weather officers formed private weather services. Inevitably, the festering problem reappeared, as it had in airline meteorology: Where did free public weather advice stop and private weather service begin? In May, 1947, the Widewing duo of Holzman and Krick debated this issue publicly at a Washington meeting of the AMS. As the head of a private firm, Krick argued that weather information beyond that in newspaper and radio announcements should fall in the domain of the private forecaster. Colonel Holzman, who had stayed in the AWS, rebutted: "To me, private meteorology does not mean setting up shop to give the U.S. Weather Bureau competition in the forecasting business." Since then, there has been a slow but continuing growth in private meteorology (there are now nearly 100 weather service firms) and in the use of former military meteorologists to present weather on television.[6] By far the most common route taken by demobilized meteorologists who wished to stay in the field was graduate school via the GI Bill of Rights. In fact, two young AWS captains, Robert M. White and George P. Cressman, obtained doctoral degrees this way and became successive directors of the national weather service during the period 1963–79.

NUCLEAR TESTING

On January 10, 1946, the Joint Chiefs of Staff announced activation of JTF-1, under the ordnance specialist Vice Adm. William H. P. Blandy. Its sole mission was to subject arrays of naval ships to nuclear detonations before an international audience of diplomats, scientists, and media representatives. Operation Crossroads featured two main events—an air blast (Test Able) and a shallow underwater shot (Test Baker). Both took place during midsummer at a remote atoll called Bikini, in the Marshall Islands. Implementing the thousand-page operational order took 42,000 men, 150 aircraft, and more than 200 ships.[7]

Blandy and his support specialists needed to know in detail the meteorological situation existing before, during, and after the detonations to ensure that no radiological fallout conditions existed for any of the wide-ranging task force units. Minimal cloud cover was also a necessity so that observers and cameras would have unrestricted views. Such weather advice was handled aboard the command ship USS *Mount McKinley* by JTF-1 staff aerologist Captain Cumberledge, his co-forecaster Colonel Holzman, and their assistant Lt. Paul A. Humphrey. Backing them up was a special Crossroads weather central established at Kwajalein Island by Major Crowson. For upper-air coverage, Crowson could use three B-29s of the 59th Weather Reconnaissance Squadron (Very Long Range), Weather.[8] A flight of navy PB4Y-1s was also based at Kwajalein to watch for unexpected typhoons or tropical storms. The weathermen had to guarantee, besides minimal cloud cover, a constant wind direction from the surface to 60,000 feet to simplify the prediction of fallout.

Following several weather delays and with all the world listening by radio, the crew of the B-29 *Dave's Dream* dropped the first nuclear weapon on ninety-three target ships on Sunday, June 30, 1946. Although the device detonated at the proper height, the drop was horizontally amiss by 1,500 to 2,000 feet. Even so, the burst sank five ships and badly damaged three others. As the shot occurred hundreds of feet above the lagoon, the explosion was self-cleansing: the column of very hot, fast-rising gases removed most of the radioactive fission products from the lower atmosphere. Within ten minutes the nuclear cloud reached an altitude of approximately 35,000 feet. It then leveled off and drifted away, although it could be spotted visually for another fifty minutes.

Because no one had ever created an underwater nuclear detonation before, the forecasting assignment for Baker Test was rather tricky. The shot on July 25 so contaminated the target area that no one could penetrate even the outer fringe of the target for two days. The shot, in fact, raised a column of radioactive water and spray 2,100 feet across, topped by a cloud of condensed water vapor reaching to 6,000 feet. The cloud subsided a bit, spread to a width of approximately six miles, and deposited a mistlike rain over the area for the next fifteen minutes.

Holzman and Cumberledge were encouraged by these tests: "It can be said that no significant meteorological influence other than purely local cloud effects resulted from the Bikini tests 'Able' and 'Baker'. . . . The tremendous energies required over considerable periods of time to cope with such large-scale natural phenomena (such as tornadoes, hurricanes and typhoons) are still not attainable in manmade explosions similar to the Bikini detonations."[9]

One thing was learned from providing aerial weather reconnaissance for these initial tests: the need to acquire fallout samples at flight altitude. By the end of the next nuclear test series (Eniwetok Atoll, 1948), AWS had installed an odd-looking air-filtering device known as the bug-catcher on the fuselages of a half-dozen B-29s. These specially equipped aircraft were then vectored on nuclear sampling missions of the highest priority for Headquarters USAF.[10] Accordingly, AWS B-29s were the first to obtain confirmed samples of nuclear debris from the first suspected Soviet fission explosion (atom bomb) in September, 1949, and from the initial Soviet thermonuclear, or fusion, explosion (hydrogen bomb) in August, 1953. General of the Army Bradley later wrote: "The detection of these radioactive samples electrified the military. . . . Sound and reliable intelligence on Soviet nuclear activities was almost impossible to come by; we depended entirely on an airborne 'detection' net, designed to scoop up telltale signs of nuclear explosions in the atmosphere."[11]

Eventually, the AWS aerial nuclear sampling mission carried far more clout with Headquarters USAF (which translated into additional aircraft and manpower) than did pure weather reconnaissance. The most popular of these multiple-use flights was the Ptarmigan mission; typically flown every other day between central Alaska (first Ladd, then Eielson Field) and the North Pole. The first such flight took place on March 17, 1947, with Capt. George A. Collins at the controls of a 59th Weather Reconnaissance Squadron B-29, accompanied by the squadron commander, Lt. Col. Karl Rauk, and the AWS commander, Brigadier General Yates. Because of the regularity of the run, Ptarmigan was also excellent for testing polar navigation techniques that could overcome radio blackout conditions and could photograph polar pack ice patterns during all seasons.[12]

COMMAND REORGANIZATION

When World War II ended, the military requirements for weather support dropped sharply. By mid-1947, for example, the navy had only twenty-seven fully operational domestic air bases, plus eleven overseas. During this cutback, the Naval Weather Service saw relatively little organizational turmoil, merely reducing the number of detachments and cutting the weather centrals from approximately thirty to fifteen.[13] Throughout the reduction, the navy's aerological desk (Op-531E) in the Office of the Chief of Naval Operations was directed by the same likeable, low-key person as during the war years—Captain Orville.

But the AWS saw many organizational changes. After spending the last twenty-seven months of the war in Asheville, North Carolina, the AWS moved to Langley Field, Virginia, on January 7, 1946. Six months later, a new move took it to a ramshackle, wooden building called Tempo-7, on the grounds of Washington National Airport. Its stay here was brief; during December, 1948, AWS headquarters moved to Andrews Field, just outside Washington, D.C.

Meanwhile, a dream came true for the AWS leadership on July 1, 1945, when it was designated a separate, independent air force command. Colonel Yates would now report directly to the AAF commanding general, Hap Arnold, and would also serve as Arnold's staff weather officer. To implement the change, on August 17, 1945, the War Department ordered that all weather units in theater commands outside the continental United States be assigned to and under the direct command of the AAF, through the AWS. The last such field unit was so assigned on October 12, 1945—a somewhat futile gesture, for by that time many were only skeleton organizations on their way to total deactivation.

AWS's long-awaited independence was short-lived. During 1946 the AAF reorganized into functional commands—strategic, tactical, air defense, and so on. To simplify and further reduce the field command structure, the AWS, along with its specialized sister services, the Airways and Air Communications Service (AACS) and the Air Rescue Service, was placed under the command of the equally global but much larger ATC. Thus, on March 13, 1946, the AWS lost its eight-month independence as a worldwide command and began to take orders from the ATC.[14]

Although the AWS was subordinate to the ATC, the fact that the AWS retained organizational autonomy was still unsettling to die-hard unity-of-command proponents. Aware of such undercurrents, General Spaatz, Arnold's successor, addressed the issue in his monthly letter (May, 1947) to the air force commanders:

> I have given a great deal of consideration to the proper place for both AACS and the Air Weather Service in the future organization of the Air Forces. I have determined for reasons which are sufficient for me, but too voluminous for detailed treatment herein, that, in the best interests of the AAF, both the AACS and the AWS must be permanent agencies in our structure. I realize to some extent this cuts across certain command boundaries, particularly at base level, but this is made necessary because of the benefits which are derived from operation of these agencies as world-wide systems, with essential ingredients of top management control and an inherent capability of extremely rapid expansion in time of emergency or war.

By then, there was another cause for rejoicing—on February 5, Yates, while in command of the AWS, had been promoted to brigadier general, thereby achieving a first for military weather organizations. Next, the National Security Act that President Truman signed into law on July 26, 1947, abolished the War Department and established the Department of Defense. It also made the air force a separate service, equal to the navy and the army. Even with that change, the AWS remained responsible for providing to the army all weather services except ballistic winds reports and, as later modified, river and flood forecasting.[15]

As of mid-1948 the 860 officers and 4,186 enlisted men of the AWS were organized along standard wing, group, and squadron lines. One wing was based in the United States; the other wing was headquartered in Japan. Under the wings came eight weather groups (one an aerial weather reconnaissance group) and nineteen squadrons, four of which were reconnaissance squadrons. In keeping with the USAF informal motto of that period— "Maintain the Air Force in Being"—one-fourth of the AWS resources were involved in reconnaissance. Consequently, between 1946 and 1950, the AWS aircraft inventory grew from forty-seven (twenty-five RB-29s, sixteen B-17s, and four B-25s) to sixty-four (sixty WB-29s and four B-17s). But a price had to be paid for this heavy emphasis on flying.

During February, 1949, the air force's new chief of staff, Gen. Hoyt S. Vandenberg, remarked to Yates's immediate superior, Lt. Gen. Laurence S. Kuter, that the AWS was rendering poor service to his flyers, particularly in forecast quality. After a quick check with Yates, Kuter, commanding the newly labeled MATS, confirmed Vandenberg's criticism. Most of the ills came from a personnel system that was still suffering from demobilization. Because of the severe shortage of experienced forecasters, moves between bases were frequent, even though housing, on and off base, was extremely tight. In 1949 only 44 percent of the AWS officers had four or more years of college, down from nearly 100 percent in 1945. Yet assignments as weather squadron commanders were made by seniority rather than by qualifications. The postwar surplus of field-grade officers also made promotion above captain almost nonexistent. To compound the problem, the number of reserve officers allowed to stay on active duty was also reduced.[16]

To overcome some of these drawbacks, Yates and his staff centralized the movement of people and the control of officer career patterns at AWS headquarters. They set up formal programs of career progression in meteorology for enlisted personnel, warrant officers, and officers and publicized them. A number of Reserve Officer Training Corps (ROTC) officers, who needed to spend four obligatory years in uniform, took one-year graduate-level courses in meteorology at MIT, Chicago, NYU, and UCLA.[17] By mid-1948 new arrangements also permitted more than a thousand wartime weather officers to hold mobilization billets in the active reserve. A corollary reserve program for officer and enlisted weathermen was initiated a year later, followed by a reserve forces section in AWS headquarters under Lt. Col. Richard M. Gill.[18] Thus, out of adversity, Yates and his staff were able to introduce much needed new command and personnel practices.

RESEARCH AND DEVELOPMENT

Demobilization did not apply to the exotic world of research and development (R & D). Rather, Congress let much of the wartime research funding continue into peacetime. At the national AMS meeting in January,

1946, the team of Professor Byers (University of Chicago), Colonel Holzman (AWS), and Comdr. Robert H. Maynard (Naval Weather Service) announced a three-year joint study of thunderstorm microstructure. Although the Weather Bureau underwrote some of the project, the military (with some assistance from the National Advisory Committee for Aeronautics) supplied aircraft, storm tracking radar, and field personnel. Final synthesis of the data would be at Chicago under Byers, whose lead analyst was Roscoe R. Braham, a former B-17 pilot and AWS weather officer.

Before the Thunderstorm Project ended in 1949, its use of scores of scientists, pilots, and field technicians had become the prototype for future large-scale meteorological research projects. The initial phase took place in mid-1946 near Orlando, Florida, where the frequent summer thunderstorms were monitored by a surface micro-observing network of fifty weather stations spaced a mile apart, supplemented by numerous Signal Corps weather radar vans. Aloft, five specially instrumented air force P-61 Black Widow fighters flew through appropriate storm cells on simultaneous traverses at levels of 5,000, 10,000, 15,000, 20,000, and 25,000 feet. Next, the ground paraphernalia was moved in twenty-two railroad cars to Wilmington, Ohio, where the Florida effort was duplicated the following summer, using frontal, as well as nonfrontal, thunderstorms.

All told, the daring pilots and their accompanying radar observers made 1,362 traverses through more than a hundred thunderstorms. As an indication of how difficult some of this flying was, air turbulence was considered heavy if vertical gusts exceeded 8 feet per second (fps). However, upward velocities were measured as high as 43 fps, a gust load sufficient for many aircraft to start disintegrating if flying at normal cruising speed into such an updraft. Downwards gusts were even worse, with many storms having sustained downdrafts of 30 fps, and a few with peak values near 90 fps. Air crews and flight records agreed that air turbulence was the most dangerous part of a thunderstorm, followed by hail damage and last by lightning strike.[19]

As 1946 turned into 1947, Congress continued generous funding of R & D. Spending such money for aerological purposes in the navy was comparatively simple. Captain Orville, as Op-531E, would request the aerological section over in the Bureau of Aeronautics to develop specific items or techniques for fleet use. If the work was done outside the navy, a contract was let. If the work was to be in-house, the bureau's task order normally went to the Naval Weather Research Facility at the Norfolk fleet weather central, for technique development. In the latter case, the effort was part of Project AROWA (Applied Research and Operational Weather Analysis). In addition, as of August 1, 1946, ONR independently sponsored meteorological research in its freewheeling Geophysical Branch.

Ironically, the same organizational principle that ensured the AWS's autonomy as the organization solely responsible for operational weather support in the air force spiked its ambitions for meteorological R&D. Because the Signal Corps had failed to improve meteorological techniques during wartime, the AWS was allowed to work in this area. However, when the Air Materiel Command (AMC) came into existence during June, 1946, its charter specified responsibility for field engineering, installation, and major maintenance of weather equipment, leaving the Signal Corps its lingering function of researching, procuring, and supplying weather equipment to the AWS and other parts of the army. Just the month before, the AWS had set up its own R & D division under Colonel Holzman. The ATC, as soon as it formally learned of the AWS incursion outside the purely operational area, challenged the legality of the AWS action. After nine months of infighting, the AAF directed by letter dated March 26, 1947, that the AWS transfer its R&D effort to the AMC.[20] There it remained until it was assumed in mid-1950 by the new Air Research and Development Command (ARDC)— redesignated as the Air Force Systems Command (AFSC) in April, 1961.

Air force meteorological research became even more byzantine when the Pentagon finally agreed to remove most of the meteorological research from the Watson Laboratories at Eatontown, New Jersey, in May, 1948. As the AAF meteorological liaison officer to Watson, Maj. Joseph O. Fletcher led its Geophysical Research Division (GRD) north to a dingy, multistory warehouse on Boston's south waterfront. There, GRD was absorbed into the three-year-old Air Force Cambridge Research Laboratory (AFCRL) complex.[21] Yates still insisted that the AWS should not be entirely ruled out of working on the frontiers of science. The AWS charter permitted the improvement of existing techniques and procedures, so during 1948 he set up the Directorate of Scientific Services at Headquarters AWS under no less than Sverre Petterssen, by then chief of the Norwegian Forecasting Service.[22]

PROJECT CIRRUS

The need to modify weather had long been considered urgent—witness Patton's fervent plea to the Almighty in 1944, asking fair weather for battle. As early as 1891, Congress authorized Robert Dryenforth to spend $9,000 to cannonade the skies for two years to determine whether artillery concussions caused rain. His results gave the experimenter a new nickname, "Dryhenceforth." Then, between 1921 and 1924, the Army Air Service installed special nozzles designed by Dr. E. Leon Chaffee on two aircraft to disperse 500 pounds of electrically charged sand over a 10-mile flight path.

This attempt to dissipate low clouds over air fields proved ineffective.[23] President Calvin Coolidge turned down the request for another $15,000 as too large a sum for such research.

Starting in the mid-1930s the meteorological profession subscribed to the Bergeron-Findeisen theory that raindrops formed around tiny ice crystals in supercooled clouds. No one tested the theory until a machinist, Vincent J. Schaefer, dropped a chunk of dry ice into a deep-freeze box on July 13, 1946. The box, already holding a fog of cold water particles, suddenly filled with a miniature snow storm of minute ice crystals. A natural-born scientist, Schaefer was then working at what some called "Irving Langmuir's university," that is, the General Electric research laboratory at Schenectady, New York. Bernard Vonnegut, a smoke expert, was brought in to determine how many ice crystals were made by a falling ice particle. Bernie also investigated other compounds that might duplicate the carbon dioxide nucleation effect; on November 14, 1946, he found that he could do so using silver iodide smoke.[24]

Those two related actions, occurring within four months, provided the building blocks for weather modification. The day before the critical Vonnegut experiment, Schaefer used a rented aircraft to drop three pounds of finely ground dry ice into a supercooled cloud east of Schenectady. As he later wrote in his laboratory notebook: "The rapidity with which the CO_2 . . . seemed to affect the cloud was amazing. It seemed as though it almost exploded, the effect was so widespread and rapid."[25]

Two months before, Langmuir had approached Colonel Yates and Dr. Michael Ference, the new meteorological branch chief at the Evans Laboratory of the Signal Corps, about government support. Both were enthusiastic. The GE general counsel was even more so when it appeared that another Schaefer cloud-seeding test on December 20 might have had something to do with Schenectady's heaviest snowfall of the year. Thus, the Signal Corps contract, signed on February 28, 1947, provided that "the entire flight program shall be conducted by the government, using exclusively government personnel and equipment, and shall be under the exclusive direction and control of such government personnel." Eventually extended into a five-year program, the contract's total cost (partly funded by the navy) came to only $790,116.

Ference quickly set up three action panels. The steering groups consisted of himself, ONR's Earl G. Droessler, and Maj. P. J. Keating, chief of the weather equipment branch at the Air Force Flight Test Facility, Middletown, Pennsylvania. The research group comprised GE researchers; ONR's Lt. Comdr. Daniel F. Rex chaired the operations group. Whenever Operation Cirrus, as it was called, conducted a major field experiment, up to forty people could be involved, including air force flight crews for seeding and monitoring, navy weather technicians for ground measurements, and civilians for support services such as time-lapse cloud photography. Three bases were used—Schenectady, New York; Puerto Rico; and Albuquerque, New Mexico. Special attention was paid to dissipating low-level wintertime stratus and ground fogs (results were promising), to attempting to increase precipitation in tropical and in summertime cumulus clouds, and to using overseeding as a possible way of suppressing thunderstorm formation.

At the Weather Bureau, Reichelderfer was cautious about the technique, as was his research chief, the former Maj. Harry Wexler of the wartime AWS. Perturbed by Langmuir's publicized hypothesis that a single silver iodide generator could modify large-scale atmospheric processes, they set up their own cloud physics project (1947–49) using another air force B-17. Their results, based on 170 field tests, were largely negative. But the general public still thought one could make it rain on demand. So Yates, as the AMS president, appointed an academic panel to evaluate the technique during 1950. Within three months, they reported: "The possibility of artificially producing any useful amounts of rain has not been demonstrated." But the potential for sometimes enhancing precipitation remained, no matter what the academics thought.[26]

SEVERE WEATHER

When the 8th and 16th Weather Squadrons departed northern Canada in early 1946, the Arctic regions were left a large meteorological blank. At almost the same time Col. Charles J. Hubbard, a wartime AAF Arctic expert, talked Congress into enacting a law calling for a joint Canadian–United States weather network. The Canadian cabinet moved more slowly, so the Joint Arctic Program, proposing that nine Arctic weather stations be jointly erected and manned, was not approved until January, 1947.[27] On April 8, 1947, C-82s of the U.S. Troop Carrier Command began to load supplies and personnel onto the sea ice of Eureka Sound, 360 miles northwest of Thule, Greenland.

The construction of such a base required airlifting 110 tons of materiel and supplies over the four months before icebreakers could arrive. All told, five stations were established in the far north: Eureka Sound, Resolute Bay (Cornwallis Island), Isachsen Fjord (Ellef Ringnes Island), Mould Bay (Prince Patrick Island), and last, on Easter Day, 1950, Alert (Ellesmere Island), 450 miles north of Thule's increasingly strategic airstrip. Although the U.S. weather observers were Weather Bureau civilians, the annual resupply of these forward bases involved both Canadian and American naval and aerial military units.

In the late summer of 1946, Admiral Nimitz, the new Chief of Naval Operations, suddenly approved Operation Highjump, to be executed by

Task Force 68 of the Antarctic Development Project.[28] No country formally owned Antarctica, so it was considered prudent to reinforce the basis for possible U.S. claims should territorial negotiations take place. For once, funding was not a problem, and on December 2, 1946, the 4,700-man task force aboard twelve ships and a submarine sailed south toward the Roaring Forties, the Howling Fifties, and the Screaming Sixties.

Although Rear Admiral Byrd was officer in charge for the overall project, Rear Adm. Richard H. Cruzen, a veteran of the previous Byrd expedition, was task force commander. Cruzen's aerologist, Captain Kosco, had the additional title Special Projects Officer (special projects abounded). Probably the expedition's most exciting moment came when six jet-assisted R4Ds flew off the carrier USS *Philippine Sea* for Little America's snow runway on the Ross Ice Shelf, 600 miles away. All told, the task force operated twenty aircraft and more than seventy over-the-snow vehicles with the loss of only four lives, an excellent record for Antarctica.

Unfortunately for the Midwest, severe weather could also exist outside the polar and the tropical regions. For example, on March 20, 1948, a tornado roared through Tinker AFB south of Oklahoma City, Oklahoma, wrecking two B-29s, fifteen P-47s, and seventeen C-54s. The AWS domestic wing was already based at Tinker, so Col. Lewis L. Mundell quickly summoned his top forecasters, Maj. Ernest J. Fawbush and Capt. Robert C. Miller, and asked if they could give better advance notice of violent weather. They had been working on a rudimentary, though empirical, technique for warning of the approach of extremely violent thunderstorms and tornadoes. Before the base was hit by the second tornado within five days, the forecasters did give some warning, even though the new storm destroyed seven B-29s, eight P-47s, and twenty PT-19s. By doing so, Fawbush and Miller were picking up where 2nd Lt. John P. Finley left off in the 1880s.[29]

By February, 1949, the Fawbush-Miller technique was reasonably reliable for forecasting the time and area of possible tornado occurrences several hours in advance.[30] To formalize its warning system, AWS created a Severe Weather Warning Center (SWWC) at Tinker AFB in Feburary, 1951. By that time, J. R. Lloyd, director of the Weather Bureau's Kansas City regional forecast office, had enough faith to authorize Fawbush and Miller, in a sharp deviation from bureau policy, to release tornado forecasts for Oklahoma to the local bureau office, as well as to the state highway patrol and the Red Cross.

Not to be left behind, the Weather Bureau set up its own Severe Local Storm (SELS) unit in 1952, under Donald C. House, and moved it from Washington to Kansas City two years later. To eliminate duplication and potential forecast confusion, AWS then moved the SWWC into the SELS facility on January 31, 1956. Unfortunately, that arrangement did not work because the Weather Bureau rigidly guarded its claim to be "the national weather service." As a result, the SWWC disbanded in March, 1961, leaving the sole responsibility for tornado forecasting to the SELS group. Even so, air force and army commands could not obtain critical weather forecasts quickly enough from the Weather Bureau unit. Because of time pressures, SELS forecasters refused to discuss their prognoses with AWS field unit forecasters, with the result that several military bases were soon struck by severe weather without warning. Consequently, AWS reestablished the SWWC at Kansas City on August 15, 1963, under a new label—the Military Weather Warning Center (Detachment 42, 4th Weather Group)—and obtained the results desired.[31]

THE BERLIN AIRLIFT

At Yalta in 1945 Churchill and Roosevelt agreed to divide Germany along a boundary running well west of Berlin, although Stalin did allow his allies to occupy postwar sectors in Germany's capital. Consequently, Allied garrison troops, as well as the populace of West Berlin, could become hostages any time the Soviets desired. In April, 1948, Stalin decided to close border posts to land traffic from the west. President Truman, believing that the best way to contend with military power was to use counterpower, authorized the military to supply Berlin by using the three 20-mile-wide air corridors agreed to by the Soviets in 1945.

The flights, which began on June 26, 1948, not only had to supply the Allied garrisons for an indefinite siege but also had to provide minimum food and fuel for some two and a half million Germans—thus the name, Operation Vittles. As the Soviets were not ready to escalate from a cold to a hot war, inclement weather became the chief threat to the operation and to the flight crews. A number of countries provided aircraft and personnel, but most of the flying was done by the RAF, the two U.S. military air cargo services (MATS and the Naval Air Transport Service), and commercial contractors such as Pan American Airways.

Although the war had ended three years before, the German weather service was still barely operational. Weather forecasting for the world's largest airlift therefore rested largely on the 18th Weather Squadron, the only AWS command left in Europe. Unfortunately, the squadron, with only 60 officers and 248 enlisted men, was at about 57 percent of authorized manpower. However, three weeks after the start of the airlift, Lieutenant Colonel Chavasse reported in as the unit's new commander. Weather stations not in direct support of Vittles were stripped of their most experienced personnel, who were reassigned to stations that were working with the airlift. Additional weather personnel came on temporary duty from the United States, but most, fresh out of technical schools, lacked field experience. Within six months the permanent weather complement in Europe grew to 155 officers and 415 weathermen; Chavasse was able to establish a weather group at Wiesbaden, Germany, composed of three weather squadrons, including the 18th.

Chavasse also served as staff weather officer to Lieutenant General LeMay, who served as commander, United States Air Forces in Europe, until October 15, 1948. To keep the airlift going during the dreary winter months, LeMay made demands on Chavasse that required near miracles in weather forecasting. Many Berlin-bound supplies such as meat and potatoes were perishable, not suitable for airfield storage. In addition, traffic control needed to know in advance which types of supplies—military, fuel, or food—had priority. LeMay started asking for thirty-day weather forecasts updated every four days, although later he modified the request to a ten-day forecast with the usual four-day update. Finally, he asked only for a four-day weather forecast supplemented by detailed climatic studies.[32]

To meet tonnage demands, the task force commander, Maj. Gen. William H. Tunner dropped Air Force minimums to 400-foot cloud ceiling and one mile of visibility at Templehof, the American intown airport at Berlin, and to 200 feet and half a mile at the other bases in use. To achieve precision, every available weather-observing technique, human and mechanical, was used. For example, markedly different ceiling values were reported by AWS weathermen using pilot balloons or rawinsondes at the terminal building and by airborne pilots. Thus, as values dropped near the minimums, the pilots came to distrust AWS reports. To overcome the difficulty, new types of ceilometers and transmissometers were used. Weather observers were also posted at the approach to the runway to count the number of runway lights that could be seen when visibility dropped to a mile. Additional weather reconnaissance flights were scheduled by the RAF and the USAF. For a while, every seventh cargo aircraft carried a radio operator to report weather conditions via code at four prearranged points along each of the three air corridors.

Unfortunately, the autumn of 1948 brought the worst flying weather on record for Germany. Two forecasting problems quickly arose—inexperience with the region and conflicting prognoses. Although the 18th Weather Squadron operated a weather central at the huge Rhein-Main air complex outside Frankfurt, the forecasters at each of the other air terminals had their own ideas for their local areas as conditions approached minimums. Chavasse initiated telephone conferences among the terminals, and the final coordinated forecast was then provided to the master air force flight service center at Frankfurt. To personalize the service further, on November 10, 1948, Maj. Bernard Pusin, the squadron's executive officer, was posted as staff weather officer to Tunner's task force headquarters.[33] To expedite the return from jammed-up Templehof, weather forecasters toured the queue of departing aircraft in jeeps to provide on-the-spot briefings, thereby avoiding the necessity for flight crews to leave their aircraft. As a result of this and similar actions, one outfit, the 15th Troop Carrier Squadron, in one 24-hour period, completed seventy-two round-trip flights between Rhein-Main and Templehof using only twelve aircraft (May 10, 1949).

The Berlin airlift continued for 321 days. Despite frequent low clouds, fog, air turbulence, freezing rain, and aircraft icing, a steady flow of C-47s, C-54s, C-82s, C-74s, C-97s, and R5Ds, plus RAF and commercial aircraft, shuttled along the air corridors to and from West Berlin. Although the land blockade ended on May 12, 1949, Operation Vittles did not completely halt until four months later. By then, 276,926 flights had been made at an estimated cost of $345 million, and forty-four British and thirty-one American airmen had been killed. On the other hand, 2,323,067 tons of vitally needed supplies reached Berlin without triggering a third world war. Thus, even hard-to-please Tunner advised Chavasse and his weary weather personnel that "these forecasts were as good as possible, being limited only by the current status of progress of the science of weather forecasting. More certainly could not have been expected."[34]

Chapter 8
A Burgeoning Era for Meteorology (1950–1961)

It is a sad commentary on the scientific status of weather forecasting that even today the methods remain so empirical and so dependent upon experience and subjective interpretation.

—Hurd C. Willett, "The Forecast Problem," (1951)

EXPANDING HORIZONS

The 1950s saw many technological breakthroughs—the development of commercial jet aircraft, color television, solid-state electronics, electronic computers, nuclear submarines, and earth satellites. But meteorology lagged. In the *Compendium of Meteorology*, a publication sponsored by the AFCRC, the dean of MIT meteorologists Hurd Willett bitterly complained: "There has been little or no real progress made during the past forty years in the verification skill of the original basic type of regional forecast, of rain or shine and of warmer or colder on the morrow." Willett urged the creation of a numerical atmospheric model that would truly fit the synoptic and climatic aspects of global weather. [1]

The biggest drawback was that most of the world's weather observations were taken north of 20° north latitude. That region, unfortunately, appeared to be the least important third of the atmosphere—thermodynamically and dynamically. Although minimally monitored, the circumpolar vortex of the southern hemisphere was, Willett believed, a far more intense phenomenon. Compounding the problem was a paucity of weather observations from the tropics, the region that is the principal heat source for global circulation. Although civilian meteorologists preferred otherwise, the requisite geographic expansion in world weather coverage had to depend heavily on military transportation, communications, man-

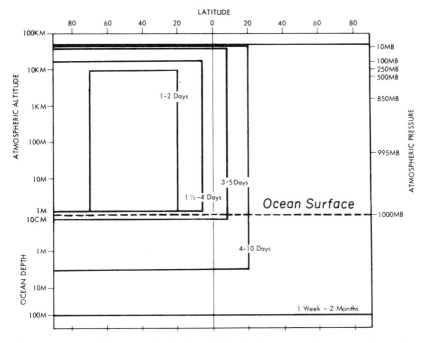

Fig. 5. Scope of data required for mid-latitude weather forecasts of varying duration. (Courtesy American Meterological Society)

power, and rocketry.[2] By the end of the decade the military had scientific stations on the Arctic ice pack, weather buoys on the high seas, Antarctic field stations, long-lived constant pressure balloons, and rockets to loft weather satellites into orbit. The question remained: Would monitoring the atmosphere from pole to pole and vertically to the ninety-ninth percentile of the earth's gaseous envelope provide the basis for scientifically based medium- and long-range forecasts of notably improved accuracy? (See Fig. 5.)

A PLETHORA OF WEATHER CENTRALS

Despite, but partially because of, demobilization, an outbreak of weather centrals developed after the war. By 1950 the AWS was operating nine regional weather centrals Stateside and overseas, including Rhein-Main (Frankfurt, Germany), Haneda (Japan), Guam, Hawaii, and the Arctic Weather Central (Elmendorf AFB, Alaska). The most significant proved to be the one formed at Offutt AFB, Nebraska, in 1949 and designated the Global Weather Central. First established under Col. James T. Seaver, who was Lieutenant General LeMay's staff weather officer with the XXI Bomber Command and Twentieth Air Force in World War II, "Global," as it came to be known, was originally dedicated to LeMay's SAC. By 1960 Global was one of three major centrals that AWS was operating (the others were the High Wycombe Weather Central in England and the Tokyo Weather Central), plus thirteen functional centers (for example, the Langley Forecast Center to support TAC), and various centralized terminal forecast facilities.

Electronic computers had come onto the scene, and the weather centrals were eager to engage in everyday numerical weather prediction using physical laws that had been known for the past century. Why had they waited so long? The paramount reason was the overwhelming number of calculations needed to make such a forecast. The first American attempt to do so came in April, 1950, when Dr. Jule G. Charney's group working at Princeton's Institute for Advanced Study under the brilliant mathematician John Louis von Neumann used the ENIAC computer at the army's Aberdeen Proving Ground in Maryland. Using simplified atmospheric equations, the group took twenty-four hours to run a twenty-four-hour forecast on ENIAC.[3] Two years later, on June 10, 1952, Princeton's new computer was unveiled. Capable of performing 10,000 instructions per second and sometimes affectionately called the JOHNIAC, after von Neuman himself, it was the forerunner of modern computers: it could do in five minutes what ENIAC took a day to do.

Now that von Neumann had ushered in the computer age, the results of his toils could be applied, with the unceasing encouragement of Rossby, to meteorology. Even a few months before von Neumann's announcement, Sverre Petterssen had urged his boss, AWS commander Oscar Senter, to involve the AWS with Air Research and Development Command's Geophysics Research Directorate in a joint numerical weather prediction project. Senter agreed. He and Dr. Bob Fletcher, who had taken over as the lead AWS scientist upon Petterssen's departure for the University of Chicago, appointed Maj. Thomas H. Lewis to the project. Fletcher also detailed Dr. Cressman to work at Princeton with von Neumann, Charney, and what was becoming a host of others, including Dr. George Platzman, Dr. Joseph Smagorinsky, and Dr. John C. Freeman.

After the IBM Corporation unveiled its new IBM-701 computer (affectionately known as the Tin Head) in the spring of 1953, Lewis visited Princeton, MIT, and the AFCRC, where Maj. Philip D. Thompson had been doing related work for four years. Lewis and Cressman then proposed that the AWS, in cooperation with the Weather Bureau and the navy, form a Joint Numerical Weather Prediction Unit (JNWPU) at Suitland, Maryland, and equip it with an IBM-701 rented for $240,000 per year. In April,

1953, the Weather Bureau chief, Commander Reichelderfer, submitted a paper outlining the plan to the Joint Meteorological Committee. All parties concurred.[4] They also agreed that the first JNWPU director would be the thirty-four-year-old Cressman from the AWS, accompanied by Lieutenant Colonel Thompson, who would head the unit's development section, and six other officers.

The joint venture got under way on July 1, 1954, but the IBM-701 was not installed until February, 1955. Using simplified atmospheric equations developed by Charney, Norman A. Phillips, Ragnar Fjortoft, and Carl Rossby, Cressman and his team issued the first machine-run forecasts on May 6, 1955. The forecasts consisted of pressure charts for three different levels up to forty-eight hours in advance. This marriage of the computer and numerical weather models was believed by many, including the popular media, to usher in a new era in meteorology.[5]

After a year or so of experience with operational numerical weather forecasting, the meteorological community began to split into two camps about the computer's value. The JNWPU frankly admitted that 500-mb forecast quality was not significantly better than subjective forecasts. Vince Schaefer worried that forecasters were becoming so addicted to computers that they believed they could not and need not function without them.[6] Yet, when new nongeostrophic models were introduced in April, 1957, the JNWPU's seventy-two hour 500-mb forecast was judged superior to its subjectively prepared counterpart. Thus, four months later, when the unit's IBM-701 was replaced with an IBM-704 that expanded output by 800 percent, the computer-produced 500-mb chart was substituted for the subjectively prepared 500-mb chart on all domestic facsimile weather circuits.

Even so, computer forecasts were far from perfect and had to be limited to a few days because the longer the forecast period, the less the computer model resembled the atmosphere. Moreover, the data grid that could be handled by a computer's memory was so coarse that it did not pick up severe local weather. Just the same, the marriage of technologies at the JNWPU survived the posthoneymoon introspection. "The initiation of the operational use of the electronic computer in the weather business," observed Dr. Fletcher in 1972, "is really the most significant accomplishment in meteorology in the United States and . . . in the world."[7] That marriage also spelled the eventual wipe-out of the plethora of postwar weather centers and centrals, where subjective forecasts were prepared.

As early as 1947 the American meteorological empire had faced another problem akin to that of the sorcerer's apprentice—raw data were flooding in faster than they could be plotted and analyzed. As during the war, the answer was "Go joint!" So the joint Weather Bureau–Air Force–Navy (WBAN) weather analysis center came into being on July 16. Under the

Weather Bureau's Joe R. Fulks, the center soon had 172 people (98 Weather Bureau, 49 air force, and 25 navy) cranking out sixty-eight weather charts a day (Table 3).[8] But it was wretchedly housed in the decrepit Weather Bureau headquarters at 24th and M streets, not far from downtown Washington. Another home was needed, and in July, 1954, the center moved to a federal complex at Suitland, which housed the U.S. Census Bureau and the Navy Hydrographic office. At about this time, the AWS was eager to move its USAF Weather Central from the basement of MATS headquarters at nearby Andrews AFB, so that central, plus one of the navy's, also moved to Suitland to form the National Weather Analysis Center (NWAC).

However, the USAF central maintained its identity behind locked doors, for it prepared a variety of specialized charts and analyses for the use of the air force, the Joint Chiefs of Staff, and the Department of Defense, and dealt with the gathering of highly classified weather data. Major General Moorman decided to move most of those functions to Global at Offutt AFB, so in December, 1957, the transfer, including thirteen forecasters and twenty-five observers, was made to the Nebraska complex. By 1959 SAC could no longer share its IBM-704 with the Global center, so the air staff approved an AWS request for a second-generation IBM-7090 computer strictly for weather use at Offutt, beginning in October, 1960, at a monthly rental fee of $64,295.[9]

The joint Suitland complex came farther apart at the seams in April, 1959, when Comdr. Paul Wolff moved the navy's Numerical Weather Research Section to the verdant grounds of the Naval Postgraduate School in Monterey, California. His rationale was that the school operated the most powerful scientific computer available—the first Control Data Corporation computer ever built. It took a year, however, for Wolff to acquire his first steady customer—the Meteorology Department of the Pacific Missile Range, Point Mugu, California.[10] The user list grew, and in February, 1961, the section became the Fleet Numerical Weather Facility. Meanwhile, back at Suitland, the NWAC was relabeled the National Meteorological Center (NMC) by the Weather Bureau in March, 1958, and Dr. Cressman was retained to run it. So within five years of the founding of JNWPU, three widely separated numerical prediction centers had come into existence in the United States.

Another center of importance was the Joint Typhoon Warning Center (JTWC) formed by the navy and the air force at Nimitz Hill, Guam, on May 1, 1959. During the 1950s the responsibility for typhoon warning in the far Pacific had become split among the navy, the air force, and the Weather Bureau. Finally, in early 1959, Commander in Chief, Pacific, petitioned the Joint Chiefs of Staff for a joint military typhoon warning facility on Guam. In its wire of April 14, the Chiefs of Staff approved the concept for streamlining reconnaissance procedures, making best use of

Table 3. **Information Flow to and from WBAN Analysis Center (1949)**

Incoming Data	Daily Frequency	Typical End Product	Daily Issuance
140 upper air soundings	2	24- and 36-hour 700 mb prognostic charts	2
350 upper wind profiles	4	12-, 18-, 24-, and 54-hour surface prognostic charts	2
200 aircraft reports	1		
750 airway reports	24	30-hour surface prognostic charts	4
800 land reports	4		
100 ship reports	4	Surface maps for North America, North Atlantic, and North Pacific Oceans	4

		Distribution	
Additional End Products	Number of Recipients		Types of Recipients
Daily weather map	3,800		Business, government, academia
Facsimile chart transmissions	160		Government (including 100 USAF and 50 USN stations) and private weather offices
Forecasts via teletype	300+		Government and private weather offices
Weather broadcasts via station NSS	Several hundred		Ships at sea (navy and merchant marine)
Weather maps	Several hundred		Newspapers nationwide
Winds aloft to 40,000 feet	Several hundred		Government and private weather offices
Radiosonde ascents (35 in USA)	Several hundred		Government and private weather offices

available personnel, and ensuring uniformity of storm warnings. They also directed that this new unit responsible for issuing storm warnings to all U.S. agencies west of 180° be commanded by the commanding officer of the Fleet Weather Central, Guam. Four days later, the Pacific command directed that the senior air force officer assigned (the first was AWS's Lt. Col. Robert M. Hoffman) be called "Director, JTWC," and be junior in rank to the commanding officer of the fleet weather central, who, at the time, was Comdr. Charles E. Tilden. Over the past quarter-century that command relationship has worked well, and warnings issued by the JTWC have helped save thousands of lives and billions of dollars in damage to military ships, aircraft, and installations.

THE KOREAN WAR

In dividing the spoils of World War II, Stalin made sure that the ancient Korean nation was broken into two parts at the 38th parallel. Then, on June 25, 1950, North Korea, with Russian backing, moved south to reunify the peninsula by force. The attack came in the midst of scattered but heavy rains at the onset of the summer monsoon, triggering what Joint Chiefs of Staff Chairman Omar Bradley later characterized as "the wrong war, in the wrong place, at the wrong time, with the wrong enemy."[11] The South Korean army (also known as the ROKs, for the Republic of Korea), a lightly armed security force supported by 500 U.S. military instructors, was in no position to stop the onslaught. The United Nations, at President Truman's urging, decided to intervene. But by August the only allied defenders left were cornered around the port of Pusan in southeastern Korea.

During this retreat the U.N. allies were heavily dependent on Japanese-based air power, primarily Fifth Air Force tactical units and the bomber command of FEAF. Beginning two days after the North Korean invasion, their attacks were directed toward interdicting lines of communication—bridges, rail yards, and supply dumps. Unfortunately, both tactical and strategic bombing depended on the weather. USAF all-weather squadrons found many periods when they could not operate because of low cloud ceilings and poor visibility in the mountains; further, certain key targets proved physically unsuitable for radar-guided bombing.[12] Visual pattern bombing likewise had problems, for suitable conditions (an undercast of not more than six-tenths cover) were all too rare during summer monsoon rains. Initially, Bomber Command used the World War II practice of determining the time to hit a designated target by relying on the weather forecast. But the forecasts so often proved to be inexact that it went to "now-forecasting," dispatching a weather aircraft ahead of the main strike force, with the senior officer aloft given authority to determine the method of attack, including whether it should be by radar, and to divert, if necessary, to alternate targets.

Britain and the United States brought to bear what sea power they had in the western Pacific against North Korean military facilities. For example, just eight days after the war's start, TF-77, including the carriers HMS *Triumph* and USS *Valley Forge*, launched air strikes against Pyongyang, North Korea's capital. Rear Adm. James H. Doyle's TF-90 (known as Amphibious Group One) also began to put raiding parties ashore to cut North Korean lines of coastal communication whenever his aerologist, Lt. Charles R. Barron, forecast favorable weather for such actions (i.e. dark, cloudy nights).[13]

When war came, neither the air force nor the navy had weather units in Korea. The navy had none in Japan, either. Fortunately, the AWS was strongly represented in Japan. Col. Tommy Moorman commanded the 2143rd Air Weather Wing, headquartered in the Meiji Building, which also contained FEAF headquarters, in downtown Tokyo. In the same building was one of Moorman's most important subordinate commands—the Tokyo Weather Central of the 20th Weather Squadron manned by approximately 100 AWS personnel plus Japanese.[14] The squadron, too, had a highly competent commander, Lt. Col. Oliver K. ("OK") Jones, who had been the VIII Fighter Command's staff weather officer in England at the height of World War II. Jones's assignment was to provide weather support to the Fifth Air Force and the U.S. Eighth Army, both based in Japan. Within forty-eight hours after the invasion Jones had one of his detachments airlifted to Korea with an advanced FEAF unit. He followed with an advanced Fifth Air Force command element and made certain that an AWS detachment was posted to each new airfield and fighter strip.

For the first year the Korean war was very fluid; opposing armies raced from one end of the peninsula to the other and halfway back again. The 20th Weather Squadron soon observed that "mobility has been one of the most important words associated with weather detachments during the Korean operations."[15] In the first four months of hostilities the eight field detachments in Korea moved approximately once every five days. Although both weather vans and air-transportable weather pods were available, the pods proved more useful because extremely rough roads kept the vans in repair shops. Sandbagged bunkers, pyramidal tents, and movable fabric-and-wood Jamesway huts became a way of life to these units, which were manned mostly by reserve weathermen who had been called to active duty and rushed to Korea without refresher courses in either meteorology or combat skills. By mid-November Moorman created a new weather squadron—the 30th, under Maj. Kenneth A. Linder—to handle Korean requirements.[16]

But the squadron was badly undermanned, with only 40 assigned officers of the 61 authorized, plus 131 enlisted men of the 273 authorized.

The Inchon Invasion   With the war little more than a week old, MacArthur, with a flare of genius, directed his staff to consider plans for an amphibious assault far behind the battle line. By early August, 1950, they had settled on the Inchon-Seoul area. On August 23, Lieutenant Barron, the amphibious force's aerologist, sat in on the key planning conference, which set the invasion during the maximum spring tides just three weeks later. Pertinent hydrographic and oceanographic data were generated both in Japan and at the Navy Hydrographic Office in Suitland.[17] Moorman's oceanographer, Capt. Robert L. Miller, prepared a study of the area, including tides, currents, sea conditions, water temperature and transparency, underwater contours, and bottom sediments.[18]

Because parsimonious Secretary of Defense Louis A. Johnson had declared that the navy would never mount another amphibious operation, the navy was able to line up only 230 ships for the invasion, a far cry from the 2,000 vessels deployed in the Okinawa invasion five years before. By early September, loading for Operation Chromite, hardly a well-kept secret, was under way at three major Japanese ports. On September 2 the Tokyo Weather Central advised that Typhoon Jane would soon strike near Kobe. Loading operations ceased, and Jane moved through the next morning with 110-mph winds and 40-foot waves, killing more than 100 persons and causing extensive damage. Soon after loading resumed, the central put out more bad news. Typhoon Kezia was threatening and might move into southern Japan about the time the fleet was to sail. Thus, keeping an up-to-date track on Kezia became an all-important task for another of Moorman's subordinate commands—the 514th Reconnaissance Squadron, Very Long Range, Weather, at Andersen AFB, Guam. During their key mission on September 8, a B-29 flying into Kezia lost an engine before locating the eye of the typhoon. Even so, the pilot, Capt. Charles R. Cloniger, feathered the propeller and finished the trip successfully on three engines.[19]

Doyle then moved up the sailing by a day, and sixty-six cargo vessels left Kobe on September 10–11 in heavy seas. MacArthur and his staff followed, aboard the USS *Mount Olympus*. Fortunately, Kezia recurved to the northeast past empty anchorages on the thirteenth, and all that remained of the storm over Inchon two days later, on D day, were high-overcast skies and a portent of light rain. This gamble was one of history's greatest strategic assaults: the North Koreans turned and raced northward to sanctuary far within their own borders.

Winter Onslaught   Through the late summer and early fall of 1950, United Nations participants built up military forces in South Korea. The

AWS was deeply involved in Project Fierce in which MATS was flying 7,000 troops per month from the continental United States to Korea.[20] To improve weather reporting at sea, the U.S. Coast Guard instituted two new weather ship locations—Sugar near the midpoint of the Tokyo-Shemya leg, and Victor near the midpoint of the Tokyo–Midway Island run—thereby creating five high-seas weather stations, one of which was operated by the Japanese. By November, 1950, the Eighth Army, now nine divisions strong, was moving aggressively northward, and on November 21 the U.S. Army's 17th Regimental Combat Team reached the Manchurian border. By then, MacArthur deemed it timely to announce that the war would be over by Christmas.

But he failed to anticipate two eventualities: a major counterattack by the North Koreans, heavily reinforced by Chinese Communist divisions, on November 25, followed by two weeks of aberrant and abominable winter weather. Although most American combat forces had cold-weather gear, the equipment was inadequate for outbreaks of polar air from Siberia, which dropped temperatures to $-25°$ F, with high winds and blowing snow. Although M-1 rifles and Browning machine guns were usable, the firing mechanisms of the carbines and Browning automatic rifles frequently froze solid. To overcome that, the troops used Wild Root cream oil or even warm urine.[21] Grenade pins stuck. Mortar base plates cracked. Rockets misfired because the propellant did not burn completely. Artillery pieces took longer to return to battery, slowing firing rates. Radio batteries froze, canceling communications. The valves and fuel pumps in the mechanized vehicles froze, requiring the engines to be run frequently, if not continuously. Repairs had to be postponed, for bare hands meant severe frostbite. Trenching tools could not penetrate the frozen earth. Rooter teeth welded to bulldozer blades broke off. Grenades and dynamite charges did little better, for such explosions merely broke the ground into chunks.

Humans fared no better. Soldiers rapidly lost weight and staying power. Socks froze to feet. When the socks came off, skin did, too. To listen for the enemy during the long winter nights, ears had to be exposed. Cases of frostbite and exposure shock skyrocketed. Once treated in warm-up tents with stimulants to overcome depressed respiration rates, the men began to suffer intestinal disorders from eating frozen food (strapping the rations against the body did not keep them thawed). One Marine Corps officer estimated that a rifleman lost 2 percent of his efficiency for every degree of temperature below zero, Fahrenheit.[22] When anyone was wounded, things got worse. Blood plasma, morphine, and water-soluble medicines froze, and the bottles broke. Because no one could work with bare hands, first-aid treatment was next to impossible. Many wounded were simply left untreated and numb with cold until they could be delivered to heated hospitals well behind the front lines.

Thus, despite heavy enemy pressure, the will to fight was frequently suppressed during late November and early December, 1950, by the over-riding instinct to stay alive. For some, the ordeal by weather proved too much. They simply lost their minds. In contrast, during the 1st Marine Division's retreat from entrapment by six Chinese divisions at the Chosin reservoir, most of its 7,000 temporary casualties from the bitter cold snapped back after a good night's sleep and some hot food.

Summertime fighting in Korea was also far from being a sinecure. Day-light broke at 5:00 A.M. and lingered for sixteen hours in a vegetation-sparse region where temperatures could reach 100° F and drinkable water was scarce. During the summer of 1950 the United States lost as many combat troops from heat exhaustion as from enemy gunfire.

Supporting the Fifth Air Force   In accordance with military doctrine, the prime use of United Nations airpower was to isolate the battlefield by interdicting the flow of enemy supplies and troops behind the front lines. Of the Fifth Air Force's total combat effort, some 70 percent was so used: the majority of AWS forecasting was for air strikes into vast areas totally devoid of weather information except that derived from pilot reports ("pireps") and aerial weather reconnaissance. If one overlaid maps so that the bound-aries of Korea and Florida roughly coincided, Seoul and Pusan would ap-proximate Tampa and Miami, respectively. Thus, forecasting for Korea would be like forecasting for all of Florida while receiving no data, except ship reports, north or west of Tampa short of the Canadian border (Russia continued transmitting weather observations in the clear). Even so, bomber commanders needed reliable forecasts of cloud cover in tenths (accurate within two-tenths) and of the thickness, bases, and tops of cloud decks between 10,000 and 17,000 feet.

Such requirements were far beyond the capability of AWS meteorolo-gists, so "now-forecasting" had to be used. On July 13, 1950, a WB-29 piloted by 1st Lt. Fred R. Spies, with FEAF's Bomber Command chief, Maj. Gen. Emmett ("Rosie") O'Donnell, on board, led the first B-29 strike from Japan against North Korean installations. Spies's plane was an aerial command post and a weather station, giving on-the-spot weather reports and directions to inbound bombers. All told, five such missions were flown with WB-29s, three with O'Donnell aboard.

In his memoirs, LeMay tells of an O'Donnell-led B-29 mission to Nak-tong on September 15, the day of the Inchon landing. "Everyone was cautioned," wrote LeMay, "against attacking that primary target unless the visibility was just about perfect. Weather didn't promise much: looked like it might be seven- or even nine-tenths cloud, and they'd have to go on to their secondary, and leave the fatal rectangle safely unbombed. Well, our weather information was off just about a hundred and eighty degrees. By the time the 29s had left their Japanese bases and flown across the sea, and were coming up from those southern islands where they had formed, the clouds all broke away. The bombers went in there with perfect visibility."[23]

Just the same, Moorman wrote O'Donnell on October 3, 1950, that AWS forecasts were accurate within operationally acceptable limits 75 percent of the time, or better than for World War II strategic bombing in Europe. O'Donnell and his field commanders remained unhappy. During the same month Colonel Moorman advised the AWS's new commander, West Point classmate Brigadier General Senter, that air force and army commanders in Korea and Japan "have all expressed varying degrees of dissatisfaction with the forecasts" and "that we can't forecast well enough to satisfy their requirements, and they are correct to a degree." In January, 1951, Lieutenant General Kuter, the MATS commander and Senter's immediate boss, wrote him about the "inaccuracy" and "unreliability" of AWS forecasts for Korea. After touring the battlefront, Senter advised Kuter that "the acid test of any military organization is how well it performs under actual combat conditions" and that certainly AWS "did not provide forecasts of the accuracy required."[24]

Wing commander Moorman could explain why his two local weather squadrons (the 20th and the 30th), backed up by two weather reconnaissance squadrons (the 512th in Japan and the 514th in Guam), could not keep customers happy. Foremost, as the 30th Weather Squadron reported, was that "the chronic disease of the Air Weather Service forecasts in Korea is 'data deficiency.'"[25] Not only was there a lack of observation points but there also was the unsolved problem of inadequate weather communications. Neither Moorman nor his squadron commander held command or control of the weather circuits, which were handled with relatively low priority by personnel of the Airways and Air Communications Service (AACS).

Most of Moorman's forecasters lacked technical depth. As of November, 1950, of 157 weather officers in the wing (excluding those at headquarters and in the reconnaissance squadrons), only 27 had university-level training in meteorology and of those, only 15 held college degrees. Compounding the problem of inexperience was the policy within the theater regarding length of tours in Korea (initially two months, then six months, and finally twelve months, as of September, 1951). In addition, because of the fluid battle situation, tactical staff weather officers at each Fifth Air Force airfield daily developed their own predawn weather forecast in conjunction with the local weather unit, then checked them by telephone with the Seoul weather central before briefing combat group commanders and aircrews. That protective mechanism could not always be used, so three different forecasts were sometimes supplied to customer units for the same area and time.[26]

To overcome such deficiencies, great emphasis was placed on mounting weather reconnaissance flights over or adjacent to enemy territory, either as a lead element of a major strike or as part of regularly scheduled missions. Fortunately, the 512th, with its twelve new WB-29 weather reconnaissance aircraft, had been declared operational on June 10, 1950. Thus, it was able to mount its first combat mission within twenty-four hours after hostilities commenced.[27] During their first ninety days of combat, WB-29 crews ran into flak over North Korea about every third mission, and their dropsondes quickly proved vulnerable to signal jamming. By early July the squadron had begun to fly at least one of two fixed tracks daily, called Buzzard, after the squadron's radio call sign. By fall, Buzzard King was being flown west to east across North Korea; this daily flight typically approached the western coast at sunset in order to traverse the peninsula in darkness.

Normally, there was no fighter escort; in fact, AWS doctrine called for aerial weather reconnaissance to avoid "areas where active enemy aerial resistance may be encountered."[28] When Senter visited the squadron in early 1952, its commander, Col. Robert C. David, reminded the AWS chief that "the regularity of these flights in time and space make the aircraft ready targets for the enemy whenever they prefer the destruction of the aircraft to the aircraft's weather reports." Apparently the North Korean and Chinese military liked these reliable reports, transmitted in the clear, for enemy fighters never bothered the WB-29s on their flights north of the 38th Parallel, which continued until June, 1952.

To supplement the wider-ranging weather flights of the WB-29s, Moorman persuaded the Fifth Air Force to attach to his wing a unit of six RB-26Cs (call sign "Snooper," later redesignated WB-26Cs) to fly tactical weather missions over the Yellow Sea and North Korea. Operating out of Taegu as the 6166th Tactical Weather Reconnaissance Flight, the unit normally ran three Snoopers a day under guidance from the Fifth Air Force staff weather officer. In Moorman's eyes these flights were so important that he ensured that each weatherman of the nine flight crews, plus the flight commander (Maj. Lawrence T. Keohane) and his deputy (Maj. Douglas S. Canning) were skilled weather forecasters. As more and more enemy jet fighters entered battle, the usefulness of the propeller-driven WB-26Cs over northern Korean diminished. By the spring of 1953 the flight's predominant use was on "Snowflake" missions flown along the politically restricted bombing line as an aid to close air-support fighter strikes.

A third important method for improving combat weather forecasts was for the forecaster to fly combat strikes. Many of the handpicked staff weather officers at air combat units were also eager fighter pilots. The Korean war's first AWS fatality was 1st Lt. David H. Grisham, who was making his forty-sixth F-51 strike from Japan on September 3, 1950. During the following seventeen months four other AWS officers and one AWS enlisted man were killed in aerial action. The AWS had no shortage of men willing to put their lives on the line to provide the best forecasts possible.[29]

As the war progressed, Lt. Col. Carl E. Wagner and staff at the 30th Weather Squadron spotted a disturbing phenomenon—the rank and the experience of newly assigned forecasters were steadily declining. Tactical staff weather officers normally held the grade of major, but in December, 1952, Wagner's ten replacements for such slots were three majors, four captains, and three first lieutenants. To overcome that deficiency, Wagner relieved tactical staff weather officers of control of local weather detachments and made them dependent upon the more experienced forecasters pooled at the squadron's Seoul weather central adjacent to the Joint Operations Center and Tactical Air Control Center (JOC-TACC). That practice was particularly favored by two members at the central, Capt. Hyko Gayikian and Maj. Ralph J. Steele. Eventually, both commanded other AWS weather centrals in the mid-1970s and were ranking colonels at AWS headquarters, where they pushed hard for a single AWS forecast production system controlled by AWS's Air Force Global Weather Central.[30]

Supporting the Eighth Army   Before the war was a month old, Jones began to contact army representatives at all command levels to ascertain the kind of weather support needed. They were extremely vague, generally like Sheridan, who was willing to take the weather as it came. The Eighth Army headquarters was just as blasé, indicating that almost any general forecast would be adequate. After all, its top officials listened to the daily Fifth Air Force briefings provided to the JOC-TACC, and the army commander— first, Lt. Gen. Walton H. ("Bulldog") Walker, then Lt. Gen. Matthew B. Ridgway—could ask for and receive twenty-four-hour and forty-eight-hour weather forecasts whenever the situation warranted.

To extend his weather observational network, Jones started placing two-man observing teams with frontline artillery units as early as August, 1950. Because they had no communications support, they accomplished little. Yet Maj. Kenneth A. Linder, as Jones's replacement in November for the newly activated 30th Weather Squadron, saw merit in the idea. By placing two-man observing teams at each corps headquarters, he created a rudimentary Eighth Army weather support program. Although Linder's scheme required approximately a dozen men, the forward teams more than paid their way. Their observations not only were useful to various corps elements but were also helpful to the Seoul weather central and to staff weather officers at supporting tactical air units.

Even after the winter debacle of 1950–51, Eighth Army had no big complaints about the lack of detailed weather support. However, at the Pentagon, the Department of the Army thought the situation needed looking into and in December, 1951, dispatched a winter environment team headed by the army's famous cold-weather expert, Dr. Paul A. Siple. After spending three months in Korea, Siple released a report the following May.

It made interesting reading. According to Siple, each echelon within the Eighth Army's chain of command believed it needed weather support, but the next echelon below did not. Thus, army headquarters did not see why corps level needed it, the corps level believed the division level did not need it, and so on. In addition, the closer a corps was to Seoul (site of the in-country weather central), the greater the satisfaction with the forecasting service.[31] Thus, I Corps, near Seoul, had few complaints. On the other hand, X Corps (First Marine Division and the army's 3rd and 7th Infantry Division), defending Korea's eastern coastal region, did not even post Seoul's daily weather forecast. Instead, the corps commander relied on prognoses developed by the weather sergeants of its own 1st Marine Air Wing, believing those predictions to be more accurate.

The Siple report also emphasized that commanders even at the lowest echelon could use tailor-made forecasts as to when valley fog would set in or lift, how much snow might fall, and the degree of cloud cover to be expected. Obviously, the Seoul weather central could not provide such pinpoint forecasting unless additional frontline weather data were available. Capt. Norman Sissenwine, an AWS World War II meteorologist who became a research climatologist for the Office of the Quartermaster General before his Korean War call-up, was already working on this problem. Largely on his own initiative, he had persuaded the Eighth Army's new commander, Lt. Gen. James A. Van Fleet, to establish weather observation capabilities near each regimental command post.

Siple's team liked the idea and recommended that the army provide its own manpower for this purpose. At the same time, Linder's successor, twice removed, at the 30th Weather Squadron, Lieutenant Colonel Wagner, had also concluded as early as April 8, 1952, that he could justify an expanded weather service for the Eighth Army. He asked for a modestly expanded Seoul weather central, placement of staff weather officers both at army and at corps headquarters, and four frontline Signal Corps weather observer teams (the army took a dim view of the use of non-combat-trained air force weathermen forward of corps headquarters).

Wagner did not get his additional resources, but he assigned Maj. Sidney A. Bird, one of his forecasters, as his liaison officer to Headquarters, Eighth Army. Bird had commanded a company of the 79th Infantry ("Cross of Lorraine") Division in 1942–43 before becoming an air force pilot and thus understood well the army's ponderous way of trying out new concepts. He worked well with his army counterpart, 1st Lt. B. J. Gudenkauf, of the Signal Corps. By late summer, 1952, the pair had sold a ninety-day test scheme by which the Signal Corps would provide forward weather observers, plus communications to transmit their data to AWS staff weather officers at the corps level. At long last, on October 5, 1952, the Eighth

Army provided the AWS command with a formal statement of weather support requirements.[32]

Late the following month, six Signal Corps lieutenants and thirty-four enlisted men, fresh out of a six-week crash training course in weather observation at Fort Monmouth, showed up to carry out the army's part of the Bird-Gudenkauf experiment. On the air force side, Wagner scraped up forecaster teams (an officer meteorologist, an enlisted weather technician, and two senior enlisted observers) for the four corps headquarters and kicked off the trial on December 14. But the corps forecaster teams contended with extremely difficult communications problems, for the wireless facsimile of the Seoul weather central was more often down than up. Piggybacking on army administrative teletype and telephone channels was just as difficult, for neither method permitted the transmission of more than nominal amounts of weather information.

The major problem with the ninety-day experiment was whether it should continue. Eighth Army officials decided that it should—but with a new twist. The Signal Corps contingent would return home as soon as its ninety-day temporary duty was up, and 30th Weather Squadron troops would then man frontline observing posts and continue to supply forecast teams at the corps level. This shift took place during late April, 1953; until the war's end the weather squadron provided a steadily improving service to army units as each better understood the other's problems. Meanwhile, the weather enthusiasts within the Signal Corps empire who had protested the meteorological withdrawal of the corps continued to agitate for an army weather service. That was not to be. In January, 1954, the Department of the Army formally announced that it would continue to rely on AWS for its operational weather support.

Supporting the Seventh Fleet   When war in Korea broke out, the nation's attention had been directed toward the "Russian Bear" in Europe, so the U.S. Seventh Fleet in the far Pacific was at minimal strength. A nonaviator, Vice Adm. Arthur D. Struble, flew his three-star flag from the cruiser USS *Rochester*; the remainder of his command consisted of the carrier USS *Valley Forge*, another cruiser (USS *Toledo*), and eight destroyers. Struble's aerological staff was just as bareboned, consisting of one chief aerographer's mate (Joseph Zaffino, three months out of advanced forecaster's school at Lakehurst NAS) and one aerographer's mate.[33]

The fleet commander liked to keep the North Koreans guessing, so he kept his force moving constantly off both sides of Korea, operating first in the Sea of Japan, then in the Yellow Sea. Unfortunately for Zaffino, receipt of radioed weather information (observations, forecasts, and canned maps) for the west central Pacific was iffy aboard the *Rochester*. The Guam and Sangley

Point (Philippine Islands) fleet weather broadcasts did not cover his operating area. Broadcasts by the air force Tokyo Weather Central did cover the area but could not be received in certain operating areas and in certain weather. So Zaffino copied whatever was available and briefed the admiral from a skimpy weather chart.

Nevertheless, by the end of three months, Struble respected his chief's weather judgment. With the war exactly a month old, on the afternoon of July 21, Zaffino offered a daring opportunity. A typhoon was moving north-northwestward just to the south of Japan's southern islands as Struble's task force steamed through the southern Sea of Japan. If the admiral wished, his ships could avoid harm by running northeast past Honshu. But if he wanted to be daring, his task force could make a fast night run into the Yellow Sea just ahead of the storm, then make daylight launches from the lee of the large island, Saishu To. The North Koreans would then be caught out in the open as they raced to annihilate the rapidly shrinking Pusan perimeter of the United Nations command. Of course, if Zaffino and Struble were wrong, the only U.S. carrier operating against the peninsula might well suffer weather damage. Struble was risking criticism like that directed at Halsey. But Struble gambled. The fleet steamed all night through the Tsushima Straits as winds and seas built up. Zaffino's forecast held. The air strikes went off on schedule, catching the North Koreans totally off guard. As Struble commented later in a commendatory letter to Zaffino, the attacks knocked out a thirty-car munitions train and two important bridges, as well as other important targets.[34]

Although the *Valley Forge* carried a lieutenant commander as its aerologist (as did her sister carrier, *Philippine Sea*), when she showed up later, Struble preferred to select attack areas for the carriers by using weather forecasts generated aboard his own flagship. With no other forecaster on board, Zaffino was under heavy stress; he had no one with whom he could confer before briefing the admiral. But Struble was quite satisfied. In fact, Zaffino's relief, Comdr. Floyd T. Thompson, as Seventh Fleet aerological officer, did not come aboard Struble's new flagship, the battleship *Missouri*, until a week after the Inchon invasion. Thus, it is not surprising that Secretary of the Navy Dan A. Kimball found it fitting, when he awarded the Bronze Star to Zaffino, to use the phrase "ceaseless efforts" in citing the chief's service as fleet aerological officer until September 21, 1950.[35]

As the war dragged on, plenty of bad weather continued—the typhoons of summer and autumn, arctic air outbreaks during winter, and a wildly active polar front in springtime. Even so, the navy and the marines carried out a wide spectrum of weather-sensitive operations: carrier strikes against land targets, amphibious landings and evacuations, close air support of ground troops, shore bombardment, mine sweeping, and maritime transport of troops and supplies.

In the meantime, the Naval Weather Service became far more capable. Its manpower grew by 60 percent, to a peak at 386 officers and 2,275 enlisted men and women just before hostilities ended. Adequately staffing the additional carriers being sent to Korea, including the *Leyte, Princeton, Bandoeng Strait, Sicily*, and *Bataan*, became less of a problem. Similarly, rotating qualified aerological staff to support the flag officers using the battleships *Wisconsin, New Jersey,* and *Iowa*, as well as the *Missouri*, was far easier to arrange.

MORE NUCLEAR TESTING

Throughout the 1950s the United States and the Soviet Union engaged in a nuclear arms race that required frequent field tests of new atomic devices. Because such tests typically were atmospheric, the pattern and the rate of the ensuing fallout were an overriding concern. When such tests were held at the Nevada Test Site, the Atomic Energy Commission (AEC) relied on Lester Machta of the Weather Bureau for upper wind and fallout forecasts.[36] If the tests were run by the Defense Atomic Support Agency (DASA) in the Pacific Proving Grounds (PPG) far to the west of Hawaii, a joint military task force conducted the field operations, as it had in the Bikini tests.

Approximately thirty of DASA's tests included huge shots in which the explosion cloud and associated fallout penetrated far into the tropical stratosphere, a poorly known region of the earth's gaseous envelope. Two of the best research teams studying that phenomenon were sponsored by the air force. At the AFCRC, Dr. E. A. Martell was the in-house specialist; the RAND Corporation in Santa Monica, California, used a trio—Dr. Stanley M. Greenfield, Dr. Robert R. Rapp, and Dr. William W. Kellogg. The elaborate meteorological service required by each test series during the decade following 1948 was directed by the staff weather officer (either an AWS colonel or a navy captain) assigned to the commander, Joint Task Force Seven. To close the meteorological loop, the staff weather officer's deputy came from the sister service.[37] Under them came the weather central element, normally based at Eniwetok Atoll.

The Eniwetok central not only served as the operation's weather analysis facility but also directed the data collection from island weather stations, specially designated ships, AWS weather reconnaissance aircraft, and pilot weather reports from P2V patrol and search aircraft. Both ship and island weather observers did their best to measure the wind field to 100,000 feet or higher. In the atolls manned by the AWS's 6th Weather Squadron (Mobile), the 800-gram rawinsonde balloons achieved an average termination height of 93,000 feet during Operation Hardtack (April–August 1958). The two destroyer divisions did equally well, for their gunfire control systems could readily track radar targets to altitudes of 100,000 feet or higher.[38]

Nuclear events carried their own special brand of excitement. In March, 1954, the Bravo shot at Bikini Atoll was supposed to go at seven megatons but achieved twice that. The associated cloud rose to more than 100,000 feet. It, and an unforecast wind shift, caused radioactive debris to fall on nearby islands (Rongerik, Alinginae, Utirik, and Rongelap) inhabited both by Polynesian natives and by military weathermen. A 28-man AWS rawin-sonde team at Rongerik quickly reported that its radiometers had gone completely off the graph paper. The range safety officer first blamed it on instrument malfunction. Then reality set in, and a quick evacuation was ordered.

Most of the 264 people involved ended up at Tripler Army Hospital in Honolulu; they suffered no permanent damage from the exposure, although radiation doses had ranged from 14 roentgens at Utirik to 175 roentgens at Rongelap. However, if the wind had shifted a little to the south, all would have received lethal doses (i.e., more than 1,000 roentgens) from the most dangerous part (about 40 by 220 miles) of the fallout stripe. Unfortunately, the misnamed Japanese fishing vessel *Fortunate Dragon* had also gone un-detected as it penetrated the announced safety zone. The ship received only a dusting but failed to wash off quickly the "white snow" that accumulated. By the time the vessel reached Japan, crew members had each absorbed about 200 roentgens. One man soon died, although the cause of death remained uncertain. The ensuing international uproar demanded cessation of nuclear testing, particularly in the Pacific. But the PPG tests continued, although with increasingly stricter controls.[39]

What this meant to the meteorological staff was vividly described by Lt. Col. Alexander R. Gordon, Jr., while serving as the weather central's staff oceanographer for the Redwing shot series. After Event Cherokee on May 21, 1956, when a B-52 dropped America's first true hydrogen bomb on Bikini Atoll, Gordon wrote from 175 miles away: "Just then the sky lighted with a yellowish-white glow; in fact, the whole world seemed lighted as if the sun had risen instantaneously. Slowly the light began to fade, and the sky in the east looked like that associated with a setting sun. . . . From here on the 'mushroom' harvest should proceed without too much hitch in schedule. Cherokee had such stringent weather requirements that for a time, many of us thought we never would get the right combination of cloud, wind and visibility."[40]

Meanwhile, the AWS continued to fly high-priority B-29 radioactive-debris sampling missions to monitor Russian nuclear tests. Starting in 1953, Russian H-bombs were detonated over Novaya Zemlya at about 73° north latitude, or two degrees farther north than Point Barrow. The Ptar-migan weather run to the North Pole was ideal for operating the "bug catchers," particularly when supplemented by other regular AWS re-connaissance runs between Alaska and Japan and between England and Spitsbergen. Such runs could be spiced with excitement; for example, on March 15, 1953, a Russian MiG-15 began firing at an AWS WB-29 off the coast of Kamchatka. Fortunately, when the WB-29's gunners fired back, the MiG pilot broke off the engagement. This bug-catching mission took on even greater stature during 1961 when the Pentagon designated AWS as the single manager of aerial sampling for the Department of Defense. This gave AWS control over secret high-altitude B-57 and balloon sampling flights—the latter involving the use of CH-21 helicopters for intermittent package recovery.

ENDS OF THE EARTH

In 1937 the Russian expedition led by Ivan Papanin landed a four-engined aircraft equipped with skis near the North Pole. On the drifting pack ice he established a scientific station (North Pole-1) to be retrieved by an icebreaker just before breakup off northeastern Greenland nine months later. Although Papanin published a book about the daring feat, few Americans knew of it, and even fewer considered duplicating the effort.[41] Then, in the midst of a routine polar mission by the 72nd Photo Reconnaissance Squadron on August 14, 1946, the aircraft's navigator noticed, when less than 300 miles north of Point Barrow, that his radar screen showed an enormous, coherent mass of sea ice more than 200 square miles in area. Because tabular icebergs of any size were foreign to the Arctic Ocean, the unique discovery was labeled Radar Target X (later named T-1) and classi-fied secret. During the next three years aircrews of the 375th Reconnais-sance Squadron (VLR) Weather—subsequently relabeled the 58th Strategic Reconnaissance Squadron (Medium) Weather—looked for similar ice masses as they flew the Ptarmigan track. None were found, and after being tracked northward for 1,500 miles, T-1 disappeared north of Greenland.[42]

Lt. Col. Joseph O. Fletcher, who took command of the squadron in early 1950, iterated the need to find more "ice islands." On July 20, 1950, one of his RB-29 crews spotted a new ice island 75 miles away. The new ice mass, located within 200 miles of the North Pole and with a corrugated surface and pronounced drainage pattern, was called T-2. Just nine days later, a third ice island (T-3) showed on an RB-29 radar 300 miles north of Siberia's Wrangel Island. The corrugated T-3, kidney-shaped and the smallest of the trio, measured approximately 4.5 by 9 nautical miles. Fletcher and his ice reconnaissance officer, Maj. Lawrence S. Koenig, had many questions about the ice islands. They proved to be slowly drifting (at about a mile a day) in a clockwise whorl between North America and the North Pole. How old were they? Where had they formed? How thick were they? But most important, could they support semipermanent airstrips, base camps, and forward outposts?

In January, 1951, Fletcher's boss, Col. Marcellus Duffy (who commanded the parent 2107th Air Weather Group at Elmendorf AFB) approached the commander of the Alaskan Air Command (AAC), Brig. Gen. William D. Old, about the possibility of putting a weather station on T-3 to determine whether the ice island could support aircraft operations. Old finally consented, but weather forced postponement throughout 1951. Project Icicle, commanded by Fletcher, commenced on March 19, 1952.[43] When the 10th Search and Rescue Squadron's C-47, piloted by Capt. Lewis Erhart and Old, touched down on T-3's rugged surface, the temperature was −49° F. Old remarked to Fletcher as they surveyed the bleak scene, "I don't see how any man can live on this thing. We're going to take off now—if we can!"

But Fletcher stubbornly stayed behind to make camp with Capt. Marion F. Brinegar and Dr. Kaare Rodahl, a Norwegian-born polar survival expert. Once the worst ice ridges had been smoothed down to make a rudimentary runway, Dr. Albert P. Crary and Capt. Paul L. Green were flown in to be the project's chief scientist and radio communicator, respectively. Before the camp facilities were complete, a navy P2V from the Barrow-based Skijump oceanographic expedition arrived to take pictures. An engine failed during takeoff, so the navy had to stay until a new engine could be flown in. Thus, before two weeks were out, the population on T-3 (later called Fletcher's Ice Island) numbered sixteen—eleven navy and five air force. But things straightened out. On May 3, 1952, a C-47 from T-3 landed at the North Pole (a technical first), where Crary made gravity and oceanic depth measurements. From there, the aircraft proceeded to Thule, Greenland, after making a stop at Rear Adm. Robert E. Peary's base camp of 1906 to check ice shelf conditions on the extreme northern tip of Ellesmere Island.[44]

For the next decade polar scientists and the AAC had an on-and-off flirtation with T-3, occupying it when its location was suitable and abandoning it when it was out of position. Ice-landing and base-establishment techniques improved steadily, and hundreds of temporary observation points came to be occupied throughout the polar basin.[45] This led directly to elaborate air-sea interaction studies of the Arctic Ocean, particularly those associated with stability of the ice cover and day-to-day behavior of the polar pack ice.

While air force meteorologists and geophysicists established drifting Arctic ice stations, former wartime meteorologists of the Navy Hydrographic Office developed ice reconnaissance and forecasting techniques for Arctic coastal waters. Suddenly the low-key effort blossomed. In early 1952 the Department of Defense decided to build a complete SAC B-29 base at Thule, just 780 nautical miles from the North Pole, during the coming summer. But because the powers-that-be would not allocate dedicated ice reconnaissance aircraft to the project, thousands of highly paid construction workers became needlessly locked in the pack ice for several weeks. As a result, the Hydrographic Office's ice team had specially assigned aircraft for the 1953 summer ice season. Steps were then made to modify the old Arctic dictum "ice is where you find it!" In the following summer specially trained aerographer's mates began to fill in for the civilian ice observers who had been flying hundreds of dangerous flight hours without receiving hazardous duty pay.[46]

The fledgling ice service faced its greatest challenge in 1955. The threat that Soviet bombers would penetrate North America from the north required the building of a chain of fifty radar stations (Distant Early Warning or DEW Line) across the top of the continent in just two summer seasons. An armada of 126 ships (52 naval and 74 cargo) were to be deployed across northern Alaska and Canada between June and October. Getting them north and safely home again during 1955 took 4,400 aerial ice reconnaissance hours, plus nearly 1,000 ice forecasts, half of which were generated in the field and half at the experimental oceanographic forecast central in Suitland. Unfortunately, during mid-August the polar pack closed in off northeastern Alaska. Authorities had visions of forty badly needed vessels, complete with crews and stevedores, frozen in throughout the winter all along the Northwest Passage. Finally, on Labor Day weekend, the Suitland forecasters spotted a pending change in storm tracks out of Siberia and rushed to advise Vice Adm. Francis Denebrink, commander of the Military Sea Transport Service, that his ships could begin their westward escape about September 10. They did so, and Denebrink later advised author Bates, who had been working closely with him, that "this was the best damned storm I ever did see!"[47]

Meanwhile, the navy was told to mount another Antarctic adventure. World politicians had been sold on the need to have an eighteen-month International Geophysical Year in 1957 and 1958. A dozen countries announced they would establish one or more bases on the earth's last undivided continent. Obviously, the United States should not only have coastal bases but also one at the more glamorous South Pole. With a century-old tradition of going south, the navy became the lead service to provide transportation (ship, air, and tracked land vehicles), site construction, and base operation, thereby freeing scientists for full-time field work.

Rear Adm. George J. Dufek, the task force commander, vividly described in his *Operation Deepfreeze* how the navy and the air force achieved a number of technical firsts in that harsh environment. The top two were setting up and operating the permanent South Pole base on the continent's high central plateau and establishing regular flight service between Christchurch, New Zealand (South Africa was also occasionally used), and the large American base at McMurdo Sound. Each Antarctic summer, Fleet Weather Central, McMurdo, came into existence to provide the world's most remote continent with a comprehensive weather forecasting service. Dufek thought highly of his staff aerologist, Lt. Comdr. John A. Mirabito: "His long-range weather predictions were always right, and the safety of the flights would depend upon him."[48]

ADMINISTRATIVE AND TECHNICAL INNOVATIONS

During the 1950s the air and naval weather services each had four different commanders, all sensible men who were well versed in meteorological matters. Of these eight, one in each uniform made positive organizational changes during his command tour. In the AWS, Maj. Gen. Oscar Senter pushed through a scheme in 1952 to tie weather groups and squadrons directly to major air force functions, such as TAC and SAC, rather than to geographic regions.[49] Then a movement formed in the Pentagon to relocate as many headquarters and organizations as possible out of the Washington area. Thus, when Headquarters MATS moved to Scott AFB in the hinterlands of southern Illinois in June, 1958, Headquarters AWS was forced to move with its parent command—dragging its heels all the way, for it was an extremely unpopular move within AWS. Nevertheless, Scott remained its home for the next quarter-century.

In the case of the Naval Weather Service, Capt. Paul Drouilhet worked from 1956 to 1958 to change his service's orientation from serving the fleet air arm to serving the entire navy. By mid-1957 he had reduced the number of fleet weather centrals from fourteen to five, putting the personnel "in a better position than ever before to handle multiple weather tasks and assignments." Among such new tasks were optimal track ship routing, antisubmarine warfare environmental prediction (the Asweps system), radar propagation pattern determination, and ice prediction. Each of the continuing centrals was directly responsible to a major fleet commander, although Drouilhet retained technical control.[50] In 1958 he achieved a major goal—the weather command function was upgraded to divisional status (Op-58 from Op-533) within the Office of the Deputy Chief of Naval Operations for Air (Op-05).

The dependence on weather centrals for most weather charts and forecasts meant that such centrals had to be able to transmit via dedicated communication circuits, the faster the better. As of the late 1940s, radio and teletype (RATT) circuits transmitted only 60 words per minute. By 1966 technology permitted digital circuits to transmit 4,000 words per minute between dedicated computers. Weather chart transmission by facsimile (both land line and radio) also greatly improved by the mid-1950s. Stateside, AWS detachments regularly received fifty charts per day; the charts prepared at the Haneda, Hickam, and Rhein-Main centrals routinely arrived by radio-facsimile at the weather analysis division of Headquarters

AWS. Communication circuits were so reliable that AWS, from its Severe Weather Warning Center at Kansas City, began to provide terminal forecasting for five air bases on November 1, 1957. The concept grew, and fifteen months later, thirty-five bases were being served. However, forecasting skills atrophied at the operational bases, and eventually a new AWS commander, Brig. Gen. Roy W. Nelson, laid the regimented concept to rest after he took over in 1963. But the shift was temporary, as it turned out, for like the Phoenix, the system rose again in 1971, only to be snuffed out again a decade later.

Once the hostilities in Korea were over, Senter, as well as his successor in 1954, Brigadier General Moorman, stressed the need to update policy directives. In December, 1956, this initiative resulted in the publication of Air Force Manual 105-6, *Weather Service for Military Agencies*—the first formal treatise on AWS doctrine. In another first, AWS published a regulation in October, 1957, outlining procedures for supporting the army. A year later the air staff ruled that the air force had the responsibility for acquiring, installing, and maintaining weather equipment on army bases, although the army could continue to furnish the associated communications. Then, on July 8, 1959, the AWS activated the 7th Weather Squadron in Heidelberg, Germany, and the 16th Weather Squadron at Fort Monroe, Virginia—the first two weather squadrons ever formed for the exclusive support of the modern-day army. Although the air staff approved their formation, it would not provide the personnel. Instead, the spaces were taken from existing AWS authorizations at a time when the air force requirements for meteorological services were also growing.

In the meantime, the Signal Corps, as the prime agent for any meteorological research and development, pursued three types of investigations—macro-, meso-, and micrometeorology (theater-wide, division-to-field-army size, and less than ten miles across, respectively). The bulk of that effort was still centered at the Meteorological Division of Fort Monmouth's Signal Research and Development Laboratory, which also taught enlisted men how to man twenty-six upper-air observing teams primarily used by the field artillery. The research efforts were varied, including cloud seeding; upper-air measurements, using rocketsondes launched by the tiny Loki and the much larger Aerobee boosters; weather radar; and even weather satellites. Then, in 1957 the U.S. Army Signal Corps Meteorological Company was formed at Fort Huachuca, Arizona. As the army's only such unit, its nine teams were widely scattered, one as far away as Greenland, in order to provide requisite meteorological support.[51] In addition, other army components, including Corps of Engineers, Quartermaster Corps, and Chemical Warfare Service, added civilian meteorologists to their staffs as necessary.

THOR'S CHARIOTS: WEATHER RECONNAISSANCE

During the 1950s the available aeronautical power plants suddenly ranged from reciprocating engines and turboprops to jets and interconti-nental rockets. As a result, aviators and meteorologists specializing in weather reconnaissance contended with an unusually wide mix of airframes (see Table 4). By 1954–56, SAC strategic reconnaissance units, equipped with RB-36s, RB-47Ks, and RB-50s, were flying weather missions, as were TAC units using WT-33s and WB-66Ds. Meteorological sensors mounted on such aircraft varied widely but could include AN/AMQ-7 temperature-humidity measuring sets, radar altimeters, psychrometers, and dropsonde chambers and receivers. In 1950 AWS used almost exclu-sively WB-29s, but it had visions of obtaining a modern aircraft off the assembly lines. It was unhappy when the Air Staff elected to give it another aircraft declared surplus to the needs of strategic bombing. Although the WB-50D was better powered and thus had more range and altitude, it was fast approaching obsolescence.

Less than a year after the prototype WB-50D was finally delivered, AWS had its first crash with one in August 31, 1956. By January 17, 1957, there were three other accidents with the trouble-prone WB-50D program. More than thirty crew members lost their lives in the four mishaps, the worst rash of accidents in AWS history. Moorman anxiously awaited reports from the accident investigation boards, only to learn they had uncovered no special trends. Between 1956 and 1960, thirteen accidents occurred with this new class of Boeing aircraft. All told, sixty-six crewmen, including ten majors, lost their lives aboard this widow maker before the last WB-50D went to the storage yard in Arizona in 1966.

The use of long-range weather reconnaissance missions as an intelligence cover was underscored on May 1, 1960, when a U-2 piloted by Francis Gary Powers was shot down over Russia. The United States first claimed that the aircraft had drifted off course while on a "weather reconnaissance" or a "weather research" mission with AWS and National Aeronautics and Space Administration (NASA) meteorological sensors aboard. What few AWS people knew was that, ostensibly, Powers's U-2 belonged to Weather Recon-naissance Squadron Provisional No. 2, one of three such squadrons orga-nized and attached to Headquarters AWS during 1956 to "obtain high-level meteorological data in conjunction with" NASA.[52]

The navy's standard weather reconnaissance aircraft between 1945 and 1953 was the four-engine PB-4Y. Like the WB-29s, which also did nuclear sampling, the weather Privateers had to perform other duties to justify their existence. Depending upon the time and place, many squadron designa-tions came and went within the navy's East-Coast hurricane-hunting mis-sion.[53] In 1952 Airborne Early Warning Squadron 4 (VW-4) started flying

Table 4. Types and Number of Reconnaissance Aircraft Assigned to the Air Weather Service (1943–1975)

	43	44	45	46	47	48	49	50	51	52	53	54	55	56	57	58	59	60	61	62	63	64	65	66	67	68	69	70	71	72	73	74	75
B-25	6	15	15	4	2																												
B-24		16	22																														
B-17			6	22	18	12	10	4	4	3	3	2	2	2																			
WB-29					25	39	67	52	60	59	46	67	80	71	39	2																	
WB-50												16	59	66	66	69	46	43	43	14	12	9											
WB-47																				33	33	32	32	25	24	24							
WC-130																					5	5	11	9	12	14	14	23	22	28	27	26	23
WB-57																				28	38	32	19	26	29	18	22	26	25	25	14	13	
WC-135																										8	10	10	10	10	8	8	7

SOURCES: Courtesy of the Air Weather Service.

two-engine P-2V Neptune aircraft with a crew of nine, including an aerologist.

But the big change-over occurred during the 1955 hurricane season, when the WC-121N Super Constellations (Super Connies, as the crews dubbed them) were phased in. A commercial aircraft redesigned to provide airborne early warning, the WC-121Ns carried a crew of twenty-nine in three teams: flight, weather, and radar. Mounted in a special hump atop the fuselage, the search radar's antenna would sweep, at altitude, an area greater than 200,000 square miles. Along with the WB-29s and WB-50s of the air force, the Super Connies of VW-4 were permitted to perform low-level penetrations of fully developed storms that had an eye diameter of at least 15 miles.[54] The "Hurricane Hunters" would make their entry at a radar altitude of only 500 feet, and, upon reaching the storm's eye, climb to the 700-mb level. They could then relay to the fleet weather central at the Miami Hurricane Center the exact locations of the "wind eye" and the "pressure eye."[55]

In 1956, following congressional prodding, the Weather Bureau set up a full-fledged national hurricane research project in collaboration with AWS, ONR, and the Army Corps of Engineers. Key to the operation was simultaneous aircraft penetration of selected storms by two WB-50s and one B-47 from the 55th Weather Reconnaissance Squadron at levels near the surface to higher than 40,000 feet.[56] New to this kind of program was the use of ONR-arranged rocket photographs designed to portray the entire storm system from altitudes higher than 50 miles.

At that time the utility of rocket photographs was unproven. As early as 1948 primitive cloud photographs were obtained up to 100 miles above the army's White Sands Proving Grounds in New Mexico, using Germany's V-2 rockets and the U.S. Navy's new Viking booster. But in 1949 Maj. Delmar Crowson inferred in "Cloud Observations from Rockets" that such photography demonstrated the earth's curvature far better than it demonstrated cloud patterns. About that time, however, the RAND team of Greenfield and Kellogg had a better idea. In April, 1951, they sent to air force headquarters a secret report entitled "Inquiry into the Feasibility of Weather Reconnaissance from a Satellite Vehicle."[57] But it went into one of the Pentagon's pigeonholes, there to reside unknown and unheralded.

Four years later the prestigious National Academy of Sciences decided that the United States should launch a series of Vanguard satellites during the upcoming International Geophysical Year. Although some of the satellites would have primitive cloud-scanning and infrared sensors, the projects would be civilian and open. Then in early 1958 the Department of Defense decided it did not need both the air force and the army to build competitive satellite reconnaissance systems. The air force was allowed to continue, but the army was told to convert its payload into a television and infrared observational satellite (TIROS) to serve the meteorological community.[58]

Events moved swiftly. The Department of Defense's Advanced Research Projects Agency (ARPA) would provide overall direction, even though it had no meteorologists on its staff. This dilemma was solved by forming yet another Washington committee. Cochaired by ARPA's very able mechanical engineer, Dr. Roger Warner, and RAND's Will Kellogg, the project was blessed with some sensible and competent people. Payload design and construction was contracted to the Radio Corporation of America (RCA) Astro-Electronics Division; the local technical direction was provided by Dr. William G. Stroud and associates at the army's nearby Signal Corps laboratory at Fort Monmouth.[59]

As a policy matter, the White House shifted the TIROS program to the newly formed NASA in April, 1959, out of military control. Even so, the project lost little momentum. By midyear, orbital parameters, payload weight, and sensor layout were fixed. RCA was well on its way to building three payloads, two for launch and one for dry runs. Because no one knew which field of view might give the most meteorological information, each satellite had two vidicon-type television cameras, one with a view of approximately 60 miles to a side, and the other with a view of about 750 miles to a side. Each camera fed a two-channel tape recorder, one channel holding thirty-two pictures taken at 30-second intervals before dumping, and the other channel providing information on the satellite's rotational position with respect to its spin stabilization. Because of intense interest in this experiment, the TIROS command-control-readout-data processing system was about as complex as one could imagine (see Fig. 6).

The headline-making launch of TIROS-1 on April 1, 1960, from the Air Force Missile Test Center at Cape Canaveral, Florida (commanded by Maj. Gen. Don Yates) was most successful. Among the best of the early earth satellites, it lasted fifteen months instead of the expected three, achieved 1,302 useful earth orbits, and sent nearly 23,000 pictures, 60 percent of which contained useful meteorological information.[60] Unfortunately, the analysts soon learned that orienting and gridding TIROS images could not be done quickly and on a mass-production basis. Stroud's team had recognized this and were already relocated at NASA's new Goddard Space Center in Maryland, working on a polar orbiting weather satellite (Nimbus) that would not have that problem.

One battle remained. Would the nation have only one weather satellite program, a civilian one, or could there be two, the second being military? Brig. Gen. Norman L. Peterson, the AWS commander, launched a marketing campaign at such commands as SAC, North American Air Defense Command, and the North Atlantic Treaty Organization (NATO). The goal was to generate support for an air force satellite that "would contribute immeasurably to the advancement of the application of meteorology in existing and future weapon systems." AWS's proposal was rejected in December, 1960, by air force headquarters. Instead, Col. Ed Roache, AWS

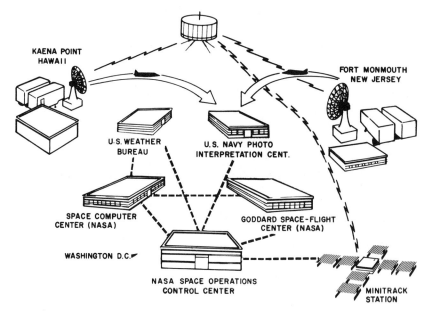

Fig. 6. Data flow within TIROS I ground complex. (From NASA Technical Report R-131, 1962)

Deputy Chief of Staff (Operations), was designated to assist in creating a national weather satellite plan under Weather Bureau leadership.[61]

By now, TIROS-II had orbited a few weeks before. Twenty-one nations, including the Soviet Union, Poland, and Czechoslovakia, were invited by NASA and the Weather Bureau to use the data cooperatively. President John F. Kennedy, at the time he took office in January, 1961, particularly liked the idea of such cooperation in space. In March, 1962, he even went so far as to write Chairman Nikita S. Krushchev: "Perhaps we could render no greater service to mankind through our space programs than by the joint establishment of an early operational weather satellite system. Such a system would be designed to provide global weather data for prompt use by any nation."[62] But no matter how spectacular the concept, it would be worthless if hostilities should occur.

As it was, the civilian community was very slow to place an advanced operational satellite into longtime circular orbit.[63] When Nimbus-II finally made it into useful orbit in mid-1966, the Department of Defense had long since allowed the air force to go ahead, in strictest secrecy, with its own meteorological satellite program.

Chapter 9
The Vietnam Period—The Home Front

Let's get the weather cleared up—the bastards have never been bombed like they're going to be bombed this time, but you've got to have weather.
—President Richard M. Nixon

PURPLE SUITERS

Once the Kennedy inauguration ceremonies were over, Defense Secretary Robert S. McNamara and his whiz kids moved swiftly to apply their management theories to the military. These included quantified measures of cost-effectiveness, elaborate mathematical comparisons of how a specified military strategy could be achieved, and rigid managerial control exerted downward from the top civilian echelon. As far as McNamara was concerned, only numbers counted. Human factors such as esprit de corps and enthusiasm were irrelevant. Instead, the armed forces were required to join the War on Poverty by making adjustments in recruiting, training, discipline, and promotion practices. McNamara maintained for years that the escalating hostilities in Southeast Asia would conclude tidily by the end of the upcoming fiscal year. He thus saw little need for specialized research and training in tropical warfare. Although the first AWS units went to South Vietnam in December, 1961, preparation of an improved *Forecaster's Guide to Tropical Meteorology* did not begin for another seven years.[1]

McNamara had another penchant that kept weather commanders nervous: bigger was automatically better. He insisted that separate military technical services in the same field be merged into composite Department of Defense entities whenever possible, for example, in logistics, communications, intelligence, and mapping. Once formed, these agencies, such as the Defense Mapping Agency, were directed by a blend of officers and men drawn from the affected services and nicknamed the Purple Suiters.[2]

During 1961 the House Appropriations Committee asked the Bureau of the Budget of the executive branch to investigate the suspected duplication of services by the various federal weather agencies. Completed the following year, the survey found that meteorological research and development programs were not well coordinated, although operational programs were.[3] The upshot was two key documents: Bureau of the Budget Circular A-62 of November 13, 1963, and an implementation plan based on the circular, published in January, 1964. Keyed to Public Law 87-843 (Section 304) enacted by Congress in 1962, the circular provided specific guidelines that reaffirmed the central role of the Commerce Department in basic meteorological services for the nation. It was to be weather's constitution, so to speak.

The associated implementation plan created the Office of the Federal Coordinator for Meteorological Services and Supporting Research (commonly abbreviated as OFCM and its head popularly referred to as "the federal coordinator") under the Commerce Department's assistant secretary for science and technology. The first of these coordinators was Dr. Robert M. White, who succeeded Reichelderfer as Weather Bureau chief following his retirement in 1963 after twenty-five years in that post. Reichelderfer had always been predictable, even slow moving. In contrast, White, a forty-year-old Bostonian, was one of the country's brightest rising stars in scientific administration.[4]

To help with his double-hatted job, White had a fifteen-man staff at OFCM's 1666 Connecticut Avenue office headed by AWS's Col. Donald F. Moore, then serving as the military adviser to White's Weather Bureau. Operational by mid-1964, the OFCM soon issued the first annual *Federal Plan for Meteorological Services and Supporting Research*. The document indicated that, by mid-1965, the total federal meteorological program would involve eighteen agencies spending $280 million annually. Although the Weather Bureau was called the government's "principal meteorological agency," the report also noted that its manpower made up only 22 percent of 20,815 persons in meteorology throughout the government. On the other hand, 69 percent of the total manpower resided in the military weather agencies (see Table 5).

From the start, in spite of White's skill, OFCM's central role in government meteorology did not go as planned by Congress and the Bureau of the Budget. One reason was that the military weather agencies (particularly the AWS) saw too much Weather Bureau in OFCM—too much program review authority and control over funds. Brig. Gen. Norman Peterson even described White's role as that of a "meteorological czar." Inviolate to the military weather agencies were in-house customers' requirements for service. Because such requirements translated into men and equipment (and bureaucratic power), OFCM had no business ruling on the validity of military requirements.

Table 5. U.S. Meteorological Resources (FY 1965, 1975, and 1985)

	Air Force			Navy			Army			Coast Guard			Commerce Dept.		
	1965	1975	1985	1965	1975	1985	1965	1975	1985	1965	1975	1985	1965	1975	1985
Cost of Services (in millions)	$82	$163	$552	$26	$44	$69	$2	$6	$8	$5	$5	$2	$99	$216	$628
Cost of Research (in millions)	$6	$3	$61	$1	$2	$18	$7	$22	$33				$8	$14	$66
Manpower (in *thousands*)	9.9	*	7.2	3.3	*	1.8	0.5	*	0.4	0.6	0.3	0.1	4.5	6.5	4.1
Surface Observation Stations															
Domestic	172	*	111	50	*	36	*	*	10	*	87†	115†	392	562	587
Foreign	100	*	66	29	*	16	*	*	2						
Marine															
Ships				118	26	30				8	88	81	15	2,550†	1,800†
Buoys				6	*	*								*	24
Upper Air Stations															
Radiosonde	46	*	42	99	*	30	37	11	11	6	23		147	127	134
Rocketsonde	12	*	2	3	*	*	3	*	2						
Weather Radars	41	15		20	*						1		32	94	150

* Data not available.
† Part-time, minimally equipped, cooperative stations.
SOURCES: Annual reports by Federal Coordinator for Meteorological Services and Supporting Research.

As a consequence, OFCM did not enjoy the military's cooperation on issues such as meteorological requirements (read *resources*). Furthermore, the military weather community snubbed White by getting him expelled from the Joint Meteorological Group (JMG) by parliamentary maneuvering. After OFCM's creation, followed by the Department of Commerce's formation of the Environmental Science Services Administration (ESSA) in July, 1965, military members of the JMG informed White that other appropriate channels existed for coordinating most civil-military weather matters. Over the next decade OFCM's power over funds and manpower steadily deteriorated.[5]

White had been the federal coordinator for only a few years when he realized that Congress was far more interested in the ocean than in the atmosphere. So instead of working hard to push the interests of Capitol Hill's pro-purple-suiters, White turned his attention seaward. Thus, when the National Oceanic and Atmospheric Administration (NOAA) supplanted ESSA on July 9, 1970, White was its administrator, a billet specifically rated as equivalent in rank to that of under secretary (or a four-star admiral).[6]

FURTHER MANAGEMENT SHIFTS

As early as 1962 the air force wanted to tidy up the administration of military meteorology by making itself the single manager for Department of Defense meteorological support. Following four years of debate, both Defense and the Joint Chiefs of Staff concluded that such a focal point was needed.[7] A compromise created a new one-star billet for a Special Assistant for Environmental Services (SAES) under the Joint Chiefs of Staff to coordinate such functions beginning June 1, 1967. Additionally, SAES inherited the functions of the JMG, thereby ending the existence of that body after more than twenty-six years. SAES also served as Defense liaison with the OFCM and other interdepartmental and international organizations, including the World Meteorological Organization (WMO), thereby closing out direct formal participation by AWS, the Naval Weather Service, and army meteorologists in interagency and international committees and working groups. To achieve some agreement, however, the SAES domain excluded meteorological research and development, oceanography, and environmental intelligence. Because 70 percent of the affected resources were from the air force, the SAES post was assigned to Brig. Gen. Roy W. Nelson, Jr., the last Cal Tech graduate and West Pointer to command AWS (1963–65).[8]

Nelson had big ideas; he asked for and got a supporting staff of forty-eight. Not being a line agency, SAES could not create or eliminate weather resources without agreement on all sides. As a consequence, to save time, military weather services began to circumvent SAES more and more. A year later, Brig. Gen. (designate) Robert F. ("Bud") Long, who had been the AFCRL commander, replaced Nelson but had no better luck in command-control. During a subsequent Joint Chiefs of Staff reorganization, the SAES fiefdom was wiped out on April 1, 1970. In its place, with a staff of twelve, appeared a lesser billet—the Deputy Director for Operations/Environmental Services (DDOES). This time around, the new DDOES charter did include the monitoring of oceanography, mapping-charting-geodesy, and astronomy, as well as meteorology.[9]

Despite the wider technical base, DDOES was even less a threat to the sovereignty of the army, navy, and air force weather services than either SAES and OFCM had been. Aside from coordinating interagency affairs and seeing that the Department of Defense was represented on interdepartmental and international committees, its most useful function through 1983 was to provide access to Defense and the Joint Chiefs of Staff on operational weather matters. In contrast, the Office of the Deputy Under Secretary (Research and Advanced Technology) served as the entry point for items about meteorological research and development. In view of this split responsibility, the military's top environmental billet in the Pentagon rated only an O-6 grade and normally rotated between air force colonels and navy captains.

CHALLENGE AND CHANGE

During the interminable war in Southeast Asia (1961–75), AWS was commanded by seven officers whose ranks ranged from colonel to major general. Their backgrounds varied as widely. Some pilots had a high school education and modest exposure to meteorology (Maj. Gen. Russell K. Pierce, 1965–70, and Brig. Gen. John W. Collens, 1974–75), but there was also the precedent-setting nonpilot, Brig. Gen. William H. Best, Jr. (1970–73), who held a *filosofi licentiat* graduate degree in numerical weather forecasting from the University of Stockholm.[10] In the same period AWS acquired a number of additional missions, including operating a rocket-sonde network (1962), performing weather modification (1965), conducting aerial photomapping (1972), and, most intriguing of all, creating and operating a solar observing and forecasting network (1962).

The AWS's first solar forecast was issued in October, 1962, under the direction of Lt. Col. Roger Olson and with the strong encouragement of AWS director of scientific services Dr. Robert D. Fletcher. As time passed, and by using equipment belonging to NASA and to the Electronic Systems and Space Systems Divisions of the Air Force Systems Command, the shoestring Solar Observing and Forecasting Network (SOFNET) monitored solar flares, the ionosphere, and the density of the upper atmosphere (a major determinant of the drag experienced by low-altitude satellites and re-entry vehicles). In August, 1964, AWS transferred its solar forecasting function to Headquarters 4th Weather Wing, Ent AFB, Colorado, where its fifty-man prediction center kept the nearby North American Aerospace Defense Command (NORAD) complex up to date on extraterrestrial phenomena. During late 1973 SOFNET was swept up into the growing AFGWC empire and, under a new acronym (SESS for Space Environmental Support System) became the Department of Defense's only real-time operational source of solar data.[11] With experience, SESS observations and forecasts became particularly useful in explaining blips on NORAD's long-range radars (thereby avoiding unnecessary alerts to the Pentagon) and in anticipating blackout of high-frequency radio communications.

With new missions, plus the continuing hostilities in Vietnam, the AWS force structure slowly grew from 10,536 personnel in 1961 to 11,702 in 1969. But a long-running policy issue continued to fester—how much AWS support should be assigned to army field units? By 1973, 13 percent of AWS manpower and operational funding were allocated, without reimbursement, to army support. That was slightly more than AWS used to assist the TAC but less than that for SAC support.

Because the army was operating more aircraft than the air force was, many considered the AWS effort on behalf of the army marginal. One in-depth analysis ruefully concluded that "progress and cooperation between the Army and Air Force (AWS) in solving these problems 'stops when resources are needed.'" As to support for the army, the study further concluded: "young AWS unit commanders—the lieutenants, the captains, the majors—and their talented enlisted men jury-rigged a system in the fox-holes and made it work year after year, despite doctrinal disagreements at high-level echelons." Unfortunately, no one "brushed with brown" (from working directly with army units) ever gained access to one of the top three command billets at Headquarters AWS.[12]

In sharp contrast to the continuing army–air force squabbling, the Naval Weather Service enjoyed relative stability during the first half of the Vietnamese fracas. Captain Drouilhet's practice of having the navy's senior meteorologist both work within the Office of the Chief of Naval Operations at the Pentagon and also be Naval Weather Service commander at the Naval Gun Factory appeared to work well. Research and development support was likewise simple and Washington-based. The Bureau of Aeronautics provided new hardware and techniques, while highly touted ONR sponsored basic meteorological research and unique field projects (such as very-high-altitude balloon flights). Additionally, the oceanographic forecasting center of the Naval Oceanographic Office developed and tested new environmental forecasting systems on its own until such systems were operational and transferred to the Naval Weather Service.

But there was a fly in the ointment. In view of oceanography's fast rising public popularity, the Congress in 1962 relabeled the venerable though dowdy U.S. Navy Hydrographic Office with a more modern designation— U.S. Naval Oceanographic Office (NAVOCEANO)—and titled its commander Oceanographer of the Navy, which merited flag rank.[13] The Naval Weather Service was not alarmed by this change because NAVOCEANO's sponsor, the innocuous Director of Naval Administration, was far removed from its own powerful sponsor, the Deputy Chief of Naval Operations for Air. But then the third oceanographer of the navy, Rear Adm. Odale D. Waters, did some fancy footwork. An updated version of the oceanographer's duties appeared in February, 1967, and included the following: "15. Provide in the Oceanographic Program organization structure the framework for including the other environmental sciences in the future."

Even so, not much happened organizationally for the next three years. In June, 1970, the highly competent and respected Capt. William Kotsch took command of the Naval Weather Service and also became Assistant Oceanographer of the Navy for Environmental Prediction Services. Because he was willing to make the billet competitive, not just a slot for the most senior aerologist, Kotsch was promoted to flag rank in April, 1971.[14] But just six months later he left to become the Deputy Director for Operations/ Environmental Services within the Joint Chiefs of Staff setup. The Naval Weather Service's top billet reverted to a four-striper, Capt. Richard M. Cassidy. As a captain, Cassidy was not in a good position to argue with the new oceanographer of the navy, Rear Adm. J. Edward Snyder, Jr., about where meteorology should fit within the navy with respect to the other geophysical sciences.

Even worse, Dr. David M. Potter, the assistant secretary of the navy (research and development) and an oceanographer himself, had already made up his own mind about where meteorology should fit within the navy structure. By late 1973 Potter was convinced of three things. There was a definite danger that Congress and the Bureau of the Budget would "purple-suit" the Naval Weather Service with the Air Weather Service; NAVO-CEANO had to be moved out of town to satisfy Congress, which believed that the navy had too many facilities in the capital; and the navy needed a geophysical corps whose mission and capabilities would range from the bottom of the sea to the top of the atmosphere.

Consequently, Potter and Snyder forced through the melding on May 5, 1975, of two officer specialties (meteorologist and oceanographer/hydrographer) into one specialty (geophysicist) for 330 affected officers.[15] Cassidy and his successor, Capt. Willard S. ("Sam") Houston, vigorously fought the idea. Houston even retired early, in 1976 in protest. But the decision stood because Potter became under secretary of the navy—the very person who arbitrated such disagreements.

Besides these organizational changes during the early 1970s, both the AWS and the Naval Weather Service persistently agitated for extra manpower and funds with which to expand the manpower-gobbling weather centrals now linked to an extensive, expensive bevy of civil and military weather satellites.[16] But the Pentagon ruled that if the dramatic new systems truly had top priority among meteorologists, other weather resources would have to be sacrificed.

In 1971 the navy's typhoon trackers (VW-1) at Guam were phased out, and on July 1, 1975, the hurricane hunters (VW-4) based at Jacksonville, Florida, were decommissioned. The Coast Guard found itself in similar trouble. To capitalize on oceanography's glamor, some sixty aerographer's mates were converted to marine science technicians during 1968. Then, in 1974, because of the capabilities of modern weather satellites, all but one of the remaining fifteen ocean station vessels were laid up; three years later the last weather ship was eliminated. Thus ended almost simultaneously two marine weather programs that had existed for three decades.

The cutbacks were every bit as bad for the Air Weather Service. With the military phaseout in Vietnam, which started during late 1970, solons demanded "peace dividends." At more or less the same time, the air force chief of staff placed extra emphasis on the air force's "teeth-to-tail" ratio, which meant modernizing with expensive new aircraft such as the F-15 fighter and the B-1 bomber. As part of the "tail" (weathermen were spear carriers, not swordsmen, and therefore "soft core"), AWS suffered drastic reductions. During FY 1972 these reductions cost AWS two wings, one group, five squadrons, nine aircraft, and 2,315 manpower authorizations, or 23 percent of its total force. By August, 1974, two-thirds of AWS's reconnaissance aircraft were in mothballs. The remaining reconnaissance squadrons numbered three, not six, and the authorized weather reconnaissance population was chopped from more than 2,700 to approximately 1,100.[17]

By then, the Defense Department was also pushing hard the "total force" concept, by which reserve forces carried more of the day-to-day work load. So the MAC commander, Gen. Paul K. Carlton, instructed his staff to "put the Air Weather Service out of the flying business." It took a year. Brigadier General Collens, head of the AWS, fought it with all the means at his disposal, but on September 1, 1975, the AWS 9th Weather Reconnaissance Wing disbanded. Its resources (seven WC-135s, twenty WC-130s, and 845 billets) were transferred to the new 41st Rescue and Weather Reconnaissance Wing (part of MAC's Aerospace Rescue and Recovery Service) at McClellan AFB, California.[18] Another seven WC-130s were assigned at the time to the newly established 920th Weather Reconnaissance Group of the Air Force Reserve at Keesler AFB, Mississippi, to help with its new responsibility of providing 70 percent of the Defense Department's aircraft committment to the National Hurricane Operations Plan. On top of that seasonal assignment, the reserve group was scheduled to fly half the necessary USAF scout, pathfinder, and synoptic weather reconnaissance missions.

EQUAL OPPORTUNITY

The Women's Armed Services Act and the Armed Forces Integration Act of 1948 required enhanced and expanded use of women and blacks in the military. However, Lyndon B. Johnson was the first president to require aggressive affirmative action. By 1967 the feminist movement was strong enough for Congress to abolish its limitation that only 2 percent of the military could be female, although women were still not to be posted to combat billets. Finally, by 1969, female officers from each service were permitted to attend the Armed Forces Staff College. And a year later, the first WAF (Women in the Air Force) entered the Air War College. It was not until 1975 that service academies accepted women for regular officer training. A year later, females were accepted for pilot and navigator training. Even so, as late as 1983, AWS would not allow its weather WAFs to enter parachute training.[19]

Notwithstanding those decades of numerical limitations and promotional barriers, a small handful of females had the ability and persistence to carve out careers as military weatherwomen between the 1940s and the 1970s.[20] For example, Margaret C. McGroarty Smith, after starting out as a recruiting officer in 1942, became a commander and assistant officer-in-charge of the Fleet Weather Facility, Alameda NAS, California in 1961. Female reserve officers also played active roles. Comdr. Mary Ellen Thomas, as a civilian, served as the longtime curricula specialist for the aerographer's mates training program; two others, Catharine F. Edgerton and Katherine J. Hinman, became captains in 1974. Enlisted weatherwomen were also becoming better accepted. Even in the Marine Corps, Jeanne Hamadyk pulled forecasting duty as far away as Okinawa and eventually became a master sergeant about 1981.

Female weather officers were probably at a greater disadvantage in the air force than in the navy. Air force promotions to upper field grades (lieutenant colonel and colonel) were weighted according to whether one was flight-rated, an academy graduate, a unit commander, had seen combat, graduated from a senior service school, and held a regular commission. In each category women were excluded or nearly so. The lingering 1958 air force policy of phasing out WAF job specialties where the representation was small did not help those who wished to continue as weather officers.

One of the women who did rise through the ranks was Lt. Col. Joyce E. Somers. In July, 1969, Somers was given command of AWS Detachment 56, the Pentagon weather unit that supported the USAF operations center and was the meteorological contact for the president's plane, Air Force One.[21] But neither she nor her sister weather officer Lt. Col. Margaret J. Perry was given command of a weather squadron or promoted. When Somers retired in June, 1974, as a senior lieutenant colonel, there were only eleven other WAF weather officers, or 0.7 percent of AWS's assigned officer force.[22]

The lot of enlisted weatherwomen was equally frustrating, for they, too, were a target in the 1958 drive to phase out peripheral female specialties. One who beat the system was Olive M. Folze. Olive enlisted as a WAC in 1944 and received her initial weather observer training at Williams Field, Arizona. Having done well in a succession of assignments, she came to Headquarters AWS and made the rank of senior master sergeant in 1961, the only WAF to have done so up to that time.[23]

A decade later another remarkable weather woman, Alice L. Hill, surpassed Folze's record. In 1949 Hill was one of the first black women to enlist in the newly integrated air force; by 1951 she was a two-striper weather observer posted to Headquarters, 18th Weather Squadron, at Wiesbaden, Germany. She proved to be a professional of the first magnitude and in 1971 became the first AWS female to achieve the coveted rank of chief master sergeant.[24]

When it came to breaking the male barrier, all pioneering women had to take a back seat to Sgt. Vickiann Esposito. In December, 1972, the twenty-year-old weather observer volunteered for weather reconnaissance flying duty. Although AWS directives specifically precluded females, Brigadier General Best favored a relaxation of the rules. His vice commander and his reconnaissance wing commander opposed the idea. Best went ahead, pushed it over the objections of the MAC commander, Gen. P. K. Carlton, and received the backing of the air staff in the Pentagon. After passing the rigorous flight physical required of males, Esposito reported to the 53rd Weather Reconnaissance Squadron in December, 1973, for duty as a dropsonde operator at Keesler AFB, Mississippi. She performed ably and in 1978 was awarded the Air Medal (another AWS female first) for fifteen typhoon penetrations as a crewmember aboard WC-130s.[25]

Making it in a predominantly white military establishment did not come easy for black males, either. The senior black weather officer in the navy, Capt. James L. Gilchrist, entered the service via officer candidate school in 1957 and served as an aerial navigator before taking up meteorology. After making the grade of O-6 in 1979, he became staff meteorologist for the commander in chief, Pacific Fleet, managing the special staff section that handled meteorology, oceanography, and charting. Another black, Capt. Corington A. Alexander, Jr., became a weather officer in 1959 and put on his four stripes in 1980.

AWS's first black colonel was James O. Ivory, a Tuskegee Institute ROTC graduate and history buff who earned a bachelor's degree in meteorology at Pennsylvania State University in 1962. Ivory touched all the right bases in his middle-level assignments, including Air Command and Staff College (1974) and Air War College (1979), followed by command of the 25th Weather Squadron at Bergstrom AFB, Texas. Eminently eligible for promotion to colonel, he appeared on the Air Force 1980 promotion list; a year later, he was followed by another black meteorologist, Walter J. Harrison, who made colonel on October 24, 1981.[26]

Following Truman's 1948 order to integrate the armed services, the lot of black weathermen in the military improved, but ever so slowly. By the early 1950s they were scattered throughout the AWS and were among the first in Korea and later in Vietnam. However, racial disharmony did not fade away by fiat, and as late as April, 1973, eight of thirty-two enlisted personnel of the weather detachment at McCoy AFB, Florida, filed formal complaints charging racial harassment by the unit's chief observer, a master sergeant. On the other hand, in 1971 Brigadier General Best had assigned a black, M. Sgt. William A. Crawford, as personal weather aide to Gen. Bruce K. Holloway, the SAC commander. Earlier, Best's automated and "dehumanized" AWS (Holloway's words) had failed to alert Holloway about an impending blizzard at SAC headquarters, but Holloway soon came to consider Crawford the best weather forecaster in the world.[27]

In the navy, the first black aerographer's mate to become chief petty officer was Charles W. Terrell, in 1963, followed by Dornice Butler two years later. In 1972 they were the first blacks to be appointed aerographer warrant officers. Butler continued to another first, when he was designated the first black mustang in the Naval Oceanography Command. Today, as a lieutenant commander, he serves as executive officer for the command's headquarters facility at Bay St. Louis, Mississippi.

THE DIGITAL REVOLUTION

Numerical weather prediction specialists learned their trade during the 1950s and by the mid-1960s began to dominate forecasting in the air force and the navy. This shift was based on five factors: the computer industry changed almost overnight from analog to digital sensing, transmission, processing, plotting, and storage of numerical data; digital data could be transmitted at megabit (millions of bits) speeds per minute, and even globally via communication satellites; improvements in midlatitude weather predictions required expanded geographic coverage; meteorological satellites could fill in global weather gaps, and electronic computers had improved by a factor of 200 between 1955 and 1965 (see Table 6).

Fortunately, the cost of exploiting those factors did not jump as fast as the increase in technical capability.[28] Such computers still could only add, subtract, multiply, or divide on command. They did not, however, have personnel predilections on how weather maps should be drawn, and they digested and plotted in near real-time the thousands of scalar points used to make a mathematically based weather analysis.

To feed these data gobblers, the Air Force Communications Service inaugurated an advanced automated weather network (AWN) on July 1, 1965. Special computers at Tinker AFB, Oklahoma daily received hundreds of thousands of weather data bits from ESSA's National Meteorological Center, from AWS weather centrals and switching stations at High

Table 6. **Growth in Computer Power at U.S. Numerical Weather Centers**

Center	Computer Type	Year of Acquisition	Relative Computing Speed
National Meteorological Center	IBM 701	1955	0.001
(Maryland)	IBM 704	1957	0.005
	IBM 7090	1960	0.02
	CDC 6600	1965	0.2
	IBM 360/195	1973	1.0
Fleet Numerical Oceanography	CDC 1604	1960	0.01
Center (California)	CDC 6500	1967	0.15
	CDC 170-175	1977	0.75
	CDC CYBER 205	1982	10
Global Weather Central (Nebraska)	IBM 704	1957	0.005
	IBM 7090	1960	0.02
	IBM 7094	1963	0.06
	UNIVAC 1108	1967	0.16
	UNIVAC 1110	1972	0.41
	UNIVAC 1100/81	1979	0.37
	SPERRY 1100/82	1981	0.70
	SPERRY 1100/72	1984	0.59
	(in conjunction with)		
	CRAY X-MP	1984	15.00

NOTE: The phrase "relative computing speed" should be treated with caution, as each manufacturer has its own method of measuring speed.

Wycombe, England, and Fuchu, Japan, and from domestic, low-speed, observation circuits.[29] Tinker's computers automatically checked, sorted, edited, and compiled the raw data into regular weather messages. Ordinary military weather units received such messages via low-speed teleprinters (60 to 100 wpm), but the master weather centrals at Offutt, Monterey, and Suitland could receive these data at rates up to 3,000 wpm.

At such a master central the data were rapidly converted by machine, with some help from humans, into myriad weather analyses and prognoses for various regions and atmospheric levels. The resultant weather information was then retransmitted digitally or by line drawing and printing equipment to customers scattered throughout the globe. However, one of the shortcomings was that each central used different computers and thus different computer programs. During 1969, for example, Global, with a staff of 414 (116 officers, 282 airmen, and 16 civilians) used four Univac-1108 computers; ESSA's Suitland complex, with 300 civilians, used two CDC-6600 computers; and at the navy's Monterey central, 126 personnel used two CDC-6500s, two CDC-1604s, two CDC-3200s, and one CDC-8090 computer. Congressman Jack Brooks, chairman of the Government Operations Committee, thought all this equipment smacked of duplication and asked the Bureau of the Budget to see whether the computer mainframes should be consolidated for weather prediction. Once again, the purple suit concept was fought off.[30]

However, manpower reductions forced the AWS to accelerate plans to centralize more computerized forecast functions at Global. In January, 1970, Global assumed the severe weather warning function when AWS disbanded its Kansas City center. Seven months later Global took over the computerized flight-planning responsibility from AWS's Suitland unit. Then in August, 1971, Global took over the Latin American forecasting chore from a center that AWS had shut down at Charleston AFB, South Carolina, and by January, 1973, Global could "direct-drive" weather facsimile products to AWS units both in European and in Pacific theaters.[31] Once that capability existed at AFGWC, the AWS no longer needed additional weather centrals, except for its climatology center (USAF Environmental Technical Applications Center), which moved from Washington, D.C., to Scott AFB in August, 1975.

When the far more powerful Univac-1108 computers were running smoothly at AFGWC, AWS launched a consolidated terminal forecast program in November, 1971, under which the master center eventually issued terminal weather forecasts for all AWS Stateside units—approximately 100 installations. As it worked out, the base weather station was responsible for a 0-to-6-hour recovery forecast only, while the 6-to-12-hour scheduling forecast came from Offutt. The program was poorly received in the field, for forecasts were in different codes, could overlap, and were often at odds with one another. Moreover, the AFGWC forecasts were accepted verbatim. Inexperienced junior forecasters let things slide so badly at base weather detachments that after Brig. Gen. Albert J. Kaehn took over the AWS command during 1978, he concluded: "We were atrophying meteorology in the weather station."[32] Kaehn wisely returned the responsibility for all the 0-to-24-hour terminal forecasts to his Stateside weather units.

However, both master military weather centrals continued to be swept up in the managerial practice in which duty as commander or vice commander at the numerical weather center was almost a prerequisite to being considered for the billet as overall weather service commander (brigadier general or commodore). The navy chiefs called this the "Monterey daisy chain" syndrome. The civilian meteorological community was dismayed that although several air force weather officers held national fame for their expertise in numerical prediction, AWS assignment practices denied them the command of Global. Instead, Global leadership fell to a series of competent but hardly numerically expert officers who (with the exception of Col. Ralph Steele) moved on before making much impact on the center's daily operations, much less introducing significant improvement in forecasting models.[33]

The situation was unfortunate, for numerical forecasting continued to have difficulty forecasting areas of localized, intense atmospheric motion such as hurricanes, typhoons, thunderstorms, tornados, and unusually heavy precipitation. Just as sadly, the latter stages of the Vietnam war proved that Global's models had very little skill when it came to tropical weather forecasting. Numerical forecasting for periods beyond five days also showed little skill. Consequently, the Fleet Numerical Oceanography Center fell back on that old, much debated technique—analog weather maps—for mandated long-range weather forecasts.

TWO CONTINGENCIES

During the Vietnam period military meteorologists temporarily focused on two other geographic areas besides Southeast Asia—Cuba and the Middle East. After scornfully rejecting the idea that the Soviets had a Cuban military buildup under way, President Kennedy, on October 22, 1962, made public the U-2 reconnaissance photographs that showed missile site construction. He called up reserves, deployed extra air and ground forces to the southeastern United States, and laid plans to blockade Cuba from the sea.

Meteorological support for all Stateside tactical air and ground forces fell within the domain of AWS's 2nd Weather Group (today's 5th Weather Wing) at Langley AFB. The group's leader, Col. Nick Chavasse, moved south on

October 28 to oversee a weather task force for the new temporary Air Force component command at Homestead AFB, Florida. There, he faced a familiar problem—a local shortage of weather personnel. His solution was the same as during the Berlin airlift—drafting forecasters and observers (forty-one and twelve, respectively) from unaffected weather units.

During the two-month period of uncertainty the White House relied heavily on aerial photographs taken at all levels to determine how the Russians and Cubans were reacting. As early as October 12, AFGWC issued "go, no go" forecasts for Cuban overflights made by the U-2 wing based at Del Rio, Texas, and maintained a continuous weather watch throughout each mission. Because of sparse weather reports for the Cuban region, Brigadier General Peterson had his 53rd Weather Reconnaissance Squadron at Kindley AFB, Bermuda, initiate WB-50 missions to Cuba. However, the weary WB-50s aborted their first two missions, so it was not until October 30 that the first successful "Easy Aces" mission was flown around Cuba—a sixteen-hour, 3,350-nautical-mile mission flown a minimum of 40 miles from the island and typically at the 500-mb level.

The other surprise came nearly eleven years later when the Yom Kippur War erupted when Egyptian forces crossed the Suez Canal on October 6, 1973. Although this unique *jihad* lasted only three weeks, nearly all of AWS's spectrum of meteorological support was exercised during the U.S. response to keep Israel from being overrun. The echoes of the first shots had hardly ceased when American air and ground commanders in Europe asked for special weather products and support for the Middle East from AWS's European command, the 2nd Weather Wing. Because of personnel reductions, there was no longer a European Weather Central at Croughton, England, and the European Tactical Forecast Unit at Kindsbach, Germany, was quickly overwhelmed. The 2nd Weather Wing immediately turned to AFGWC for help.

After some delays due to coordination problems, AFGWC began to send special forecast products over facsimile circuits from Offutt to Europe, including wind prognoses (800-, 700-, 500-, and 400-mb levels) and forecasts for such localities as Cairo, Alexandria, Tripoli, Port Said, Damascus, El Arish, and Lod International Airport at Tel Aviv. On October 17, as the requests for special forecasts snowballed, AFGWC began to transmit a standardized weather support package every six hours to all interested commands, including domestic ones. The package contained not only information of the type already noted but also forecasts for the Mediterranean and adjacent land masses from Spain to the Middle East, a discussion of the synoptic situation from the Azores to the Middle East, en route flight hazards, and clouds and significant weather throughout the Middle East.

As in the Cuban crisis and other military contingencies, intercepts of routine weather observations from affected countries (Egypt, Syria, and

Iraq, in this case) dropped to zero, and observations from Jordan were spurious. To help fill that gap, the computer of the AWS's Environmental Technical Applications Center at the Navy Yard annex in Washington worked round the clock to generate conditional climatic tables.

President Richard M. Nixon directed the air force to launch a mammoth airlift of aircraft, weapons, tanks, ordnance, and supplies to Israel to replace that which had been lost in the surprise attack. In the Mediterranean, Spain, Italy, and Turkey refused landing rights, so Lajes Field in the Portuguese Azores became an important pit stop. It also became a bottleneck because of its small size. As in 1943, Lajes had a terrible crosswind problem. MAC's chief, General Carlton, had to inform the air force vice chief of staff on October 13: "We can't move a muscle" because of the 50-knot crosswinds.[34]

To overcome the problems at Lajes, some of the F-4 fighters delivered to Israel were ferried nonstop from Stateside bases. Answering an urgent call from TAC, a WC-135B (with augmented crew) from the 55th Weather Reconnaissance Squadron at McClellan AFB, California, flew four round-trip weather scout missions across the Atlantic to Torrejon air base near Madrid, Spain, between October 15 and 22. Fortunately, flying weather at Tel Aviv remained nearly perfect throughout the war—except in the early morning hours of October 23 when fog at Lod went below landing minimums (only the second time in eight years during October), causing the diversion of a C-5A and four C-141s to nearby Ramat David airfield.

Otherwise, AFGWC forecasts stood up well despite a lack of local weather data, thanks primarily to the availability of defense weather satellite information. An AWS postmortem concluded that the service's weather support had been excellent, leading Brig. Gen. Thomas A. Aldrich to reflect: "We've proven ourselves, but we want to make it [AFGWC] more responsive."[35]

Chapter 10
The Vietnam Period—The Open War

"As far as I am concerned, the—this weather {satellite} picture is probably the greatest innovation of the war . . . . This is something that no commander has ever had before in a war."

—Lt. Gen. William W. Momyer, USAF
(TV interview, Tan Son Nhut Air Base,
May 4, 1967)

SETTING THE STAGE

For the past two millennia, Indochina (today's Vietnam, Cambodia or Kampuchea, and Laos) has been the scene of unending territorial wars and almost constant occupation by outsiders (see Map 4). During the latter part of World War II, Ho Chi Minh received modest U.S. military support to facilitate removal of the Japanese from Vietnam. But Ho's Viet Minh organization also sought to eject the French in the postwar period.

By April, 1954, Gen. Vo Ngyen Giap's forces had cornered 15,000 of France's best troops in North Vietnam's rainiest valley, at Dien Bien Phu. President Eisenhower ordered the USAF to airlift reinforcements from France to Indochina. AWS forecasters were quickly positioned at cooperating airfields along the way, in Egypt, Pakistan, Ceylon, Thailand (Don Muang airport), and South Vietnam (Tourane airport, now called Da Nang). But the airlift was not enough, and the battered French troops surrendered on May 7, 1954.[1]

The following day, international conferees in Geneva, Switzerland, agreed to make Vietnam, Cambodia, and Laos independent nations, free of French influence. Vietnam would be temporarily divided at the 17th parallel (buffered by a demilitarized zone, or the DMZ) and run as two countries until nationwide elections could be held in 1956 to decide the nation's fu-

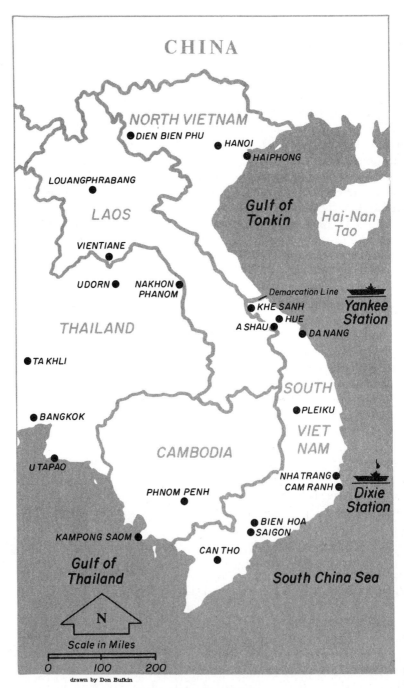

Map 4. Southeast Asia.

ture. That plan did not come to pass. Instead, South Vietnam's French-designated premier, Ngo Dinh Diem, and Ho Chi Minh ran their designated parts of the country as separate and feuding fiefdoms for the next five years. In South Vietnam there also appeared in mid-1957 a supposedly indigenous communist movement (Viet Cong, nicknamed the VC) whose goal was to overthrow Diem's regime by guerilla tactics.[2]

When the French pulled out of South Vietnam, they left behind a small civilian Department of Meteorology in the Department of Public Works and Communications. Its French equipment was either obsolete or nearly worn out by 1961. Of the department's twenty weather stations, only the one in Saigon conducted rawinsonde ascents. Weather forecasts were generated at three locales: downtown Saigon (general forecasts) and in two airport locations, Da Nang and suburban Saigon's Tan Son Nhut. The fledgling and inept Vietnamese Air Force (VNAF) also had a small weather service comprising two professional forecasters on loan from the Department of Meteorology's eleven-man forecaster corps, one enlisted forecaster, and twenty-two weather observers. However, the VNAF lacked weather communication facilities, did not use measured visibility checkpoints, and failed to make routine on-base dissemination of meteorological observations. Overall, the VNAF was a fair-weather air force—it seldom flew at night or in instrument weather, so there were no equipment or methods for measuring cloud ceilings during darkness.

During the 1950s Eisenhower's administration chose to improve the VNAF by giving it better aircraft. John F. Kennedy, upon taking over in early 1961, was willing to introduce additional training and even combat personnel into South Vietnam. By September, 1961, Col. William S. Barney, commanding AWS's 1st Weather Wing at Fuchu, Japan, confided to a subordinate that members of the command were likely to be needed to support counterinsurgency operations within ninety days. His guess was correct. Between October and December, 1961, Pacific Air Forces (PACAF) units initiated Operation Farmgate (counterinsurgency using a "Jungle Jim" unit based at Bien Hoa), Operation Pipe Stem (photo reconnaissance using RF-101s out of Tan Son Nhut and Don Muang), Operation Ranch Hand (defoliation spray runs using C-130s), and Operation Mule Train (tactical airlift for Vietnamese army troops from Da Nang, Qui Nhon, Pleiku, Nha Trang, Ban Me Thuot, Da Lat, and Camau).[3]

Barney, by mid-November, knew that the Thirteenth Air Force had orally requested field support within South Vietnam, and Maj. Edward E. Ellis, his personal envoy, arrived at Tan Son Nhut on December 12, 1961, to determine what was needed. Even before his arrival, the Thirteenth had submitted a formal request for weather support at Tan Son Nhut, Bien Hoa, and Don Muang. The initial cadre of twenty-three weathermen (eleven forecasters, eleven observers, and one clerk) were equipped for "extended" temporary duty by December 15 and arrived in Vietnam before New Year's Day.

Ellis took over as staff weather officer to Brig. Gen. Rollen H. Anthis, who had arrived a month before. Anthis's job was to command the Thirteenth Air Force's 2nd Advanced Echelon (2nd ADVON), coordinate ongoing field operations, and expedite VNAF training. Ellis also started a joint AWS–Vietnamese weather forecast central at Tan Son Nhut in January, 1962. A month later two VNAF pilots came by for advice. As Ellis described it later:

> [The two] asked for a three-day forecast for the Saigon area. There is nothing unusual about a request like this. . . . Two days later they asked for a forecast for the Saigon area for the next morning. They were given a forecast of 700 feet broken, 1,200 feet overcast, no rain, and good visibility except in clouds. The next morning the two pilots bombed the President's [Diem's] palace. The forecast verified right on the nose. They bombed, strafed, rocketed, and napalmed the palace for twenty minutes. . . . Being an old fighter pilot, I admired their ability. I don't see how anyone could have survived.[4]

As it turned out, one attacker was shot down, but the other escaped to Cambodia.

During the same month, the Pentagon discarded the low-profile MAAG concept and activated the U.S. Military Assistance Command, Vietnam (USMACV, or MACV for short) led by a four-star army general, Paul D. Harkins. This was followed on February 8, 1962, by the activation of a similar unified command in Thailand (USMACTHAI), also led by Harkins.[5] In-theater resources of the air force and the navy also were under Harkins's control. At the suggestion of Gen. Curtis LeMay (by then USAF chief of staff), the AWS also established the Weather Squadron Provisional (1st) at Saigon on May 25, 1962, to support both the 2nd ADVON and the army-oriented USMACV.

According to joint force concepts, the squadron commander, Lt. Col. Chandler R. Brown, was supposed to serve as staff weather officer to General Harkins as well as to Brigadier General Anthis. However, Anthis frowned on the use of AWS resources to support USMACV and its subordinate army commands—a bit of tit-for-tat because Harkins had not signed off on air force doctrine that specified the air force as the single manager of all air assets within a joint force arena.[6] So for the next two years, AWS support to USMACV headquarters was provided as needed. It consisted primarily of climatology briefings and the compilation of weather annexes for USMACV and USMACTHAI war plans.

On November 8, 1962, the provisional weather unit was replaced by the full-fledged 30th Weather Squadron led by Lieutenant Colonel Brown. Headquartered at Tan Son Nhut, Brown's formal command consisted of seven detachments in Vietnam and Thailand and an authorized strength of sixteen officers and seventy-four enlisted men. Initially, the work was not too demanding. During July, 1962, the VNAF and USAF had flown only 227 tactical missions in Vietnam. By November, however, VNAF crews were better trained: they flew 1,500 sorties, using 410 USAF and VNAF aircraft for close air support, photo reconnaissance, and airlift. One of the biggest handicaps faced by squadron forecasters was a lack of experience in tropical meteorology. Until mid-1962 the University of Hawaii had offered training in the subject, but a gap existed until July, 1963, when the Air Training Command instituted a four-week course of its own at Clark AFB in the Philippines.

Even so, the one-year Vietnam tour policy (comparable to that in Korea) meant that most of the unit's forecasters never became truly proficient in tropical forecasting. Unfortunately, continuity could not be provided by VNAF meteorologists. As late as December, 1963, that service provided only one of the three promised meteorologists for the joint Vietnamese–30th Weather Squadron central in Saigon, which had to turn out a twenty-four-hour planning forecast each morning, three twelve-hour forecasts daily, and, if needed, severe weather warning advisories. At Tan Son Nhut the squadron's Detachment 2 operated a centralized forecasting unit that was located with the 2nd Air Division's command post, which controlled all air strikes within South Vietnam. Detachment 2 forecasts were also provided to AWS forecasters posted to each of the ARVN corps areas (I Corps at Da Nang, II Corps at Pleiku, III Corps at Saigon, and IV Corps at Can Tho); these forecasts were the basis for localized weather predictions for specific operations and sites.[7]

Theoretically, suppressing the insurgents was left to the South Vietnamese, with Americans only observing and advising. Consequently, a key element in the 30th Weather Squadron's overall mission was training Vietnamese to operate a weather service that could support combat operations without American assistance. During 1962, Capt. Sey Katz, at Barney's suggestion, surveyed the situation and submitted a five-year plan calling for an eighty-nine-man VNAF weather squadron. Approved at first in U.S. channels, the plan was scuttled as far too ambitious. Instead, emphasis was to be placed upon on-the-job training for VNAF and civilian weather personnel at base weather stations that the squadron operated.[8]

Although simple in concept, the fallback approach was hard to implement. Both language and cultural barriers existed, despite the availability of translators and translated teaching material. To American weathermen, their Vietnamese students often seemed lethargic. Once a Vietnamese adjusted to the methods, techniques, and habits of an American adviser, the adviser would return Stateside and be replaced by someone with different techniques and personality. By early 1964, the 30th Weather Squadron decided that it no longer had a direct training responsibility, thereby leaving the VNAF weather service a paper organization manned by only a handful of well-qualified forecasters. Meanwhile, political events went from bad to worse, particularly after President Diem was executed by his own troops in November, 1963.[9]

COMBAT BEGINS

On February 7, 1965, a Viet Cong raid against the American compound at Pleiku, in Vietnam's west central highlands, killed eight U.S. Army personnel. President Lyndon B. Johnson immediately ordered U.S. dependents out of Vietnam "to clear the decks" for increased reaction. Retaliatory air strikes north of the DMZ were ordered the same day. Six days later Johnson approved Operation Rolling Thunder, a sustained air force–navy bombing campaign against North Vietnam. Before the year ended 184,000 American troops were in Vietnam, a number that steadily escalated to more than a half-million by mid-1969.[10]

Throughout the buildup, the USMACV command structure remained basically unchanged. In the far north the III Marine Amphibious Force used the 1st and 3rd Marine divisions, plus the 1st Marine Air Wing. USMACV's naval component consisted of U.S. Naval Forces, Vietnam/Naval Advisory Group, which was headquartered in Saigon, and conducted coastal and river blockades (Operations Market Time and Game Warden, respectively). USMACV's army component (known as U.S. Army Vietnam, or USARV) operated as a field army headquartered at Long Binh just northeast of Saigon and directed two corps-level units called I Field Force (Nha Trang) and II Field Force (Long Binh). The Seventh Air Force, activated in April, 1966, at Tan Son Nhut to replace the 2nd Air Division, served as USMACV's air component and controlled fifteen wings of aircraft, plus the 314th Air Division (airlift). Additional airpower outside USMACV's direct control was also brought to bear, particularly against North Vietnam proper, by Carrier Task Force 77 of the Seventh Fleet and from a SAC B-52 bomber wing and supporting KC-135 tankers based initially in Guam and later at U-Tapao (Sattihip), Thailand.

Although South Vietnam was only approximately as large as California, moving about was not easy (see Map 5). Most of the country was mountains or swampy deltas. The coastal railroad no longer worked. The few roads were often impassable because of rain, flooding, or guerilla attacks. USMACV pushed air mobility as the answer. By late 1966, the Seventh Air Force operated more than 1,000 aircraft. Of these, 400 were based at Tan Son Nhut, where the air traffic density (up to 1,600 takeoffs and landings daily) made it the busiest airport in the world. Even so, the army's air mobile

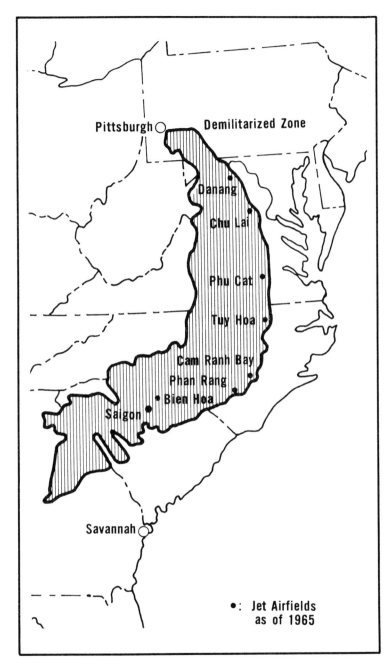

Map 5. Comparative sizes of the United States and South Vietnam. (From *The United States Air Force in Southeast Asia, 1961–1973*)

concept gave that service more helicopters (chiefly Bell UH-1s and Vertol CH-47s) in Southeast Asia than the USAF had aircraft. As a result, the United States had more troop-carrying and cargo helicopters in-theater than existed in the combined armies of the communist world.[11]

IN-THEATER MANAGEMENT OF THE AIR WEATHER SERVICE

With the quadrupling of U.S. air and ground forces in Southeast Asia during 1965, the 30th Weather Squadron was swamped by urgent requests for support. To complicate matters, bad fighting weather was common. Between April and August, the southwest monsoon brought high heat and humidity, plus some rain and cloud. But the worst weather, particularly in the region's northern half, came during the northeast monsoon (October–February) when weak frontal surges out of China created what the French called *crachin* weather—periods of drizzle, rain, and fog that lasted for days to sometimes weeks. Further complicating the seasonal patterns were tropical storms and intense typhoons that could penetrate the area anytime between July and January.

In his *A Rumor of War*, Philip Caputo vividly described combat in such a climate: "We were fighting more and more actions against main force guerillas and, in some instances, against North Vietnamese Army units. I didn't know if the enemy had started his rainy season offensive. I only knew . . . that the weather often grounded our planes and helicopters, that it was difficult to move supply convoys, tanks, and big guns down the muddy roads, that the enemy was fighting harder, and we were losing more men. The expedition had become a war of attrition, a drawn-out struggle in the mud and rain."[12]

At first the 30th Weather Squadron coped by adding more detachments at Cam Ranh Bay, Phan Rang, and An Khe in Vietnam and at Korat, Ubon, and Nakhon Phanom in Thailand, swelling the detachment total to twenty-three. The authorized manpower nearly tripled: 152 forecasters, 197 observers, and 52 support personnel by the end of December, 1965. When problems concerning span of control arose, Col. Alexander Kouts, the unit's fifth commander in three years, asked that a weather group be formed in-theater. But the necessary paperwork to do so bogged down.

The following June, the MAC commander, Gen. Howell M. Estes, visited Vietnam and was briefed on the problem. Estes immediately wired his staff to petition the Air Staff for not just a group, but for three subordinate weather squadrons as well. Stirred by the general's firm hand, the MAC staff under Estes saw to it that USMACTHAI, USMACV, the Pacific Command, and the Air Staff granted approval in just twenty-two days—an administrative record. The new setup, effective July 8, 1966, located the 1st Weather Group at Tan Son Nhut, along with two of its subordinate squadrons—the 30th, specializing in supporting Seventh Air Force within Vietnam, and the 5th (moved to Long Binh in August, 1967), which supported the USARV (except for field artillery units).[13] Phased out of Southeast Asia two decades before, the reactivated 10th Weather Squadron became the group's third subordinate command. The prime mission of the 10th, with headquarters in Udorn in remote northeastern Thailand, was to support Seventh Air Force units throughout that country.

Even though the group's manpower grew to a peak of 701 by March, 1970, the basic organizational alignment worked well until the summer of 1971 when forces began to be withdrawn from the theater. Its leadership, which rotated yearly under the one-year-tour policy, by and large performed satisfactorily. In the demanding period July, 1966, through January, 1968, Col. Lewis J. Neyland, Col. Robert B. Hughes, and Col. Edwin E. Carmell successively showed initiative and imagination in commanding the 1st Weather Group; seven other colonels rotated through the top command slot before the group was deactivated on June 30, 1972. But with such a turnover, instances of poor assignments were inevitable; for example, lieutenant colonels were sent to command the 5th Weather Squadron in combat, even though they had no experience in supporting army field units.

During the late 1960s the remote 10th Weather Squadron became a favorite unit for AWS leadership to run in "anointed sons" and "fast-burner" lieutenant colonels who were "ticket punching" to comply with the "leadership" part of their officer effectiveness reports. By so doing, they once more became competitive for promotion, after having been promoted ahead of their peers while homesteading in such insular specialties as weather satellites, computer meteorology, centralized system support, or highly classified "special strategic programs." In Thailand, momentum buttressed their unfamiliarity with things tactical; no inspector general looked over their shoulders for technical incompetence; and they were not there long enough to get their noses bloodied by irate tactical air commanders. Although such leadership was extremely barren and uninspiring in some instances, after a year the favorite sons returned home to their quasipermanent specialties, with combat command time on their records and promotion folder photographs showing both a Bronze Star and a Legion of Merit on their dress blues.

In a war zone, manpower allocations were based on a sixty-hour, six-day work week rather than the conventional forty-eight-hour work week. One rationale was that men who were kept busy had less time to think of home and get into trouble. By and large, this practice worked well, even though few WAF weatherwomen were permitted into the theater to share the work load.

End-of-tour reports were required between 1969 and 1973 of all key weather personnel in Southeast Asia, including detachment commanders and senior enlisted men. Most of those reports, whether filed by company-level or field-grade personnel, reflected extremely high morale. Morale was high for two reasons: tangible professional accomplishment, fortified by the comforting knowledge that one could leave without question at the end of twelve months even if no replacement showed up. Further, with roughly only 7 percent of the AWS in Southeast Asia at any given time, few, if any, forecasters ever pulled involuntary second tours.[14]

That policy also meant that most young lieutenants and captains arriving in-theater had little unit command and weather-briefing experience. Colonel Neyland observed that many "didn't know how to operate without centralized products" and "didn't know how to hand-massage data," so "we had to teach them from scratch." Neyland's successor, Colonel Hughes, likewise found a peacetime "Weather Bureau" mentality among his replacements. "A lot of people who came over here . . . took . . . six months to find out that this was no longer a game," Hughes said. "The intentions were good; the difference was there's a war on."[15]

To ameliorate the problem, each successive group commander usually returned to the Korean practice—putting the most capable weather forecasters in the AWS's principal forecast center (at first in Saigon but moved in 1967 to suburban Tan Son Nhut). Before mid-1965 three main centers existed: Detachment 1 (Don Muang Airport at Bangkok) provided all area and terminal forecasts for air bases in Thailand; Detachment 2 at Tan Son Nhut did the same for all operations in South Vietnam; and Detachment 14's Maj. Ray B. Coffman and associates within USMACV's Cholon compound turned out weather forecasts for North Vietnam, Laos, and Cambodia. The forecasts from the Cholon compound were used to support USMACV's highly classified covert operations by the Studies and Observation Group (SOG) in those politically sensitive countries. Forecasts issued by the three centers overlapped and were sometimes at odds, so Colonel Kouts resolved the issue by making Detachment 14 responsible for all area weather forecasts for South and North Vietnam, Thailand, and Laos.[16] Shortly thereafter, the AWS domestic concept of centralized forecasting was further adjusted, but in the opposite direction. With the buildup in the number of South Vietnamese air strikes plus the inability of the communication system to provide up-to-the-minute strike forecasts, the local weather detachments were finally freed to prepare their own terminal and strike forecasts as needed.

WEATHER RECONNAISSANCE, SATELLITES, AND
OTHER DATA SOURCES

When the sustained Rolling Thunder air operation against North Vietnam got under way in February, 1965, the big question was how to obtain prestrike information over potential targets. As all AWS reconnaissance aircraft were unarmed, the 2nd Air Division began to fly an average of six weather sorties a day (at a cost of $18,000 per sortie), using F-4Cs or RF-101s, at random to avoid tipping off planned strike areas. Although such weather scouting flights penetrated even to the fringes of Hanoi and Haiphong, the division's operation chief, Brig. Gen. George B. Simler, was far from happy with the system and growled to Colonel Kouts: "I am wasting six perfectly good fighter bombers on your goddam weather reconnaissance!" [17]

When SAC began to use B-52s to pattern bomb targets in both Vietnams the following June (30 monthly sorties, escalating to 1,800 sorties per month by March, 1968), AWS's air arm was brought in on August 7 to help scout the air-refueling areas. Initially, SAC requested four weather scout flights per week, but the requirement grew to two weather scout sorties per day, using WB-47Es out of Clark AFB, between July, 1966, and June, 1969. Using fixes supplied by ground radar stations at Bien Hoa, Pleiku, and Dong Ha in Vietnam and Nakhon Phanom in Thailand, the B-52 virtually became a night and an all-weather bomber, for ground controllers advised aircrews when the bomb release point was reached. AWS units furnished the radar sites with wind speeds up to 30,000 feet (at 5,000-foot intervals) and "D" values (drift allowances for bomb release). Fortunately, the northeast monsoon had little effect on that type of operation, for thunderstorms were rare and the weather at refueling altitudes was generally good. Synchronous bombing in formation became more of a challenge during the southwest monsoon because thunderstorms, though occasional, were intense enough to obscure offset aiming points on the planes' radar scopes. Then the bombs were either not released or fell off-target. [18]

The occasional typhoon also caused much concern. During 1965 the B-52s had to evacuate Andersen AFB, Guam, four times, and the KC-135 refuelers at Kadena AFB, Okinawa, had to evacuate nine times. But 1967 set a record, for approaching typhoons flushed out Andersen's B-52s three times and Kadena's KC-135s twelve times. As late as July 8, 1973, Typhoon Anita caused AWS headaches when it appeared to be headed for the Seventh Fleet minesweepers that were clearing the approaches to Haiphong as part of the ceasefire agreement. Unarmed WC-130s of the 54th Weather Reconnaissance Squadron normally abided by a "no-fly" line dictated by the Joint Chiefs of Staff. The line lay 100 nautical miles off North Vietnam and

Communist China. However, the commander in chief, Pacific Fleet, urgently needed to know Anita's track and persuaded the Joint Chiefs to relax the no-fly line to 12 miles. An aggressive WC-130E crew flew up the Gulf of Tonkin, with both navigation and radar gear jammed, tracked by Chinese radar all the way. The aircraft finally penetrated Anita 102 nautical miles south of Haiphong but could not complete the storm fix until it was over the North Vietnamese coast. The hasty escape was a clean one, but MAC commander Gen. Paul K. Carlton finally heard of it and directed his inspector general to investigate. Once the facts were in, Carlton raised such a fuss that the Joint Chiefs of Staff temporarily suspended all weather reconnaissance flights into the Gulf of Tonkin. [19]

As in previous wars, the acquisition of good-quality aerial photography was extremely weather dependent. In addition to conventional camera platforms, there were three newer types—the C-130-launched drone, the U-2 powered glider, and SAC's high-speed, high-altitude SR-71 Blackbird. For the glider and Blackbird, the amount of cloud cover, haze, or smoke at the target should normally be four-eighths or less. Although drones were relatively cheap ($7,000 per mission versus $70,000 a mission for an SR-71) and could fly at very low altitudes below the cloud decks, they had to be flown in daylight for recovery by a CH-3 helicopter. Providing in-flight weather support to the Blackbirds was a particularly interesting assignment. Initially, some SR-71 missions were flown nonstop from Beale AFB, California, to target areas in Southeast Asia and back, with in-flight refueling. Later, SR-71s were based at Kadena AFB, and replacements were flown out from Beale about every six months. Either way, all of the 9th Weather Reconnaissance Wing's squadrons—the 54th at Andersen AFB, the 55th at McClellan AFB, California, the 56th at Yokota AFB, Japan, and the 57th at Hickam AFB, Hawaii—assisted by flying scout weather reconnaissance missions in the SR-71s' air refueling areas, an assignment that grew to 578 long-range meteorological sorties during the three years following July, 1969.

Unquestionably, the greatest technological advance that military meteorologists used in Vietnam was the weather satellite. Detachment 2 acquired its first civil satellite cloud picture from TIROS VIII on January 30, 1964, using an AN/MKR-9 mobile satellite readout station on Tan Son Nhut. Later, two other AWS detachments were also equipped for monitoring the ESSA and the Nimbus satellite series. But the satellite system that sold Lieutenant General Momyer was the covert Defense Meteorological Satellite Program (DMSP). [20]

DMSP control was dominated by strategic considerations. The exception was a DMSP satellite orbited during 1965 to meet some of the Seventh Air Force's specific tactical needs in Southeast Asia. When Under Secretary of the Air Force John L. McLucas finally revealed at a Pentagon press conference in March, 1973, the existence of the DMSP effort, Congress had to be publicly informed of the duplication with the civil meteorological satellite program. At half the orbiting altitude (486 versus 900 nautical miles), DMSP birds offered nearly twice the fine resolution (0.3 versus 0.56 nautical miles) than did those of NOAA, plus an advertised capability to orbit a replacement satellite in forty-five days versus the six to twelve months it took for civilian satellites. In addition, DMSP customers required data in early morning, noon, and midnight hours; NOAA's was a midmorning requirement. Philip J. Klass had, in fact, already speculated that the DMSP birds were needed to inform reconnaissance satellite programmers when small areas of strategic interest in Russia and China were cloud free so that precious spacecraft film would not be wasted.[21]

In South Vietnam, Tan Son Nhut's highly secret Site VI readout unit regularly sent processed pictures of cloud patterns over heavily defended North Vietnamese targets by microwave to Seventh Air Force headquarters. Security was so tight that few air force officers and even fewer of their army counterparts knew of the capability. One notable exception was that satellite pictures and data were regularly used to brief General Westmoreland (and General Abrams) and his top MACV staff, generally at the regular Saturday morning situation conference when a seven-day weather forecast for the coming week was presented. The navy, too, was cut in on the system and had one experimental unit aboard the carrier USS *Constellation*. Not a parabolic dish receiver, the navy's antenna system ran just below the edge of the flight deck so that on two occasions it acted as an additional protective barrier when fighters swerved out of control after landing. Although the navy's DMSP readout van took up an entire aircraft parking space, the ship's skipper considered the trade-off more than justified.

The regional forecasters at Detachment 14 also used weather data from other sources. Surface and upper-air observations taken to World Meteorological Organization standards were regularly available for all of Asia (except for North Vietnam and southern China after 1964) via teletype from Kadena and Clark AFBs. Vessels of the Seventh Fleet always lay offshore, and what were cryptically called "classified sources" sent weather information from enemy-infested territory. Climatology helped, as did fascsimile charts and bulletins issued by AWS's Asian Weather Central in Japan. The AWS pilot-to-forecaster service was also highly developed (10,057 contacts at Tan Son Nhut alone during 1967).[22] After five years of tribulation, by 1970 the 1st Weather Group had five long-range (AN/CPS-9 or AN/FPS-41) and thirteen short-range (AN/FPS-103) weather radars blanketing Southeast Asia.

SUPPORTING THE SEVENTH AIR FORCE

As in the Korean conflict, Southeast Asia's air war, including West-moreland's extravagant use of SAC B-52s as "artillery," was totally tactical. In practice, two distinct and separate air wars were fought there.[23] One was the "in-country" war over South Vietnam, in which meteorological support, despite the monsoonal climate, played a relatively small role. The second was the "out-country" war, which emphasized tightly controlled interdiction attacks against targets in Laos, Cambodia, and particularly North Vietnam and in which political decisions in Washington, D.C., repeatedly overrode local weather conditions and vagaries—to the despair and safety of those doing the flying.

Either way, the elements helped make it a miserable war. Water concentrations in dense monsoonal rainclouds induced compressor stalls in intricate jet engines and blanked out radar signals. Summer heat could be so bad that an inferior potting compound in the F-4s melted; the electrical insulation of 367 of these fighters had to be redone, at an average cost of $59,000 per aircraft. The steady rains of summer could quickly wash out the subsoil beneath aluminum runway matting, closing the strip until repairs could be made.[24] All in all, weather so tempered the targeting, tactics, timing, and type of ordnance employed that the Seventh Air Force's two major omnibus air plans were entitled "Northeast Monsoon Campaign" and "Southwest Monsoon Campaign."

In the in-country aerial campaign, enemy aircraft did not exist. Accordingly, there evolved a unique tactical air doctrine in which airborne Forward Air Controllers (FACs) were used extensively. Flying propeller-driven O-1, O-2, and OV-10s, the FACs (typically flown by fighter pilots) became the final on-scene authority on whether a launch should strike a specified target or divert to secondary and tertiary targets.[25] With experience, the Seventh Air Force found preplanned strikes to be most efficient, so during the 1965–68 period, approximately 70 percent of its strength went into such missions (the remainder was used for "immediate strikes" or to support "troops-in-contact" with the enemy).

A typical preplanned strike began with an army ground commander who planned an action two or three days hence. His air liaison officer would advise the type of air support needed. Once the local Vietnamese province chief concurred, the request went through channels to the master Tactical Air Control Center (TACC) at Tan Son Nhut. After approval, the TACC staff matched the request against aircraft that would be available the following day. That done, the staff considered the upcoming weather, based on the thirty-six-hour weather forecasts supplied by the 1st Weather Group forecaster on duty, as an aid in choosing the most opportune strike time. Finally, fragmentary orders ("frags," as they were commonly called) were issued to the air units involved and, except for monitoring the mission, the TACC's task was over.

From then on, the key player was the local FAC who flew over the target at the designated time on the following day. With the aid of the nearby army ground commander, the FAC verified the location and, weather permitting, called for the strike.[26] By then, pilots of the fighters, after briefings (including weather) at their home base, were vectored to the area under guidance of local air traffic control agencies until they were turned over to the FAC about five minutes before in-flight rendezvous. Once the fighters were in sight, the FAC marked the target with smoke and called in the strike aircraft. After the strike, the FAC reported the damage to the fighters. If the target was obscured by weather, the FAC simply shifted the attack to secondary or tertiary targets or passed his strike aircraft to other FACs who had workable, weather-free targets (weather could vary from one side of a mountain to the other).

The potential importance of weather forecasts for recovery from such raids was offset by a bevy of circling tanker aircraft, ready to provide midair refueling if needed. In view of the small area involved, the region might well have ten or more accessible airfields should air controllers advise returning pilots of adverse weather at home base. Even so, air support of ground forces fell off sharply during adverse weather because FACs found it difficult to direct strikes. Air support was similarly limited at night, a time when the VC preferred to do their fighting, although flares and ground radars were used in critical situations.

Although tactical photo reconnaissance units were inclined to think they operated free of weather constraints, nature disagreed. Imagery, whether visual light, radar, or infrared, eroded when visible moisture occurred between the sensor and the target. Although his 1st Weather Group received as many as 1,400 target reconnaissance requests monthly during early 1966, Colonel Neyland later observed,

> We could never get the recce [reconnaissance] people to use a system of optimizing their scheduling of targets based on weather. The system used was: "We'll write the frag today for tomorrow's mission; we'll give the guy all the targets he has fuel for; we'll give him three times as many as he has film for, and he'll go out and fly until he uses up his film or runs out of targets." . . . And it was ineffective, grossly ineffective. . . . We had some of the most expensive recon photographs that you have ever run into. Miles and miles of cloud pictures.[27]

In Neyland's opinion, the disregard of weather advice was "shameful," for proper utilization could have cut tactical reconnaissance costs by a third. Paradoxically, photo reconnaissance pilots flying over North Vietnam saw it the other way. Taking unarmed aircraft into the world's most heavily defended airspace put a premium on each flight. Accordingly, operations officers were more willing to listen to the forecasters, and many missions were scrubbed because of postulated poor weather. Those that did go north turned in a relatively low rate of unsuccessful photo sorties. Even many of the air aborts attributed to poor weather were not caused by poor photographic conditions but by clouds that just happened to be over the target during pass-by.[28]

The out-country war was far more complicated than that in South Vietnam. Both Presidents Johnson and Nixon practiced the tenet attributed to Clemenceau that "war is much too serious a thing to be left to the military." Accordingly, both commanders in chief reserved for themselves and their immediate subordinates the pace, locale, and nature of the air war against North Vietnam. By introducing complex rules of engagement that would supposedly keep Russia and Mao's China from directly intervening in the conflict, Johnson badly hobbled American airpower.[29] No important target or area could be hit without his consent. His decisions were relayed through Defense Secretary McNamara to the Joint Chiefs of Staff, who then transmitted an approved list of targets (with accompanying strike instructions) to the Commander in Chief, Pacific (Adm. Ulysses S. Grant Sharp, as of 1965–66). In turn, Sharp's command on the hill above Pearl Harbor apportioned targets and approach routes between the Seventh Air Force and the navy's CTF-77.

Although Johnson and Nixon exerted a tight rein on U.S. armed forces half a globe removed from the White House, they could not control the weather. Because they often ignored it, some critical diplomatic maneuvering that should have been backed up by airpower was allowed to take place during the annual northeast monsoon, even though that period brought predominantly poor flying weather to North Vietnam between mid-October and mid-March. Moreover, each day's best bombing weather tended to occur between late morning and late afternoon. Because of the time difference, these were awkward hours for Johnson's frequent White House pronouncements to the media about how "his boys" were punishing the North Vietnamese. He thus preferred early morning strikes, even though fog and mist had not yet burned off.

A steep price was paid for that cavalier attitude. Between December 1 and December 25, 1965 (the latter was the effective date of a Johnson-ordered temporary moratorium on air operations over North Vietnam), 58 percent (or 952) of all scheduled air strike sorties into North Vietnam were canceled because of weather. In jettisoned bombs alone, it cost the U.S. taxpayer over three hundred 750-pound bombs, fifty-five 1,000-pound bombs, twelve 2,000-pound bombs, and forty-two 3,000-pound bombs. When the moratorium was rescinded on January 30, 1966, the Joint Chiefs of Staff directed resumption of air strikes irrespective of the weather: of 132 strikes scheduled for the opening day, all but 58 were canceled because of weather, and just 10 of the sorties flown were effective.[30] Overall statistics for 1966 were nearly as depressing (Appendixes E and F). Of 57,440 strike sorties scheduled against North Vietnamese targets, 24,013 were affected by weather—and the figure was even higher for approved targets in the Hanoi-Haiphong area.

Strangely, weather advice was often ignored by top Seventh Air Force officials.[31] Later in 1966 Colonel Neyland noted:

> The targets had to be fragged strictly on the basis of the priority of targets, without regard for any weather input. . . . So the only weather input made was this: "Since we are going to go to 'Yen Bay' tomorrow, if it's bad, where are we likely to have good weather for a secondary target? Or if we had two high priority (primary and secondary) targets and they are both bad, then what area is likely to have acceptable weather for tertiary or a target of opportunity?" . . . A very high percentage of strikes were directed to secondary or tertiary targets prior to takeoff . . . They never had any intention of going to the primary target, but it still shows up on the books as being a weather divert.[32]

During 1967 the vexatious situation continued, for targets were politically rather than strategically chosen. Once, when the new commander of the Seventh Air Force, Lt. Gen. William W. Momyer, vented his frustrations on a Detachment 14 forecaster over an incorrect thunderstorm prognosis, Col. Edward Carmell, commander of the 1st Weather Group, visited his top customer to see if more could be done in weather support. "Well, Ed," Momyer replied, "it isn't the weather support that I'm frustrated about; it's the actual weather that's happening."[33]

But Momyer tended to be short of patience with weathermen, no matter their rank or stature. Col. Ralph Suggs, a weather wing commander, once visited Momyer to make a sales pitch for using target forecasts prepared by the Detachment 14 weather center under Lieutenant Colonel Gayikian, who had extensive war experience in Korea. Momyer threw him out of the office, saying he could not use such information. A few months later Colonel Barney, then the AWS vice commander, tried to pay a call on the three-star general, only to be told that Momyer did not have time for the air force's number-two weatherman.[34]

Momyer's "fair-haired boy," Col. Jacksel M. Broughton, was the only fighter pilot who has yet written a book about Vietnam. *Thud Ridge* was based on Broughton's 102 missions over North Vietnam in the F-105 Thunderchief (the "Thud") while vice commander of the 355th Tactical Fighter Wing at Takhli Air Base, Thailand. Broughton was irritated by several weather phenomena, including the "murk . . . like somebody painted your sunglasses white" caused by indigenous haze and burning croplands. But what bothered him most was what he termed "inaccurate bombing wind forecasts." "The weatherman can force you to go back to a target several times," Broughton observed; "the most obvious way is a bum forecast." "Our degree of accuracy on vital details like bombing winds over the target is abominable," he continued; it was not "due to lack of desire to do the job right on the part of the weathermen; they simply are not prepared to give accurate winds over a strange spot on the ground."[35]

Because of frustration felt by wing and squadron commanders like Broughton, the Seventh Air Force continually appealed up the chain of command, imploring Headquarters USAF and the weapons industry to deliver the all-weather capability that had been widely advertised as early as the Korean War fifteen years before. The F-4s tried bombing using Loran-C with some success, but thunderstorms still disrupted the highly accurate navigational signals. Then McNamara's personal hobby, the F-111A fighter-bomber (the TFX), was sent to Thailand during March, 1968, for combat evaluation. In theory, the TFX, with its terrain-following radar, should have been all-weather, but the unique radar also blanked out in heavy rainshowers. So even F-111s tried to avoid thunderstorms and showers en route to targets. To make fighter-bombers more all-weather, electro-optical and laser-guided bombs were also hung on the aircraft. But even these "smart bombs" could be stupid in the presence of haze, mist, cloud, and pronounced atmospheric refraction.[36] Although the weathermen could provide accurate cloud forecasts, they did not prove very skillful in predicting line-of-sight visibility for such bombs.

Despite such shortcomings, Detachment 14 won the 1966 Moorman Award (named after Lieutenant General Moorman) as the best centralized AWS forecasting facility. The Seventh Air Force's new commander, Gen. George S. Brown, also commended the unit that November. But a few months after rotating out of the theater during 1970, he bluntly told the MAC commander (in front of AWS commander Brig. Gen. William H. Best, no less) that "the weathermen never knew what the hell was going on [in Southeast Asia]. I used to fuss at them, but you know, they're not a goddam bit better today. They've got satellite pictures, worldwide communications, and they aren't batting a goddamned percentage point better calling the weather than they were in 1942."[37]

CLEWING IN THE COMMANDER IN CHIEF

After becoming AWS commander during 1970, Brigadier General Best came to believe that a primary reason that his organization had been virtually ignored in target selection was that meteorological advice was too filtered before it reached top White House and Pentagon decision makers. Yet the decision makers had some weather consciousness. In congressional testimony in February, 1967, McNamara frankly stated: "at the present time, the level of activity [against North Vietnam] is limited not by aircraft but by weather." And in early May, 1970, while defending the debatable intrusion of a few days earlier into Cambodia, Defense Secretary Melvin R. Laird told Congress: "I am sure that the motivation of the president was to take advantage of this three to six week period [of good weather] while we have an opportunity to destroy these [North Vietnamese] sanctuary facilities [before the southwest monsoon]."[38]

As a matter of practice, Detachment 14's area forecasts for Laos, Thailand, and Vietnam were transmitted daily to the Pentagon in time for the morning briefing at the National Military Command Center (NMCC). The center also received daily weather satellite pictures. In addition, an AWS detachment not only briefed key air force officers but also provided forecasts, weather summaries, and climatic studies for the White House.[39] Forecast packages were carried to the White House by the president's military assistant. Even so, Best perceived a problem. The weather products were going across the Potomac River only when requested; were handled by a nonmeteorologist military aide who might—or might not—pass them on to his boss; and often they were, as Best liked to call them, "wash day forecasts."

A good example of what could go wrong took place in late 1971. Although President Nixon had begun to pull American forces out of Vietnam the year before, the North Vietnamese were putting on more military pressure than appeared merited. When the traditional Christmas ceasefire ended, Nixon authorized five straight days of the heaviest air attacks since 1968 against North Vietnam. As might have been anticipated, Operation Proud Deep Alpha ended up fighting northeast monsoon weather as much as it did the human enemy. Of the nearly 150 fighter-bombers used in the first attack wave on Sunday, December 26, all but 46 returned home without having bombed their targets because of low cloud, fog, and rain caused by a "freak weather change" that had not been forecast by Detachment 14.[40] The next four days brought more of the same bad weather, although it was correctly forecast (which did not help the valiant aircrews, for all the bombing had to be done under instrument flight conditions).

Finally, Brigadier General Best decided that a method was needed for inserting meteorological advice directly to the "geopolitical decision makers"—perhaps by a staff weather officer to the secretary of defense or to Dr. Henry A. Kissinger, Nixon's special assistant who seemed to call so many of the signals.[41] To bypass the ponderous paperwork system of the Joint Chiefs of Staff, Best turned to weatherman Lt. Col. Keith R. Grimes, who was on good terms with two of Kissinger's Southeast Asia aides, Dolf M. Droge and Sven Kraemer. In September, 1972, Grimes met with them and with the National Security Council's science adviser, Dr. Vincent V.

McRae. All agreed that the council needed better weather input. But a good idea died aborning because AWS did not follow through.

The following month Kissinger announced from the Paris talks that "peace is at hand," but on December 13 the North Vietnamese broke off negotiations. Nixon ordered round-the-clock air strikes on previously untouched military targets in the Hanoi-Haiphong area to begin on December 18. That final, eleven-day bombing campaign, code-named Linebacker II, resulted in the war's heaviest air assault, including the loss of fifteen B-52 bombers among other aircraft. However, it was a very difficult effort, as Admiral Thomas H. Moorer, chairman of the Joint Chiefs of Staff, told Congress later: "We were then in the middle of . . . the northeast monsoon period. . . . Therefore, it was necessary to use those resources, namely, the B-52's, the F-111's, and A-6's that had an all-weather capability. As a matter of fact, as it turned out, during the period that we were conducting the operations . . . with the exception of a 36-hour standdown for Christmas, there were actually only about 12 hours which were suitable for visual bombing, including use of the so-called "smart bombs."[42]

WEATHER SUPPORT FOR THE U.S. ARMY, VIETNAM

The U.S. Army's ground war in South Vietnam was largely unconventional. Primarily, it was seesaw warfare that used elements ranging from brigades to rifle squads because the ubiquitous enemy, whether VC guerilla or North Vietnamese regular, preferred to use hit-and-run tactics—set an ambush, strike, then retreat to a sanctuary, either in the Vietnamese countryside or across the border in Cambodia or Laos. The counterplay of the U.S. Army, Vietnam (USARV), was air mobility: a division's combat elements were airlifted to the battle scene, generally by army helicopters. The field test of the concept came when the 1st Cavalry Division (Airmobile) and its 440 choppers arrived during the summer and fall of 1965. The method was so successful that it was extended to the other army divisions brought to Vietnam.

Because the USARV had the status equivalent to that of a field army, it rated its own AWS weather squadron, the 5th (a designation in limbo since 1941–42, when the unit was wiped out in the Philippines by the Japanese). Numbering 180 by mid-1969, the squadron had nine detachments—one at the headquarters of I Field Force and of II Field Force, plus one each at the seven permanent army airfields that operated independently of either field force. A weather detachment assigned to a field force or to a corps (XXIV Corps) consisted of both forecasters and observers—as did subordinate operating locations that supported the six army divisions. Below that level, three-man meteorological observer teams, who reported to the divisional weather station, were assigned to dependent brigades that operated away from the parent division and sometimes, for special situations even to regiments.

"Broad-picture" weather forecasts were provided to the army general in overall command of South Vietnam forces primarily by USMACV's staff weather officer, the commander, 1st Weather Group. Although routine briefings included daily weather summaries and forecasts, the big catch was Westmoreland's (and later Abram's) demand for a seven-day forecast each Saturday. Because predictions beyond seventy-two hours could not be made accurately, the forecasters, playing it safe, made prognoses that were vague and pessimistic which generated criticism from time to time.[43] The Detachment 14 forecasters had no better luck advising on periods of 2 or more inches of rain in any twelve-hour period, a forecast needed as an aid in moving armored vehicles after the Tet offensive of 1968. But the unit had the greatest trouble with the four-to-six-week prediction of the onset of the seasonal monsoons. Consultation with AWS headquarters was not helpful, either; their guidance was "make them iffy!"

Outside the Saigon area, the use of weather support varied from area to area, unit to unit, commander to commander, battle to battle, season to season, and year to year. Two out of every three end-of-tour reports filed by officers and senior enlisted men attached to army units reflected a belief that the army as a whole was unaware of or had little use for their services. Four years after the 5th Weather Squadron began to operate in Vietnam, the weather group commander, Col. Daniel B. Mitchell, observed: "Adequate weather support to the Army is still a problem. The Army personnel are not trained or experienced in use of weather in their operations. Our people coming over are not, in most instances, familiar with Army operations. So it is sometimes difficult to get the two together. Once Army personnel get a sample of the support available . . . they are the easiest customers to please because, not knowing what is available, they are happy to get practically anything."[44]

If the army was uninformed about the support AWS was decreed to provide, much of the responsibility rested on the AWS doorstep. The typical 5th Weather Squadron forecaster had no training or experience with army operations, either in the field or at doctrinal schools such as Carlisle Barracks and Fort Leavenworth. The squadron's commander, Lt. Col. William E. Cummins II, sensed an undercurrent in the AWS that officers assigned to army support were automatically playing on the "second team."[45] Although AWS policy technically prohibited the weatherman from flying special weather reconnaissance and forecast check missions in light army aircraft and helicopters during weather that was significant to operations, many flew anyway. But army pilots did not want noncombatant observers aboard, so the more gung-ho weathermen qualified, on their own initiative, as door gunners, to gain access to the battlefield.[46]

Military rank also carried far more weight in the army, making it difficult for enlisted AWS observers at brigade headquarters and company-grade officers at division headquarters to compete for supplies, facilities, communications, and other services. AWS tactical weather observing equipment was also too sophisticated to be kept in proper repair in Vietnam's dust and mud.[47] By the last half of the 1960s, the younger generation of AWS forecasters had been brought up on 100 wpm teletype and the dependable receipt of weather facsimile charts. Neither existed in the army communications system in Vietnam. Unbelievably, requests for a facsimile capability at army weather units, plus an upgrade from 60 wpm to 100 wpm teletype, took from 1966 to 1970 to be implemented. By then, the troops were going home.

Fortunately for the reputation of military weathermen in general (and the AWS in particular), Lieutenant Colonel Cummins and, during 1968, the staff weather officer to the 1st Cavalry Division (Airmobile), Capt. Thomas E. Taylor, were among those who motivated their men yet worked smoothly within the army system. Cummins, who had the 5th Weather Squadron from August, 1968, to October, 1969, pointed out that "our men wear the patches of the Army units we support. We live with them, eat with them, and, if there's some trouble, we fight alongside them." The Georgia-born Taylor found Major General Tolson eager to make weather count.

The two-bar captain thus dealt directly with the two-star general rather than through the divisional intelligence officer, as the field manual said to do. In return, Tolson found: "I had A-Number-One support from Taylor and the Air Force all during that time [of the Khe Sanh siege and the A Shau Valley assault]. It was terrific. I would have been in one hell of a fix if I hadn't had it." Taylor's prognoses were "a major consideration every time," Tolson offered, and "they were damned good forecasts." In that respect, Taylor served primarily as the forward area briefer, leaving the forecasting to 1st Lt. James P. Reilly, CWO Wilbur Sunday, and S. Sgt. John R. Fix at Camp Evans, the division headquarters.[48]

During the height of the Tet offensive in late February, 1968, the 1st Weather Group at Tan Son Nhut directed that Detachment 14 be responsible for the official terminal forecasts for such heavy combat sites as Hue, Khe Sanh, and the A Shau Valley. Unfortunately, the one-way teletype to the 5th Weather Squadron's forecasting units would be down as much as 60 percent of the time. When Capt. Ronald W. Clarke, the staff weather officer of the 101st Airborne Division, asked for a sole-user telephone circuit to improve his service, the signal officer abruptly replied, "tough shit." So most ground-combat-support forecasting was done at the local level, which suited the field detachments fine, as most had little use for, or faith in, the centralized forecasts from faraway Saigon. Instead, the field forecasters used seat-of-the-pants or rule-of-thumb (single-station) prediction techniques. Often the short-period prognoses (three to twenty-four hours) were mere extensions of the most recent (when available) hourly observations from their brigade observer teams. Delivering such forecasts to the brigade commanders and other forward users was further complicated by an AWS directive that prohibited enlisted observers from interpreting weather reports to the commands they were assigned to. Instead, the verbatim forecasts received by phone were to be passed on to the brigade intelligence officer without comment, a practice that some innovative and aggressive enlisted men learned to work around in the heat of battle—to the benefit of all concerned, particularly when the forecasts did not arrive at all.[49]

THE TET OFFENSIVE AND ITS AFTERMATH

South of the Demilitarized Zone (DMZ), Ho Chi Minh's forces lacked airpower of any kind, so their intelligent counter was to take advantage of poor weather and darkness whenever possible. Quite logically, the VC's largest offensive of the war began during the evening hours of January 30, 1968, at the height of the northeast monsoon. It was Tet, the Vietnamese New Year's Day, which called for a week-long celebration; the South Vietnamese army (the ARVN) was in a relaxed state of readiness, and many soldiers were on home leave. In contrast, 84,000 determined North Vietnamese and VC troops, ready to die on the spot, simultaneously struck a hundred places—from the DMZ to the southernmost Ca Mau Peninsula. One of the small suicide units even penetrated the lower floor of the American embassy in Saigon, giving American television crews ideal footage for the "living-room-war" back home.[50] After thirty days of fighting, 37,000 of the attackers had died (44 percent fatalities), more than the United States had lost since entering the war seven years before. But mopping-up was long and hard because American airpower continued to be hamstrung by prevailing low cloud, fog, and mist. The battles for Hue, Khe Sanh, and the A Shau Valley illustrated the effects of those conditions all too vividly.

During heavy fog, Hue, the ancient walled imperial capital of all Vietnam, was overrun by perhaps ten battalions of North Vietnamese and VC. Because Hue was just 40 miles north of Da Nang, retaking the city was the responsibility of the marines' III Amphibious Force (whose headquarters were at Da Nang), reinforced by 45,000 USARV troops of the 1st Cavalry and 101st Airborne divisions. Bad weather and poor visibility persisted, negating air support. So it became house-to-house fighting reminiscent of bitter World War II battles. Finally, on February 24, the last enemy position was wiped out. As the III Amphibious Force commander Lt. Gen. Robert E. Cushman, Jr., noted ruefully afterward, "with a break in the weather, the [three-week] battle would have been fought and won in half the time."[51]

By then, one of Cushman's reinforced marine regiments was also in highly publicized trouble in another part of his command area. The unit was stationed in a mountain valley (similar to Dien Bien Phu) near the Laotian border to prevent troops and supplies from moving along Highway 9 and reaching Da Nang. General Giap's regulars began to encircle this Khe Sanh base on January 21, 1968. With Joint Chiefs of Staff approval, General Westmoreland, believing that air supply could keep the base going without great trouble, decided to make a firm stand for strategic and psychological reasons. He made his decision knowing that "we were in the midst of the northeast monsoon with no prospect of relief from bad weather until the end of March," and that "poor visibility . . . because of low clouds and persistent ground fog, made helicopter movement hazardous if not impossible much of the time," thereby posing "major problems for close air support and supply by air."[52]

Climatic studies furnished Westmoreland's staff by the 1st Weather Group indicated that the Khe Sanh valley would normally have cloud ceilings below 2,000 feet and visibilities of less than 2.5 miles on more than half the mornings through April, with ceilings rising to more than 3,000 feet in the early afternoon. Unfortunately, Khe Sanh's weather conditions this particular February were far worse than average. During evening, early morning, and late afternoon hours, mist and fog frequently kept visibilities to less than a mile. During the best day of the month, good weather lasted only six hours. Even then, visibility was less than 5 miles, and the cloud cover was scattered to broken at 1,000 to 2,500 feet. During the seventy-three-day siege, fog kept the 3,900-foot runway closed almost 40 percent of the time. Supply drops were made by USAF C-123s and C-130s, plus Marine Corps C-130s, from 400-foot altitudes to prevent parachute-supported materiel from drifting over to the waiting North Vietnamese.[53] Some C-130 passes were made 5 feet above the runway centerline to deliver extraheavy construction cargo.

When the situation became critical or helicopters needed to land at the airstrip, an armada of USN, Marine Corps, and USAF gunships and jet aircraft covered the area with napalm, rockets, 20-mm cannon, smoke, and high-level B-52 pattern bombing. Eventually, the air strikes supporting Khe Sanh totaled 27,650 sorties. Because of the prevailing poor weather, 62 percent of all the strikes were directed against the close-in targets by AN/MSQ-77 ground radar crews. All told, more than 11,000 tons of supplies and ammunition were air-delivered to the 6,680 besieged marines, and 3,387 passengers arrived or departed from the much-repaired airstrip.[54]

Westmoreland was anxious to have the siege lifted. Yet he knew that "a study of weather . . . revealed that not until about the first of April could I count on good weather for airmobile operations."[55] To clear Highway 9 into Khe Sanh, Westmoreland turned to Major General Tolson and his "1st Cav" division of 19,000 men and 500 helicopters, backed by 10,000 marines and 3 ARVN battalions. To mount Operation Pegasus, Tolson's force operated from Landing Zone Stud, a 1,500-foot airstrip defended by bunkers, just 11 miles northeast of Khe Sanh.

Tolson's weatherman went wherever the general went. So April 1 found Captain Taylor and his three-man weather observer team at Stud fending off daily questions from the impatient commander and his staff about burn-off time for the low scud and fog, which seldom was before 1:00 P.M. In Tolson's opinion "good weather was considered to be any condition where the ceilings were above 500 feet and the slant range visibility was more than a mile and a half." Yet when Tolson's troops finally moved forward, resistance was slight, and Khe Sanh was relieved on April 8.[56]

Two days later, without warning, USMACV ordered Tolson to pull the 1st Cav out of Khe Sanh, turn south, and join the 101st Airborne Division in Operation Delaware, a "reconnaissance in force" of the A Shau Valley, where the enemy maintained a large logistics base.[57] Westmoreland's abruptness stemmed from a Detachment 14 long-range weather forecast that a short period during mid-April offered the best chance for assaulting the valley before the onset of heavy rains of the southwest monsoon. The final operations plan for Delaware came out on April 16, and D day was tentatively set for the following day.

Tolson, however, stipulated the D day would be contingent upon there being three consecutive days of favorable weather. By April 16 the weather was still bad, so with Taylor's backing, Tolson got USMACV to slip D day to April 19. Even though the assault could be delayed no further, the weather proved worse than forecast for the first few days. It was bad in the valley and just as bad at Camp Evans, where scores of helicopter pilots had to climb through the overcast, reassemble in formation on top of the clouds, fly to their target areas, then search for a hole in the clouds to make their descents and final runs.

Finally, on April 22, the weather improved, and two of Tolson's brigades began to get the job done. By May 3, C-130s were landing in the valley's A Luoi airstrip, where Tolson promptly put his forward command post. But heavy monsoonal showers were setting in, even washing out enough of the A Luoi strip to halt C-130 traffic. Extraction via choppers began on May 10 and wound up a week later. The enemy lost many supply depots and suffered at least 839 casualties; Tolson's forces lost twenty-one helicopters, primarily to 12.7-mm antiaircraft fire because the low cloud ceilings kept the choppers at a vulnerable altitude. In Tolson's subsequent analysis of the campaign, he said that he would have preferred the heavy but sporadic monsoonal storms of mid-May to the persistent and widespread low clouds and fog of mid-April. In other words, "one must be very careful to pick the proper weather indices for an airmobile operation. An inch of rain that falls in thirty minutes is not nearly as important as a tenth of an inch which falls as a light mist over 24 hours."[58]

By the time the Tet offensive and its counterattacks were drawing to an end, the North Vietnamese leaders had learned a major lesson. By June 30 they had lost roughly 120,000 men from attacking the allied forces head-on. For example, the siege of Khe Sanh was a "killing ground" of North Vietnamese, for they suffered some 10,000 to 15,000 fatalities; the U.S. Marines lost 205 men, and the U.S. Army far fewer than that. Unfortunately, press objectivity in Vietnam was lacking, and the American public came to think of the Tet battle as a defeat, rather than the military victory it was.

Weather detachment commanders at the separate headquarters of the two field forces were at odds during Tet 1968 over the use made of their forecasts. In the south, the commanding general of II Field Force used weather information primarily for long-range planning, showing special interest in illumination data (particularly moonlight), rainfall accumulation, tropical storm tracks, and general meteorological trends. In the north, I Field Force saw it the other way. Helicopters increasingly became the fast-response lifeline to troops in trouble. That weather detachment's commander reported that "go/no-go decisions based on the weather forecast occurred almost daily during periods of bad or marginal weather."[59]

Another difference of opinion appeared internally, among the 5th Weather Squadron staff members—should observer teams be deployed as far forward as brigade? Conservatives argued that being that far up front could be dangerous. During January, 1968, alone, the enemy launched forty-seven attacks (mortar, rocket, or physical assaults) against twenty-one army installations where weather squadron personnel were housed. Eventually, Capt. Tom Taylor and one of his observers received shrapnel wounds during a rocket attack in September, 1968, against Camp Evans. Even worse, three men of the 5th Weather Squadron were killed in action during Tet—S. Sgt. James C. Swann and Sgt. Edward W. Milan at Ban Me Thout on March 4, 1968, and S. Sgt. Eduardo Garcia, Jr., two weeks later just north of Landing Zone Baldy. The other two weather squadrons of the 1st Weather Group lost only one man between them—A 1c. Kenneth E. Baker, Jr.—in an attack on Binh Thuy on March 22, 1968.

In the final analysis, in the military it is not how many casualties you take but whether you accomplish the assigned task reasonably promptly. As a brigade commander of the 1st Cavalry Division succinctly expressed it: "We fight three things: the enemy, the terrain, and the weather, and the 5th Weather Squadron provides us with the answers about the weather."

WEATHER SUPPORT FOR NAVAL AND MARINE CORPS OPERATIONS

Although the first naval unit (Helicopter Squadron HHM-362 of the U.S. Marine Corps) arrived in South Vietnam on Palm Sunday, 1962, major involvement did not come until more than two years later. As a result of the Gulf of Tonkin incident in early August, 1964, President Johnson used aircraft from the carriers USS *Ticonderoga* and USS *Constellation* to attack North Vietnamese coastal bases. In 1965 came Operation Market Time, a blockade along the South Vietnamese coast. A year later, Operation Game Warden, an expansion of the Market Time concept, ensured safe river passage and reduced Viet Cong taxation and confiscation of goods in transit.

Despite the boarding and search of more than 240,000 skiffs, junks, and ships between mid-1965 and mid-1966 under the joint aegis of the tiny Vietnamese navy and Commander, Naval Forces, Vietnam (COMNAV-FORV), the latter command remained too small to rate a weather unit. Just the same, several hundred patrol craft of COMNAVFORV were extremely sensitive to monsoonal winds. For example, the commander of River Patrol Section 512 reported that his craft were hindered by high winds and heavy seas almost 50 percent of the time during July, 1966.[60]

For help, COMNAVFORV turned to the 1st Weather Group's Detachment 14, and, as Colonel Neyland colorfully put it, "we were up to our ass in navy support." Until December, 1968, the detachment issued a daily twenty-four-hour maritime coastal forecast (including one for the interior of the Mekong River delta), as well as twenty-four-, forty-eight-, and seventy-two-hour maritime operations forecasts for the Gulf of Tonkin. In part, those forecasts were based on products from the Fleet Weather Central on Guam's Nimitz Hill and, in part, on reports exchanged with aerologists aboard carriers operating in the Gulf of Tonkin.[61]

In addition to the modest meteorological service of the self-contained III Marine Amphibious Force in northern South Vietnam, the navy also ran a minimal surf observation and forecasting service to assist the huge Naval Support Activity, Da Nang, between early 1967 and mid-1970. An aerologist posted to Da Nang was supported by individual aerographer's mates assigned to over-the-beach unloading points at Cua Viet, Tan My, Chu Lai, and Cam Ranh Bay. By using their wave reports and sneaking perhaps four hours of sleep a night, the lieutenant or the warrant officer provided a 10:00 P.M. forecast on the probability that loaded LCMs and YFUs could safely cross the surf zone and off-load the following day. As Lt. Frederick Martin, one of the forecasters, observed later, "It was good duty for they usually did as I recommended!"[62]

Even busier duties faced aerological staffs assigned to the big attack carriers stationed offshore between 1964 and 1972. Those ships, with crews of up to 5,000 men and a complement of as many as 100 of some of the world's most sophisticated aircraft, served as tightly controlled political instruments free of mud, dust, and sabotage. Such ships drew their meteorological advisories from the "Weather Division," also known as Code OA (O stood for Operations Department, A for Aerology). As in World War II, the combat manning allowance provided for a divisional staff of twenty, led by a commander, if available. But in sharp contrast to AWS practice, the ranking enlisted forecaster on board played a major role in briefings. Although it varied from carrier to carrier, one method was to have the three-striper brief the admiral and his staff (when aboard), plus the ship's captain and interested department heads. That left the chief aerographer's mate to handle the many demands of the air group and the scores of pilots and air crews.[63] All told, the aerologist and his chief worked eighteen- to twenty-hour days, stretching out on the deck in the weather shack for catnaps. Such continuous professional pressure caused, in more than one case, the nervous breakdown of otherwise fine weathermen.

In the hectic days of 1964 through 1966, the technical basis for issuing weather advisories varied widely. Radio teletype and facsimile receivers monitored the unclassified broadcasts that could be received clearly. With luck, it was the broadcast from Fleet Weather Central, Guam, but transmissions out of Communist China or the Japanese Meteorological Agency were useful, too.[64] In 1966 two attack carriers finally obtained prototype automatic picture-taking (APT) receivers for monitoring civil weather satellites. And pilots soon knew the difference, for one said, "You aren't just guessing any more!" Yet the big improvement came a year later when all carriers were given a full-time encrypted weather teletype channel as part of the new multichannel communications service. Because each ship made great efforts to keep the service readable by continually adjusting frequencies, receivers, and antennae, the amount of weather data received jumped five- to tenfold. In return, the carriers were to feed upper-air data back to the global weather centrals. Oddly enough, that took some doing, for the newer, "big-deck" carriers of the Forrestal and Midway classes were equipped with missile-tracking radars too sophisticated to track mere weather balloons. Thus, the older Essex-class carriers, which had antiaircraft radars, and destroyers had to track balloons for the "big ones."

During Operation Rolling Thunder, CTF-77 operated two or even three carriers at Yankee Station, a hypothetical point roughly abeam of the DMZ. On station roughly thirty days at a time, one carrier would launch attack aircraft while the other was flying fighter cover and "flak suppression," plus refueling and rearming strike aircraft. The next day, the roles might be reversed. During standby periods, one carrier might fly nights and its companion days, giving ship crews a modicum of rest and ship maintenance time. It was a killing exercise, not only for the North Vietnamese but also for those aboard the carriers. For instance, during the good weather of June, 1966, CTF-77 launched 5,665 attack sorties, 3,078 of which were against North Vietnam and some of the world's deadliest antiaircraft fire and surface-to-air missiles.[65]

As with the Seventh Air Force, the adverse monsoon weather heavily favored the enemy rather than the attacking naval pilot. Vice Adm. David C. Richardson, the CTF-77 commander in 1966–67, later wrote in a lament like that of AWS Brigadier General Best, "With the centralized control of the war from afar, Washington could not keep in touch with the ever-changing weather which often required on-the-scene changes in target and weapon assignments."[66] Weather-canceled missions were also dangerous in their own right. For example, the USS *Oriskany*'s assigned morning strike of October 26, 1966, had to be canceled because of bad weather over North Vietnam. While magnesium parachute flares were being removed from the readied aircraft, one ignited and set off 700 more flares in the storage locker. Once the terrifying fire was out, forty-four officers and men were dead, including twenty-five hard-to-come-by pilots.

During the northeast monsoon, the "balloon busters" needed to be adept at forecasting the passage of true frontal systems and diffuse cold air surges out of China. Otherwise, from October through March at Yankee Station, the ship's force played a waiting game; the weather typically consisted of multilayered, stratiform cloud decks from near the surface to 10,000 feet. Although there were sometimes stretches of many days without suitable strike conditions, carrier flight support and aviation personnel remained at the ready on the slight chance that the aerologist was wrong and that an unpredicted weather window would appear both at the target area and at the carrier. According to the weathermen, these spells were "sucker holes" because overeager air group and task force commanders sometimes insisted on launching without sufficient acceptable weather over the targets.

In the case of the southwest monsoon that dominated Yankee Station from April through August, the weather was largely convective clouds and showers. Tropical waves and storms, plus typhoons, were merely imposed on this pattern. Normally, winds would be very light, even calm, during late evening and morning hours but would pick up during the afternoon. Alert carrier skippers could handle that type of weather and had their aerologists diligently searching for the best conditions. On the synoptic chart the weather might appear to be the same day by day, but actually each day was different locally. The gradient wind might be slightly weaker or stronger, more southerly or more westerly, depending upon the migration of the Intertropical Convergence Zone (ITCZ). There might also be changes in upper-level strength or direction, plus other elusive factors.

Capt. Conley R. ("Dick") Ward, the only officer ever to be designated director of naval oceanography and meteorology, recalled from his days as the USS *Oriskany*'s aerologist during 1966–67:

> One of the most critical forecasts . . . [I] had to make was where the carrier should be at the start of its twelve-hour period of flight operations—and how strong the winds would be. Lots of wind translated into larger ordnance and/or fuel loads, or, if the load remained constant, the carrier would require less speed through the water. In such an instance, you might operate with six or less of the ship's eight boilers on the line. This was extremely valuable to the ship's maintenance force (our ship was twenty-three years old), for work could only be done in the boilers after twelve hours of cooling.[67]

Ward's memoirs pointed out that bad wind forecasts could also cause other things to go wrong. Aircraft too heavy to launch, even with the carrier at maximum speed, would have to be lightened. But that led to disastrous consequences: the launch was delayed and the aircraft had to tank up aloft before it could penetrate enemy airspace. Generally, CTF-77 air strikes were coordinated, often with air force strikes from the south. Thus, a delayed launch offshore meant that, instead of hitting the enemy simultaneously from different directions and obtaining an element of surprise and confusion, the navy strike would hit when the North Vietnamese were on full alert and waiting, a heavy price to pay for a bum prediction.

The area held another meteorological trap—the directional variability of Tonkin Gulf winds caused by showers and by Hainan Island. Nevertheless, carriers, while launching or recovering aircraft, had to be steered into the wind. If that meant approaching Hainan, the carrier had to be brought around quickly to avoid exposing airborne aircraft to Chinese antiaircraft fire or even placing the ship herself under attack. Reflecting further on those problems, Ward observed: "Although it was embarrassing, you could interrupt a launch, but recovery was tough. You had aircraft low on fuel, frequently damaged aircraft, and occasionally a wounded pilot or crewmember."[68] Contributing to such problems was the possibility of reduced visibility and ceilings, as well as certain sea conditions that, by synchronization, magnified the motion of carrier flight decks.

Naval forecasters on Yankee Station had an additional way of generating nervous tension. When tropical storms originated within or were tracked into the South China Sea, the question quickly became whether the storm would continue westward toward Vietnam or recurve northward. If the storm did approach the Asiatic mainland, it might pull clear, dry air over the target area from China. If so, it would provide perfect bombing weather until the storm drew close to the Tonkin Gulf. The aerologists hoped that such a storm would move westerly, then recurve just northeast of Hainan Island. In such a situation CTF-77 could slip to the south of Yankee Station as the weather worsened but then quickly return when conditions improved. If the storm moved steadily westward, the task force could be trapped between Hainan Island and North Vietnam with no place to run and no place to hide. As Ward succinctly put it, "Leave Yankee Station too soon or unnecessarily, and you miss superb bombing weather. Wait too long and you court disaster!"[69]

In summing up aerological duty on Yankee Station, Ward noted that "The demands on the carrier weather officer were truly extreme. But they performed as professionals and were accepted as such."[70] Fortunately, the carrier's meteorologist was not alone but was backed by an equally dedicated team of aerographer's mates. Because the men worked together closely, the nine-month Yankee Station tours would eventually slide by with maximum accomplishment despite the frustrating political controls on when, where, and how to attack.

C hapter 11
The Vietnam Period—Covert Operations and Withdrawal

"Enemy too close now!"

—Appendage to final radioed weather report
from Phnom Penh, April 17, 1975

THE GEOPOLITICAL SITUATION

Besides the war in South Vietnam, which appeared daily in living color on America's television sets, vicious combat occurred throughout all of former French Indochina.[1] Although both Russia and the United States, as signatories to the Geneva accords of 1962, withdrew military advisers from the small neutral country of Laos, which borders Vietnam to the west, the North Vietnamese did not. Instead, they reinforced the local communist forces (Pathet Lao), built sanctuaries across the border in Vietnam, and expanded the Ho Chi Minh trail, which snaked from North Vietnam through Laos and Cambodia to end near Saigon (see Map 6).

The political structures in Cambodia and in Laos were extremely weak. Publicly, the two governments generally looked the other way when the North Vietnamese blatantly abused their neutral territory. Privately, they often welcomed American help, provided it was covert and deniable. That approach also satisfied U.S. political leaders, who were anxious not to advertise America's increasing involvement in what became referred to in Congress as "the secret war."

KEITH R. GRIMES—GUERILLA WEATHERMAN

Numerous AWS weathermen participated in that super-secret, cloak-and-dagger warfare in Southeast Asia between 1965 and 1975. However, one meteorologist stood out as truly exceptional—Keith R. Grimes.[2]

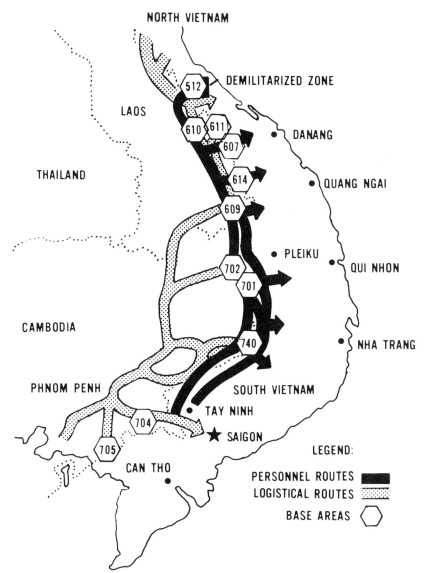

Map 6. Infiltration routes along the Ho Chi Minh Trail. (From *The United States Air Force in Southeast Asia, 1961–1973*)

Trained as a petroleum geologist at the University of Texas, twenty-two-year-old Grimes joined the air force in 1957 and received a master's degree in meteorology the following year from Pennsylvania State University. An outsdoorman who had the ability to inspire the confidence of others, Grimes began training a detachment of commando weathermen (Detachment 75 of the 2nd Weather Group) in 1963 at Eglin AFB's Hurlburt Field in northern Florida. Their mission was to provide local weather support to the army's Special Forces and to the USAF's own air commandoes. Grimes's group first came under fire during early 1965, when Col. Edward E. Mayer of the army's 7th Special Forces Group used their services during the Dominican Republic crisis.

By then, the ground war in northern Laos near the Plaine des Jarres was being spearheaded by a guerilla army of some 3,500 Meo tribesmen under the leadership of Brig. Gen. Vang Pao, a brilliant, courageous man with a pathological hatred of the North Vietnamese—which they reciprocated. Pao's ragtag army could not stand up against Giap's forces in sustained combat. But it carried out ambushes and hit-and-run raids, supported by modified Lao T-28 trainers carrying bombs and machine guns. However, about one-third of those strikes were aborted or ineffective because of bad weather. Therefore, in mid-July, 1965, Captain Grimes discussed the problem in Vientiane, the Laotian capital, with the very able career diplomat Ambassador William H. Sullivan, who directed both open and covert American assistance programs.[3]

Grimes learned that a key problem was the primitive Meo's lack of a workable air strike system. Sullivan made an offer: "You get these guerillas to where they can use air support, and then come back. If you're still convinced you need weather support, we'll talk about it further." On July 19, 1965, Grimes met at Na Khang with Vang Pao and his Central Intelligence Agency (CIA) adviser.[4] Signaling his decision primarily through eye contact and facial gestures, Pao accepted Keith's offer of help and friendship. During the month of steady combat that followed, and working with a small air operations center in Vientiane run by the American embassy's air attache, Grimes built an air support system which he used to personally direct Laotian T-28 strikes, plus occasional strikes by USAF F-4s and F-105s flying out of Thailand.

In setting up guerilla ambushes, Grimes had several close calls in which his "liberated" Soviet AK-47 rifle came in handy. Yet he also had his day as a weatherman. The Meos knew of a limestone cave in which one of Giap's brigadiers made his headquarters. After patiently waiting for good weather, Grimes called in an F-4 to strike with 1,000-pound bombs. They collapsed the cave despite its 20-foot-thick overburden, halting local North Vietnamese operations for several weeks as well. All told, Grimes's private air war probably killed more than 1,200 of Giap's troops.[5]

Because of Grimes's credentials, Ambassador Sullivan agreed to supplement the Meo air strike systems with a rudimentary weather reporting network of some dozen stations manned by Grimes-trained Laotian observers. The first went in at Long Tieng (Lima Site 98), the site of Van Pao's headquarters. When the results paid off, Sullivan permitted a few more

AWS weathermen into Laos. Keith signaled for two commando weathermen from Detachment 75, M. Sgt. Thomas M. Watson and A1c. Andrew V. Wilder, plus the Thai-speaking S. Sgt. Maurice D. Kunkel from the AWS detachment at Udorn, Thailand. As of December, 1965, the situation was well enough in hand for Grimes to return home.

Detachment 75 personnel continued to work in Laos with native weather observers and the part-time assistance of Air America (a clandestine airline) personnel, primarily the airline's radio operators. By 1968 twenty-eight clandestine weather observation points were generating 4,500 meteorological reports monthly to assist in-country decision makers and to aid Detachment 14 forecasters in Saigon. A year later Congress publicly began asking why U.S. military personnel were involved in a secret war in Laos. Twice thereafter, nervous AWS commanders ordered Detachment 75 personnel out (March, 1970, and February, 1973), only to have them sent back at the request of the U.S. ambassador in Vientiane.[6]

During the next five years (1965–71) Grimes drew a series of assignments as instructor at the Air Command and Staff College and as an Army War College student. His lecture on Laos became famous, and he gave it more than a hundred times to such high personages as the Joint Chiefs of Staff and Secretary of the Air Force Harold Brown. In addition, the U.S. Junior Chamber of Commerce named him one of America's outstanding young men during 1967 for his skill in unconventional warfare.

At the request of his Dominican Republic coworker Colonel Mayer, Lieutenant Colonel-select Grimes (a promotion achieved after twelve years, one month of active duty) was suddenly placed on special secret duty at the Pentagon in early June, 1970. His assignment was staff weather officer to air force Brig. Gen. Leroy J. Manor and army Col. Arthur D. ("Bull") Simons, who were to plan and execute a liberation raid on a branch of the "Hanoi Hilton" prison at Son Tay, not far from Hanoi. Grimes soon found that the most suitable weather windows for launching the night raid started in late October and ran well into November. Scores of domestic rehearsals were held; Grimes worked with every element of the raiding force and knew every facet, inside and out, before the force's deployment to Thailand.

Mid-November, 1970, found Grimes and three others in Southeast Asia to make final arrangements with the appropriate squadron, wing, and base commanders for necessary support. One of Grimes's first contacts was Col. Leonard E. ("Zip") Zapinski, commander of the 1st Weather Group. Zapinski denies it, but Grimes claimed to have sought access to the highly classified DMSP weather satellite data and, later, the temporary loan of two top forecasters from the Detachment 14 weather center. A disagreement arose between the two officers concerning security clearances and access rights; the disagreement was not settled (according to Manor's after-action report) until the USAF director of operations in Washington, D.C., wired the vice commander of the Seventh Air Force.[7] Eventually, Zapinski released the DMSP data to Manor as well as the services of S. M. Sgt. Dennis H. Van Houdt and M. Sgt. Loyola E. Ralston, the best forecasters of North Vietnamese weather within Detachment 14, to help Grimes.

While all that was being sorted out, Manor and Grimes flew to Udorn to talk with two of Zapinski's field commanders—Lt. Col. Albert J. Kaehn, Jr., at the 10th Weather Squadron and Lt. Col. Franklin A. Ross, the boss of Zip's hush-hush rain-making WC-130s detailed from the 54th Weather Reconnaissance Squadron. With Ross, the topic was special weather reconnaissance for late Friday afternoon, November 20. In Kaehn's case, Grimes wanted to ensure that Sgt. Wayne E. Fuiten, one of his first observers in Laos and even then still working the back country of Laos and Cambodia in secret, could crank up the Laotian weather reporting net for a rescue effort should the raiders run into trouble.

By then, as was true of many other weather-critical military operations, the meteorological situation was the worst in years. Roughly five years' worth of typhoons moved through the area in just eight weeks. In addition, cold surges of air out of central Asia were far stronger and more frequent than normal. At noon on November 18 (Wednesday) Typhoon Patsy moved westerly from the Philippines while another cold front pushed south from northern China. In the wee hours of Friday morning, the Ralston–Van Houdt forecasting team advised Manor that Patsy would roar ashore in Vietnam by Saturday evening (November 21), the day originally targeted for the raid. The ensuing cold front would move into the prison area the following day, with at least four more days of very poor weather to follow. Even then, North Vietnam and Laos were cloud-covered, but their forecast indicated that an induced high-pressure ridge with dry air from China would form between westerly moving Patsy and the southerly moving cold front. Should the ridging continue southward, as the most recent DMSP imagery had shown, the Red River Valley surrounding Son Tay should break wide open by about sundown that very evening (Friday).[8]

"Of all the decisions made, the most difficult one was based on weather," Manor wrote later: "I was concerned about the weather in the Tonkin Gulf because I wanted the Navy diversionary force to go." So the raid's overall commander had a long talk with Grimes and asked, "What's your conclusion?" "My conclusion," he responded, "is if we don't do it tonight, we'll never do it because I don't think we can keep this operation secure for that long."[9] So Washington's approval was sought and received to jump off a day early. At 5:00 P.M. on Friday, the final briefing took place at Takhli airbase, Thailand, minutes after a RF-4C landed following a weather sortie across Laos to the North Vietnamese border; Lieutenant Colonel Ross, the weather reconnaissance specialist, was in the rear seat. Ross's finding was as forecast—the ridging had cleared out the target area, and visibilities were unlimited in the Red River Valley.

The raid to the vicinity of Hanoi took place as planned and rehearsed. For thirty minutes in the darkness of early morning on Saturday, November 21, fifty-six Americans (fifty-three army led by Bull Simons, plus a three-man USAF HH-3 helicopter crew) mounted a search of the cells of Son Tay Prison, looking for U.S. prisoners. Unfortunately, the raid came too late. No prisoners were there. Despite having left many enemy dead, the attackers got away without a serious casualty during a five-and-one-half-hour mission under conditions about as hair-raising as they can get. As to the weather, Grimes had been absolutely right. For eight consecutive days before the raid, Son Tay had been below flight minimums, and the site again went below minimums on November 21 and stayed that way for a month.

Although Brigadier General Best, the AWS commander at the time, proclaimed Son Tay a textbook case on how to use weather support in a military operation, the personal feeling was sour. Lucius Clay, Jr., the Seventh Air Force commander, claimed that Typhoon Patsy's landfall at the DMZ was so atrociously forecast that it had adversely affected some of the navy's diversionary raids, even though the cyclone's actual landfall was only 50 miles north of the position forecast by the Joint (navy–air force) Typhoon Warning Center in Guam. The superb forecasting of Sgt. Van Houdt and Sgt. Ralston drew warm letters of commendation from Brigadier General Manor, but Colonel Zapinski and his successor at the 1st Weather Group, plus their boss at 1st Weather Wing, did not believe those forecasters merited any medals solely for their work on Son Tay.[10]

As for Grimes, Best never deigned to hear his briefing on the raid. When Grimes returned to the Air Command and Staff College, his superior, irked by Grimes's long absence, wrote up a damaging effectiveness report. After graduating from the Army War College in 1972, Grimes (who did win a Legion of Merit for his role in Son Tay) was offered a job by Best on the AWS staff, even though the AWS commander did not have the courtesy to tell Grimes that the man he would be working for was Colonel Zapinski.

RAIN MAKING AND WEATHER MODIFICATION

Until the mid-1960s, the U.S. Weather Bureau generally succeeded in keeping the federal government out of rain making. However, the bureau's ingrained pessimism did not influence the freewheeling Naval Ordnance Test Station (NOTS, China Lake) in the remote California desert. There, Pierre St. Amand, the station's ranking geophysicist, tinkered with many aspects of global earth science. One of his brainstorms was to drop silver or lead iodide flares into suitable cloud buildups over areas of the earth so remote that they could not support a ground-based network of smoke generators for making rain on demand.

As part of the Vietnam "laboratory assist" program, St. Amand during 1966 tested over Laos a NOTS-developed rack capable of dispensing 104 silver or lead iodide flares per aircraft sortie. Each such flare consisted of a 40-mm aluminum photoflash-type cartridge plus primer and candle assembly. Enthusiasm for St. Amand's early results wended its way to the Pentagon's Office of Defense Research and Engineering. Then that office's meteorologist, navy Capt. Sam Houston, was flown by White House helicopter to Camp David. After cooling his heels from 10:00 A.M. to 8:30 P.M., Houston was finally allowed to present a thirty-minute briefing to President Johnson on the technique. The theory was that rainfall enhancement during the southwest monsoon might well slow supplies moving down the Ho Chi Minh trail.

Johnson approved an operational evaluation of the concept. In early 1967 the AWS 54th Weather Reconnaissance Squadron was allocated three WC-130As, plus the use of two RF-4Cs already at Udorn, for that purpose. The handful of high-ranking Defense and State Department officials who knew of the test considered it to be extremely sensitive politically, particularly in the international arena. For example, what if friendly Thailand claimed that its rice paddies were being denied the water that was artificially precipitated over Laos? Accordingly, the U.S. ambassadors to South Vietnam, Laos, and Thailand were not informed of the operation, and neither were the governments they were accredited to. Within the military, the project went by various code names: Popeye, Intermediary, Compatriot, and, in AWS, Motorpool. In the combat area only four general officers, including Generals Westmoreland and Abrams, were privy to the mission. Besides the assigned aircrews, only about half a dozen 1st Weather Group members knew. Even the RF-4C squadron commander was intentionally left in the dark, for he also flew photo surveillance flights over North Vietnam.

Rain-enhancement missions were typically flown out of Udorn at the freezing level, generally found at approximately 18,000 feet. A total of 2,602 such sorties were flown between mid-March, 1967, and the end of the project on July 5, 1972, reaching a peak of 737 sorties in 1968.[11] Determining whether cloud-seeding enhanced rainfall in the target areas was difficult, but Defense Intelligence Agency experts concluded that rainfall had been increased by as much as 30 percent in limited areas and that the movement of enemy supplies had been somewhat slowed. In contrast, Westmoreland claimed that the operation resulted in "no appreciable increase" in rainfall over the Ho Chi Minh trail.[12] The general may have been feeling conservative. After all, he probably remembered that when Major

General Tolson was bitterly complaining about rainy weather during the Khe Sanh and A Shau Valley battles, rain-making aircraft under USMACV command were making daily runs over the nearby countryside. Nonetheless, Motorpool was relatively cheap; it required no sacrifice of American life and cost a mere $3.6 million per year.

In March, 1971, nationally syndicated columnist Jack Anderson broke a story about air force rain makers in Southeast Asia. The story set off a spate of articles and inquiries. Even Senator Claiborne Pell, a reserve Coast Guard captain, had a Senate resolution passed calling for the United States to seek a treaty banning environmental (weather and climate) modification as a weapon of war. Until 1974, when Pell finally consented to listen to a top-secret Defense Department briefing on the subject (which the solon promptly placed in the public domain), Defense and State Department officials steadfastly refused to comment publicly on press allegations.

In a closed hearing of the U.S. Senate on March 20, 1974, Pell assessed the technique: "An elephant labored and a mouse came forth." Even so, as a high-ranking member of the Senate Foreign Relations Committee, Pell kept pushing the matter in disarmament and environmentalist circles. The idea caught on, and, in December, 1976, the United Nations General Assembly approved a treaty banning environmental warfare. Russia and the United States signed it the following May. Ironically, it was communist-controlled Laos (where the U.S. rain-making effort first began, when Laos was neutral) whose ratification on October 5, 1978, put the treaty into force![13]

By then, AWS was involved in a number of other ways of modifying weather. During the grim days at Khe Sanh in early 1968, fifteen highly classified C-123 missions dispensed salt particles over that base, in hopes (without success, as AWS had cautioned) that the hygroscopic particles would cause the warm fog particles to coalesce and thus improve visibility. By then, while contending with supercooled fog over the runways at Elmendorf AFB, Alaska, AWS C-130s had flown thirty-seven seeding missions, using crushed dry ice, between November, 1967, and February, 1968. At Elmendorf, holes appeared where they should, permitting ninety-one aircraft recoveries and ninety-four departures that otherwise would have been delayed or diverted.[14]

The Department of Defense also arranged other rain-making flights, provided the request carried enough political clout. For example, between April and June, 1969, two WC-130Es of the 54th Weather Squadron, with St. Amand serving as scientific director, flew seventy-six cloud-seeding missions in the Philippines during a drought-relief exercise labeled Gromet II. Then a Texas drought in 1971 generated the requirement for domestic AWS cloud-seeding flights under the general direction of Dr. Archie Kahan, once the AWS's ace forecaster in the Aleutians and subsequently the director of the Texas A & M University Research Foundation (1954–63). However, by 1970, Kahan was in charge of the Bureau of Reclamation's Division of Atmospheric Water Management. The air force was not eager to participate, though AWS was. Governor Preston Smith got President Nixon into the act, and Project Cold Rain came into being. The 55th Weather Reconnaissance Squadron detailed two WC-130Bs to Kelly AFB, Texas, for such flights during June, 1971; the results, according to the Texas press, were an unqualified success.[15]

The following year drought appeared in the strategic Azores Islands. Air force Brig. Gen. Thomas A. Aldrich, commander of U.S. forces there and a former AWS vice commander, suggested to Governor Machaco Pires that cloud seeding be tried. AWS wished to participate but was overruled by a general at MAC. The U.S. Navy's irrepressible St. Amand soon showed up with a WP-3A aircraft, ready to drop silver iodide flares. Even so, it was Aldrich, the commander of AWS a year later, who was referred to in one local newspaper as "St. Thomas of Lajes," having replaced St. Peter as the island's traditional celestial patriarch.[16]

PHASE DOWN

Richard Nixon entered the White House in January, 1969, with a promise of peace, and the troops started coming home near the year's end. By December, 1971, the Seventh Air Force had 277 fighter and strike aircraft, down from a high of 737 aircraft in June, 1968. With fewer resources, U.S. air commanders employed their assault forces far more judiciously. When the AWS's Brigadier General Best visited the new commander of the Seventh, Gen. John D. Lavelle, at Tan Son Nhut in mid-September, 1971, Lavelle advised: "You're damn right we're using weather; we just don't have enough ordnance to spread around!"[17] Lavelle quickly acquired the reputation of being the Seventh Air Force's most weather-conscious commander, but he was relieved of command in April, 1972, for conducting unauthorized air strikes against North Vietnam.

Even as Lavelle was being fired, the North Vietnamese were taking the offensive. As Joint Chiefs of Staff chairman Admiral Moorer explained on April 20, 1972, to a sceptical Congress, on March 30 General Giap moved a complete division (including some 160 tanks plus motorized artillery and antiaircraft guns) across the DMZ under the cover of very low ceilings and low visibility. "It was under these conditions," Moorer added, that the North Vietnamese "were able to operate without much air opposition for a rather long period." That was an understatement. During the first twelve days of the invasion, weather conditions were suitable for tactical air strikes on only one day. Even President Nixon was griping to his aides about Vietnam's weather.[18]

Although Nixon authorized a long series of air strikes (called Operation Linebacker) against North Vietnam during May–October, 1972, the pressure on South Vietnam continued. Regardless, the American phaseout in South Vietnam proceeded, and the last AWS unit—the 1st Weather Group—closed down on June 30, 1972. The residual U.S. effort in Southeast Asia re-formed at Nakhon Phanom air base, Thailand, under the complex label U.S. Support Activities Group/Seventh Air Force (USSAG-7AF). As of mid-1974 the command numbered 34,000 Americans, of which 27,000 were air force personnel who were operating approximately 400 combat aircraft (F-4s, F-105s, A-7s, F111s, B-52s, KC-135s, and C-130s) at four bases (Udorn, Nakhon Phanom, Korat, and U-Tapao). By then, the command's main mission was to keep Lt. Gen. Lon Nol and his friendly forces in Cambodia from being overrun by the North Vietnamese and the indigenous communists, the Khmer Rouge.

An updated congressional dictate permitted Lon Nol's units to receive only military assistance funds and supplies, plus unarmed photo reconnaissance and aerial resupply missions. The handwriting was on the wall. Yet it was somehow fitting that Lieutenant Colonel Grimes returned to the theater to command the 10th Weather Squadron during its closeout in 1974 and 1975.[19] Grimes arrived at the squadron's headquarters at Nakhon Phanom in mid-July 1974 and began, with typical vigor, to visit all his detachments. By the month's end he had reached two conclusions—morale was low, and weather factors were inhibiting both types of daily unarmed flight missions (i.e., aerial photography over South Vietnam and Cambodia, and supply airdrops within Cambodia). When Grimes explained to his weathermen that the war was truly still on and where they fit in, morale climbed steeply, as did their work performance.

In the case of aerial photography, the RF-4Cs were flying, because of enemy air defenses and fuel shortages, only during forecasted periods of cloud-free photography (50 percent or less undercast). Although the forecasts were of good quality, the North Vietnamese and Khmer Rouge had also figured out the criteria and chose to remain under cover during such situations. Grimes persuaded commands to make random changes in flight times, and the rate of target detection rose. And after an integrated ballistic wind forecast to the C-130 crews was introduced, the number of food and ammunition drops that fell outside besieged garrisons was reduced from approximately 20 percent to 1 percent by November.

Grimes quickly learned that there was barely a semblance of a Cambodian weather service, either civil or military. There were no upper-air observations, and for the first half of 1974, only seven weather observations came out of the country—and those from one site. Grimes was authorized to visit Cambodia to correct the situation. Upon arriving at Phnom Penh's Pochentong airfield, he located 1st Lt. Heng Touch, acting commander of the Khmer Air Force's (KAF) Air Weather Service. Although French-trained Touch was competent, his service had not launched a pilot balloon for nearly a decade because it could not afford twenty-nine-cent balloons![20] By late August, 1974, S. Sgt. Paul C. Ferris, from Grimes's squadron, had volunteered to train and upgrade Touch's weather observers. Within a month, surface and upper-air observations were regularly being passed to Nakhon Phanom, and Ferris was on his way to being named the 1974 "AWS Observer of the Year." Unfortunately, no one in the AWS chain of command bothered to advise Gen. P. K. Carlton of Grimes's new project. The MAC commander angrily closed the AWS's Cambodian program; two months later, the Air Staff approved a formal PACAF request for continuing it.[21]

THE COLLAPSE OF PHNOM PENH AND SAIGON

By late 1974 it was common knowledge at USSAG/7AF headquarters that the definitive battle for Phnom Penh would begin in January, 1975. Grimes and S. Sgt. Steven D. Roush (Ferris's replacement), along with S. Sgt. Miguel C. Salas (a weather-equipment repairman), worked valiantly to help Touch and Deroo get ten military and civil weather observation stations operational by then. On February 5, 1975, the Khmer Rouge turned back the last attempted supply convoy up the Mekong River to Phnom Penh, and eight days later the capital had to rely totally on American-financed commercial air carriers for food, medical supplies, and ammunition. Grimes made his final visit to Pochentong airport on February 10, even as it was under fire from 107-mm rockets.[22] The meteorological system that Grimes put together permitted the commercial air shuttle to land hundreds of times at Pochentong without weather incident while delivering more than 35,500 tons of supplies. On April 1, Gen Lon Nol fled the country. On April 12, U.S. Ambassador John Gunther Dean, his staff, and others were airlifted to Thailand via Operation Eagle Pull, a carefully planned and well-executed military helicopter evacuation.

Although Cambodia's top leadership had left, Lieutenant Touch's people kept taking and transmitting weather observations of paramount importance, for by then, the only way to supply the capital was by Birdair's C-130s (on bailment from the USAF), which airdropped rice and ammunition to Pochentong. Lt. Gen. John J. Burns, the USSAG/7AF commander, decided to continue the airdrops as long as Grimes's weathermen were receiving observations from Pochentong. So the airdrops continued; fifty-six missions were flown over the beleaguered airfield between April 11 and April 17.

Finally, on April 17, the Cambodian government capitulated. Thirty minutes later, a new weather report came from Pochentong, but the brave observer added the poignant final message, "enemy too close now." With the final communication link severed, the airdrops halted. All that was left was to write epitaphs about some very brave weathermen and their sad fate.[23]

Even as Phnom Penh was falling, so was South Vietnam. On April 15, 1975, when all communication with the Cambodian capital was severed except for the weather link, the large ARVN base at Bien Hoa, not far from Saigon, came under communist fire. Shortly before, Pleiku, Hue, Da Nang, Qui Nhon, Cam Ranh Bay, and Nha Trang had fallen to the North Vietnamese and the Viet Cong. Obviously, it was the beginning of the end. Two weeks later, on April 29, President Gerald Ford ordered the closeout of Operation Frequent Wind by evacuating the last Americans and certain Vietnamese from Saigon by military helicopter in the face of sixteen attacking North Vietnamese divisions.

In planning for Operations Eagle Pull and Frequent Wind, the 10th Weather Squadron's forecasters at USSAG/7AF headquarters supported the two evacuations the same way. Mission forecasts for Frequent Wind included a brief overview of the synoptic situation, en route and air refueling area forecasts, and prognoses for helicopter and fixed-wing landing sites at Saigon, the beach at Vung Tau, and the naval amphibious group, which would be lying offshore. In addition, on April 19 the Air Force Global Weather Central began to issue computer flight plans for C-130 and C-141 traffic between Tan Son Nhut and Clark, Kadena, and U-Tapao airfields.

On April 22 Guam's Joint Typhoon Warning Center pointed out a typical meteorological headache—a tropical depression that was forming south of the Philippines might affect the area. Although the evacuation was picking up momentum, an estimated 64,000 persons still needed to be removed from Saigon. The following day Seventh Fleet recommended to Lieutenant General Burns that USSAG/7AF consider advancing the final evacuation of the American embassy to April 25 because the storm might drape Saigon in thunderstorms followed by low clouds, perhaps trapping U.S. personnel while the city was being overrun. However, Capt. Steven L. Richter, after checking the squadron's climatological records, told Lieutenant General Burns that tropical depressions spawning that far south should not adversely affect the weather in Saigon. On April 25 the depression, approximately 300 miles off Vung Tau and moving westerly, still alarmed Carrier Task Force 77. Fortunately, the storm followed the postulated climatic norm and curved northward without seriously hampering operations.

By April 28 the vast Tan Son Nhut airfield was receiving artillery fire, and the final observations were transmitted from its weather relay center at 1900 hours Greenwich Mean Time that day. A force of eighty navy, marine, and air force helicopters shuttled to and from offshore aircraft carriers extracting Americans and Vietnamese. With the disappearance of Vietnamese weather observations, the 10th Weather Squadron forecasters at Nakhon Phanom relied almost solely on weather satellite imagery and data from their own DMSP readout site. Fortunately, the weather proved flyable and as forecast—intermittent rain with thunderstorms, plus surface winds low enough not to trouble chopper landings and takeoffs. The results of Frequent Wind's last seventeen hours were reasonably impressive—1,373 Americans and 5,595 Vietnamese rescued via 638 helicopter sorties. Even so, more than 400 designated Vietnamese did not get out before Saigon surrendered unconditionally on April 30, 1975.

THE SS MAYAGUEZ INCIDENT

Two weeks later, on May 12, the Khmer Rouge captured the U.S. merchant vessel SS *Mayaguez* while she steamed through international waters off Cambodia. President Ford ordered the Joint Chiefs of Staff to have the military recapture the ship and crew immediately. No one knew for sure, however, whether the thirty-nine-man crew was on the ship, on an adjacent island (Koh Tang), or on the mainland 30 miles away. The Joint Chiefs turned over the assignment to Commander in Chief, Pacific, who passed the final action to Lieutenant General Burns and his USSAG/7 AF command at remote Nakhon Phanom. The fleet commander also swiftly assembled elements of the necessary joint task force: the carrier USS *Coral Sea* and the destroyers USS *Holt* and USS *Wilson*; 300 marines flown to the air force base at U-Tapao, and General Burns's own strike aircraft.

At that time of year Koh Tang was under the influence of the southwest monsoon. Lieutenant Colonel Grimes and his weather people worked feverishly to ensure that bad weather would not foil the rescue attempt. By then, with no weather observations available from Cambodia or Vietnam, Nahkon Phanom's DMSP readout unit proved invaluable. Because early morning was a lull in the diurnal thunderstorm pattern, Grimes and his forecasters were of the opinion that an early morning assault offered the best chance of minimal cloud cover over Koh Tang. Others agreed, and the Joint Chiefs ordered the assault to get underway at 3:50 A.M. (Thailand time) on Thursday, May 15. Eleven air force helicopters airlifted the marine contingent south from U-Tapao along a relatively weather-free route picked by Grimes and his people. Sixty-five marines went to the USS *Holt*, from which they boarded the SS *Mayaguez*, only to find it abandoned.

The other 240 marines were inserted on Koh Tang and immediately met deadly fire from the Khmer Rouge. Throughout the day the air force provided good fighter support, but by nightfall, when the marines left the island, five U.S. helicopters had been destroyed.[24] By then, the missing *Mayaguez* crew had been recovered unharmed from a fishing boat. Still, the price paid in American casualties was high: fifteen killed, fifty wounded, and three missing at the battle scene, plus another twenty-three men lost when a USAF CH-53 helicopter crashed in Thailand.

The U.S. presence in Thailand was drawing to a close. On September 30, 1975, the 10th Weather Squadron was deactivated, and its three remaining detachments (Udorn, Korat, and U-Tapao) began to report directly to the 1st Weather Wing in Hawaii.[25] Early the next year, only the U-Tapao unit remained. On May 20, 1976, its turn came to turn over its weather facilities to the Thais. It was a sad departure, for Thai meteorologists, both military and civil, had been hospitable, intelligent, courteous, eager to learn, industrious, and imbued with a deep sense of national pride. The feeling of respect was mutual. On the night that AWS closed its Nakhon Phanom station, an anonymous Thai weather observer disseminated via electrowriter the following message:

All G.I.
    I am sorry and don't need G.I. go America. I need all G.I. stay here.
    But government don't need G.I.
    I say sawad dee [farewell]. I hope G.I. will come back to stay NKP [Nakhon Phanom] again.
    Sawad dee.[26]

Chapter 12
Almost Present Tense
(1976–1985)

*You can put your computers back-to-back, and the maps, and the charts,
and the airplanes . . . but you've got to have the people too, or you've got
nothing. People are what it is all about.*
—Brig. Gen. William H. Best, Jr., USAF

THE HUMAN EQUATION

During the Vietnam era, the armed services had a growing problem
with disciplinary misfits and drug abusers. But in 1975 the tide turned.[1]
Officials again recognized that military weather recruits should be drawn
from the upper decile (or nearly so) of volunteers. Moreover, in view of the
changing times, such potential specialists no longer had to be categorized as
just meteorologists or aerographer's mates, for such work was also being
done by geophysicists (U.S. Navy), ballistic meteorological crewmen (U.S.
Army), and marine science technicians (U.S. Coast Guard). By mid-1983
that environmental specialist corps added up to 7,439 military personnel
(Table 7), or 24 percent more than in the civilian-operated national weather
service.

The weather specialty continued to be attractive to women particularly
those in the enlisted ranks. In 1983, for instance, AWS had 401 females in
weather specialties, or nearly 14 percent of personnel in that category. The
navy's percentage was twice that—449 female aerographer's mates in a total
of 1,158. However, the need for high scores on technical aptitude tests
(plus the related educational background) kept the number of enlisted
blacks with weather specialties to 3 percent in the AWS and at 5.5 percent
among aerographer's mates.[2] Hispanics, at about a third of those percent-
ages, fell behind even more.

Table 7. Weather Personnel in Uniform (Estimate for mid-1983)

Service	Officers and Warrant Officers	Enlisted Personnel	Total
Air Weather Service	1,165*	3,037	4,202†
Naval Oceanography Command	400	1,725‡	2,125
Army	47	609	656
Marine Corps	15	300	315
Coast Guard	1	140	141
Total	1,628	5,811	7,439

*The last warrant officer, CWO Billy G. Hance, retired from AWS on March 1, 1977.
†Does not include USAF meteorological reconnaissance and communications support personnel.
‡Aerographer's mates only.

The navy closed its venerable aerographer's school at Lakehurst NAS during 1979 and shifted such training to the Department of Defense's Weather Training Center at Chanute AFB. There, apprentice seamen and Marine Corps privates joined the "corn field navy" and attended a wide spectrum of courses offered by the air force's Weather Training Branch, 3330th Technical Training Wing. The beginning weather observer course, which lasted eleven weeks, drew as many as seventy airmen, twenty sailors, and five marines. The graduates, after two years in the field, could then return for a twenty-two-week technician course in which they learned to make and issue forecasts. In fact, it was mandatory that such personnel progress from observer to forecaster status if they wished a full twenty-year career in the military.[3]

Despite the practice at Chanute, training officers for weather duty did not go purple-suit. Air force policy remained basically the same as in the late 1940s—recruit new holders of bachelor's degrees in engineering, science, or mathematics and send them to a year's meteorological course at one of thirteen selected universities. By 1983 approximately a hundred young officers, thirty of them women, were enrolled in the program before being sent to a base weather station for hands-on meteorological experience.[4] Following one or more tours of weather forecasting, qualified AWS officers then returned to academia to acquire advanced degrees. In 1983, out of 1,125 air force weather officers, 693 held bachelor's degrees, 385 master's degrees, and 46 had doctorates. However, it was a career pattern that did not appeal to Air Force Academy graduates. In 1983 the AWS averaged 51 percent of its officer accessions from officer training schools (OTS), 47 percent from reserve officer training corps (ROTC) programs, and only 2 percent from the service academies.[5]

The navy method for creating officer forecasters differed radically from the air force method. Since 1975, three types of naval forecasters have existed: special duty geophysicist relabeled "oceanographer" (SDO) in mid-1984, limited duty meteorologist/oceanographer (LDO) and CWO (aerographer). In October, 1985, there were 510 officers in these sequential categories: 450, 44, and 16, respectively. Warrant officers came from the ranks, as did the LDOs. The warrant officers were aerographer's mates whose unique skills and performance warranted long-term retention; the LDOs, or mustangs, upgraded their skills by extra voluntary training, such as earning bachelor's degrees in off-duty hours. As graduates of the Naval Academy or selected universities, SDOs were regular naval officers from the very first; however, because of their specialization, they could not command warships. Instead, they did graduate work, including a research thesis, in the joint fields of oceanography, meteorology, geodesy, and mapping before becoming lieutenant commanders. They could thus assume any command within the geophysical field, including the flag-designated billet in charge of the Naval Oceanography Command.[6]

All oceanographers trained at one location—the Naval Postgraduate School, Monterey—and took just one packet of courses, the air-ocean science curriculum. Of the thirty-seven courses a prospective oceanographic officer needed to take, only fourteen had to be meteorological. As of mid-1983, forty-seven officers, including thirteen women, were enrolled in that curriculum. Such training was costly, for the instructor corps (primarily civilian) consisted of eleven meteorologists and twenty-seven oceanographers. To spread the expense, four related curricula were offered to outsiders, including one in pure meteorology, which was attended by nine USAF officers. In 1983 the outsiders numbered thirty-eight, including officers from France, Canada, New Zealand, Korea, Taiwan, Egypt, and Great Britain.

Whether the navy's rigid in-house method of training environmental officers was better than the flexible air force method remained debatable. However, when the Joint Chiefs of Staff mounted the most weather-sensitive of joint operations during the early 1980s, it chose AWS as the sole source of weather support for the mission.

OPERATION EAGLE CLAW

Within two days of the American embassy takeover in Teheran, Iran, on November 4, 1979, President Carter asked the Joint Chiefs of Staff to develop a military means of extricating the fifty-two hostages. He also specified that any final plan should not be one of brute force, as in the *Mayaguez* raid, but one that would cause minimal casualties on both sides. Such a plan would necessitate the use of maximum stealth and strict operational security. Rather than choosing to use an existing military task force, the Joint Chiefs decided to create an ad hoc unit.

Army Maj. Gen. James B. Vaught took overall command and planned a mission that would use three sequential airlifts. Eight RH-53D Sea Stallion minesweeping helicopters (navy) were to be piloted by marine and navy officers hastily trained in low-level desert night flying. They would launch just before dusk from the nuclear carrier, USS *Nimitz*, off Iran's southern coast in the Gulf of Oman, and fly north under the cover of darkness to a remote desert site (Desert One) 600 miles closer to Teheran. There, the helicopters would be met and refueled by six USAF C-130s carrying the army's Delta Team of ninety commandos under Col. Charles A. Beckwith.[7] The RH-53Ds, with the commandos on board, would then go to a site east of Teheran manned by undercover agents. During the second night the team would go in trucks to the center of Teheran to release the hostages, after which all Americans would be taken by helicopter to another airfield not far from Teheran. There the entire party would board a pair of MAC C-141s for the last phase of Operation Eagle Claw.

Vaught's joint task force chose Capt. Donald G. Buchanan, a thirty-two-year-old AWS climatologist in the Pentagon, to be its "environmental officer." In direct support was a small, specially created AFGWC cell at Offutt AFB (Maj. Frank H. Wells and Maj. Malcolm P. Chase, plus Capt. Domonic A. Ruggeri, served as principals) that made practice daily forecasts for the entire operational area of the eastern Mediterranean region and the Arabian Peninsula. Using the AFGWC global satellite data base and numerical modeling, plus conventional weather reports, those special forecasts (which were verified after the fact as best they could be) included short-range predictions, long-range outlooks, and aircraft route weather and winds.

For climatological support, Buchanan drew on the AWS's USAF Environmental Technical Applications Center at Scott AFB, plus climatic data that AWS had contributed to the CIA *National Intelligence Survey* series on Iran and Afghanistan published in July, 1970.[8] These data suggested that the best assault time would be late winter, when there would be sufficient hours of nautical darkness, plus some moonlight, and air temperatures and densities suitable for heavy helicopter operations. The climatological summary also suggested special weather problems and hazards, such as thunderstorms and suspended dust, but Buchanan never gave a specific briefing on Iran's climate to Eagle Claw's planners and decision makers. Instead, most of his climatological information was written and eventually included in a weather annex to the Eagle Claw operations plan.

To stay beneath Iran's detection radars, the mission would be flown at very low level (below 500 feet) and would use visual navigation and night vision goggles. Thus the special JTF was justifiably concerned about how well

Captain Buchanan and his supporting AFGWC could forecast acceptable weather for the two-day raid. But with experience, the JTF gained considerable confidence in the AFGWC's ability to predict the required "Visual Meteorological Conditions" (VMC—generally, 1,500-foot cloud bases and a minimum visibility of 3 miles). As a consequence, alternatives for executing Eagle Claw under conditions other than VMC were not pursued. Security ruled against a suggestion by Brig. Gen. A. J. Kaehn that WC-130s be used for weather reconnaissance or as pathfinders. In addition, the mission C-130s would be traversing the same ingress route as the RH-53Ds, and there was a high climatic probability of clear weather.

In a highly unusual practice, Captain Buchanan was not allowed to visit the U.S. training areas and chat with the RH-53D and C-130 crews about his forecasts or about weather problems that they were having or might run into. Instead, he was forced to follow the army practice: intelligence officers who had no meteorological training presented Buchanan's prognoses to the aircrews. Feedback, if any, was by the same indirect means. Thus, the traditional relationship between pilot and weather forecaster was severed— procedure that exacted a considerable price later.

On the evening of April 16, 1980, President Carter was again briefed on Eagle Claw by Vaught, Vaught's deputy (Maj. Gen. Philip C. Gast, USAF), and Colonel Beckwith. The situation looked favorable, so Carter authorized final deployment.[9] Three days later the balance of the players were dashing to battle posts nine time zones away, including the RH-53D pilots to the USS *Nimitz*. Once aboard, the pilots were isolated from the ship's force, including the on-board aerologist, Lt. Comdr. Donald E. Hinsman.

By then, a three-man AWS contingent of Captain Buchanan, Maj. Clifford F. Gilbert (2nd Weather Wing), and Frank Wells (AFGWC's weather satellite expert) was operational with a weather satellite capability, facsimile receivers, weather teletypes, and dedicated circuits at an advanced command center supporting General Vaught in Egypt.[10] By noon on launch day, April 24, a weak weather front trailed southwestward across Iran. Thunderstorms loomed over the Zagros Mountains west of the ingress routes. However, skies over southwestern Iran were clear. When Captain Buchanan briefed Vaught, no mention was made of blowing sand or dust in the operational area. The decision was made to "go."

Dusk found the eight RH-53Ds, whose markings had been removed, penetrating the Iranian coast in the same place and at approximately the same time as the C-130s. The faster C-130s arrived first at Desert One, where the weather was as Buchanan forecast: light surface winds, good visibility, and the right amount of moonlight with some high cirrus cloud cover.[11] There, with engines running, the six C-130s were forced to wait much longer than planned, for the helicopters were slow in appearing.

About three hours out from the *Nimitz*, one RH-53D aborted because of mechanical difficulties. The other seven ran into a cloud of suspended dust 50 miles east-northeast of Bam. It was the first of several unforecast walls of suspended dust that, although invisible on the weather satellite imagery, spanned 225 miles along the lee side of the Zagros Mountains. Visibility dropped sharply. Flight discipline was lost as helicopter crews could not maintain visual contact with ground references or one another.

The RH-53Ds separated into flights of one and two aircraft each. When several navigation and flight instruments failed on another RH-53D, an already difficult problem became impossible, so its crew also aborted and returned to the *Nimitz*. Unfortunately, they were unaware that they were within twenty-five minutes of exiting the last suspended dust area. Finally, when the sixth and last helicopter touched down at Desert One eighty-five minutes behind schedule, with the navy flight commander on board, his aircraft could not continue because of an irreparable hydraulic problem. The mission was now short one helicopter for the upcoming flight. President Carter, contacted by the radio, agreed that Eagle Claw must abort.

During the abort process, the thirty-six powerful engines of the C-130s and the RH-53Ds caused new visibility problems. While repositioning an RH-53D so that another could top off fuel tanks for the return flight, the first chopper crashed into the nose of a C-130 refueler when the pilot lost vision in dust clouds kicked up by his own rotor blades. Both aircraft burned, and eight crewmen were killed. The remaining task force quickly boarded the remaining five C-130s, which then departed for Masirah, a small island off Oman's coast, from which the C-130s had been launched.

Early the next morning (Washington time) President Carter went on national television to take full responsibility for the failed rescue attempt. There was an immediate outcry for answers. Congressional committees and subcommittees sprang into action and requested hearings. Even Captain Buchanan appeared before Senator John C. Stennis's Armed Services Committee—the first time an AWS company-grade officer had been summoned before solons. During questioning, Buchanan iterated that the problem had been unpredicted suspended dust, not dust storms. Asked whether the weather support had been sufficient, major generals Vaught and Gast replied affirmatively and without reservations.

Still, there was intense pressure for details. On April 30, Brigadier General Kaehn was called to the Pentagon and, through Major General Gast, directed by Joint Chiefs chairman Gen. David C. Jones (USAF) to conduct a postmortem of the AWS weather support. Captains Buchanan and Ruggeri, Major Wells, and two other officers formed a team assembled for that purpose by Kaehn. The result of that three-day review was a white paper that concluded that all AWS forecasts for the entire operational area had been accurate, failing only to predict the suspended dust.[12]

The study speculated that air rushing down from mountain thunderstorms could have been "of sufficient magnitude to lift and spread fine, powdery dust into the air and along the route of the helicopters." [13] Emphasizing the difference between such dust and the dust storms or sand storms noted in press reports, which implied the presence of high winds, the review team concluded that it was simply beyond the state of the art to reliably forecast such a condition. The Defense Department immediately included the white paper in a formal report on the rescue submitted to Congress on May 6 and also used it to refute misrepresentations and unsubstantiated allegations by the press.

Nevertheless, AWS failed to placate its critics. On May 16 Kaehn was instructed by Gast to approach the civil sector of the federal weather community about an independent, unbiased appraisal of the AWS support effort. Kaehn contacted the deputy of the federal coordinator of meteorology, William Barney (a former vice commander of the AWS), who, after touching base with National Weather Service director Richard Hallgren (also a former AWS officer), corralled three experts to form an independent study group (all of whom were distinguished AWS alumni). The trio consisted of two senior NOAA meteorologists—Leonard W. Snellman, one of the nation's foremost synoptic meteorologists, and Vincent J. Oliver, one of the country's finest satellite meteorologists—and Robert E. Beck, a climatologist who had supervised the development of the National Intelligence Survey's weather coverage for the Defense Department. Kaehn labeled it a very thorough review, but, in fact, the three experts spent the equivalent of one working day in the Pentagon pouring over pertinent weather data. They concluded that AWS support had been professionally planned and executed and that its forecasts had been as accurate as available data and state of the art would permit. [14]

Considerably more thorough was an inquiry by a special review group commissioned by General Jones. Made up of six senior-ranking officers, active duty and retired, the blue-ribbon panel was chaired by Adm. James L. Holloway III, a retired aviator and former chief of naval operations (1974–78). Another member was retired air force Lt. Gen. Leroy Manor who had skillfully used Keith Grimes's meteorological talents in planning and executing the Son Tay prison raid a decade earlier. Submitted in August, 1980, the Holloway report concluded that the mission concept was valid, the operation feasible, and success dependent upon the maintenance of secrecy.

"Planning was adequate except for the number of backup helicopters and provision for weather contingencies," the admiral's introductory statement read, and "preparation for the mission was adequate except for the lack of a comprehensive, full-scale training exercise." The group unanimously concluded that no one action or lack of action caused the operation to fail, but "two factors combined to directly cause the mission to abort: unexpected helicopter failure rate and low visibility flight conditions en route to Desert One." [15]

Of the eleven major issues spotlighted by the report, four related to weather and weather support. The critique group harbored strong reservation about the failure to use C-130s for weather reconnaissance and as pathfinders, particularly as the DMSP satellite proved unable to spot low dust clouds at night. The study was also critical of the fact that AWS weather specialists never had direct contact with flight crews: the RH-53D pilots were thus unaware of the possibility of suspended dust and had never trained for such an occurrence. [16] Moreover, the weather prediction for the night of April 24 did not mention possible instrument flight conditions along the land route taken by the helicopters.

Despite the broken forecast and the critics' charges, Brigadier General Kaehn said repeatedly that he was proud of the effort made by Captain Buchanan and the other AWS weathermen. However, he was slow to officially and formally convey that praise to his men; in fact, he remained very sensitive about their efforts, saying often that six choppers had made it to Desert One (the minimum number needed). More than two years passed before Kaehn conveyed to Buchanan and the others the appreciation that had been expressed by Vaught and the MAC commander right after the rescue attempt. It was November, 1981, when Buchanan received the Joint Service Commendation Medal (roughly equivalent to an Air Force Commendation Medal) that the Joint Chiefs had authorized. But because of AWS delays in the necessary paperwork, it was 1983 before eight other AWS weathermen received the same medal for Eagle Claw.

TODAY'S MILITARY WEATHER SERVICES

United States Air Force   When Gen. P. K. Carlton relinquished the reins of the Military Airlift Command in April, 1977, AWS no longer had to endure more than its fair share of drawdowns. With such external pressure to defend AWS size out of the way, Kaehn and his successor at AWS headquarters, Col. George E. Chapman, could turn their attention to upgrading the quality of their organization. [17] The most popular AWS commander since Tommy Moorman, Kaehn also worked hard to sort out which weather stations should be directed by a weather officer and which by a enlisted detachment chief. The "Benevolent and Protective Association of NCOs," as he affectionately referred to them, held strong views on the subject, but a compromise eventually placed NCOs in charge of fixed weather units that were not scheduled to move elsewhere during military emergencies.

Over the past two decades AWS placed heavy emphasis on upgrading AFGWC hardware, on data transmission links, and on the centralized weather support system as an entity. Kaehn believed the time had come to upgrade the physical capabilities of the weather detachments. He emphasized three new system developments: the Automated Weather Distribution System, the Next Generation Radar (NEXRAD, a joint doppler radar effort funded jointly by NOAA and the Federal Aviation Administration), and the Battlefield Weather Observing and Forecasting System. Equally important was the need for a better algorithm to use in target selection, one that would allow the decision maker to determine the greatest probability of success for a given target per target acquisition method (visual, infrared, television, or laser), tactic, and probable weather condition. Finally, as the best manned and equipped U.S. military weather service, AWS was assigned responsibility as the primary environmental support element for the nation's new Rapid Deployment Joint Task Force.

United States Army   The late 1970s still found the land forces uncertain about how best to use weather knowledge organizationally. The Army Audit Agency investigated that problem during early 1978 and issued a blunt report on June 12 of that year: "Activities responsible for various aspects of meteorology are fragmented among different Army organizatons, and a central focal point does not exist to provide guidance, supervision and coordination in the field of Army meteorology. Consequently, tactical meteorological data support requirements have remained largely undefined, training of officer personnel in the consideration and application of meteorological effects data is inadequate, personnel resources are under-utilized and misaligned, and research and development funds were not utilized efficiently." [18]

Meteorological program management proved to be split between two headquarters components (Intelligence and Corps of Engineers), two field army commands (Training and Doctrine Command, or TRADOC, and the Materiel, Development and Readiness Command, or DARCOM), one subordinate command, two training schools, a field operating agency, and the Atmospheric Sciences Laboratory (ASL) at the White Sands Missile Range, New Mexico. ASL was the dominant player, for it used a staff of 330 meteorological observers, plus 68 other military personnel, to provide weather support to research projects at fourteen army installations from Panama to Alaska. [19] These observers were buttressed by a meteorological equipment repairman group that included an additional 84 personnel.

Totally independent of the ASL empire were twenty-six artillery meteorological sections that used 260 artillery meteorological crewmen. The size of such sections varied from eight to fifteen crewmen (for no apparent reason as far as the auditors were concerned). In addition, the audit found 51 meteorologically qualified army officers, only 13 of whom were assigned duties requiring that skill.[20] When 175 civilian staff and 575 AWS support personnel were counted, the army was found to be using approximately 1,750 weather personnel—or almost one-third the total population of AWS.

For once, an audit received attention, although three years slid by before the army's vice chief of staff, Gen. John W. Vessey, Jr., directed implementation of a "Meteorological Plan for Action." According to that plan, the army's assistant chief of staff for intelligence would serve as lead agency, with the meteorological desk to be handled by a civilian, James M. Beck, a former AWS officer and pilot. In the Vessey-Beck plan, ASL lost all military observer billets; in return, the laboratory was to gain 230 civilian positions to handle noncombat weather functions. Furthermore, by September, 1984, specialty codes for enlisted weather observers and repairman would disappear from the books.[21] However, ballistic meteorological crewmen would continue to train at the Field Artillery Center and School, Fort Sill, Oklahoma. Of the other numerous army schools, only two would teach the impact of weather—the Army Aviation School at Fort Rucker, Alabama, providing rudiments of aeronautical meteorology, and the Combined Arms Center at Fort Leavenworth, Kansas, portraying effects of weather on field operations, personnel, and weapon systems.[22]

United States Navy   By the mid-1970s more navy admirals were wearing "dolphins" than "wings of gold." Astute naval politicians knew that oceanography was becoming more important than meteorology in the eyes of navy brass and congressional politicians. So in early 1976 Capt. Sam Houston, Jr., arranged for his Naval Weather Service command billet to be renamed Director of Naval Oceanography and Meteorology (DNOM), a step that the Royal Navy in Great Britain had already taken. It was hoped that this step would ease Capitol Hill pressure to merge the Naval Weather Service into a military purple-suit weather service. Houston's initiative backfired by the time he left the navy in March, 1976.

After having been brought back from retirement a year earlier by navy under secretary Dave Potter, Rear Adm. J. Edward Snyder reassumed his role as Oceanographer of the Navy on October 1, 1976. Snyder concentrated on speeding the move of the navy's oceanographic and geophysical program from Washington, D.C., to the semiabandoned, alligator-infested grounds of NASA's Space Technology Laboratories (NSTL) in Mississippi. As part of this mandatory hegira, the new DNOM, Capt. Dick Ward, moved his command to office trailers sited in what seemed to be perpetual mud. Ward also kept tangling with Snyder (the last of the battleship admirals until the 1980s) about the utility of numerical weather prediction. At one time the admiral even tried to have the Naval Postgraduate School cease teaching the subject. In despair, Ward retired early (October, 1978), hoping that Snyder would quit pressuring meteorology. But Ward's replacement was not another aerologist but, rather, a submariner turned oceanographer—Capt. John R. McDonnell.

Then followed several months during which options for melding the charting, environmental, and geophysical services into a single entity were studied. The results were foreordained. When the Naval Oceanography Command came into existence on October 1, 1978, it absorbed the Naval Weather Service Command, even though, as one of those involved commented, "Never have so many dragged so many feet for so long!" Snyder was not through, however. He ordered that the term *oceanography* replace *meteorology* throughout the naval lexicon. Editors of naval dictionaries were instructed to delete any explanation of *meteorology* and to insert the phrase "see oceanography." Sign painters went to work. The four weather centrals became oceanography centers. Seven weather facilities were converted to "Naval Oceanography Command Facilities," and fifty-odd environmental detachments were relabeled "Naval Oceanography Command Detachments."

Events ultimately moved so swiftly that AGCM Ronald W. Palmer performed four separate functions during one duty tour (1974–79): last leading chief of the Naval Weather Service Command, first and last leading chief for the DNOM organization, and first leading chief of the Naval Oceanography Command.[23] To old-timers, it was a soul-wrenching series of actions. But the powers-that-be believed just as firmly that the new command was necessary if the fleet was to receive economically and efficiently a total spectrum of geophysical services in an age of fast-moving global warfare. Just the same, even in 1985, the facts suggested that in the field, 80 percent of personnel time was devoted to weather support, 10 percent to oceanographic support, and the remainder to administration and supply.

United States Marine Corps   Although few meteorologists were aware of it, the Marine Corps continued to operate a low-key but viable weather program, tucked away in the Aviation Logistics Support Branch of service headquarters just up the hill from the Pentagon. As of 1985, the meteorological desk rated a captain (Capt. Larry L. Swope), although the rank had risen as high as lieutenant colonel during the Vietnam period. In that low-key service, essentially everyone had come up through the ranks. At the top were six LDOs plus eight WOs. Below were approximately 100 enlisted forecasters (staff sergeant or higher), backed up by approximately 200 enlisted observers of lesser rank.

In accordance with current practice, new Marine Corps weather observers and forecasters were trained at Chanute AFB. However, specialized course work in such topics as sea, swell, and surf forecasting, plus the use of specially equipped, forward-area weather vans, was taught at Chanute by well-seasoned marine and navy military instructors rather than by air force civilian or uniformed staff. The graduates then joined weather detachments assigned to all Marine Corps air wings and air bases, where the forecasting services were basically local and regional, and extended not more than twenty-four hours ahead.

United States Coast Guard   The least of the armed services also had the least of weather services. The potential existed for a respectable weather capability, but the resources and priorities did not. During FY 1984 the Coast Guard used 97 personnel at an approximate yearly cost of $2 million. Eighty-one cutters were able to take weather observations, using either quartermaster or marine science technicians. However, the larger potential rested with USCG coastal stations, 128 of which reported weather conditions to the National Weather Service. Unfortunately, the coastal task was secondary and lacked quality control and funding.

The talents of the 140-person corps of marine science technicians trained at the Coast Guard Reserve Training Center, Yorktown, Virginia, had also been drifting away from meteorology since the last USCG-operated weather ship had been laid up in 1976. In 1984 such technicians were specializing more and more in marine safety problems, particularly those associated with oil and chemical spills. The service was using just eight weather briefers, who had received three weeks of specialized training at Yorktown before being posted to air stations (Kodiak, Cape Cod, and Mobile), to an ice breaker (USCG *Glacier*), or to the ice observing program for the Great Lakes operated by the 9th Coast Guard District headquarters at Cleveland, Ohio.[24] Coast Guard weather forecasters, graduates of the four-month prediction course at Chanute AFB, were even fewer. One chief served as a Yorktown instructor, another was assigned to the Pacific Area Strike Team to assist with oil spills, and the third operated the ice program at Cleveland.

AN APPRAISAL

Despite humanity's best hopes, warfare has been rampant ever since mankind formed social groups. But few such conflicts have been won by simple, one-dimensional shows of military might. In the sixth century B.C., the brilliant Chinese strategist Sun Tzu pointed out: "Know the enemy, know yourself; your victory will never be endangered. Know the ground, know the weather—your victory will then be total."[25] Sun Tsu's advice has been borne out in the American military over the past 170 years. Despite vagaries in the ways military weather advisories were generated, disseminated, and acted upon, the ledger definitely came out on the side favoring the importance of weather warriors.

In the United States there has been a century-long debate, sometimes quite acrimonious, over the advantages and disadvantages of having a single federal agency discharge both the civil and military weather functions of the nation. Except for 1904–17, the program consolidators have always lost. Instead, the branches of the armed forces have fostered separate internal weather services, developing them so as to be responsive to each service's unique roles and missions. As long as the country's military branches remain separate, no overwhelming evidence can be marshaled to support the formation of a purple-suit weather agency. [26]

Today's military meteorologist works with products derived from fifth-generation weather satellites and sixth-generation electronic computers. But the question remains, how good are the men and women who operate this hardware and provide meteorological advice to a highly varied clientele whose interests now run far beyond conventional weather? In fact, for the past decade, these specialists have been dealing with thinking by the Joint Chiefs of Staff that calls for the use of "environmental officers" to provide a spectrum of geophysical information from the bottom of the sea to the top of the atmosphere, and even beyond. Fortunately, the meteorological community has generally been able to adjust. Leaders in the Air Weather Service and the Naval Oceanography Command believe that today's corps of military environmentalists is the finest all-volunteer group yet assembled during peacetime. [27]

Just the same, stresses exist. In the air force, service academy graduates have not provided a leadership cadre since the World War II era when West Pointers such as Yates, Senter, and Moorman opted for military meteorology as a profession before going on to three-star rank. Today's Air Force Academy graduates, once they have earned the right to wear wings, see more glamor and potential for career advancement in flying units. Thus, when General Carlton put AWS out of the flying business in 1975, out went the opportunity for a flying career within the field of weather. AWS has not had a rated-officer commander since Carlton's action and is not likely to have one in the future.

Conversely, Carlton's decision elevated the morale of AWS nonflying weather officers, for it meant that, for the first time ever, the brigadier general billet in the AWS command aerie was one they could compete for. But the situation is not likely to produce daring leaders. Rather, it will generate managers—"ticket-punching" technicians who touch all the right bases during their careers, adroitly avoiding the fatal habit of "making waves" because they are not members in good standing of that close-knit fraternity who wear silver pilot wings, much less the even more shadowy "ring knocking" academy club.

The army situation continues to be grim, despite the Vessey-Beck plan's goal to [provide] "effective, responsible weather support to Army tactical commanders, and maximize the efficiency of meteorological intelligence resources."[28] The army's weather program continues to be directed at the technical level, as it has been since World War II, by a civilian. No matter how skilled, articulate, and devoted she or he may be, the system still works against such a director's acceptance as a "true insider" by the army's top command.

Now that six years have elapsed, the navy is largely over the trauma generated when a naval oceanography command was substituted for the sixty-year-old weather service. But transition and growth pains remain. For example, a geophysical officer, who may be called upon to make weather forecasts, may have spent as little as a third of his time on that skill while doing postgraduate work at Monterey. Moreover, in certain quarters a tradition lingers that one who wishes to become director of the Naval Oceanography Command, had better serve either as executive officer or as commander of the Fleet Numerical Oceanography Center (the "Monterey daisy chain"), confirming the mandate that massive electronic computers and communications systems are the key to modern weather forecasting. The catch-22 problem, which equally applies to that held by AFGWC's proponents, is what do battle area forecasters do when communications are severed or the master computer bank malfunctions?

There also remains the issue of how well military meteorologists are used to help top commanders make tactical and strategic decisions. In Eagle Claw the task force environmentalist was a company-grade officer who was not permitted to talk to the pilots who were risking their necks in the operation. It can be done far better. As Capt. Dick Ward noted about his days on Yankee Station: "The carrier meteorologist was consulted at every turn and brought into the planning and execution of all attack operations, no matter how sensitive, in order to turn the weather pattern into a friend or neutral, rather than an enemy. Had the White House and the Pentagon seen it that way, far fewer missions would have accomplished the same target attrition rate."[29]

Communications being what they are today, Washington will, in all likelihood, continue to make tactical military decisions without firsthand weather advice. Before Vietnam and satellite communications, such a practice was nonexistent; tactical decisions were traditionally the domain of the overall commander at or near the battlefield. It therefore behooves a commander of today's weather warriors not only to be on good terms with the battlefield commander but to ensure, with all vigor and by all means at his disposal, that vital weather information is available to and used by decision makers at 1600 Pennsylvania Avenue and the Pentagon.

Continuing advances in electronics have exacerbated the issue of whether new weapons and tactics have finally freed the battlefield from adverse weather conditions. During the Korean War munitions makers and hard-

ware enthusiasts proclaimed that modern technology could negate anything introduced by Mother Nature. But Adm. Thomas H. Moorer, while
commander in chief of the Atlantic Fleet during 1966, was far more correct
when he observed: "It is peculiar, that while weather has always been a
factor in the prosecution of wars, that as military technology has advanced
and become more complex, military operations have become *more* sensitive
to the environment."[30]

In the age of radar, lasers, infrared detectors, microcomputers, inertial
guidance, smart bombs, and navigational satellites, meteorological considerations remain extremely important. As the recent Falkland Islands episode has shown, an all-weather military force does not exist, nor is one on
the horizon. This consideration was very much on the mind of John F.
Lehman, Jr., a naval aviator and the secretary of the navy, during an address
on May 26, 1982: "In a military balance where the navy of our principal
adversary is superior in numbers and near in comparable technology, it is
likely that the navy with the better knowledge of the environment will have
the war end on its terms."[31] This comment can, in all probability, be
applied to the other armed services.

We believe that military meteorologists (environmentalists, if you will)
will continue to play an important role in negating, minimizing, and
exploiting the effects of weather on warfare. Their services are worth too
much for today's commanders to ignore.

Que desideret pacem, praeparet bellum.

Appendixes

US TELEGRAM OB 2 extra RUSH PRIORITY
COLUMBEY LES BELLES 19 Oct. 1918

SEND the following Message:

TO:
NEMO TEN VIA WABASH
SIGNALS SECOND ARMY WABASH

WEATHER FORECAST NO J269 CONFIDENTIAL LORRAINE UN-
TIL 6 P.M. 20 OCTOBER

A.   Weather good for infantry, poor for aviation and observation. parag.

B.   Wind at surface weak—0 to 3 mps—northerly night, 0 to 6 mps.
north to northwest day,
>   At 2000 M weak—3 to 8 mps—north
>   At 5000 M weak—8 to 15 mps—northeast, parag.

C.   Sky overcast first part of night with occasional breaks or clear spaces
before midnight. Fog early morning and forenoon. Overcast afternoon.
parag.

D.   Cloud height 1000 meters night, 200 meters morning becoming
1000 meters afternoon. parag.

E.   Visibility poor—0 to 2 km—night and morning, 2 to 5 km afternoon. parag.

F.   Mist or wet fog in morning. parag.

G.   Minimum temperature 3 deg. maximum 10 deg. parag.

H.   Conditions favorable for use of gas by enemy opposite sectors facing
northwest, north, and northeast, parag.

K.   Odds in favor of forecast 7 to 1, except cloud 3 to 1. Issued 5:30 P.M.

NEMO

A TRUE COPY

W. R. BLAIR
MAJOR, S.C.

Local Time	Duty Undertaken
0500	AGC reports to Weather Office and starts map analysis.
0530	Weather Officer arrives and checks maps for prognosis.
0545	Commence map discussion, develop prognosis, and make rough forecast.
0600	Leading Petty Officer (LPO) holds reveille for weather division.
0630	LPO supervises morning upper air sounding by watch section.
0645	Weather Officer completes forecast, and LPO commences making up smooth copies.
0700	Weather Officer proceeds to appropriate areas for briefing Flag Officer and vessel's Commanding Officer. CPO signs smooth printed forecast; office messenger takes smooth forecast stencil to Operations Office for duplication and surface/upper air maps to Photographic Lab for reproduction.
0745	Weather Officer finishes briefings and goes to breakfast; messenger distributes maps and forecasts throughout ship, including appropriate embarked aviation squadron personnel. CPO secures.
0815	Weather Officer briefs department heads and division officers.
1100	CPO arrives Weather Office to analyze noon map; Weather Officer checks synoptic map against forecast for signs of major error. Holds short map discussion and revises forecast as needed.
1130	CPO to lunch.
1200	Weather Officer to lunch.
1300	Weather Officer rebriefs appropriate officers as necessary.
1345	Weather Officer secures, and CPO takes forecast duty.
1630	Weather Officer returns to office, and CPO and LPO to dinner.
1800	Weather Officer to dinner, CPO to quarters, and LPO stands office watch.
1900	Weather Officer rebriefs as necessary; LPO supervises upper-air sounding by watch section.
2000	Weather Officer and LPO to quarters; CPO takes watch.
2230	Weather Officer/CPO sketch and analyze "midnight" map; recheck the night forecast and morning outlook; rebrief if any major changes.
2300	Weather Officer/CPO retire.

SOURCE: U.S. Navy Weather Research Facility, *The Carrier Weather Officer*, NWRF Report 25-0959-025 (Norfolk, Va.: U.S. Naval Air Station, 1959).

AIR FORCE WEATHER STATION
12TH WEATHER REGION
MOBILE UNIT NO. 2

March 14, 1944

WEATHER FORECAST FOR BATTLE SECTORS: 0000A-2359A,
MARCH 15.

ANZIO   Clear tonight. Few low clouds early morning. Increasing high and middle cloudiness late afternoon and evening. Light rain probable late evening. Visibility unrestricted. Wind north and northwest 15–20 mph, diminishing during morning and shifting to west 12 mph. Moderate temperatures.

CASSINO   Clear tonight. Partly cloudy during morning. Increasing high and middle cloudiness afternoon and evening. Light rain probable at night. Visibility unrestricted. Wind north 15–20 mph. diminishing in morning and shifting to west 12 mph. Moderate temperatures.

GENERAL ANALYSIS

Frontal system over France yesterday morning has moved rapidly southeastward, passing this station about 0600A. The attendant low pressure center has joined with the low off Southern Italy and formed a large trough of low pressure over Southern Yugo-Slavia and Greece. Northwesterly circulation brought rapid clearing behind the front except in higher mountain areas. A shift of wind is expected tomorrow about noon which will bring increasing cloudiness as another low now over Ireland approaches the Western Mediterranean. Light rain is probable late on the 15th. The prospects for March 16th and 17th are not promising as the Azores High has weakened considerably. This will allow low pressure centers from the North Atlantic to enter the Mediterranean zone.

DAILY ALMANAC   MARCH 15–16, 1944

	Sunrise	Sunset	Moonrise	Moonset	
15	0608	1810	2337	0915	FULL
16	0607	1811	——	0952	MOON

DISTRIBUTION
   1-ASC CG
   1-ASC CS
   2-ASC A-2, A-3
   1-ASC REAR
   5-5TH ARMY

WEATHER DATA: PRESENT AND
24 hrs. ending at 1800A

Highest Temperature: 60
Lowest Temperature: 35
Precipitation   0.10"

DAVID M LUDLUM
Capt, Air Corps
Weather Officer

Weather Report of 5 June 1944, 05.00[h]

Only for Official Use!

Shooting-light (Brest):
  Ending on June 5: 23 hrs
  Beginning on June 6: 5.37 hrs

Weather at St. Germain (headquarters site): 05.00 hrs: . . .

General weather situation:
  As expected, the strong central low-pressure system in the area between Iceland and Scotland has largely overcome the high-pressure
  ridge present over Western Europe. Thus the road to Western Europe
  has been opened for the pertinent frontal zones. An initial bad-
  weather zone appearing as a cold front will be crossing the area of C-in-
  C West. In the course of today, clouds will disperse in its rear with
  isolated showers in between. It is to be supposed that more secondary
  depressions will develop at the west and south sides of the central low-
  pressure system.

Forecast until midnight:
  Moderate to fresh wind from west to northwest. After a bad weather
  front from the west has passed in the course of the day, the clouds will
  break up again, and some showers will form from time to time.
  Visibility mostly good, only sometimes slightly reduced in showers.
  Daytime temperatures around 15° to 20°C.

Outlook until tomorrow evening (June 6, 1944):
  Moderate to fresh wind from west to northwest, sky clearing locally
  during the night; during the day more or less changing cloudiness
  with interspersed showers occurring particularly in the afternoon. In
  between, clearing in places. Temperature at night around 10°C., and
  in daytime around 15° to 20°C. Visibility mostly good, sometimes
  reduced by showers; in the morning, mist also in places. . . .

Italy: clear sky, visibility good. Mediterranean Sea: Hotter, good visibility.

Outlook for enemy attacks until tonight:
  Departure from the British launch areas generally possible without
  difficulty, in particular if only small formations are put into action.
  Operations of larger formations probably impeded by frontal showers
  with thick clouds. Air activity in the C-in-C West's area not impeded

in southern France, but in the other areas rendered more difficult by a zone of bad weather with thick clouds and rain. Later on, clouds will clear from the west, and conditions for attacks will be more favorable.

SIGNED: Dr. Müller,

NOTE: This forecast was issued from the Saint-Germaine headquarters of General Field Marshal von Rundstedt, commander in chief, West. Translation courtesy of Suzanne Roll, Hamburg, FRG. A photograph of this document in German appeared in 1979 in *Der Spiegel*, no. 27.

Target	Sorties Scheduled	Canceled (%)*	Diverted (%)†	Ineffective (%)‡	Total Aborted
North Viet-nam	57,440	7,312 (12.75)	16,048 (28.00)	653 (1.14)	24,013 (41.90)
Laos	34,036	2,275 (6.67)	3,713 (10.89)	392 (1.15)	6,380 (18.71)
South Viet-nam	69,420	1,189 (2.62)	2,124 (3.08)	618 (0.89)	4,561 (6.58)
Total	160,896	11,406 (7.12)	21,885 (13.63)	1,663 (1.04)	34,954 (21.75)

SOURCE: John F. Fuller and Allan B. Milloy, *The Air Weather Service in Southeast Asia* (Scott AFB, Ill.: MAC, 1968).

* Canceled because of bad weather at base, en route, or at the primary, alternate, or tertiary targets.
† Diverted before takeoff on basis of forecast of bad weather at target or after takeoff because of adverse weather reported or encountered at primary target.
‡ Declared ineffective against primary target because of adverse weather encountered en route, in refueling area, or at the target. These aircraft expended their ordnance against another target, jettisoned it, or returned to home base with it aboard.

APPENDIX F: Weather Effects on Naval Air Operations in Southeast Asia (Late 1966)

Service	Aircraft Type	September		December	
		Sorties Flown	Sorties Canceled by Weather	Sorties Flown	Sorties Canceled by Weather
Navy	A-1	1,042	36	237	35
	A-3	374	6	—	—
	A-4	3,726	150	1,536	1,227
	A-6	249	0	263	36
	F-4	1,275	25	1,397	554
	F-8	325	8	359	121
	Totals	6,961	225	3,792	1,973
Marine	A-4	—	—	210	33
Corps	A-6	—	—	83	3
	F-4	—	—	148	36
	F-8	—	—	75	2
	Totals			516	74

SOURCE: John F. Fuller and Allan B. Milloy, *The Air Weather Service in Southeast Asia* (Scott AFB, Ill.: MAC, 1968).

Notes

1. John F. Fuller, *Weather and War* (Scott AFB: MAC, 1974), p. 1.

2. Alfred J. Henry, "Early Individual Observers in the United States," *U.S. Weather Bureau Publication 11, Part II* (1894): 295–97; Alexander McAdie, "Simultaneous Meteorological Observations in the United States during the Eighteenth Century," *U.S. Weather Bureau Publication 11, Part II* (1894): 303–304; William M. Davis, "Was Lewis Evans or Benjamin Franklin the First to Recognize That Our Northeast Storms Come from the Southwest?" *American Philosophical Society Journal* 45 (1906): 129–30. Franklin might be called America's first military meteorologist, for he organized and served as captain of a militia company on the Pennsylvania frontier during 1756. George Washington also had a deep interest in weather. The last words penned in his diary a day before he died on Dec. 14, 1799, were meteorological. See Clarence J. Root's "A Faithful Record," AMS *Bulletin* 7, no. 3 (1926): 50.

3. Reuben G. Thwaites, ed., *Original Journals of the Lewis and Clark Expedition*. vol. 1 (New York: Dodd, Mead, 1905).

4. Thomas Lawson, *Army Meteorological Register for Twelve Years, from 1843 to 1854, Inclusive* (Washington, D.C.: Public Printer, 1855), p. v.

5. As early as 1817, Lovell observed: "It is not until [the recruit] begins to feel the want of dry and comfortable clothing and to be exposed to changes of weather without sufficient clothing or exercise that he suffers from diseases of the lungs and bowels. . . . It is very common after a cold and rainy night when the sick are in tents, to find several who appeared fast recovering dead within 24 hours." U.S. armed forces deaths listed as "other" during the Civil War (Union troops only), Spanish American War, and World War I were 61%, 84%, and 64%, respectively, of the total casualties reported. U.S. Bureau of the Census, *Historical Statistics of the United States: Colonial Times to 1970*; Part 2 (Washington, D.C.: GPO, 1975), p. 1140.

6. H. H. C. Dunwoody, "State Weather Service Organizations," *U.S. Weather Bureau Publication 11, Part II* (1894): 285–86.

7. In submitting the *Meteorological Register for 1843–54* to the secretary of war,

Bvt. Brig. Gen. Thomas Lawson noted that the report was based on more than 8,000 monthly registers containing nearly 4 million observations.

8. William M. Davis, "The Redfield and Espy Period, 1830 to 1855," *U.S. Weather Bureau Publication 11, Part II* (1894): 305 – 16; Eric R. Miller, "The Evolution of Meteorological Institutions in the United States," *Monthly Weather Review* 59, no. 1 (1931): 1 – 6. As early as 1838, Espy petitioned the U.S. Senate to provide awards "for rainmaking by burning woodlands"; he also arranged for the Pennsylvania Lyceum to ask Congress to establish a national weather service.

9. James P. Espy, *First Report on Meteorology, Made to the Surgeon-General, U.S. Army* (Washington, D.C.: Public Printer, 1843), pp. 1 – 4, plus 29 charts. In addition to the army "clerkship" Espy served as "professor of mathematics" during 1842 – 45 in the navy's Depot of Charts and Instruments. By 1848 his work orders came from the navy secretary and his second, third, and fourth reports on meteorology were submitted through navy channels to Congress in 1849, 1850, and 1852, respectively.

10. As the Depot's successor, the U.S. Naval Observatory eventually published an unbroken sequence of weather observations for Washington, D.C., taken from 1838 through 1902.

11. U.S. Congress, House, *Appropriations for Naval Service, 1842*, 27th Cong., 2d sess. (1842), H. R. 673, p. 22.

12. Matthew F. Maury, *Explanations and Sailing Directions to Accompany the Wind and Current Charts* (Washington, D.C.: Public Printer, 1851).

13. Maury's optimal ship tracks were the first application of "pressure-pattern navigation" based on scientific principles. Long-range aircraft flights using the concept began in 1944, nearly a century later.

14. W. H. Beehler, "The Origin and Work of the Division of Marine Meteorology," *U.S. Weather Bureau Publication 11, Part II* (1894): 221 – 32. Until about 1910, federal scientific instructors and researchers were carried on the payroll as professors. The first American Ph.D. degree in meteorology was granted in 1899 by the Johns Hopkins University's department of geology to Oliver L. Fassig, a Weather Bureau employee.

15. Marc I. Pinsel, *150 Years of Service on the Seas, Vol. I (1830 – 1946)* (Washington, D.C.: Government Printing Office, 1982). The participating countries were Belgium, Denmark, France, Great Britain, the Netherlands, Norway, Portugal, Russia, Sweden, and the United States. As of that time, the British already had a nineteen-station land-reporting network. However, only after an unpredicted storm of Nov. 14, 1854, wrecked the combined French-British fleet off Balaklava did the two governments institute formal weather observation and prediction services. See H. Landsberg in *Scientific Monthly* 79, no. 6 (1954): 347 – 52.

16. Matthew F. Maury, *The Physical Geography of the Sea and Its Meteorology*, ed. John Leighly (Cambridge: Harvard University Press, 1963); Harold L. Burstyn and Susan B. Schlee, "The Study of Ocean Currents in America before 1930," in *Two Hundred Years of Geology in America* (Hanover, N.H.: University Press of New England, 1979).

17. As late as the 1960s pilot charts of the Naval Oceanographic Office carried the legend "Founded upon the researches made in the early part of the nineteenth

century by Matthew Fontaine Maury while serving as a Lieutenant in the United States Navy."

18. R. H. Weightman, "Establishment of a National Weather Service—Who Was Responsible for It?" (unpublished report, U.S. Weather Bureau, 1952), p. 35.

19. U.S. National Archives, *List of Climatological Records in the National Archives*, Special List No. 1, prepared by Lewis J. Darter, Jr. (Washington, D.C.: GPO, 1942; reprinted, 1981).

20. Samuel P. Langley, "The Meteorological Work of the Smithsonian Institution," *U.S. Weather Bureau Publication 11, Part II* (1894): 216–20.

21. Eric R. Miller, "The Pioneer Meteorological Work of Elias Loomis at Western Reserve College, Hudson, Ohio, 1837–1844, *Monthly Weather Review* 59, no. 5 (1931): 194–95.

22. Frederick J. Hughes, "Albert James Myer: Army Physician and Climatologist," *Transactions of the American Clinical and Climatological Association* 81 (1969): 119–29; Paul J. Scheips, "Albert James Myer, Founder of the Army Signal Corps: A Biographical Study" (Ph.D. diss., American University, 1966), p. 685. A combative, acquisitive individual, Myer had been a telegraph operator and had based his doctoral thesis, "A New Sign Language for Deaf Mutes," on dot-dash principles. While an assistant surgeon between 1854 and 1857 on the West Texas frontier, he observed Comanches signaling with lances. Eventually, he proposed to the secretary of war a visual communication system, using flags by day and torches by night, to replace battlefield couriers on horseback. After the system was favorably studied by a board headed by Lt. Col. Robert E. Lee, Myer was appointed Signal Officer of the Army with rank of major on June 21, 1860, a date known as the official birth date of the Army Signal Corps, whose insignia still incorporates flags and torches. In late 1863 Myer disagreed with Secretary of War Edward M. Stanton regarding the proper role of the quasiprivate "U.S. Military Telegraph" and was relieved of military service the following year. It was not until 1867 that he was recalled to active duty and reinstated as bureau chief—albeit a bureau authorized only 6 officers and 100 enlisted men, all on detail from other components of the army.

23. Eric R. Miller, "New Light on the Beginnings of the Weather Bureau from the Papers of Increase A. Lapham," *Monthly Weather Review* 59, no. 2 (1931): 65–70. The resolution provided "that the Secretary of War be . . . authorized and required to provide for taking meteorological observations at the military stations . . . and for giving notice on the northern lakes and on the seacoast by magnetic telegraph and marine signals, of the approach and force of storms."

24. At an annual salary of $2,004, Lapham's pay was equivalent to that of Col. Myer, who drew a base pay of $1,320 plus $657 in subsistence allowances. U.S. Weather Bureau, "Chronological Outline of the History of Meteorology in the United States of North America," *Monthly Weather Review* 34, no. 4 (1909): 146–49.

25. Donald R. Whitnah, *History of the U.S. Weather Bureau* (Urbana: University of Illinois Press, 1961), p. 26. The meteorological budgets (by fiscal year) were as follows: 1869–70—$15,000; 1870–71—$50,000; 1871–72—$102,000; and 1872–73—$250,000. The military payroll's cost (more than half the total) was

picked up separately by the army-wide appropriation for military pay and allowances. In 1872 nearly 230 weather personnel were paid in that manner. A typical weather station was commanded by an "observer-sergeant" backed up by a telegrapher with the rank of corporal. Such units numbered 24 in 1870, 55 in 1871, and 78 in 1873. Although primarily meteorological, these army stations provided up-to-the-minute status reports to Washington on the great railroad strike of July–August, 1877, and established a military presence at local emergencies such as yellow fever epidemics and the great Chicago fire of 1871.

26. Myer increased Abbe's pay from $3,000 to $4,500 per annum within a two-year span, making Abbe one of the two highest-paid civilians in the executive branch (Joseph Henry, the Smithsonian Institution's secretary, was the other). Abbe, as dean of federal meteorologists, did not retire until 1913.

27. Cleveland Abbe, "The Meteorological Work of the U.S. Signal Service, 1870 to 1891." *U.S. Weather Bureau Publication 11, Part II* (1894): 232–84. In Oct. 1871, Lt. H. H. C. Dunwoody, USA, began an official comparison of published predictions versus the daily weather map values. Verification factors of 76.8% and 77.6% were reported for 1871–72 and 1872–73, respectively (see Cleveland Abbe in *U.S. Weather Bureau Bulletin* 11, no. 2 [1895]: 252).

28. Truman Abbe, *Professor Abbe and the Isobars: The Story of Cleveland Abbe, America's First Weatherman* (New York: Vantage Press, 1955).

29. U.S. Army Signal Corps, "Weather and the Signal Corps" (unpublished press packet assembled by P. J. Scheips, Office of Chief Signal Officer, for the ninety-sixth anniversary of the Army Signal Corps, 1956), p. 22.

30. The Signal Corps' second expedition during 1881–83 for the International Polar Year took 1st Lt. P. H. Ray and his party to Point Barrow, Alaska, without difficulties.

31. U.S. Congress, Senate, *Testimony before the Joint House-Senate Commission to Consider the Present Organization of the Signal Service, Geological Survey, Coast and Geodetic Survey, and the Navy Hydrographic Office*, 49th Cong., 1st sess. (1886), S. Misc. Doc. 82, p. 1002.

32. U.S. Senate, *Final Report of the Joint House-Senate Commission to Consider the Present Organization of the Signal Service, Geological Survey, Coast and Geodetic Survey, and the Navy Hydrographic Office*, 49th Cong., 1st sess. (1886), S. Rep. 1285, p. 59. Observer-sergeants were frequently drunk on duty. One of the most flagrant violators was John Timothy O'Keefe, a Naval Academy dropout. Assigned to the station atop Pikes Peak during the late 1870s, he would make up weather reports ahead, leave them with the corporal to transmit at the proper time, and take off on a spree. Civilian staff likewise came under criticism. For example, during 1888, a Signal Corps inspector mentioned to the press that the civilian forecaster at Washington, D.C., was such a pure scientist that he could not convert his theories into accurate public weather forecasts.

33. Greely went on to build up the Signal Corps' communication function as a major general. Even in retirement, the amazing man continued to be a prolific writer of books. By the time of his death in 1935 at age 92, he had written a dozen books on meteorology, the American Arctic, Alaska, and the climatology of the arid American West, a record unsurpassed by any other military weatherman before or since. Three of his military records stand out: he was the first volunteer Civil War

private to achieve the grade of brigadier general in the regular Army; he was probably the only man to jump in grade from captain to brigadier general in one day; and he was the only officer to receive the Medal of Honor while in his nineties.

CHAPTER 2

1. Theodore Roosevelt, Presidential Executive Order, July 29, 1904.

2. Mark W. Harrington, "Systematic Explorations of the Upper Air With Estimates of Cost," *Monthly Weather Review* 42, no. 11 (1914): 619–21.

3. Willis R. Gregg, "Aerological Investigations of the Weather Bureau During the War," *Monthly Weather Review* 47, no. 4 (1919): 205–208.

4. Academic members were drawn from Johns Hopkins, Stanford, Northwestern, and Columbia universities. Naval membership consisted of naval constructor Holden C. Richardson and Capt. Mark L. Bristol. U.S. Weather Bureau, "National Advisory Committee on Aeronautics," *Monthly Weather Review* 43, no. 10 (1915): 500–501.

5. U.S. Weather Bureau, "Influence of Weather on Military Operations," *Monthly Weather Review* 47, no. 1 (1919): 84–85.

6. H. G. Lyons, "Meteorology During and After the War," *Monthly Weather Review* 47, no. 1 (1919): 81–83; Clarence L. Meisinger, "Notes on the Meteorological Service of the German Army from Translations of German Documents," ibid. 47, no. 12 (1919): 871–74.

7. Robert A. Millikan, *Autobiography* (New York: Prentice Hall, 1950). Millikan's fame and the first Nobel Prize to an American came from his work in 1910–11 measuring the charge of a electron by suspending aerosols in electrical fields (i.e., by fogmaking).

8. Artillery tables of the time assumed that local surface wind, temperature, and barometric conditions remained constant through a shell's entire flight. But if there was an opposing wind aloft of, say, 22 miles per hour, a 75-mm artillery shell reaching a height of 6,600 feet would fall nearly 1,320 feet short. See Bertram J. Sherry and Alan T. Waterman in *Monthly Weather Review* 47, no. 4 (1919): 215–22.

9. All five had notable postwar careers. Blair and Sherry stayed in the Signal Corps, Gale rose to dean of physical sciences at Chicago, Bowie returned to the Weather Bureau, and Waterman became the founding technical director for the Office of Naval Research and for the National Science Foundation.

10. George O. Squier, "Meteorological Service of the Army," *Monthly Weather Review* 47, no. 1 (1919): 84. One of Marvin's strong points was his ability to work well with the military. A graduate in mechanical engineering from Ohio State University, he had been recruited by Hazen in 1884 for the Signal Corps Meteorological Service.

11. Robert H. Kargon, *The Rise of Robert Millikan* (Ithaca, N.Y.: Cornell University Press, 1982).

12. Philip M. Flammer, "Meteorology in the U.S. Army, 1917–1935" (Master's thesis, George Washington University, 1958).

13. U.S. Army Office of the Chief Signal Officer, Meteorological Division, "Plan for the Meteorological Service, A.E.F." (ca. early 1918, typescript, Office of the

Historian, MAC, Scott AFB). As Chief of Air Service, Army Group, Brig. Gen William Mitchell had on his desk at every hour the updated weather conditions for the next 36 hours.

14. Oliver L. Fassig, "A Signal Corps School of Meteorology," *Monthly Weather Review* 46, no. 12 (1918): 560–62. More than 90% of these trainees were college graduates. By specialties, there were civil engineers—100; mechanical or electrical engineers—75; Weather Bureau observers—40; teachers—30; and chemists—20. Among the students were Ivan Ray Tannehill, who later wrote the classic book about hurricanes, and C. Leroy Meisinger, who soon became an upper-air specialist of considerable renown. Twenty-five of the graduates were sent directly to the navy, undoubtedly at Millikan's suggestion, to become badly needed underwater sound apparatus operators in antisubmarine warfare.

15. Charles F. Brooks, "Collegiate Instruction in Meteorology," *Monthly Weather Review* 46, no. 12 (1918): 555–60. A weather instructor at Texas A&M whom Brooks described as the keenest of the lot was Sgt. Don McNeal, a 1913 graduate of Ohio State who was commissioned a second lieutenant in October, 1918, and who went on to a series of assignments between the wars before emerging in 1940 to exert more influence on meteorological training in World War II than any other individual.

16. Millikan developed an unspoken love-hate relationship with his superior, Brig. Gen. Squier. In Millikan's *Autobiography*, he notes that the general was a strange character who prided himself on being a scientist. In no degree, Millikan claims, could Squier be thought of as a manager with balanced judgment, although he did have the much needed ability to get things moving on a large scale.

17. Bertram J. Sherry and Alan T. Waterman, "The Military Meteorological Service in the United States During the War," *Monthly Weather Review* 47, no. 2 (1919): 216–22.

18. Robert A. Millikan, "Some Scientific Aspects of the Meteorological Work of the United States Army," *Monthly Weather Review* 47, no. 2 (1919): 213–16.

19. John F. Fuller, "WWI Brings Military Weather into Its Own," *AWS Observer* 25, no. 1 (1978): 2. Allied pilots were primarily interested in cloud cover and wind speed/direction at altitudes up to 15,000 feet. With cruising speeds of about 85 knots, their planes tended to drift over German lines during combat because of the prevailing westerlies; the strong headwinds thus made the return difficult, particularly if the planes were damaged.

20. Thomas R. Reed, "Some Meteorological Observations of a Bombing Pilot in France," *Monthly Weather Review* 48, no. 4 (1920): 216–17; U.S. Weather Bureau, "The Signal Corps Meteorological Service, A.E.F.," ibid. 47, no. 12 (1919): 870–71.

21. The golden fleur-de-lis in the emblem of the Air Weather Service commemorates the World War I duty in France. "History of the Meteorological Section, Signal Corps, American Expeditionary Forces" (1918, unsigned typescript, Office of Historian, MAC, Scott AFB).

22. To halt the outflow, early in 1919 Capt. Sherry stood on a New York dock for three hours, reviewing the situation with a hundred weathermen just back from France. As Sherry advised the Signal Corps Personnel Division later (see Sherry memo, Mar. 8, 1919, to Col. J. C. Moore, Chief Signal Officer, RG 111, file

665.2, National Archives), "none of the enlisted men desire to stay in the Army under any circumstances. This whole detachment desired immediate discharge to a man."

23. As of early 1917 the U.S. Navy had 54 aircraft, most of which were unsuitable for combat. The aviation corps of the navy had 43 officers and 239 enlisted men, and the marine aviation corps 5 officers plus 30 enlisted personnel. At war's end the navy operated 1,865 flying boats and seaplanes, 242 land planes, 205 kite balloons, 15 dirigibles, and 10 free balloons, manned by 3,117 officers and 43,452 enlisted personnel. Fifty-one aviation units operated overseas at twenty-seven stations in Great Britain (including Ireland), France, and Italy for antisubmarine patrol, convoy protection, scouting, bombing of naval and land targets, support of marine land combat units, and dispersal of propaganda leaflets (see secretary of the navy's annual report for FY1919). Roswell F. Barratt, to Francis W. Reichelderfer, Jan. 4, 1973, copy in author Bates's files.

24. After graduating in physics from the City College of New York during 1881, McAdie became another Hazen "observer-sergeant" acquisition for the Signal Corps. McAdie continued in the federal weather service for the next thirty-two years (except for a year's break) before becoming director at Blue Hill.

25. U.S. Chief of Naval Operations, Weekly report of Naval Aviation Division for Nov. 26, 1917, states Naval Air Detachment, MIT, holding aerological discussions with Blue Hill Observatory; Alexander G. McAdie, "The Work of the Aerographic Section of the Navy," *Monthly Weather Review* 47, no. 4 (1919): 225–26; Alexander G. McAdie, *Annual Report of the Blue Hill Observatory for the Year Ending 30 June 1918* (Cambridge: Harvard University, 1918).

26. S2c. Roswell F. Barratt, U.S. Naval Air Detachment, MIT, to Chief of Naval Operations, Jan. 5, 1918, file NAD-762-15 (National Archives RG 78, box 257).

27. Roswell F. Barratt to author Bates, Dec. 1, 1982.

28. Chief of Naval Operations (Aviation) to BuNav, file 7151, Jan. 25, 1918, subject: Meteorologist for Naval Aviation; U.S. Navy Department, *Register of Commissioned and Warrant Officers* (Washington, D.C.: Navy Department, 1919). Listing shows that McAdie enrolled as lieutenant commander, USN Reserve Force, on Feb. 1, 1918.

29. Of 58 candidates, the training program recommended 52 for commissioning. Of these, 24 were Ivy Leaguers, and 5 were from MIT. Only 3 came from schools south of the Mason-Dixon Line. Princeton had the most candidates—8. Because of McAdie's overseas duty and frequent "disappearing spells" at Blue Hill, most of these classes were taught by the facility's chief observer, L. A. Wells, and by newly commissioned ensigns—Ellsworth B. Buck, Clarence N. Keyser, Ivor O. Mall, Elven Parsons, Walter A. RuKeyser, and Bailey Townshend.

30. C. T. Jewell, "Work of the Naval Observatory in Connection with Naval Aerography," *Monthly Weather Review* 47, no. 4 (1919): 226–27. The list included a barograph, anemoscope, anemobiagraph, thermograph, hydrograph, sunshine recorder, lightning recorder, psychrometer, aneroid barometer, balloon equipment, recording theodolite, clock, and thermometers (solar radiation, maximum-minimum, and gross minimum). Central stations also received nephoscopes, rain gages, aerographs, and hygrometers (see Chief of Naval Operations [Aviation] to Naval Observatory, letter file 086-199, Feb. 26, 1918, box 266, RG 78, National

Archives). McAdie, quite dissatisfied with Weather Bureau equipment, required the observatory to follow his predilections. Ruy Finch, "Meteorology in the Naval Aviation Service Overseas," *Monthly Weather Review* 47, no. 4 (1919): 227–28. Despite the promises, Barratt's group found it wise to order materiel from three sources—the British Hydrographic Office, the British Meteorological Office, and the Bureau Centrale Météorologique—for they still never received two of any item (Barratt to author Bates, Dec. 20, 1982).

31. McAdie's high opinion of what had been accomplished in a little more than four months is given in his report of June 10, 1918, to Assistant Secretary Roosevelt, written at the blimp station near Paimbouef, France: "The work of organization and equipment has now reached such a point that the officer in charge feels that the special duty which he was asked to undertake by the Assistant Secretary of the Navy has been essentially completed; and that the Navy now has an efficient aerographic service equal to the best foreign service." McAdie was probably hinting that he did not want his active duty orders extended. If so, the hint did not work for he was kept on active duty until May 29, 1919, with the title "Senior Aerographic Officer."

32. U.S. Naval Air Station Aerological Detachment, Pensacola, Aerological Log, vol. 1. Entry of May 4, 1918, describes reconnaissance flight piloted by Ens. Maxwell.

33. Clifford L. Lord, "The History of Naval Aviation, 1898–1939, Part III," unpublished MS of Naval Aviation History Unit, 1946, p. 775, copy filed in Navy Department Library.

34. David Beaty, *The Water Jump* (London: Martin Secker & Warburg, 1976); Percy Rowe, *The Great Atlantic Air Race* (Toronto: McClelland and Stewart, 1977).

35. Willis R. Gregg, "The First Trans-Atlantic Flight," *Monthly Weather Review* 47, no. 5 (1919): 279–83.

36. Barratt to author Bates, Dec. 20, 1982. Commanders of large naval aircraft in those days were the navigators, not the pilots. Pilots on Read's NC-4 were the Coast Guard's Lt. Elmer Stone and the navy's Lt. Walter Hinton. NC-1's senior pilot was Lt. Marc Mitscher, who later became a famous World War II aircraft carrier commander.

37. Gregg, "First Trans-Atlantic Flight," p. 283.

CHAPTER 3

1. From Aug., 1919, through Mar., 1920, the Aerial Mail Service, in 1,111 trips, had to make 203 forced landings—154 because of bad weather and 47 because of mechanical trouble. See U.S. Weather Bureau, "Effect of Weather on the Aerial Mail Service," *Monthly Weather Review* 48, no. 6 (1920): 335–36.

2. Frederick J. Nelson, "The History of Aerology in the Navy," *U.S. Naval Institute Proceedings* 60, no. 371 (1934): 522–28.

3. Alfred J. Henry et al., *Weather Forecasting in the United States*, Weather Bureau Publication No. 583 (Washington, D.C.: GPO, 1916), p. 5. For example, Charles L. Mitchell started as an assistant weather observer shortly after 1900. In 1915 he was designated a forecaster. By the 1930s he was considered the most accurate of the

Weather Bureau's forecasters, but no one, including Mitchell himself, could write down just how he did it.

4. As the war dragged on, Europeans became more malnourished. Bjerknes's top student at Leipzig, Harald U. Sverdrup, found studying extremely difficult, for he preferred to spend the time thinking about his single meal of the day—a lone egg in the evening. Bjerknes, his family, and his students lived and worked in a large house. Carl-Gustav Rossby, who joined the group in 1918, remembered the professor as having only a vague interest in his students and a parsimonious way with his family.

5. Ralph Jewell, "The Bergen School of Meteorology," *AMS Bulletin* 62, no. 6 (1981): 824–30; Jacob Bjerknes, "On the Structure of Moving Cyclones," *Geofysiske Publikasjoner* 1, no. 2 (1918): 1–8 (rpt. *Monthly Weather Review* 47, no. 2 (1919): 90–99.

6. This is the northern hemisphere condition in which storms rotate counter-clockwise. The situation is reversed in the southern hemisphere. Air masses were classified by geographic source (arctic, polar, tropical, and equatorial) and by moisture content (e.g., maritime, continental). Thus, North America featured nine main types, such as Tropical Gulf (of Mexico) (T_g) and Polar Continental (P_c).

7. Jerome Namias, "The History of Polar Front and Air Mass Concepts in the United States—An Eyewitness Account," *AMS Bulletin* 64, no. 7 (1983): 734–55; George W. Platzman, "A Retrospective View of Richardson's Book on Weather Prediction," ibid. 48, no. 8 (1967): 514–50.

8. U.S. Army, *Annual Report of the Chief Signal Officer to the Secretary of War, 1923* (Washington, D.C.: GPO, 1923), p. 43.

9. This assignment did not please air power enthusiasts. As late as June 1, 1933, Mitchell testified before the joint congressional committee to investigate dirigible disasters: "Now, in this country our weather is under the Agricultural Department that is concerned with the raising of onions, potatoes, and such things, and the air outfit has no control over it whatever. Every other country in the world has a meteorological service under the air or the war department."

10. Francis W. Reichelderfer to author Bates, Apr. 20, 1980.

11. Carl G. Rossby, "Organization of Weather Service for Safe Flying on an Airway," *Seventeenth Annual Safety Congress Transactions* (Chicago: National Safety Council, 1928), pp. 675–99.

12. Victor Boesen, *Storm: Irving Krick vs. the U.S. Weather Bureaucracy* (New York: G. P. Putnam's Sons, 1978), p. 18.

13. Von Karman's laboratory grew into today's vast Jet Propulsion Laboratory. After the war, he chaired the air force's first science advisory board.

14. As naval officers could go no higher than lieutenant commander in aerological billets, Reichelderfer took his mandatory sea duty in other specialties such as gunnery. His annual navy pay, including allowances, was about $8,000, a figure eventually matched when Secretary Wallace raised his Weather Bureau job to the grade eight professional level.

15. Nelson, "History of Aerology," p. 524.

16. U.S. Navy Department: Chief of Bureau of Navigation to Chief of Naval Operations, file N152-RMG-JJ, Oct. 23, 1919, subject: Pigeons, Photography and Meteorology.

17. U.S. Navy, *Report of the Secretary of the Navy, 1922* (Washington, D.C.: GPO, 1922), p. 366.

18. Before departing, Keyser designed the seal of the American Meteorological Society. Francis W. Reichelderfer, "The Bulletin Interviews: Dr. F. W. Reichelderfer," *WMO Bulletin*, July, 1982, pp. 171–84. A chemistry graduate from Northwestern University, Reichelderfer qualified in heavier-than-air (1919) and lighter-than-air (1929) aircraft. He died, aged 87, on Jan. 25, 1983.

19. Early navy pibal stations were at Rockaway Inlet, N.Y.; Lakehurst and Cape May, N.J.; Hampton Roads, Va.; Pensacola, Fla.; San Diego, Cal.; and Coco Solo, Panama. Marines took similar runs at Parris Island, S.C.; and Santo Domingo, Haiti. In addition, the Army Signal Corps operated fourteen pibal units and the Weather Bureau, thirteen.

To ensure acquisition of radioed weather messages, aerographer's mates often became proficient at copying the Morse code weather broadcasts. Robert Currie was particularly famed because he could plot a weather map directly as the signals came in over the air. Radio teletype, of course, did not exist until about the middle of World War II.

20. Aerographer's mate training was shifted to NAS Lakehurst in 1929, where it remained until merged with that of the other armed forces at Chanute AFB, Ill., in Feb. 1978.

Among those who achieved this grade early on (with their initial skills) were Albert Francis, R. J. Brown, and R. L. Welles (machinist's mate, aviation), Robert Currie (quartermaster), T. Thomas (signalman), E. M. Brown (yeoman), and J. B. Chamberlain (boatswain's mate). Most of these men had notable careers. Francis became chief meteorologist for Pan American Airways (Pacific Division) and then operations manager for China National Airways. R. J. Brown became chief meteorologist for Pan American (South American Division); Thomas held the same position in Pan American's Atlantic Division. Currie was a ranking meteorologist with American Airlines, and Welles became chief meteorologist of United Airlines' Western Division. In 1931 several other navy chiefs, led by Paul Gareau, left to set up American Airlines' first weather service. However, in 1935, Krick was given the task of reorganizing that activity and placed his own graduates, led by Dr. George Taylor, in the key positions. Robert L. Welles to Comdr. Neil F. O'Connor, ca. 1970, copy in author Bates's files.

21. Among the aviators exposed to aerological training were Felix B. Stump (later commander in chief, Pacific) and Adolph P. Schneider, a hotshot aviator later killed in the Curtiss Cup Races, thereby rating a trophy named after him for the pilot achieving the highest speed in a seaplane.

22. Dwight R. Messimer, *No Margin for Error—The U.S. Navy Trans-Pacific Flight of 1925* (Annapolis: U.S. Naval Institute, 1981), p. 61.

In still air, the PN-9 class's maximum range was 100 nautical miles short of the distance to be traveled. Thus the aircraft captains, Comdr. John Rodgers and Lt. Allen T. Snoddy, needed northeast trade winds to overcome the fuel shortage. The critical weather forecasts were the joint effort of Thomas R. Reed (San Francisco Weather Bureau station chief) and Lt. Wyatt, the aerologist at NAS, San Diego, (Wyatt also made all necessary field arrangements). A low overcast covered most of the flight track, making accurate underway wind measurements impossible. (See

Thomas R. Reed, "Meteorological Aspects of the San Francisco–Hawaii Airplane Flight," *Monthly Weather Review* 53, no. 9 [1925]: 384–87).

23. The initial class's outstanding student was Charles J. ("Molly") Maguire. He replaced Reichelderfer at the Bureau of Aeronautics aerology desk in 1928, obtained a lighter-than-air rating in 1931, and wrote the textbook *Aeronautical Meteorology (Aerology)* (New York: McGraw-Hill, 1931). Eventually, he commanded NAS Richmond, Fla. (1943), and the cruiser, USS *Cleveland* (1945). Upon retirement, he was promoted to rear admiral on the retired list, thereby becoming a "tombstone admiral."

24. C. G. Andrus, "Meteorological Aspects of the International Balloon Race of 1920," *Monthly Weather Review* 49, no. 1 (1921): 8–10.

25. Reichelderfer, for example, participated in the national balloon races of 1919, 1923, 1928, 1929, and 1930, as well as the International Balloon Races of 1923 in Belgium. In Belgium one race was run in threatening weather. Reich's balloon landed before going to sea, but the U.S. Army's team was hit by lightning, and both the pilot and the copilot were killed, as were three other participants in the race. See C. Leroy Meisinger in *AMS Bulletin* 4, no. 1 (1923): 50–51.

26. Francis W. Reichelderfer, "Weather Forecasting for Airships," *Aero Digest*, Aug. 1924, pp. 84–87.

27. Louis H. Maxfield, to President, Naval War College, Jan. 25, 1921 (BuNav file 5901-4647).

28. U.S. Congress, *Investigation of Dirigible Disasters—Hearings before a Joint Committee to Investigate Dirigible Disasters*, 73d Cong., 1st sess. (1933). Testimony cited: New York *Daily News*, p. 188; Charles L. Mitchell, pp. 196–224; Rear Adm. Ernest J. King, pp. 596, 604, and 607; Col. Charles A. Lindbergh, p. 659; and Brig. Gen. William Mitchell, p. 695. Eight months after these hearings, Krick submitted an analysis to the Chief of Naval Operations claiming he could have forecast the unforecastable for the USS *Akron's* fatal flight (see Irving P. Krick's MS report, "Weather Conditions Associated with the AKRON Disaster," to Chief of Naval Operations and forwarded to the Bureau of Aeronautics by Op-23-H-EMW memo of Feb. 7, 1934, file ZR4/L11-1-18, 340207). Krick, citing air mass analysis, wrote: "The afternoon map [1600 EST] would certainly leave no doubt as to the situation, and all flights along the south Atlantic coast should be suspended until the Npc cold front passage." This alienated naval aerologists, because Reichelderfer had been using air-mass analysis nine years before this Army reserve lieutenant of coast artillery had ever drawn a weather map.

29. U.S. Congress, *Airship Investigation—Report of Col. Henry Breckenridge: Committee Print for Use of Joint Committee to Investigate Dirigible Disasters*, 73rd Cong., 1st sess. (1933), p. 35.

30. Ibid., p. 7.

31. Lt. Howard T. Orville, another of the class's four naval officers, went on to command the Naval Weather Service for a decade (1940–50). However, the class's star student was 1st Lt. Randolph P. Williams of the Army Air Corps, who later became known as the "Father of the Air Weather Service."

32. Wilbert M. Lockhart to Commander, Naval Service Weather Command, ca. 1970.

33. Shirley was famed for his ability to plot a weather map simultaneously in

three colors, using three separate pens strapped together and rotated as necessary. He could stay even with several Weather Bureau plotters who were copying the same reports as a joint exercise.

34. Homer W. Ball, "Meteorological Course Given at the Signal Corps School at Camp Alfred Vail, N.J., during 1920," *Monthly Weather Review* 49, no. 2 (1921): 85–87. When 1st Lt. Thomas W. Moorman, Jr., reported in to be the weather officer at Randolph Field, Tex. (the "West Point of the Air"), in 1937, the station staff consisted of two operations clerks and one Signal Corps man busily copying radioed-in weather reports. Alfred H. Thiessen to General Saltzman, Sept. 11, 1924 (Copy in National Archives, RG 111, file 665.2). Ernest A. McKay, *A World to Conquer: The Epic Story of the First Round-the-World Flight by the U.S. Army Air Corps* (New York: Arco, 1981).

35. "Dr. C. Leroy Meisinger, 1895–1924," *AMS Bulletin* 5, no. 6 (1924): 81–87. Dr. Meisinger's personal sacrifice has since been memorialized in an annual award in his name by the AMS for notable upper-air research. The society has also donated a plaque, mounted on a Scott Field hangar, citing Meisinger and Neely's last flight.

William E. Kepner, "Flight of RS-1, San Antonio, Tex., to Scott Field, Ill.," *Monthly Weather Review* 59, no. 10 (1931): 386–88. Although without a high school diploma, Kepner rose through the air force hierarchy until, as a major general, he commanded the all-important VIII Fighter Command in England during World War II. Moreover, he was sure to point out to new staff weather officers that he, too, had been involved in weather forecasting.

36. *New York Times*, Sept. 9, 1933, pp. 1–2.

37. Arthur F. Merewether, interview with author Bates, July 24, 1982.

38. 1st Lt. James H. Doolittle was the first American pilot to intentionally fly blind. On Sept. 24, 1929, he took off, traversed a 15-mile course, and landed at Mitchel Field without ever seeing the ground or the exterior of his aircraft. Merewether had earned a master's degree in chemical engineering from MIT in 1924. Before that, he was on the roster of the Pittsburgh Pirates, a major league baseball team. His times at bat: one!

39. In researching Air Corps records for a master's degree, Philip M. Flammer found that only 1,187 out of 3,140 scheduled mail flights arrived on time. Another 841 flights were completed but with appreciable delay. Of these delays, 446 were caused by adverse weather. Of 571 flights only partially completed, 424 were halted because of bad weather. Of the 664 flights that did not get off the ground, 618 had to be canceled because of dangerous flying conditions.

40. Between 1923 and 1937 the Signal Corps program for improving meteorological equipment was spotty. Until 1928 the work was handled by a small military laboratory at McCook Field, Ohio. Then the work moved to Washington, D.C. A year later, it again moved to become part of the general signal section at Fort Monmouth, N.J. When Lt. Col. Blair established the Signal Corps Laboratories there the same year, he included a meteorological section. However, productivity remained low, and work on a mobile meteorological station muddled along for a dozen years after the first try in 1930.

41. The weather command structure became unbelievably intricate. Capt. Williams reported from Langley Field (see his letter of Feb. 9, 1936, to Commanding

General, General Headquarters Air Force, now in AWS historical files): "At present, . . . the [weather] station is serving the GHQ Air Force and the 2nd Wing, and thus is under orders from constituted Air Corps authority. At the same time, the Signal Corps personnel assigned to this duty are parcelled out from a [meteorological] company with headquarters in Baltimore and taking orders from a control officer at Bolling Field and from the office of the Chief Signal Officer."

42. U.S. Army Air Forces Weather Wing Headquarters, "History of the AAF Weather Service I, 1935–1941," typescript, Office of MAC Historian, Scott AFB, pp. 43–59.

43. At one stage of planning, a 1st Weather Group under Captain Williams would have been based at Bolling Field. For purposes of simplification, this plan was dropped, and Williams left for other duty. The "Father of the Air Weather Service" was killed during a photo reconnaissance flight over France on Sept. 5, 1944.

44. This organizational concept did not eliminate the issue of who controls a base weather station—the air field commander, who needs work details, parades and inspections, or the regional control officer/weather squadron commander located many miles away but still responsible for quality of weather service provided by his remote detachments.

45. Merewether, interview, July 24, 1982. Unfortunately, Losey was creating his own death warrant. After Germany's surprise invasion of Norway the following April, Losey helped America's minister to Norway, Mrs. Florence Jaffray Harriman, escape to England. Placing her in a railroad tunnel on Apr. 21, 1940, Losey moved to its mouth to observe a German dive-bombing attack. A bomb fragment hit his heart, making him the first officer to be killed by hostile action while in the service of the United States during World War II.

CHAPTER 4:

1. Wilbert Lockhart to Commander, Naval Weather Service Command, ca. 1970.

2. Henry H. Arnold, *Global Mission* (New York: Harper Brothers, 1949), p. 166.

3. Arthur F. Merewether, interview, June 24, 1982. Krick's technique: Assume that a ten-day forecast is required. First, type the current weather at the point of interest and upwind (if in the westerlies) for several hundred miles. Second, machine sort the previous forty years of weather types in the analog weather type file to obtain the best match possible. Third, study maps of the matched periods and project the weather conditions by assuming that the earlier pattern will repeat for the next ten days. Krick's accuracies, although not achievable by others, were said to be nearly 95% for the short term (one day to two weeks) and 80% for longer-term forecasts.

The Weather Bureau (with navy and air corps support, including the services of 1st Lt. Moorman) set up its own long-range forecasting unit under Jerome Namias in May, 1941. However, its forecasts were for five days or less. If needed, they were supplied to the navy's chief long-range forecaster, Cdr. Anderson, in the contiguous navy weather central, to be transmitted via Cdr. Orville to users for such pending invasions as North Africa, Italy's Anzio beachhead, Normandy, and southern France (see NAVAER Report 50-45T-5, 1946, *Operations of the Navy Wartime Long Range Forecast Unit, 1940–46*).

4. Howard T. Orville, file report, Jan. 24, 1941, concerning interdepartmental meteorological meeting, Jan. 21, 1941. Participants were as follows: Air Corps— Capt. Merewether and Capt. Anthony Q. Mustoe; Navy—Cdr. Maguire and Lt. Cdr. Orville; Civil Aeronautics Authority—W. Sibley; and Weather Bureau— Rossby, Tannehill, and Reichelderfer, who served as chairman. A poll at the meeting suggested the following inventory of qualified weather forecasters: Weather Bureau—150, civil airlines—94, army—62, navy—46, and educational and other institutions—25. Immediate additional needs were army—175; navy—80; and the Weather Bureau—30. When the war was over, approximately 700 of the bureau's 2,400 employees were in uniform. Before 1942 only two women held observer ratings; by autumn of 1945, more than half of the bureau's weather observers were female. For additional details, see U.S. Department of Commerce, *World War II History of the Department of Commerce, Part 10: U.S. Weather Bureau* (Washington, D.C.: Department of Commerce, 1948), pt. 10 (multilithed).

5. U.S. Dept. of Commerce, *World War II History*, pp. 8–10.

6. Harry Wexler and Maurice Tepper, "Results of the Wartime Historical and Normal Map Program," *AMS Bulletin* 28, no. 4 (1947): 174–78.

7. Merewether, interview, June 24, 1982.

8. Noted meteorologists involved in the training program included: MIT— Hurd Willett, Bernhard Haurwitz, Henry G. Houghton, and Thomas F. Malone; NYU—Athelstan Spilhaus and James Miller; Chicago—Helmut E. Landsberg, Philip Church, Victor Starr, Oliver Wulf, Herbert Riehl, Molly and Vincent J. Oliver, and Michael Ference (subsequently Ford Motor Company's vice-president for research); Cal Tech—Robert E. Elliott; and UCLA—Jacob Bjerknes, Jörgen Holmboe, Harald Sverdrup, Morris Neiburger, Jule Charney, Robert D. Fletcher, and the radiation expert Joseph Kaplan.

Dozens of these cadets became outstanding academicians, businessmen, and scientists after the war. Among the more notable were Kenneth A. Arrow (Nobel Laureate in economics, 1972), Robert M. Allan, Jr. (president of Cyprus Mines Corporation), and Silas B. Phillips, Jr. (president of the major utility Central & South West).

9. Wesley F. Craven and James L. Cate, eds., *Services Around the World*, vol. 7 of *The Army Air Forces in World War II* (Chicago: University of Chicago Press, 1958), pp. 314–16.

10. Lt. Comdr. Frederick A. Berry, a 1937 Cal Tech weather graduate, directed the Annapolis aerology course. Berry and two coeditors (Lt. Comdr. Eugene Bollay and Lt. Comdr. Norman R. Beers) published the very useful *Handbook of Meteorology* (New York: McGraw-Hill, 1945).

11. Alexander R. Gordon, Jr., to author Bates, Jan. 25, 1980.

12. USAF Air University, Historical Division, "Weather Training in the AAF, 1937–1945." Air Historical Study No. 56 (typescript, 1952), pp. 15–52.

13. Orlando Ward, *The Women's Army Corps*, U.S. Army in World War II series (Washington, D.C.: GPO, 1953), p. 147.

14. U.S. Air Force Simpson Historical Research Center, "USAF Unit Lineage and Honors—3d Weather Squadron" (typescript, 1975), p. 11.

15. John F. Fuller, *Air Weather Service, 1937–1977: An Illustrated Chronology* (Scott AFB: Office of MAC History, 1977), p. 6.

16. Following World War II, van Straten continued as a civilian research meteorologist in the aerology section until she retired in 1973. She wrote the book *Weather or Not* (New York: Dodd, Mead, 1966) and reached the rank of commander in the naval reserve.

17. U.S. Navy Bureau of Aeronautics, "Aerology," vol. 15 of "World War II Administrative History, Bureau of Aeronautics" (typescript, 1957, 81 pp.)

18. John F. Fuller, "Black Weathermen Train at Tuskegee," *AWS Observer* 30, no. 2 (1983): 8.

19. These officers were Capt. John B. Branche, 1st Lt. Robert M. Preer, and 2nd Lt. Grant L. Franklin and 2nd Lt. Paul E. Wise.

20. Of this class, Dale F. Leipper founded departments of oceanography at Texas A&M University (1949) and the U.S. Naval Postgraduate School (1968); author Bates and Boyd E. Olson served as successive technical directors of the U.S. Naval Oceanographic Office (1964–79); and John C. Crowell became a member of the illustrious National Academy of Sciences (1980).

21. Fuller, *Air Weather Service*, pp. 4–6.

22. "Winds, Weather and Warships," *Naval Aviation News*, Oct. 1957, pp. 1–7.

23. In 1937 the Signal Corps appropriation for weather research and new meteorological equipment came to $31,000. By 1945 the annual allocation stood at $10,233,802. However, the expenditure for meteorological equipment and supplies in FY 1946 dropped to $2,593,622 (see Signal Corps Historical Division report, "Meteorology in the U.S. Army Corps, 1870–1960," written by Karl Larew in 1960).

Whedon earned a bachelor's degree in physics and aeronautical engineering at MIT in 1924. After a fourteen-year stint in the Signal Corps, she became staff meteorologist for the Army's Office of Research and Development before retiring with accolades in 1971.

24. To clarify their military status, a special congressional act effective Jan. 1, 1943, made Spilhaus (a citizen of South Africa) and two Arctic specialists (Bernt Balchen of Norway and Paul-Emile Victor of France) temporary officers in the AAF.

25. Athelstan F. Spilhaus, interview, Feb. 11, 1976, for Oral History Collection, Texas A&M University Library, pp. 21–22.

26. George R. Thompson, *The Signal Corps: The Outcome (Mid-1943 through 1945)*, United States Army in World War II series (Washington, D.C.: GPO, 1966), pp. 426–68.

27. Wartime funds for aerological equipment and supplies were, rounded to the closest thousand (K): FY 39—$60K; FY 40—$168K; FY 41—$485K; FY 42—$967K; FY 43—$2,848K; FY 44—$3,400K, and FY 45—$2,844K. (For details, see the unpublished U.S. Navy Bureau of Aeronautics, "Aerology.")

28. U.S. Navy Office of Chief of Naval Operations, "Naval Aerological Research and Development, 1935–1945" (typescript, n.d., 18 pp.).

29. At the war's end, aerology units were aboard 42 CV-class, 8 CV-Light-class,

and 16 CV-Escort-class carriers; 10 AGC-class command ships also carried such units, as did 9 AV-class aircraft tenders.

30. What is commonly recognized as the first premeditated flight by a military aircraft into the eye of a hurricane took place on July 27, 1943. Col. Joseph B. Duckworth, officer in charge of the AAF's instrument flying instructor's school at Bryan, Tex., and 1st Lt. Ralph O'Hair, a navigator, took off from Bryan in a single-engine AT-6 Texan trainer and penetrated the eye while flying between Galveston and Houston. Upon landing at Bryan, Duckworth was met by 1st Lt. William H. Jones-Burdick, commander of the base weather station, who persuaded the colonel to repeat the flight that afternoon with Jones-Burdick along as observer. For details, see Ivan R. Tannehill, *The Hurricane Hunters* (New York: Dodd, Mead, 1955); and John F. Fuller, "Weatherman Third to Enter Hurricane's Eye," *AWS Observer* 25, no. 11 (1978): 11.

31. U.S. Navy Office of Chief of Naval Operations, *Operational Aspects of Hurricane Warning Service (Atlantic)*, NAVAER-50-IT-29 Report (Washington, D.C.: Bureau of Aeronautics, 1945), 25 pp.

32. Malcolm F. Willoughby, *The U.S. Coast Guard in World War II* (Annapolis: U.S. Naval Institute, 1957), pp. 127–30.

33. The three colonels who successively directed the AAF weather service during 1942–45 eventually became general officers. Zimmerman made one-star rank and retired in 1958 after serving as the first dean of faculty at the Air Force Academy. Harold H. Bassett, who held the weather desk between March 9, 1943, and January 9, 1945, later became a major general and served as deputy commander of the Taiwan Defense Command. Donald N. Yates then served as weather chief until August 1, 1950, and ultimately retired from the post of deputy director, Office of Defense Research and Engineering, Department of Defense, as a lieutenant general.

34. No matter where the young weather officer went, he was in a setting in which a broken forecast might mean the lives of aircrews, not just a low grade in class. For example, in January, 1944, the great master Jacob Bjerknes came through Stephenville, Newfoundland, en route to Scotland. A severe cold front had preceded him and lay over the warm Gulf Stream just offshore. The question facing the duty forecaster (Bates, a Bjerknes student of the preceding year) was whether the professor's unpressurized C-54 could skirt, without icing up, the front's towering cumulonimbus tops. If not, the flight should be postponed until the following night. After Bates briefed him on the situation and tried to evoke an opinion, Bjerknes blurted, "Lieutenant Bates, you must remember I'm a meteorologist, not a forecaster!" and disappeared into the passenger lounge. Fortunately, the evening crossing to Prestwick took place without difficulty.

35. Norman A. Riley, interview with author Bates, Jan. 16, 1980.

36. David S. Merrihew to author Bates, Oct. 6, 1944.

37. Earlier, Chicago's Philip Church had provided advice on anticipated meteorological problems such as atmospheric dilution of the fireball.

38. Jack M. Hubbard to author Bates, Aug. 29, 1983.

39. Kenneth T. Bainbridge, *Trinity*, Report LA-6300-H (Los Alamos: Los Alamos Scientific Laboratory, 1976), pp. 22–23. Lead individuals for the four subsections were 1st Lt. C. D. Curtis, Sgt. J. C. Alderson (previously on Canton

Island), Sgt. P. A. Tudor, and Sgt. S. W. Blades (formerly of Greenland's Sondrestrom Fjord).

40. Peter Goodchild, *J. Robert Oppenheimer: Shatterer of Worlds* (Boston: Houghton Mifflin, 1981), p. 154.

41. John E. Wallace, to author Bates, Sept. 2, 1983.

42. Later, Groves said of the meeting: "Since it was obvious that they [the weathermen] were completely upset about the failure of the long-range predictions, I soon excused them. After that it was necessary for me to make my own weather predictions—a field in which I had no special competence." See Leslie R. Groves, *Now It Can Be Told: The Story of the Manhattan Project* (New York: Harper, 1962).

CHAPTER 5

1. Basil Clarke, *Atlantic Adventure: A Complete History of Trans-Atlantic Flight* (London: Allan Wingate, 1958). Electronic navigation did not exist until July, 1943. When Greenland's first Loran-A tower was completed near Frederiksdal on Dec. 31, 1942, the associated wooden buildings blew away the following night in a gale whose wind speeds reached 162 mph.

McTaggart-Cowan later directed the Canadian weather service (1959–64) and eventually served as the executive director of the powerful Canadian Science Council.

2. On July 1, 1942, the Ferrying Command was designated the ATC. Its North Atlantic Division was headquartered in the remote potato town of Presque Isle, Me. (as was that of the 8th Weather Squadron) for twenty months following June, 1942. Lt. Col. Merewether took over as the squadron's RCO and commanding officer in September, 1942.

To handle huge number of North Atlantic crossings (clearing flights of fifty bombers at a time was not unknown), large American facilities were built across the runways from Canadian complexes already operational at Gander Lake and Goose Bay. Any difficulties in the duplicate operation were ironed out by a Joint Central Commission, the meteorological members of which were Merewether for the ATC and McTaggart-Cowan for the RAF Ferry Command.

3. "Thunder Over the North Atlantic," *Fortune* 30, no. 5 (1944): 153–60, 197–206.

4. Some famed weathermen came out of this crucible of adverse weather and extensive flight operations. In the postwar period, Merewether became American Airlines' chief meteorologist; his deputy, Maj. Leo Kiley, eventually commanded the Defense Atomic Support Agency's Field Activity as a brigadier general. Gander's Maj. Lynn Irish acquired a reputation second only to that of McTaggart-Cowan for skillful North Atlantic forecasting. Capt. Ray Roda and Capt. Alfred K. Blackadar of Stephenville earned a vice-presidency in Trans-World Airlines and a presidency of AMS, respectively; 1st Lt. Norman A. Phillips of squadron headquarters became a U.S. pioneer in numerical weather prediction.

5. Malcolm F. Willoughby, *The U.S. Coast Guard in World War II* (Annapolis: U.S. Naval Institute, 1957), pp. 192–205.

6. The *Natsek* was one of ten Grand Banks fishing trawlers commandeered by Rear Adm. Edward H. ("Iceberg Eddy") Smith to occupy weather observing points off Labrador, Greenland, and Iceland during the war's early days. AerM1c Saul Singer recalls that in Oct., 1942, he was ordered to the *Atak* for Denmark Strait duty, the former weather observer having come ashore spitting blood because of chronic seasickness. Two weeks later, a day away from port-call, Singer was in a semicoma from dehydration caused by the same problem.

7. Saul Singer described the station routine: "Each 24-hour period we entered and drew two surface maps of the area from Newfoundland to the English Channel, and made . . . two 36-hour forecasts of our immediate area. We took and worked up four pibal soundings and two radiosondes. Weather permitting, we [also] made daily aerograph hops in a N3N, a [open-cockpit] Navy-built trainer" (letter to author Bates, Dec. 23, 1982).

8. Vannevar Bush, *Pieces of the Action* (New York: William Morrow, 1970), pp. 87–92.

9. 9th Weather Squadron, "USAF Unit Lineage and Honors, Form 3825-0-34" (1975, 28 pp).

10. The southerly route between London and New York City extended more than 8,170 nautical miles, but the direct great circle route took only 3,000 nautical miles. Even so, regular westbound ATC winter flights over the North Atlantic were not permitted until regular C-54 weather reconnaissance flights began over the region early in 1944.

Forecasting for the Lajes runway could be tricky. Lying between two ridges, the single strip became inoperable when gusty gale winds set in before the passage of a cold front. Because of the U-boat threat, no ships (except weather ships) filed weather reports west of the Azores, so timing such frontal passages was "by guess and by God," a condition made more critical because there were no authorized alternate airstrips in the Azores.

11. On July 5, 1943, Col. Raymond T. Lester, staff weather officer to the Ninth Air Force, crash-landed his P-40 fighter 60 miles east of the Nile River while en route from Cairo to Luxor. Luxor did not know the plane was down, and Lester died of heat prostration and dehydration while walking toward the river.

12. T. H. Vail Motter, *The Persian Corridor and Aid to Russia*, U.S. Army in World War II series (Washington, D.C.: GPO, 1952), pp. 105–106, 265.

13. Air Weather Service, "Mission Environmental Support" (unpublished white paper, May 2, 1980, re Iranian rescue mission).

14. Horace R. Byers and Dawson C. McDowell, "Weather on the Southeast (Atlantic) Route," *AMS Bulletin* 26, no. 6 (1945): 220–34. The best of the Rio Piedras instructors was 28-year-old Herbert Riehl, a naturalized citizen of German birth. As a weather cadet at NYU, he found military discipline too much, so he ended up a civilian on the University of Chicago's payroll.

15. 8th Weather Squadron to Commanding General, North Atlantic Wing, ATC, Feb. 4, 1946, subject: Discontinuance of USAAF Forecasting Facilities at Goose Bay.

16. Samuel E. Morison, *The Two-Ocean War* (Boston: Little, Brown, 1963), pp. 222–23; B. H. Liddell Hart, *History of the Second World War* (New York: G. P. Putnam's Sons, 1970), pp. 316–17.

17. George F. Howe, *Northwest Africa: Seizing the Initiative in the West*, U.S. Army in World War II series (Washington, D.C.: GPO, 1957), p. 43.

18. Winston Churchill, *The Hinge of Fate*, vol. 4 of *The Second World War* (Boston: Houghton Mifflin, 1950), p. 535; Dwight D. Eisenhower, *Crusade in Europe* (New York: Doubleday, 1948), p. 79.

19. H. Kent Hewitt, "The Landing in Morocco, November 1942," *U.S. Naval Institute Proceedings* 78, no. 11 (1952): 1245.

20. Boesen, *Storm*, pp. 51–54. Although Krick's wartime reserve commission was in the navy, his criticism of the USS *Akron* incident made him persona non grata with Capt. Orville. Finally, Gen. Arnold engineered his transfer as a major to the Weather Central Division as of Aug., 1942. Once there, he attempted to be named staff weather officer to Gen. George C. Marshall, the army chief of staff. This effrontery was quickly laid to rest by the chain of command (Arthur F. Merewether statement to author Bates, July 24, 1982).

21. U.S. Navy Chief of Naval Operations, *Operations of the Navy Wartime Long Range Forecast Unit, 1940–1946*, NAVAER-50-45T-5 Report (Washington, D.C.: Bureau of Aeronautics, 1946), p. 2. On Jan. 6, 1943, Secretary of the Navy Frank Knox sent a secret letter to the secretary of commerce asking him to thank the Weather Bureau's Charles L. Mitchell, Jerome Namias, and Kenneth Smith for making "an important contribution to operations which resulted in the successful completion of landing operations by the largest landing forces in history."

22. K. A. Willard, "Note on R.A.F. Meteorological Reconnaissance," memorandum to Chief, Weather Central Division, Feb. 6, 1943 (also in "History of AAF Weather Reconnaissance Squadron [Test] No. 1, August 21, 1942–December 5, 1943," Appendix, section 1, pp. 63–69). Army Air Corps weather forecasts out of London and then from Gibraltar were arranged by Maj. Lee P. Dahl, who had been sent to England for that purpose in September, 1942.

23. Martin Blumenson, *The Patton Papers, 1940–1945* (Boston: Houghton Mifflin, 1974), p. 100; Eisenhower, *Crusade*, p. 98; Richard C. Steere, "The Weather Factor during Operations TORCH, HUSKY, and AVALANCHE" (MS, 1976, 19 pp.).

24. Steere to author Bates, Apr. 1, 1983.

25. Howe, *Northwest Africa*, pp. 69–70.

26. Hart, *History*, pp. 321–22.

27. 12th Weather Squadron. "History and War Diary of the 12th Weather Squadron, Sept. 14, 1942–March 31, 1944" (typescript, 1944), pp. 1–3.

28. Churchill, *Hinge of Fate*, p. 661; Eisenhower, *Crusade*, pp. 116–18.

29. John F. Fuller, "A Lesson from History: Win in North Africa Comes Behind Weather," *AWS Observer* 42, no. 2 (1977): 4.

30. U.S. Army Chief of Staff, *General Marshall's Report: The Winning of the War in Europe and the Pacific* (New York: Simon & Schuster, n.d. but known to be 1946), pp. 9–10.

31. Churchill, *Closing the Ring*, vol. 5 of *The Second World War* (Boston: Houghton Mifflin Co., 1951), p. 32.

32. Hanson Baldwin, *Battles Lost and Won: Great Campaigns of World War II* (New York: Harper & Row, 1966), pp. 188–235.

33. Albert N. Carland and Howard M. Smyth, *Sicily and the Surrender of Italy*,

U.S. Army in World War II series (Washington, D.C.: GPO, 1965), pp. 10, 88–89.

34. U.S. Navy Chief of Naval Operations, *The Invasion of Sicily*, NAVAER 50-30T-1 Report (Washington, D.C.: Bureau of Aeronautics, 1944).

35. U.S. Army Weather Wing Headquarters, message to War Department (Radio Branch, Office of Public Relations), Aug. 7, 1943, copy in files of MAC historian.

36. Donald C. Taggert, *History of the Third Infantry Division in World War II* (Washington, D.C.: Infantry Journal Press, 1947), p. 53.

37. Steere, "Weather Factor," p. 15.

38. Eisenhower, *Crusade*, pp. 172–73; Churchill, *Closing the Ring*, p. 32.

39. Omar N. Bradley, *A Soldier's Story* (New York: Henry Holt, 1951), p. 127.

40. Carland and Smyth, *Sicily*, pp. 108–11.

41. Willoughby, *U.S. Coast Guard*, p. 227.

42. Churchill, *Closing the Ring*, p. 32.

43. 12th Weather Squadron, "History and War Diary," pp. 14–16, 27, 43–44, and 46–48.

44. On August 6, three days after the infamous slapping of a hospitalized soldier he suspected of malingering, Patton took on a mobile team of the 12th Weather Squadron while it was unloading at the Palermo docks. The LST doors would not open, so some weathermen, wearing fatigue hats instead of helmet liners, were trying to help. Enraged, Patton stepped up, grabbed the offending hats, and threw them in the water. As the weather team reported later, "Then, secure in the knowledge that he had helped us to the best of his ability, and given us the full benefit of his more mature intelligence, he swung his immaculately pressed trousers back inside his well guarded staff car and went on to straighten out other tangles" (12th Weather Squadron, "History and War Diary," p. 47).

45. Steere, "Weather Factor," pp. 18–19.

46. U.S. Army Weather Service, "History of the Air Weather Service, 1943–45" (typescript, 1945), 5: 120–30.

47. Although the AWS hired and fired commanders of continental U.S. weather squadrons, it could only make recommendations to and through theater commanders in the case of overseas squadrons, over which it exercised neither command nor operational control. Miller was a tried and proven wartime squadron commander, not only well liked by his men but one who enjoyed the confidence of his meteorological superiors and of the air and ground commanders he served. Eight months later, he was killed on Oct. 21, 1944, while serving as an observer aboard a B-26 bomber destroyed by flak on a bombing run over northern Italy.

48. The observatory was located just 2 miles from the crater, which erupted violently in mid-March, 1944. Up to 3 feet of soot, ash, and clinkers fell on Pompeii air field some 5 miles distant, completely destroying eighty-six B-26 bombers valued at approximately $25 to $30 million. Robert C. Bundgaard, "Sverre Petterssen, Weather Forcaster," *AMS Bulletin* 60, no. 2 (1979): 182–83.

49. Martin Blumenson, *Salerno to Cassino*, U.S. Army in World War II series (Washington, D.C.: GPO, 1969), pp. 293–315.

50. Martin Blumenson, "General Lucas at Anzio," in *Command Decisions*, ed. Kent R. Greenfield (Washington, D.C.: GPO, 1960), pp. 323–50.

51. 12th Weather Squadron, "History and War Diary," p. 2.

52. Ernie Pyle, *Brave Men* (New York: Henry Holt, 1944), p. 235.

53. Freyberg began his career as a dentist and received the Victoria Cross for high valor at Gallipoli in 1915. He had the unique distinction of having been wounded eighteen times in two wars. See Wesley F. Craven and James L. Cate, eds., *Europe: Argument to V-E Day, January 1944 to May 1945*, vol. 3 of *The Army Air Forces in World War II* (Chicago: University of Chicago Press, 1951), p. 195.

54. Irving Ripps, "Air Support Weather: I," *AWS Bulletin* 3, no. 8 (1945): 21–25.

55. A former high school history teacher with a Ph.D. from Princeton (1938), Ludlum joined the Army Air Corps as a private in 1941. During a ten-day period on the Salerno beachhead he and his sixteen-man enlisted team were shelled constantly. However, so many of the shells were duds thanks to the sabotage by the underground at the German munition factories that some of the soldiers started living above ground in tents, rather than in foxholes. One was Ludlum, who even slept in pajamas, rather than in uniform, after removing combat boots. One morning, his men were sitting in the captain's tent when there was the unmistakable lethal whine of "incoming." All dove for trenches, but as Ludlum ran, he fell into a pile of manure. The German shell did, too. The shell did not explode; Ludlum did! Years later, Ludlum became the founding editor of the journal *Weatherwise* and author of several popular books, including *Weather and the American Scene, American Weather Book*, and the *New England Weather Book*. See also David Ludlum, "Weather at the Fronts," *AWS Bulletin* 2, no. 1 (1944): 1–2.

56. "Operation Ludlum: Cassino Bombing Underlines Lesson," *Newsweek* 23, no. 13 (1944): 25–26.

57. Blumenson, *Salerno to Cassino*, pp. 438–48. Ludlum demurs on the point that he totally "blew" the forecast. First of all, he did not know that Freyberg demanded three days of good weather, and his own forecast was not optimistic for good weather on March 16 and 17. Second, his 24-hour forecast did call for probable light rain in the evening of March 15 (Ludlum to Bates, Mar. 22, 1983).

58. John F. Fuller, "Lesson from History: Weathermen Aid Flights Behind Nazi Lines," *AWS Observer* 24, no. 1 (1977): 6.

59. Fuller, *Weather and War*, p. 6; Arnold, *Global Mission*, p. 375. The initial, much vaunted, daylight en masse Eighth Air Force bombing raid came on Oct. 9, 1942, when 108 heavy bombers pounded Lille, France.

60. Fuller, *Weather and War*, p. 6.

61. John F. Fuller, "Lesson from History: WWII Weather Intercepts," *AWS Observer* 32, no. 4 (1984): 3 and 32, no. 5 (1984): 3.

62. 18th Weather Region, "History of the 18th Weather Region" (typescript, ca. 1944, 7 pp. plus two-page addendum on Lt. Col. Murray O. Jones).

63. Additional modifications to the weather B-24s included adding a radar altimeter, a flare-pot drop tube, and extra fuel tanks. For oceanic runs, guns and armor were also removed to increase cruising range. Such reconnaissance flights determined wind fields, moisture content, and pressure altitudes for the 850-, 700-, and 500-mb levels, and also made occasional vertical ascents to the 400- and even the 300-mb levels.

64. John R. Deane, *The Strange Alliance* (New York: Viking Press, 1947), pp. 74–77.

65. John F. Fuller, "A Lesson from History: The Raid Against the Ploesti Refineries," *AWS Observer* 23, no. 1 (1976): 7.

66. Leading one of the four bomber groups over Ploesti was Col. Leon W. Johnson, one of the twenty-two original AWS officers in 1937. Eleven B-24s in Johnson's group were destroyed during the raid. The colonel was among five recipients of the congressional Medal of Honor for extraordinary heroism during the low-level attack. A West Pointer (class of 1926), Johnson had been one of Krick's first Air Corps students at Cal Tech. When he left meteorology in mid-1940, he stood second in seniority among AWS officers. Eventually he and William S. Stone became the only four-star generals who had meteorological service time.

67. For an understanding of weather forecasting techniques and procedures for strategic bombing operations, particularly those of the Eighth Air Force, see the following *Weather Service Bulletin* articles: Anthony Q. Mustoe, "How It Works," 1, no. 2 (1943): 19–22; Robert T. Poole, "Weather Briefing for European Theater Bombing Missions," 1, no. 2 (1943): 23–24; and Morris Hendrickson, "Metro Aspects of Bombing, 3, no. 9 (1945): 12–17. Also see John F. Fuller's "A Lesson from History" series in the *AWS Observer*: "The Schweinfurt Raid of October 14, 1943," 22, no. 10 (1975): 7; "Weather Hits WWII's Operation Argument," 25, no. 9 (1978): 11, and "Argument Defeats Weather, Nazis," 25, no. 10 (1978): 7.

Cloud ceilings at takeoff were to be at least 1,000 feet and visibility at least 1.5 miles. The assembly areas should have no thick cloud layers or multilayered cloud decks. En route, bomber pilots did not want severe icing conditions, contrails, or thick cloud layers at the cruising altitudes of 20,000 to 25,000 feet. Over target, the under-cloud cover should not be greater than four-tenths. For landing, bombers needed cloud ceilings of 1,000 feet or more, with visibilities of at least 2.5 miles. Although marginal home-base weather would permit takeoffs, the condition definitely had to hold or improve for the next five to six hours as the B-17s (depending on winds aloft and routes taken) made their way more than 1,000 miles from England to east-central Germany and back.

68. U.S. Strategic Air Forces in Europe. "History of Office of Director of Weather Services, USSTAF" (typescript, 1945), pp. 14–16.

69. Arnold called Yates in and asked that he pick the senior members of the weather team that would not only go with him to forecast for Operation Argument but also for the subsequent cross-channel invasion in May, 1944. Yates immediately picked Lt. Col. Benjamin G. Holzman, a former Cal Tech associate of Krick's, as his "number two." But Arnold wanted Krick involved. So Yates asked, "But will I have total command over this team?" The four-star general exploded, "Why, certainly!" But Yates hung in there, "Even over lieutenant colonels?" "Damn right—and now get the hell out of here!" (related by Samuel Solot to author Bates, June 25, 1982).

70. Although German aircraft factories turned out more than 7,000 fighter aircraft during the next three months, most were inferior in workmanship. New German pilots, because of training fuel shortages, were even more inferior. Thus, during Feb. 1944, the Luftwaffe lost 1,300 aircraft because of pilot and mechanical failures.

71. U.S. Strategic Bombing Survey (Chairman's Office), *Weather Factors in Combat Bombardment Operations in the European Theatre*, Report 62 (1947; not placed on public sale).

72. Arnold, *Global Mission*, p. 166; U.S. Department of the Air Force, *Report of the Chief of Staff, United States Air Force, to Secretary of the Air Force* (Washington, D.C.: GPO, June 30, 1948), p. 89; Ira C. Eaker, "The Evolution of Air Command," in *Impact: The Army Air Forces' Confidential Pictorial History of World War II* (New York: James Parton, 1980), vol. 1, p. xv.

73. Haywood S. Hansell, Jr., *The Air Plan That Defeated Hitler* (Atlanta: Higgins-McArthur/Longino & Porter, Inc., 1972), pp. 121, 294–95; James H. Doolittle, "Daylight Precision Bombing," in *Impact*, vol. 6, pp. xv–xvi.

74. Twenty-seven years later, James M. Stagg, the lead forecaster, wrote the authoritative *Forecast for Overlord* (London: Ian Allen, 1971). Several other participants published journal articles, including Charles C. Bates, "Utilization of Wave Forecasting in the Invasions of Normandy, Burma and Japan," *New York Academy of Sciences Annals* 51 (1949): 545–59; C. K. M. Douglas, "Forecasting for the D-Day Landings" *Marine Observer* 22, no. 155 (1952): 16–26; Lawrence Hogben, "He'll Remember with Advantages—The D-Day Weather Forecasts," Imperial Chemical Industries *Magazine* 42 (1964): 102–104; and Robert C. Bundgaard, "Sverre Petterssen, Weather Forecaster," American Meteorological Society *Bulletin* 60, no. 3 (1979): 182–95. The thoughts of Lt. Col. Krick and Lt. Col. Holzman have been documented by two professional writers: Victor Boesen, in *Storm*, and Patrick Hughes, in *A Century of Weather Service* (New York: Gordon and Breach, 1970). Several historians have also mentioned the weather factor in their treatises on the battle for Normandy. Among the best of these are Gordon A. Harrison, *Cross-Channel Attack*, in the U.S. Army in World War II series (Washington, D.C.: GPO, 1951); Samuel E. Morison, *The Invasion of France and Germany, 1944–1945* (Boston: Little, Brown, 1957); and J. Piekalkiewicz, *Invasion Frankreich 1944* [*Invasion of France, 1944*] (Munich: Südwest-Verlag, 1979).

75. With favorable weather, it would still take another thirteen weeks before the Allied divisions equalled in number the sixty German divisions already deployed throughout northern France and Belgium.

76. Eisenhower, *Crusade*, p. 239. Excerpt from *Crusade in Europe* by Dwight D. Eisenhower (copyright 1948 by Doubleday & Company, Inc.; reprinted by permission of the publisher). In practice, D day's meteorological parameters had been worked out in detail in Washington, D.C., by an AAF Weather Service climatological team led by Dr. Woodrow C. Jacobs and David Blumenstock. For details, see Jacob's *Wartime Developments in Applied Climatology*, American Meteorological Society Meteorological Monographs, 1, no. 1 (1947).

77. The Swell Forecast Section was intentionally misnamed to hint that the invasion might occur in an exposed area, such as south of Brittany. Because Cdr. Steere, now staff aerologist to R. Adm. Kirk and his Task Force 122, could supply no U.S. Navy meteorologists, the section's forecasters were one Royal Navy meteorologist (Lt. Harold W. Cauthery) and two 21st Weather Squadron oceanographers (1st Lt. John C. Crowell and 1st Lt. Charles C. Bates). To provide forecast verification data, His Majesty's Coast Guard reported wave conditions thrice daily from sixty-one coastal points between Land's End and East Anglia.

78. After World War II, Holzman, as a brigadier general, commanded the Air Force Office of Scientific Research (1958–60). His final tour before retirement in 1964 was as commander, AFCRL.

Author Bates, who worked elbow-to-elbow with Wolfe and Hogben for eight months during 1944, sharply disagrees with Stagg's evaluation. As the only forecasters in the group familiar with war at sea (after all, it was an invasion), they provided sane middle ground between Dunstable's pessimists and Widewing's optimists.

79. A rather formal officer, Fleming held the Distinguished Service Cross for having helped sink the pocket battleship *Scharnhorst*. He had served as chief forecaster and officer in charge, Admiralty Forecast Section, during 1940–42, and fleet meteorological officer, the Home Fleet (1942–44). He eventually became director of the Naval Educational Service (1956) and was later knighted (1960).

80. Donald N. Yates to Arthur F. Merewether, Mar. 2, 1953.

81. Stagg, *Forecast for Overlord*, p. 96. At the time of the recall, Southwick House was experiencing clear, calm weather. When an advance mine-sweeping unit got this signal, it was already within 36 miles of the French coast. However, with the cold front dominating the channel by Sunday night, German patrol and minelaying vessels stayed in harbor and missed an opportunity to learn that the Allies might be up to something out of the ordinary.

82. John Fleming, "Recollections of Weather Forecasts Issued for the Normandy Landings in June, 1944" (MS of Sept. 21, 1981, in possession of author Bates).

83. Robert C. Bundgaard, "Sverre Petterssen, Weather Forecaster," Kaman Aerospace Corporation internal report (ca. 1978), p. 20; Harrison, *Cross-Channel Attack*, p. 276.

84. Stagg, *Forecast*, p. 115; Yates to Merewether, Mar. 2, 1953; Lawrence Hogben, to author Bates, Aug. 17, 1982.

85. John F. Fuller, "A Lesson from History: Normandy—June 6–July 1, 1944," *AWS Observer* 24, no. 7 (1977): 7. During 1944–45, Moorman wore as many as four hats: staff weather officer for the Ninth Air Force (Maj. Gen. Hoyt S. Vandenberg); staff weather officer for the 12th Army Group (Gen. Omar N. Bradley), RCO for the 40th Mobile Communications Squadron, and RCO for the 21st Weather Squadron. To help out, Maj. August W. Throgmorton was the 21st's commanding officer, but final authority rested with Moorman.

The first man to jump, S. Sgt. Charles J. Staub, became a casualty from multiple gunshot wounds before ever taking a weather observation. His teammate, S. Sgt. Robert A. Dodson, spent the first thirty-six hours acting as a rifleman before finding time to send out hourly weather observations. On D + 15, he finally reached a field hospital for treatment of a knee injured on landing.

Life was equally difficult with the ASPs. Cpl. Eugene Levine with the 82nd Airborne Division left England for France aboard a C-47 towed glider flying at 500 feet. Over Normandy the C-47 was hit by flak and crashed, although Levine's glider landed satisfactorily. Going ashore on D day from an LST proved nearly as exciting for Sgt. Patrick L. Kelley, attached to the 4th Infantry Division. When driving his radio-equipped jeep to the beach from 600 feet offshore, he was greeted with heavy gunfire and noted what at first appeared to be floating logs—the bodies of soldiers killed earlier.

Detachment YF was the first ashore at Omaha Beach via an LCT late on D day. As the craft approached the assigned landing spot, German mortar, small arms, and 88-mm artillery fire became so thick that the vessel was directed to lie offshore overnight. Following two aborted tries in the morning, the truck moving off just ahead of the weather van took a direct hit from an 88-mm shell. Pushing the wreckage out of the way, the weather team drove on to the beach, only to find German lines about 300 feet away.

86. John Fuller, "A Lesson from History: The Mulberry Harbor Disaster," *AWS Observer* 25, no. 8 (1978): 7. In a memoir composed during 1981, Fleming wrote: "If previously I had never experienced sheer misery, I certainly did now. . . . Since then, my only consolation has been that independent analyses of the situation then prevailing have confirmed that my forecast was correct on the evidence available. But the feeling that one has been, however inadvertently, the main contributor to what was almost a major disaster is something not easily put aside."

87. Stagg, *Forecast*, p. 126.

88. Chief Lloyd White operated a small aerological unit at Cherbourg. However, the senior navy beachmaster at Omaha advised Bates he had little need for wave forecasts as he "preferred to keep a sharp eye on the glass." Charles C. Bates, "Utilization of Wave Forecasting in the Invasions of Normandy, Burma, and Japan," *New York Academy of Sciences Annals* 51 (1949): 558–59.

89. During the postwar period, Pritchard and Reid became nationally known oceanographers. The former became the founding director of Johns Hopkins University's Chesapeake Bay Institute, and in 1982 the latter became chairman of Texas A&M University's Department of Oceanography.

Later, 1st Lt. Crowell and 1st Lt. Bates received squadron commendations for "making the science of oceanography a significant factor in an assault landing." On Nov. 7, 1944, the Ninth Air Force awarded them Bronze Star medals for "meritorious service in connection with military operations against the enemy in June 1944." The same general orders also awarded identical medals to fellow squadron members Maj. N. Allen Riley and Maj. Maynard E. Smith, as well as to T. Sgt. Richard B. Batten, T. Sgt. Donald M. Pherson, and S. Sgt. Wiley A. Smith. It was typical of Moorman to give as much consideration to his enlisted men as to his officers. All told, eighty members of his weather command received these awards before war's end.

90. The best primary sources on Market-Garden weather support are Kent's "Weather Report on Airborne Invasion of Holland" (Mar. 13, 1945) and the Kent-Jacobs joint report "Weather-Market" (ca. 1945). Author Fuller used both studies in "Weather Decisive in Market-Garden," *AWS Observer* 26, no. 4 (1980): 4–5; and in "Market-Garden," MAC Recurring Publication 50-1, *Airlift Operations Review* 2, no. 4 (1980): 24–28.

The best secondary source on the airborne phase is John C. Warren, *Airborne Operations in World War II, European Theater*, USAF Historical Study No. 97 (Maxwell AFB, Ala.: Air University, 1966). See also Charles B. MacDonald, *The Siegfried Line Campaign* (1963) in the U.S. Army in World War II series, and his chapter, "The Decision to Launch Operation Market-Garden," in *Command Decisions*, ed. Kent R. Greenfield (Washington, D.C.: GPO, 1960); David G. Rempel, "Check at the Rhine," in vol. 3 of *Army Air Forces in World War II* (Chicago:

University of Chicago Press, 1951); and Cornelius Ryan, *A Bridge Too Far* (New York: Simon & Schuster, 1974).

91. Thirty-six years later, on Sept. 20, 1980, the Arnhem jump was reenacted when 120 paratroopers of the U.S. 82nd Airborne Division and the British 4th Parachute Brigade (both units in the original battle) jumped from three (MAC) C-130s above the battle site. Most of these jumpers were not even born when the battle occurred, but some British 1st Airborne Division survivors were there to explain what had happened.

92. Eisenhower, *Crusade*, p. 310.

93. Ibid., p. 345.

94. Fuller, *Weather and War*, p. 6; Blumenson, *Patton Papers*, p. 605.

95. Bradley, *Soldier's Story*, p. 343.

CHAPTER 6

1. The state of readiness in the Pacific area is well delineated in the following: Forest C. Pogue, *George C. Marshall*, vol. 2: *Ordeal and Hope: 1939–1942* (New York: Viking Press, 1966); Louis Morton, "Japan's Decision for War," in *Command Decisions*, ed. Kent R. Greenfield (Washington, D.C.: GPO, 1960); Mark S. Watson's chapter, "Chief of Staff: Prewar Plans and Preparations," in the U.S. Army in World War II series (Washington, D.C.: GPO, 1950); and John E. Costello, "Remember Pearl Harbor," *Proceedings of the U.S. Naval Institute*, Sept. 1983. Hickam's ranking weather noncommissioned officer, M. Sgt. Harry Gordon, was in the base stockade because of a scrape he had been in before the attack. He was released during the bombing raid and was cited for bravery under fire while going to the aid of his fellow weathermen.

2. On July 15, 1943, the AAF reinstated its own weather forecasting unit at nearby Hickam Field, using a teletype link between the two centrals. U.S. Navy Fleet Weather Central, Pearl Harbor, "History of the Fleet Weather Central, and Pearl Harbor, June 1941–15 August 1945." (typescript, n.d., 35 pp.).

3. The Agana station chief, CAerM Luther B. Jones, escaped capture until Sept. 1942. Following several days of torture, during which he refused to reveal other hiding places for escapees, he was summarily beheaded.

4. Maj. Gen. Davenport Johnson, U.S. Army, to Comdg Gen, AAF, "Report on D/F Facilities, South Pacific Area (Rickenbacker Accident)," Jan. 7, 1943; Maj. Gen. George E. Stratemeyer, Chief of Air Staff, Hq AAF, to Comdg Gen, ATC, "Report of Capt. Eddie V. Rickenbacker on his South and Southwest Pacific Area Mission," Feb. 8, 1943; Rickenbacker, *Seven Came Through: Rickenbacker's Full Story* (Garden City, New York: Doubleday, Doran and Co., 1943), pp. 6–11, and *Rickenbacker* (Englewood Cliffs, N.J.: Prentice Hall, 1967), pp. 297–300; and Col. L. G. Fritz, et al., "Official Statement: Interrogation of Captain William T. Cherry, Jr.," Dec. 11, 1942, 10pp. See also Capt. Henry P. Lona, 11th Ferrying Gp, ATC, to Comdg Gen, West Coast Wg, ATC, "Narrative Report on Rickenbacker Trip," Dec. 29, 1942. All the letters cited above are on file in the MAC history office. Information was also provided in a letter from Lestor Gaynor to author Fuller, Oct. 13, 1983. Gaynor was assigned to the Hickam weather station in January,

1940, and met Feeley in March, 1942. Gaynor claimed that Feeley (currently residing in Fort Myers, Florida) was unfairly "made the goat" for the incident; that DeAngelis dropped his octant when the crew left a party for Rickenbacker "roaring drunk"; and that an hour after Cherry took off from Hickam with Rickenbacker aboard, another plane departed Hickam for Canton using the same forecast and arrived as planned.

One of the three officers who interrogated Cherry was the West Pointer and Cal Tech graduate weatherman, Lt. Col. Milton W. Arnold, one of the twenty-two original weather officers of the AAC Weather Service in 1937, who General Arnold also used as a troubleshooter along the North Atlantic ferry route in 1942–43.

5. See Jonas A. Jonasson, "The AAF Weather Service," in *Services Around the World*, vol. 7 of *The Army Air Forces in World War II*, ed. Craven and Cate (Chicago: University of Chicago Press, 1958), pp. 329–31; AWS, "History of the AAF Weather Service, 1941–43" (typescript), 3: 242–48, 254–57; AWS, "17th Weather Squadron" (typescript prepared by AWSDI/Historical Division, June 8, 1966).

Blessed with a lagoon, swaying palm trees, ideal climate, and a light work load, the Aitutaki weathermen found the natives hospitable and friendly. According to the squadron's history, "The native girls, some of them lovely even by Hollywood standards, were especially attentive to lonely GI's, giving rise to the much circulated rumor that it would be necessary to use MP's [military police] to force the American soldiers to return home after the war."

6. Sidney E. Wheeler, "Marine Fog Impact on Naval Operations," (Master's thesis, U.S. Naval Postgraduate School, 1974), pp. 18–19; Lewis Morton, ed., *The Fall of the Philippines*, U.S. Army in World War II series (Washington, D.C.: GPO, 1953); Arnold, *Global Mission*; Richard A. Watson, "Pearl Harbor and Clark Field," in *Plans and Early Operations, January 1939 to August 1942*, vol. 1 of *The Army Air Forces*, ed. Craven and Cate, p. 203.

7. Destruction of U.S. forces in the Philippines was so complete that no weather squadron records survived. Because the whereabouts of 5th Weather Squadron personnel and records were unknown, the unit was not officially inactivated by the Pentagon until Apr. 2, 1946. Despite its wipeout, the squadron shared three distinguished unit citations for 1941–42 that were awarded broadly to personnel and units in the Philippines. The outfit also received the Philippines Presidential Unit Citation and official credit for the Philippine Campaign. See letter and attached form 3825 by Gerald F. Hasselwander, Simpson Historical Research Center, Maxwell AFB, Alabama, to HQ MAC (CSAH): "Revised History of 5th Weather Squadron to Replace History Prepared on 23 July 1975" (Sept. 10, 1975).

8. Cook was later executed by the Japanese on Mindanao Island.

9. U.S. Military Sea Transportation Service, retirement ceremony brochure for Rear Adm. Denys W. Knoll, May 1, 1967.

10. Zemo C. Tarnowski to author Bates, Jan. 30, 1983; Stephen Marek, *Laughter in Hell* (Caldwell, Idaho: Caxton Printers, 1954), pp. 62–63, 101–104, and 240. For such outstanding leadership, Tarnowski, in 1946, was retroactively appointed warrant officer (1942), ensign (1943), and lieutenant, junior grade (1945). Remaining in the naval weather service, he retired with the rank of commander in 1965.

11. Carrol V. Clines, *Doolittle's Tokyo Raiders* (Princeton, N.J.: Van Nostrand Reinhold, 1964), pp. 32, 235, and 237; Ted W. Lawson, *Thirty Seconds Over Tokyo* (New York: Random House, 1943); and Jack A. Sims, "The Tokyo Raid—An Avenging Call," *The Air Power Historian* 4, no. 4 (1957): 175–85.

12. U.S. Navy Chief of Naval Operations, "The First Raid on Japan," NAVAER 50-40T-4 Report (Washington, D.C.: Bureau of Aeronautics, 1947), 6 pp.

13. Upon the raid's completion, Pacific fleet commander Adm. Nimitz radioed embattled Corregidor that the canned weather maps being sent out by Knoll's unit were invaluable for current operations (Knoll to Bates, Feb. 21, 1983).

14. John F. Fuller, "A Lesson from History: Doolittle Raiders Fight Weather, Japanese," *AWS Observer* 23, no. 4 (1976): 7.

15. U.S. Navy Chief of Naval Operations, "The Battle for the Coral Sea," NAVAER 50-IT-12 Report (Washington, D.C.: Bureau of Aeronautics, 1944), 16 pp.

16. Hubert E. Strange, *A Full Life* (privately printed, 1980), pp. 61–64.

17. Florence W. van Straten, *Weather or Not* (New York: Dodd, Mead, 1966), pp. 11–16.

18. U.S. Navy Chief of Naval Operations, "The Battle of Midway," NAVAER 50-40T-1 Report (Washington, D.C.: Bureau of Aeronautics, 1944), 14 pp. Lt. Cdr. Strange, as TF-17's aerological officer during the battle for Midway Atoll, disagrees with the idea that Yamamoto could plan to use bad weather that far ahead. In a letter to author Bates on Apr. 7, 1983, Strange (who made rear admiral upon retirement in 1947) maintains: "The Japs took off in order to reach Midway at a certain time. They and we didn't know the timing of any weather systems." We have relied, however, on U.S. Navy Chief of Naval Operations, "The Battle of Midway."

19. E. B. Potter, "The Crypt of the Cryptanalysts," *U.S. Naval Institute Proceedings* 109, no. 8 (1983): 52–55.

20. Samuel E. Morison, *The Coral Sea, Midway and Submarine Actions* (Boston: Little, Brown, 1960).

21. Ernest J. King, *First Official Report to the Secretary of the Navy, March 1, 1944* (reprinted Philadelphia: J. B. Lippincott, 1947, p. 553, as *War Reports* by Fleet Admiral Ernest J. King). The following provide excellent background material about war in the Aleutians: Samuel E. Morison, *Aleutians, Gilberts, and Marshalls* (Boston: Little, Brown, 1951) and *Two-Ocean War: A Short History of the United States Navy in the Second World War*. (Boston: Little, Brown, 1963); Louis Morton, "Strategy and Command: The First Two Years," in *The War in the Pacific*, U.S. Army in World War II series (Washington, D.C.: GPO, 1962); Kramer J. Rohfleisch, "Drawing the Battle Line in the Pacific," in *Plans and Early Operations*, vol. 1 of *Army Air Forces in World War II* (Chicago: University of Chicago Press, 1948); Historical Office, Headquarters Army Air Forces, *Army Air Forces in the War Against Japan, 1941–1942*, pp. 111–17 and 149–56, and the unit history, "History of the 11th Weather Squadron, 11 January 1941–31 May 1944" (typescript, 1944), pp. 8–9, 12.

22. Benjamin F. Taylor, and O. N. Serbein, Jr., "Temperature and the Probability of Aircraft Icing in the Alaskan-Aleutian Area," *AMS Bulletin* 27, no. 10 (1946): 580–88.

23. Archie M. Kahan to author Bates, Aug. 4, 1982. Kahan's skill and luck held. In Dec., 1943, while still a reserve officer and just twenty-one months out of Cal Tech, he was awarded the Legion of Merit by the Army's Alaskan Department for outstanding weather predictions used in the successful bombing of Paramushiru in the Kurile Islands. To hold off people who frequently demanded long-range weather forecasts, he made up a pack of calling cards with enough weather sequences on their backs to give several months of coverage. As he wryly admitted in a letter to Bates, Aug. 4, 1982: "If you make enough statements, random chance will let some of them pan out!"

24. Nine of House's men were promptly captured. House avoided capture and escaped to the other side of the island, where he held out for 50 days before exposure and starvation drove him to surrender to the Japanese. House and his men survived the war as prisoners. The weathermen left a dog, which the Japanese adopted and which was waiting when the Americans landed on Kiska the following year. See John H. Cloe and Michael F. Monaghan, *Top Cover for America: The Air Force in Alaska, 1920–1948* (Missoula, Montana: Pictorial Histories Publishing Co., 1984), p. 63.

When naval families started to live on Adak during 1963, school bus use fell into three categories: (1) service as scheduled; (2) bus service, but small children must be led or carried to and from buses; and (3) service canceled because of hurricane-force winds. See Virgil E. Sandifer, "CAVU at Paramushiru," *Air Force*, July, 1944, pp. 31–32; Army Air Forces School of Applied Tactics, *A Meteorologist's Report on Aleutian Campaign* (Chanute Field: Army Air Forces Training Command, 1944); and U.S. Navy Chief of Naval Operations, *Fleet Air Wing Four Strikes*, NAVAER 50-40T-2 Report (Washington, D.C.: Bureau of Aeronautics, 1945).

25. John F. Fuller, "A Lesson from History: Weather—Enemy's Friend in Aleutian Battle," *AWS Observer* 25, no. 3 (1978): 11.

26. U.S. Navy Chief of Naval Operations, "The Occupation of Kiska," NAVAER 50-30T-2 Report (1944), 17 pp.

27. Wheeler, "Marine Fog," p. 29.

28. U.S. Army Air Forces Weather Wing Headquarters, "Intelligence Summary: Organization of the Japanese Weather Services" (typescript, 1945); John F. Fuller, "A Lesson from History; Bismarck Sea, World War II," *AWS Observer* 23, no. 9 (1976): 7.

29. John F. Fuller, "A Lesson from History: Weather Fights Invasion, Paradrop, Road," *AWS Observer* 23, no. 9 (1976): 7.

30. Suggs became the AWS vice commander before retiring as a colonel during 1970.

The central also controlled several weather spotter stations set up at isolated advance points in New Guinea such as the Markham Valley and in the Owen Stanley Mountains, as well as other secret sites in Papua's interior. 15th Weather Squadron, "The Early History of the 15th Weather Region (to Early 1943)" (typescript, n.d.), pp. 31–32, 50, and 58; 15th Weather Squadron, "History of the 15th Weather Region (22 April 1942–25 September 1945" (typescript, n.d.), pp. 27, 40, 43, 56, and 58–59; U.S. Navy Chief of Naval Operations, "Operations of the Seventh Amphibious Force, 30 June 1943 to 2 January 1944," NAVAER 50-30T-3 Report (Washington, D.C.: Bureau of Aeronautics, 1944), 25 pp.

31. John F. Fuller, "A Lesson from History: Weathermen Fight Japanese Behind Enemy Lines," *AWS Observer* 24, no. 10 (1977): 7.

32. One night in May, 1944, the weather guerilla, T. Sgt. Max E. Hoke, boarded a submarine at Darwin. A month later, the ship placed him ashore on Mindanao. His weather gear was so cumbersome that it took him and assisting natives three days to move the materiel through the jungle and into nearby hills. There, at a concealed Filipino radio station, he found two Americans who had escaped capture two years before. Almost as soon as his weather station went on the air, Japanese patrols moved in, just five hours' away. "It wasn't very pleasant," Hoke noted later, "waiting a week to see what they were going to do," for a favorite enemy tactic was to surround a suspicious area during the night and attack at dawn. (See Martin Fleer, "Combat Weather Pacific Style" in the 12th Weather Squadron's newspaper, *Snojob* 2, no. 9 (Sept., 1945).

33. Ralph G. Suggs, Memorandum to Office of Assistant Chief of Staff, Sixth Army, Dec. 18, 1944, subject: Sixth Army Weather Office (See also attachment to 15th Weather Squadron, "History of the 15th Weather Region"); John F. Fuller, telephone conversation with Dr. Dean Allard (Head, Operational Archives Branch, Naval Historical Center, Washington, D.C.), Aug. 19, 1977.

34. Karl C. Dodd, *The Technical Services: The Corps of Engineers, The War Against Japan*, U.S. Army in World War II series (Washington, D.C.: GPO, 1966), pp. 570–71, 573, 576, and 578–86.

35. U.S. Navy Chief of Naval Operations, "The Assault Landings on Leyte Island," NAVAER 50-30T-6 Report (Washington, D.C.: Bureau of Aeronautics, 1944), 13 pp; Craven and Cate, eds., *The Army Air Forces in World War II*, vol. 5: *The Pacific: Matterhorn to Nagasaki* (1953), pp. 341, 348, 355–56, 373, 376–79, and 383–89; Steve Birdsall, *Flying Buccaneers: The Illustrated Story of Kenney's Fifth Air Force* (Garden City, N.Y.: Doubleday, 1977).

36. Two decades later, Rottman became the AWS public information director. After retiring as a lieutenant colonel in 1968, he began a second career as a popular television weathercaster in Colorado.

37. 15th Weather Squadron, "Early History," p. 239.

38. William Manchester, *American Caesar: Douglas MacArthur, 1880–1964* (Boston: Little, Brown, 1978), p. 395.

39. U.S. Navy Chief of Naval Operations, "Amphibious Landings in Lingayen Gulf," NAVAER 50-30T-9 Report (Washington, D.C.: Bureau of Aeronautics, 1945), 9 pp.

40. Far East Air Force Weather Central, "The Role of the Far East Air Force Weather Central in Planning (initially) the Attack and (finally) the Occupation of Japan, June to September 1945" (typescript, 1945), 9 pp. Officers in charge for these centrals were Lt. Col. Henry T. Harrison, the senior United Air Lines meteorologist for Chicago and a member of Byrd's first Antarctic expedition (1928–29), and Capt. Ross R. Kellerman, USN. Ultimately, the building's most famed inhabitant was a lowly duty forecaster, 1st Lt. Robert M. White, who became president of the National Academy of Engineering in 1983, after a distinguished military and civilian career.

41. U.S. Navy Chief of Naval Operations, "The Occupation of the Marshall Islands," NAVAER 50-30T-5 Report (Washington, D.C.: Bureau of Aeronautics, 1944), 12 pp.

42. Warren C. Thompson, Discussion of C. C. Bates, "Utilization of Wave Forecasting in the Invasions of Normandy, Burma, and Japan," *New York Academy of Sciences Annals* 51, no. 3 (1949): 569–72.

43. Thompson recalls that the Scripps course offered no guidance on how to communicate surf observations and forecasts to the operators, much less indicate the accuracy of aerial wave observations. His own work, based on flying at an altitude of 1,000 to 2,000 feet over Hawaiian beaches, suggested that surf heights could be called to the closest foot if breakers did not exceed 6 feet.

Onshore, the situation was equally inhospitable. Supposedly, the island of Angaur was secured on Sept. 20, although mopping up continued for another month. Then, during the night of Oct. 24, nine Japanese filtered through the defense perimeter and were slain near the 7th Weather Squadron detachment's camp, where officers and enlisted men lived in separate pyramidal tents. About 4:30 A.M. the unit's commander was awakened by a phone call warning of further Japanese infiltration. Running outside the tent, he came face to face with a Japanese soldier. He turned quickly and ran back into the tent for his rifle. The enemy soldier was right behind, screaming "*banzai*" and firing a pistol with one hand while clutching a hand grenade and a land mine in the other. 2nd Lt. Robert L. Shaw, who had been asleep, jumped from his cot and grabbed the enemy. While the men wrestled, the grenade exploded, killing both instantly. Ten other weathermen in that tent, plus one next door, were wounded by the shrapnel, but most of the explosion was absorbed by Shaw, who had made himself a human shield. For "gallantry in action against the enemy," Shaw was posthumously awarded a Silver Star, a Bronze Star, and the Purple Heart. He was survived by his father, Chet L. Shaw, managing editor of *Newsweek* magazine. (See "Angaur Wxmen Wounded," in *Weather Merchant*, Jan., 1945, a monthly newspaper issued by AAF Weather Service, Pacific Ocean Area.)

44. During the Leyte operations Johnson's escort carrier, USS *Fanshaw Bay*, was heavily shelled by enemy surface craft, and Murphy's *Kitkun Bay* was badly damaged by a Japanese suicide plane. On the USS *Bismarck Sea*, only 700 were saved from a ship's complement of 1,100. Thompson proved to be so calm that he was the last survivor into the water (but the first to be picked up). In 1953 he and author Bates were the first recipients of doctoral degrees in oceanography granted by Texas A&M University.

45. Warren C. Thompson, "Hydrographer for the Navy," *UCLA Magazine*, Dec. 1945, pp. 5, 21–26.

46. Commander in Chief, Pacific Fleet, ALNAV letter to fleet commands concerning heavy weather in western Pacific, declassified Sept. 26, 1955, and reprinted in H. C. Adamson and George F. Kosco, *Halsey's Typhoons: A Firsthand Account* (New York: Crown, 1967). Many consider that incident the greatest marine disaster from natural causes in modern naval history. Two books with opposing viewpoints describe the event. One is Adamson and Kosco, *Halsey's Typhoons*. Capt. C. Raymond Calhoun, one of the destroyer skippers whose ship came close to sinking, later wrote *Typhoon: The Other Enemy* (Annapolis: Naval Institute, 1981), in which he pointed out amazing lapses in mariner's judgment.

47. William F. Halsey, Jr., Twelfth endorsement to Court of Inquiry findings into heavy weather losses suffered by 3rd Fleet, Sept. 29, 1945, reprinted in Calhoun, *Typhoon*, pp. 207–208.

48. Nicholas H. Chavasse, "AAF Hurricane Reconnaissance, Western Pacific, 1945," *AMS Bulletin* 27, no. 9 (1946): 510–18; John F. Fuller, "A Lesson from History: Typhoon Reconnaissance," *AWS Observer* 22, no. 5 (1975): 7. On Aug. 24, 1945, the plan was to occupy Tokyo two days later. However, four typhoons were strung out in an arc, Hong Kong–Iwo Jima–Hokkaido, forcing a two-day delay because of the forecasted positions of Ruth and Susan. By then, AAF weather centrals at Manila and Guam were jointly assigning feminine names to tropical storms. During July–August, 1945, the FEAF central christened eight such storms west of longitude 130° east with names ranging from Mary through Tess; the Tinian central used the names Eva through Helen. In 1947 masculine names were used for tropical storms south of the equator. Because such depressions never crossed the equator, Typhoon Donna and Hurricane Don could never affect each other. Atlantic hurricane forecasters, however, used sequential numbers through 1948 for storm designators, followed until 1953 by the use of phonetic words such as Able, Baker, and Charlie. After that, feminine names came into exclusive use, a practice further modified during 1979 when masculine names were included north of the equator.

49. Lockhart's Hawaiian duty assignment was dual: coordinator of navy weather centrals, Pacific Ocean area, and fleet aerological officer on the staff of Commander in Chief, U.S. Pacific Fleet.

50. U.S. Navy Chief of Naval Operations, "Operational Aspects of Typhoon Warning Service, 1945–1946," NAVAER 50-45T-8 Report (Washington, D.C.: Bureau of Aeronautics, 1948), 23 pp.

51. Much of the aviation gas was delivered by converted B-24s; however, additional fuel went by rusty 55-gallon drums lashed down in the bellies of twin-engined C-46s and C-47s. Air turbulence easily caused leaks; as late as Jan., 1945, a single Hump storm resulted in the loss of nine aircraft; thirty-one people aboard were killed or missing.

52. Surface and winds aloft data were largely transmitted by radio using the international five-digit weather groups expressed in Morse code. If the AACS radioman copying the data was competent and dedicated, the weather office got a good set of charts. If not, there would be a string of excuses—static had been heavy, Indian radio transmitters were screwed up, equipment had failed, and so on. If all three AACS radiomen assigned to weather duty were nonproductive, there was no way the station could get usable weather charts.

53. 10th Weather Squadron, "History of the 10th Weather Squadron, June, 1942–September, 1945" (typescript, 1945), pp. 21–25. While a first lieutenant, Dale J. Flinders served as the 10th Weather Squadron's historian for a time. Remaining in the AWS, he retired as a colonel during 1974. Because of his knack for writing droll poetry, he became informally known as the "Poet Laureate of the Air Weather Service" and added levity to many a banquet.

54. Although only 1,709 officers and men were authorized for the 10th Weather Squadron by war's end, approximately 2,000 were carried on its rolls—the largest squadron in AWS history and nearly half the size of today's AWS population.

55. Carrots included reassignment to civilization after a good job in the steamy Assam Valley, a promotion, ten days of leave in the Vale of Kashmir, or time to participate in sport events such as the India All-Services Championship (in which "weather Wallah" Capt. A. R. Gordon, Jr., won the 800-meter run).

As squadron CO, Ellsworth flew 400 combat missions. Using Betsy, he helped pioneer night flying over the Hump, a period of minimal enemy fighter intercepts and reduced thunderstorm activity. By 1953 he was a one-star general commanding the SAC's 28th Strategic Reconnaissance Wing, which flew B-36s out of Rapid City, S.D. On Mar. 13 of that year, he tried to penetrate American airspace undetected from Lajes during an air-defense exercise by relying on Col. Edward Jess's long-range forecast, which called for fog and stratus in a storm over Newfoundland. Intentionally flying low through the soup, Ellsworth's plane hit the top of a hill near Nut Cove, killing all twenty on board. Another thirteen men died when their search plane crashed on takeoff. Had Jess's forecast been wrong, thirty-three men might have lived. As it was, the Rapid City installation was renamed Ellsworth AFB, the only major air force installation to be dedicated to the memory of a military weatherman.

56. In May, 1943, the monthly lift rate for air cargo was set at 10,000 tons. In Jan., 1945, with a flight leaving the Assam Valley every 2 minutes, the rate hit 46,000 tons. John F. Fuller, "A Lesson from History: Richard E. Ellsworth, Air Weather Service, 1942–49." *AWS Observer* 15, no. 5 (1968): 7.

Craven and Cate, eds, *Army Air Forces in World War II*, vol. 3, *Services around the World*, p. 325. The first 10th Weather Squadron personnel to reach China by the Burma Road arrived on June 22, 1945. The convoy of twenty jeeps and four trucks took forty-seven weathermen (including author Bates as convoy commander) twelve days to drive the 1,365 miles from Chabua, Assam, to Kunming, China.

57. The war's longest single-stage B-29 raid took place the night of Aug. 10–11, 1944. Fifty-three B-29s from China Bay, Ceylon, left to bomb refineries at Palembang, Sumatra, through a patchy undercast; thirty-nine succeeded, making it a 3,853-mile round-trip.

To ensure the top-level forecasting skills at the central, the Weather Bureau lent two of its best station chiefs—Robert Fletcher from Los Angeles and Gordon Dunn from Miami (Dunn was at that time the bureau's best forecaster for tropical weather).

58. Many other weathermen also engaged directly in combat. Flinders, who spoke fluent Burmese, followed right behind Sherman tanks of the British Fourteenth Army as they moved into Kalaw, Burma, where he had taught in the high school prior to the Japanese takeover. S. Sgt. Howard E. Leach, supporting the British 17th Armored Division in Meikitila, patrolled with the Ghurkas and eliminated six Japanese soldiers, for which he won a Bronze Star medal. Sgt. Henry M. Yates, a truck driver in civilian life, distinguished himself by killing several enemy during a bloody Japanese counterattack at the all-important Myitkyina airstrip.

59. Maj. Charles R. Dole, commander of the China Weather Central, used analogs to make these 72-hour forecasts. The central's lead forecaster was Maj. Delmar L. Crowson, who became a brigadier general expert in atomic warfare during the postwar period. Another of the central's veterans, Capt. Clarence E. ("Ed") Roach, went on to become AWS director of operations.

60. Charles R. Dole. "Analogs When Isolated," *AWS Bulletin* 2, no. 4 (1944): 9–12; 2nd Weather Reconnaissance Squadron, "History of the 2nd Weather Reconnaissance Squadron, February–December 1944" (typescript); L. P. Bachman, "Where Weather Is Born," *Air Force Magazine*, Aug., 1945, pp. 20–21.

61. LeMay later wrote, "That mission helped in the end but there is no way in which any weather personnel—however experienced, discerning, hard-working and/or devoted—can make good bombing weather out of bad bombing weather." Curtis LeMay and Mackinlay Kantor, *Mission with LeMay: My Story* (Garden City, N.Y.: Doubleday, 1965), p. 343. The American weather team at Yen-an grew with the addition of 1st Lt. Demetrious H. Russell, three more enlisted men, and, in the summer of 1945, Major Spilhaus. As the ranking American, Spilhaus met Chairman Mao on several occasions but came to know Madame Mao better. At the war's end, Spilhaus left Nationalist China very carefully; by then, General Tai Li, Chiang's chief of secret police, had a price of $20,000 on Spilhaus's head, dead or alive. In a typical Spilhaus adventure, he had helped smuggle out a Chinese Communist lady to India as a quid pro quo for Mao's aiding the 10th Weather Squadron. Tai Li hated communist collaborators and had even been accused of murdering his own mother. (For additional details on Yen-an by Spilhaus, see his interview of Feb. 11, 1976, Texas A&M University Oral History Collection.)

62. John F. Fuller, "A Lesson from History: China-Burma-India Theater Challenges 10WS." *AWS Observer* 26, no. 7 (1979): 7.

63. Charles C. Bates, "Utilization of Wave Forecasting in the Invasions of Normandy, Burma, and Japan," *New York Academy of Sciences Annals* 51, no. 3 (1949): 559–65.

64. As staff weather officer for the Tenth Air Force, Ellsworth needed to ascertain quickly whether British naval forces might abort the marine landings, thereby leaving paratroopers on their own deep inside Japanese-held territory. So he developed a trip-wire. As soon as Capt. Crowell and Capt. Bates provided the key 36-hour surf forecast to the East Indies Fleet weather officer, instructor Commander S. W. O. Pack, they drove to the nearby American airbase at Ratmalana and radioed Ellsworth by urgent top-secret message their opinion of what the Royal Navy might accomplish in the next two days.

65. Milton E. Miles, *A Different Kind of War* (Garden City, N.Y.: Doubleday, 1967), p. 18.

66. The Army chain of command up to and includng Gen. Marshall detested the SACO setup. Here were U.S. forces largely independent of Stilwell and Wedemeyer conducting joint field operations with the notorious Tai Li. Furthermore, the U.S. Navy had no business conducting a land guerilla war on army turf.

67. Using trucks that moved slowly over abominable roads, SACO set up intelligence outposts throughout northern and eastern China. The one at Shanpa, a windy, desolate spot in Inner Mongolia, was unique. Although the area came only nominally under Chiang's control, this far northern spot was useful both for radio direction-fixing and for Class-A weather observation purposes. As a goodwill gesture, the local governor, Gen. Fu Tso-yi, even provided horses. Consequently AerM 1c. Robert Sizemore became one of the "sailors on horseback" portrayed in a movie of the 1950s entitled *Operation Gobi*.

68. As might be expected, the director of China activities for the 10th Weather Squadron, Lt. Col. William Crawford, was very unhappy about SACO's weather caper. In his analysis of the situation prepared in late 1945 for the U.S. Forces China Theater Investigation Board, Crawford claimed that it was "a striking example of uncoordinated effort," that "the Navy had no use for a separate weather reporting

system," and "that Navy efforts to establish such a network were completely abortive."

69. Frederick A. Brown, "U.S. Navy Weather Stations in Siberia," *U.S. Naval Institute Proceedings* 87, no. 7 (1962): 76–83.

70. Elmer R. Reiter, *Jet Stream* (Garden City, N.Y.: Doubleday, 1967).

71. "Despite the forward push of 8,800 horsepower generated by four great engines, several B-29s sailed backward during their attempted approach to Japan," noted one account: "weathermen aboard described that sensation as the eeriest they had ever experienced." Rossby, Bjerknes, John Bellamy, and other top meteorologists were dispatched to the Pacific to help cope with the unforeseen weather problems over Japan. See Bob Speer and Richard Dugan, "Japan's Invisible Ally," *Weather Service Bulletin* 3, no. 6 (1945): 1–3.

72. "The Air War on Japan, Part II," *Fortune* 32, no. 4 (1945): 133–37, 249–70. "That damned front" made navigation so difficult that many crews missed their landfalls completely. When wind velocities reached such high values, lateral drift was difficult to correct for, so bomb runs had to be made directly upwind or downwind. Fighting upwind over a heavily defended Japanese city was unthinkable. This meant going downwind at speeds neither bombsights nor bombardiers could function properly at. Moreover, such high winds made a second pass impossible if the first one failed. When a navigational error brought a plane in downwind of the target, getting back into the proper flight line could leave a plane too short of fuel to get home.

73. At night, cloudiness over Japan tended to thin out and loran reception cleared, making navigation easier. Low-altitude bombing runs reduced fuel consumption, thereby permitting heavier bomb loads. They also lengthened engine and airframe life and, most important, increased bombing accuracy. On the long flight home, the B-29s met an early dawn near Iwo Jima, which made it easier to ditch damaged planes safely.

The pertinent climatic analyses were prepared in large part by Dr. Helmut Landsberg, ultimately America's greatest climatologist of the midcentury, and Dr. George Benton, a superb dynamic meteorologist who is now provost of the Johns Hopkins University main campus. Although posted to the AAF's operational analysis office, they drew heavily on synoptic climatologies developed by the AWS's outstanding climatic team, which included Dr. Woodrow C. Jacobs and Dr. Robert F. Stone, assisted by David Blumenstock and Katherine Hafstad. See David Blumenstock, *The Ocean of Air* (New Brunswick, N.J.: Rutgers University Press, 1959); Helmut Landsberg, George S. Benton, and H. Bond, *Weather Conditions in Relation to Incendiary Bombing of the Tokyo Area*, Operations Analysis Division, 20th Air Force, report dated Apr. 20, 1945.

74. See Robert F. Futrell and James Taylor, "Reorganizaton for Victory," in *The Pacific: Matterhorn to Nagasaki*, vol. 5 of *The Army Air Forces in World War II*, ed. Craven and Cate, pp. 696, 709, 712–17. Gen. Arnold started target selection for the untried nuclear weapon in February, 1945. In typical Arnold fashion, he asked Krick for a long-range weather forecast five months or so ahead. Krick suggested good bombing weather between August 5 and 6, an estimate Tibbets claimed verified quite well. See Paul W. Tibbets, "Training the 509th for Hiroshima," *Air Force Magazine* 56, no. 8 (1973): 49–55.

75. Louis Morton, "The Decision to Use the Atomic Bomb," in *Command Decisions*, pp. 514–15. LeMay to Cmdg. Gen., AAFPOA, Apr. 18, 1945, subj: Reporting Efficiency of AAF Weather Service: "A large measure of the success of the recent operations of the 21st Bomber Command has been attributed to the accuracy with which weather, particularly at the target, has been predicted." As LeMay rose higher, first as commander of SAC, then as air force chief of staff, he never forgot the value of high-quality weather support. His belief was specially valuable to the AWS in the 1950s and 1960s when the role of weather in aerial operations was extensively debated.

76. *The Pacific*, vol. 5 of *The Army Air Forces in World War II*, ed. Craven and Cate, pp. 696, 709, and 712–15; U.S. Army Air Forces Weather Service, Pacific Area, "History of the Service" (typescript, 1945), p. 30.

77. The two inboard engines of Sweeney's B-29 conked out for lack of fuel as the returned aircraft taxied off the runway at Okinawa's Yontan airstrip. Frederick L. Ashworth, "Dropping the Atomic Bomb on Nagasaki," *U.S. Naval Institute Proceedings* 84, no. 1 (1958): 12–17; Bruce Goldfarb, "He Was on Both Atom Bomb Flights," *Washington Post*, National Weekly Edition, June 10, 1985, pp. 10–11.

After researching declassified Allied and Japanese assault and defense plans, Alfred Coppel, a former AAF fighter pilot, wrote an exciting historical novel *The Burning Mountain* (New York: Harcourt Brace Jovanovich, 1983) about what might have happened if nuclear devices had not been used.

CHAPTER 7

1. Alexander Kendrick, *Prime Time: The Life of Edward R. Murrow* (New York: Little, Brown, 1969). Reprinted by permission of the publisher.

2. Air Weather Service, "History of the Service, 1945–46" (typescript, 1946), 3: 46. By May 15, 1946, Greenland's largest air base, Narsarssuak, had the following weathermen: one captain, one first lieutenant, one staff sergeant, twenty privates or privates first class, and three Danish civilians. River Clyde in far northern Labrador, which should have been filing hourly weather reports, was down to one experienced weather observer who also had radio duty.

3. Headquarters North Atlantic Wing, Air Transport Command, to Commanding General, Atlantic Division, Air Transport Command, Mar. 19, 1946, subject: Need for Weather Forecasters in the North Atlantic Area, copy in author Bates's files.

4. Weather Service Headquarters, Army Air Forces, letter signed D. N. Yates to author Bates, Jan. 29, 1946. Maj. Archie Kahan, despite his Legion of Merit, chose to stay out. A misunderstanding in 1945 had caused Col. Yates to snap Kahan to attention and use him "as a dartboard for barbed insults." Kahan wrote, "It was a fine bit of irony that the man who had the most to do with my preference for civilian life was asking me to make a career in the military." By 1954 Kahan was the executive director of the Texas A&M University Research Foundation, a position he held for the next nine years.

5. In late 1945 the society, with a membership of 2,883, had a yearly cash inflow

of $37,899. Twenty-five years later the membership was more than 12,000, and the annual cash flow was approximately $2.5 million.

6. Benjamin G. Holzman, "Remarks Concerning Industrial Meteorology," *AMS Bulletin* 28, no. 9 (1947): 411. The boundary between federal and private weather services remained a turbulent issue for years. In 1953 the under secretary of commerce established an advisory committee on weather services, chaired by Brig. Gen. J. J. George of the Air Force Reserve, to investigate the situation. Other ex-military meteorologists on the panel were Col. Merewether, Capt. Orville, Col. Spengler, Maj. Spilhaus, and Lt. Robert Elliott, a former Cal Tech faculty member. Their views, which were favorable toward private firms, appeared in a report, *Weather Is the Nation's Business* (Washington, D.C.: GPO, 1953). Charles C. Bates, "Status of Applied Meteorology in the Post-War Period," *AMS Bulletin* 30, no. 6 (1949): 199–203, and "Industrial Meteorology and the American Meteorological Society—A Historical Overview," ibid., 57, no. 11 (1976): 1320–27. According to a 1954 National Science Foundation survey, of 5,273 professional meteorologists in the U.S., 43 percent were still in uniform. Of the civilians, 1,325 held USAF reserve commissions, and 650 were in the naval reserve. Thus, almost a decade after World War II, 80% of U.S. civilian meteorologists still had military ties.

7. Joint Task Force One, *Operation Crossroads—The Official Pictorial Record* (New York: William H. Wise, 1946).

8. John F. Fuller, to Col. F. A. Post, USAF (Lincoln Laboratories Summer Studies Program), May 18, 1970, subject: Synopsis of Air Weather Service Reconnaissance Program. The unarmed B-29s carried such meteorological sensors as the ML-313 psychrometer and the SCR-718 and APN-1 radar altimeters. The AN/APQ-13 radar already aboard the B-29s was also used for cloud detection.

9. Benjamin G. Holzman, and Arthur A. Cumberledge. "Weather and the Atomic Bomb Tests at Bikini," *AMS Bulletin* 27, no. 5 (1946): 247–48 and 27, no. 8 (1946): 435–37.

10. Fifty-ninth Weather Reconnaissance Squadron (VLR), "Squadron History, January–March, 1947" (typescript, 1947), p. 9; John F. Fuller, "A Lesson from History: B-29, RB-29, WB-29: Faithful Bird Fills Big AWS History Page," *AWS Observer* 25, no. 4 (1979): 7.

11. Omar N. Bradley and Clay Blair, *A General's Life: An Autobiography by General of the Army Omar N. Bradley* (New York: Simon & Schuster, 1983), p. 514. Also in Bradley's autobiography, he relates: "This detection net was first proposed—*urged*, I should say—in 1947 by [the] Atomic Energy Commissioner. . . . Responsibility for operating it had been delegated to the Air Force. . . . It had been in full-time service barely one year when one of its aircraft, a B-29 operating under the guise of a weather plane, picked up signs of the [first] Soviet atomic explosion (radioactivity in the atmosphere) near Alaska on September 3, 1949" (p. 514).

12. Early B-29 flight highlights include the discovery of the first large ice island (Target X) in the Arctic Ocean on Aug. 14, 1946; the first flight over the top of a hurricane on Oct. 7, 1946; and the first low-level night penetration of a hurricane's eye on Oct. 19, 1947.

13. Between early 1945 and May, 1950, the number of naval weather detachments fell from 1,588 to 271; aerological officers dropped from 1,318 to 221, and

approximately 5,000 warrant officers and aerographer's mates dwindled to 1,470 (see *Naval Aviation News*, Oct., 1957, p. 3).

14. From that date on, AWS remained assigned under ATC or its successor airlift organizations, namely, MATS (June 1, 1948), then MAC (January 1, 1966). Ironically, throughout its growth after 1937, the entity that became AWS was opposed by proponents of the unity-of-command doctrine, not the least formidable of which within the AAF (to say nothing of elements within the Army) were ATC and the Air Training Command. In 1945–46, however, ATC did not actively campaign to acquire the AWS.

15. John F. Fuller, *Air Weather Support to the United States Army: Tet and the Decade After*, Air Weather Service Historical Study No. 8 (Scott AFB, Ill.: MAC, 1979); Joint Chiefs of Staff, memorandum of policy No. 46, subject: Responsibility for River and Flood Forecasting for the United States Armed Forces, June 24, 1948.

16. AWS, "History of the Service, 1949" (typescript, 1949), pp. 45–55. Many wartime AWS lieutenant colonels and colonels remained in grade until they retired ten to fifteen years later. William Barney, who stayed a colonel about as long as anyone while working up to being AWS vice commander, commented that if one had to be frozen in grade, that of colonel was as good as any.

17. Cal Tech quit teaching meteorology by late 1948. Upon Dr. Millikan's retirement a year before, his replacement was an MIT academic, Dr. Lee DuBridge. One of DuBridge's early actions was to phase out meteorology, thereby causing Krick to leave the campus.

18. "Composite (Reserve) Weather Squadrons Organized," *AMS Bulletin* 29, no. 4 (1948): 145.

19. Horace R. Byers and Roscoe R. Braham, *The Thunderstorm* (Washington, D.C.: GPO, 1949), 287 pp.; Horace R. Byers, "Thunderstorms," in *Compendium of Meteorology*, ed. Thomas F. Malone (Boston: American Meteorological Society, 1951), pp. 681–93.

20. The AAF letter was signed by Maj. Gen. LeMay, who by that time held the research desk at Headquarters AAF. LeMay additionally tagged Yates for Holzman's services, an action that caused Holzman to spend the rest of his military career on the research side of the air force. At the time of the LeMay letter, AWS technical and research projects underway included chemical warfare meteorology at Camp Detrick, tropical meteorology at the Institute of Tropical Meteorology, possible use of electronic computers at Princeton University's Institute for Advanced Study, fog modification, arctic meteorology, statistical meteorology at MIT, minimal flight planning by Maj. D. C. Williams that ultimately led to computer-derived flight plans, and special climatic summaries used in Joint Army-Navy Intelligence Surveys.

21. Over the years, AFCRL and GRD melded into what was known by 1976 as the Air Force Geophysics Laboratory. The AWS became a leading client of that laboratory's meteorology division. Besides Brig. Gen. Holzman, a number of weather colonels commanded the organization, including Marcellus Duffy (1948–49), Leo A. Kiley (1964–65), Robert F. Long (1965–68), and Dale J. Flinders (1968–71).

22. The directorate's highly creditable research staff included George P.

Cressman, Karl Johannessen, Leonard W. Snellman, and Robert G. Stone. Reporting to the directorate was AWS's Climatic Center, headed by Woodrow C. Jacobs. In 1970 Jacobs became the first director of ESSA's Environmental Data Service.

23. Clark C. Spence, *The Rainmakers: American "Pluviculture" to World War II* (Lincoln: University of Nebraska Press, 1980), 182 pp.

24. A one-gram pellet of dry ice falling through a supercooled cloud forms about 10,000 trillion sublimation nuclei. Vaporizing a gram of silver iodide creates about 600 trillion particles, enough to fill 0.2 cubic miles of sky after distribution by normal processes.

25. Barrington S. Havens, James E. Jiusto, and Bernard Vonnegut, *Early History of Cloud Seeding* (Socorro: New Mexico Institute of Mining and Technology, 1978), 75 pp.

26. Irving Langmuir, "A Seven-Day Periodicity in Weather in the United States during April, 1950," *AMS Bulletin* 31, no. 10 (1950): 386–87; Richard D. Coons and Ross Gunn, "Relation of Artificial Cloud-modification to the Production of Precipitation," in Malone, ed., *Compendium of Meteorology*, pp. 235–41; Bernard Haurwitz, et al., to the President, AMS, Aug. 16, 1950, *AMS Bulletin* 31, no. 9 (1950): 346–47. Cloud seeders of note during the 1950s included Irving Krick's Global Weather Resources Development Corporation and Archie Kahan, who later became chief, Office of Atmospheric Resource Management, in the Rocky Mountain region of the U.S. Bureau of Reclamation. The topic became such an issue that President Eisenhower, in 1953, established an Advisory Committee on Weather Control chaired by Capt. Orville and including AWS reserve officers Brig. Gen. George and Col. Spengler.

27. Canadian Department of Transport (Meteorological Division), *Joint Arctic Weather Stations Programme, 1946–1951* (Toronto: Department of Transport, n.d.), 147 pp.

28. Kenneth J. Bertrand, *Americans in Antarctica, 1775–1948* (New York: American Geographical Society, 1971), pp. 483–513; Lisle A. Rose, *Assault on Eternity: Richard E. Byrd and the Exploration of Antarctica, 1946–47* (Annapolis: Naval Institute Press, 1980).

29. Joseph G. Galway, "J. P. Finley, the First Severe Storm Forecaster," *AMS Bulletin* 66, no. 11 (1985): 1389–95. The Fawbush-Miller bad weather prediction technique was described in a series of six papers published in the *AMS Bulletin* between 1951 and 1954. In 1956 the society also gave them the Meisinger Award.

30. Of fourteen tornado forecasts they issued in 1949 for the Kansas-Texas-Oklahoma area, thirteen verified. In 1950 the Gulf Coast states and most of the Middle West were added to Tinker's responsibilities. Of the thirty-three tornado forecasts issued in 1950, twenty-nine verified. However, on Sept. 1, 1952, an unforecast tornado struck Carswell AFB, Tex., causing an estimated $48 million in destruction and damaging 106 of SAC's huge B-36 bombers. Congress was disturbed, for it meant SAC's main atomic striking force had been severely crippled by weather. Ernest Fawbush, Robert C. Miller, and L. G. Starrett, "An Empirical Method of Forecasting Tornado Development," *AMS Bulletin* 32, no. 1 (1951): 1–9.

31. Robert C. Miller, "Chronology: Evolution of Severe Weather Forecasting Responsibilities" (typescript, USAF Severe Weather Warning Center, May, 1972).

32. John F. Fuller, "A Lesson from History: The Berlin Airlift," *AWS Observer* 23, no. 3 (1976): 7.

33. As airfield conditions approached values at which they would be closed, dispatchers demanded that ceilings and visibilities be given to the closest 50 feet and quarter-mile, respectively. They also asked that these criteria be forecast for three hours in advance. Maj. William J. Norton commanded the Rhein-Main weather central during those trying days.

Bernie (more popularly pronounced "Barnie") Pusin later teamed with another famous Barney in the AWS, William S. Barney, to oversee support of U.S. nuclear testing in the Pacific region during the 1950s. By retirement time, Pusin had served as AWS public information officer (while Barney was the AWS's vice commander) and as commander of two weather squadrons—the 6th and 25th.

34. William H. Tunner to Commanding Officer, 2105th Weather Group, Aug. 13, 1949, subject: Support Given to Airlift Task Force.

CHAPTER 8

1. Hurd C. Willett, "The Forecast Problem," in Thomas F. Malone, ed., *Compendium of Meteorology* (Boston: AMS, 1951). Willett believed the modeling failed for three reasons: the atmosphere was too complex to be categorized as simply consisting of specified air masses and front discontinuities; cyclogenesis rarely, if ever, duplicated the idealized Bjerknes wave-cyclone model, and the basic impulses that triggered large-scale cyclogenesis and anticyclogenesis frequently came from far outside the specific area of interest.

2. The first global surface weather map was drawn by Leo Alpert in early 1950 by combining daily sea-level synoptic analyses of the Southern Hemisphere (a joint Weather Bureau–MIT effort) with the equivalent Northern Hemisphere surface analyses issued by the bureau. One of the Air Corps' first 150 weather officers, Alpert had developed a wartime specialty of forecasting for the Panama Canal Zone.

3. In 1904 Jakob Bjerknes's father suggested that all one needed to do was integrate the atmosphere's equations of motion, using appropriate raw data. Then in 1922 the British pioneer Lewis F. Richardson agreed that this could be done by filling a computing theater with 64,000 mathematicians who would rapidly crank desk calculators so that the end product would appear before the weather pattern did. When attempted on a small scale, the Richardson technique went wildly astray, as when it predicted a jump of 145 mb in pressure during a six-hour forecast. However, his book, *Weather Prediction by Numerical Processes*, written in 1922 and reprinted in 1965 (New York: Dover), became the classic treatise and was used as a starting point by post–World War II researchers. See Philip D. Thompson, "A History of Numerical Weather Prediction in the United States," *AMS Bulletin* 64, no. 7 (1983): 755–69; and Jules Charney, R. Fjörtoft, and John von Neumann, "Numerical Integration of the Barotropic Vorticity Equation," *Tellus* 2 (1950): 237–54.

4. In practice, AWS wrote the paper and Oscar Senter persuaded Reichelderfer to present it. However, Reichelderfer and his research chief, the former AWS wartime major Harry Wexler, had strong reservations about whether numerical

weather prediction was economical and ready for use. The AFCRC was equally reluctant.

5. The IBM-701 had an electrostatic memory of 2,048 words of 36 binary bits each (including sign), an addition time of 60 microseconds, a multiplication time of 456 microseconds, and the ability to make 10,000 numerical operations per second by using stored programs. Output was in two formats: punched cards and by a printer that generated 120 72-digit lines per minute. To generate a 12-hour prediction took 72,000 arithmetic operations per one-hour time step, or 864,000 operations. A one-hour time step could be accomplished in 35 seconds, of which only 8 seconds were spent in calculations and the remainder in data handling and internal housekeeping. Such housekeeping tasks included conversion of magnetic-tape data to a transmittable teletype format and subsequent printout. With the 100-wpm teletype circuits then used Stateside and the 60-wpm circuits overseas, an average numerical weather prediction bulletin (approximately 325 five-digit groups) took 3.5 and 5.25 minutes, respectively.

6. Joint Numerical Weather Prediction Unit Staff Members, "One Year of Operational Numerical Weather Prediction," *AMS Bulletin* 38, no. 5 (1957): 263–68.; Vincent J. Schaefer, "Can We Do It Better?" ibid., 39, no. 1 (1958): 90–92.

7. John F. Fuller, "Text of Interview with Dr. Robert D. Fletcher (Chief Scientist, Air Weather Service)," June 22, 1972, p. 1.

8. "Operations of the WBAN Analysis Center," *Weather Service Bulletin* 2, no. 1 (1948): 4–8; Joseph Vederman, "The Weather Bureau–Air Force–Navy Analysis Center," *AMS Bulletin* 30, no. 10 (1949): 335–41.

9. Air Weather Service, "History of the Service, July–December, 1959" (typescript, 1960), p. 415.

10. Wolff remained in charge of the navy's numerical weather prediction program until he retired in 1972 to set up his own weather service, Global Weather Dynamics. In Nov., 1983, he reappeared in federal service as director, National Ocean Service, of the National Oceanic and Atmospheric Administration (NOAA).

11. Roy E. Appleman, *South to the Naktong, North to the Yalu: June–November, 1950*, in *United States Army in the Korean War*, ed. Stetson Conn (Washington, D.C.: GPO, 1961), p. 21; Joseph C. Goulden, *Korea: The Untold Story of the War* (New York: Times Books, 1982), p. xvii. Captured documents later revealed that the North Koreans timed their major ground assaults to coincide with poor flying weather in order to negate the air superiority of the United Nations Command.

12. The air force's official history of the Korean War, by Robert Futrell, read: "Korean operations demonstrated that the USAF had not become an all-weather air force."

13. Walter Karig, Malcolm W. Cagle, and Frank A. Manson, *Battle Report—The War in Korea* (New York: Rinehart, 1952), p. 152.

14. AWS's last detachment in Korea was inactivated on Sept. 10, 1949, at Kimpo Airfield south of Seoul, when the last of the postwar U.S. forces departed. After the end of Japanese control in 1945, weather service in both Koreas rapidly fell into disrepair. Nothing either occupying power could do restored them to their former efficiency.

Maj. John J. Jones ably directed the Tokyo Central, whose prime customer was

General of the Army MacArthur's United Nations Command. The navy eventually set up a small weather unit under Capt. John Tatom down the hall; however, an independent weather central was not activated at the huge Yokosuka Naval Base south of Tokyo until Dec. 15, 1952.

15. The weather station in direct support of the Joint Operations Center—Tactical Air Control Center (JOC-TACC) of the advanced headquarters of the Eighth Army and the Fifth Air Force also suffered this yo-yo effect. Under Maj. Robert A. Taylor, the station opened at Taegu in late July, 1950, moved south to Pusan by mid-August, then pushed back to Taegu a month later. October, 1950, found the station in Seoul, followed by a new retreat to Taegu in December, and finally back to Seoul for good on June 15, 1951. U.S. Air Force 20th Weather Squadron, "History of the 20th Weather Squadron, July–September, 1950" (typescript, 1950).

16. After events stabilized, the 30th Weather Squadron operated ten to fifteen detachments, two of which temporarily got as far north as Pyongyang, the North Korean capital, during the fall of 1950.

17. Naval commanders took a dim view of the proposed landing site. The heavier assault ships needed 23 feet of water to clear the Inchon mud flats, and the maximum tidal range was but 31 feet when the moon was at perigee. Fortunately, the North Koreans thought the same and left the region lightly defended. Should the target date of Sept. 15 have been missed, the ensuing month's delay would have had many adverse effects.

18. John F. Fuller, "A Lesson from History: [Preparations for Inchon Landings]," *AWS Observer* 22, no. 9 (1975): 7. The companion top-secret study was prepared and typed by author Bates in his role as chief, Marine Geography Section, U.S. Navy Hydrographic Office, then used to brief President Truman.

19. For his airmanship under trying conditions, Cloniger received the Distinguished Flying Cross, probably the first in the AWS to do so for tropical storm reconnaissance.

20. AWS also helped to shift ninety SAC B-29 bombers and ninety-six C-119 troop carrier aircraft from the continental U.S. to the Far East, including a ninety-day loan of thirty AWS navigators to help move the aircraft.

21. There was reason to believe that Communist China waited to join battle until after North Korea's rivers had frozen, thereby nullifying the United Nations Command's destruction of the key bridges south of the Yalu River and the Manchurian border. Appleman, *South to the Naktong*, in *U.S. Army in Korea*, pp. 139, 262, and 744; see also Walter G. Hermes, *Truce Tent and Fighting Front*, in ibid., pp. 178–80; Fred Decker, Russell L. Lincoln, and John A. Day, *Weather Effects on Army Operations*, fourth quarterly report (15 Apr.–15 July, 1955), Army Signal Corps contract DA-36-039-SC-63206 with Department of Physics, Oregon State College, Corvallis; Matthew B. Ridgway, *The Korean War* (Garden City, N.Y.: Doubleday, 1967), p. 70; and Karig et al., *Battle Report*, p. 403.

22. Goulden, *Korea*, p. 367.

23. LeMay and Kantor, *Mission with LeMay*, p. 463.

24. Moorman, Thomas S., Jr., to Brig. Gen. William O. Senter, Oct. 20, 1950; Laurence S. Kuter to Senter, Jan. 21, 1951; Senter to Lt. Gen. Kuter, Apr. 2,

1951. Inaccurate forecasts of high-velocity winds over Korea during winter were particularly troublesome when close-interval pattern bombing attacks were being marshaled. They could cause the times over target to vary by much as sixteen minutes early or late from scheduled release time. Sometimes the winds varied so much with altitude that lower-level bombers might be underflying the higher flights, a hazardous thing to do.

25. U.S. Air Force 30th Weather Squadron, "History of the 30th Weather Squadron, 16 November–31 December 1950" (typescript, 1951), p. 21.

26. Robert F. Futrell, *United States Air Force Operations in the Korean Conflict: 1 November 1950–30 June 1952*, USAF Historical Study No. 72 (Maxwell AFB, Ala.: Air University, 1955), pp. 46, 251.

27. WB-29s were distinguishable from regular bombers by the absence of all armament and gun turrets except for the tail turret, which carried twin .50-caliber machine guns. Bombardier equipment had also been removed to make room for a weather instrument panel and a place for a weather observer crew member.

During February, 1951, the 512th was deactivated and replaced by the 56th Strategic Reconnaissance Squadron (Medium), Weather. Between them, the two units earned all eleven U.S. campaign streamers awarded for the Korean "police action."

28. John F. Fuller, "A Lesson from History: Recon Flights Plug Hole; Both Sides Use Data," *AWS Observer* 25, no. 5 (1978): 7.

29. One of the 6166th pilot-forecasters, Capt. John W. Collens III, went on to command the AWS as a brigadier general during 1974–75. A staunch weather reconnaissance advocate, Collens went to the mat with his four-star MAC commander in 1975 about taking that mission away from the AWS; unfortunately for the meteorologists, he lost, hands down.

Another Grisham—Capt. Leon Grisham—served as staff weather officer to the 51st Fighter Interceptor Wing and flew 100 combat missions in the F-80 Shooting Star over Korea. After making colonel, he commanded the 55th Weather Reconnaissance Squadron. During his military career he earned three Distinguished Flying Crosses, thirteen Air Medals, a Bronze Star Medal, and two Purple Hearts, undoubtedly an AWS record.

The other pilot/weather forecasters lost were: Capt. Warren G. Harding and Capt. Gerald L. Brose. In addition, Capt. Bruce K. Nims, 1st Lt. James M. Schouley, Jr., and T. Sgt. Carl M. Spence were killed while serving as weather observers in combat aircraft over Korea.

Also of note, a former AWS chief of staff, Col. John K. Arnold, had transferred out of the AWS earlier in 1950. On Jan. 12, 1953, aboard a B-29 of the 581st Air Resupply and Communications Wing, Arnold was shot down near the Yalu River. After capture, he was convicted as a spy by a Chinese military tribunal in Peiping (now Beijing). After thirty-one months of imprisonment, finally he was released in August, 1955.

30. By 1975, when he became AWS chief of staff, Gayikian had a reputation as a likable but highly opinionated officer. He had a right to be—he had served as an enlisted man, a warrant officer, and commissioned officer through seventeen pay grades, private to colonel, over a thirty-seven-year period!

31. Siple was the Boy Scout chosen to go on Rear Adm. Richard E. Byrd's first

expedition to Antarctica (1928–29). As an army major in 1945, he toured the western Pacific, briefing troops on how to contend with the cold, rainy weather during the upcoming invasion of Japan during the winter of 1945–46.

By April, 1952, the Seoul weather center provided a dozen specialized weather forecasts for the Eighth Army: an eighteen-hour and a five-day general forecast for all Korea, a special twenty-four-hour forecast for each corps sector, advisories of impending severe weather, and a twenty-four-hour forecast for the Signal Corps, Corps of Engineers, and any antiaircraft unit that had sent in a request.

32. In the States, Brig. Gen. Senter was also trying to smoke out formal weather support requirements from the Army Field Forces (later redesignated the Continental Army Command) based at Fort Monroe, Va. He, too, was lucky when Gen. John R. Hodge, the force commander, approved a formal package of domestic army needs the same month—Oct., 1952.

33. Because of the Truman-Johnson defense austerity program, the navy had fifty more weather detachments than it had aerological officers.

34. U.S. Navy carriers chose not to launch nighttime interdiction strikes, and the North Koreans learned to move trucks, armored vehicles, and trains at night during good weather. Arthur D. Struble, letter of commendation to AGC Joseph Zaffino, Sept. 14, 1950.

35. Dan A. Kimball, citation for Bronze Star Medal to AGC Joseph Zaffino, n.d.

36. As an AAF weather officer, Machta had spent the last half of World War II, as had his fellow officer George Cressman, instructing meteorological cadets at NYU. The first test director for the Nevada shots was another former NYU instructor—Dr. Athelstan Spilhaus. Upon his return from China, Spilhaus and Rear Adm. Thomas G. W. Settle convinced President Truman and the AEC that the Buster-Jangle shot series should not be conducted on Amchitka Island in the Aleutians because of environmental and geological conditions. Even so, the AEC later detonated three nuclear explosions on Amchitka—Longshot (1965), Milrow (1969), and Cannikin (1971).

37. In the PPG, light easterly tradewinds existed up to 25,000 feet. From 25,000 to approximately 50,000 feet existed a layer of westerlies—actually west-southwesterly winds. Then came the "Krakatoa easterlies," which gradually diminished at approximately 100,000 feet. In this vertical profile, the westerlies were the most variable and the most critical in determining the pattern of radioactive fallout.

In this highly workable system of staffing the tests, the staff weather officer exerted operational control over all JTF weather components. A test series often lasted four months or longer, so everyone cooperated to achieve the universal personal goal: "Get the test series over so we can get back to civilization!" Two of the best staff weather officers were Col. Charles D. Bosenot (Redwing series) and Capt. Daniel Rex of the Navy (Hardtack series).

38. Joint Task Force Seven, "Description of Major Hardtack Weather Units," Enclosure to Staff Weather Officer's Report on Operation Hardtack (1958), p. 4, copy in author Bates's files.

39. AWS reconnaissance aircraft often intentionally penetrated the atomic

clouds, exposing crew members to a dosage of as much as 25 Roentgens (i.e., a dosage about twice that experienced during a seventy-year lifetime from medical/dental X-rays and natural radiation backgrounds). Crew members carried dosimeter badges, and after atomic cloud penetrations, the aircraft was washed down, a process known as cooling the aircraft. Since cessation of atmospheric tests in 1963, various veterans and other citizens have claimed that they suffer physical maladies, generally cancer, from fallout. However, as late as 1981, the Interagency Task Force on Compensation for Radiation Related Illnesses steadfastly maintained that the low level of the fallout posed little or no risk of adverse health effects. See testimony of Lt. Gen. Harry A. Griffith, USA, Director, Defense Nuclear Agency, before U.S. Senate Committee on Labor and Human Resources, Oct. 27, 1981; and R. Jeffrey Smith, "NRC Finds Few Risks for Atomic Vets," *Science* 228, no. 4706 (1985): 1409.

The amount of air support required for a PPG test series was mind-boggling. During 1951–52, twenty-five such tests required 2,664 aerial sorties, generally with highly instrumented aircraft. And this was well before the flap about fallout from Shot Bravo!

40. Alexander R. Gordon, Jr., to author Bates, May 21, 1956.

41. The expedition's hydrometeorologist was Yevgeniy Federov, who became director of the Soviet Hydrometeorological Service five years later and worked with the U.S. military weather services. Ivan Papanin, *Life on an Ice Floe*, trans. Fanny Smitham (London: Hutchinson, 1947).

42. Joseph O. Fletcher and Lawrence S. Koenig, 58th Strategic Reconnaissance Squadron (M) Weather, *Floating Ice Islands*, Special Report No. 5 (1951). The Ptarmigan ice photographs were compiled by Maj. Alexander Gordon, the AWS liaison to the Hydrographic Office, into a definitive report on polar ice conditions (H. O. Publication 611) and later used by author Bates to encourage naval policy makers to send nuclear submarines below the Arctic Ocean's ice canopy.

43. After the Pentagon heard of "Crazy Joe" Fletcher's ice island project, Fletcher was asked to defend it in Jan., 1952, before a group chaired by no less than Brig. Gen. Don Yates, then the director of R&D at Headquarters USAF. Yates liked daring experiments, so the go-ahead came easily.

44. Although Papanin claimed to have made the first North Pole landing in 1937, later estimates suggest he was about 10 miles off. Participants in the USAF's 1952 flight were Lt. Col. William Benedict (pilot), Lt. Col. Fletcher (copilot), 1st Lt. Herbert Thompson (navigator), M. Sgt. Edison T. Blair (recorder), S. Sgt. Harold Turner (flight engineer), A1c. Robert L. Wishard (radio operator), A2c. David R. Dobson, Dr. Crary (geophysicist), Robert Cotell (assistant geophysicist), and Fritz Ahl (bush pilot). Mike Wise, *Ice Islands of the Arctic: Alaskan Air Command's Arctic Experience* (Elmendorf AFB: Alaskan Air Command, 1979), pp. 11–12.

45. T-3 slowly orbited the Canada Basin clockwise and in 1959 was moving westerly when just 20 miles north of Point Barrow. As of mid-1983, T-3 was again near the North Pole and apparently would exit east of Greenland and undergo certain destruction (NOAA press release 83-39, June 12, 1983). Meanwhile, Fletcher became NOAA's Assistant Administrator for Oceanic and Atmospheric

Research in Jan., 1984, beginning his forty-third year of federal service. Joseph O. Fletcher, "Origin and Early Utilization of Aircraft-Supported Drifting Stations," in *Arctic Drifting Stations* (Washington, D.C.: Arctic Institute of North America, 1968), pp. 2–13.

46. Charles C. Bates, Thomas F. Gaskell, and Robert B. Rice, *Geophysics in the Affairs of Man* (Oxford: Pergamon Press, 1982), pp. 143–46. The Hydrographic Office's ranking ice observer, Henry Kaminski, was killed, along with his star pupil from the Naval Weather Service, when their P4Y2 aircraft crashed into Ellesmere Island, Canada, on Apr. 16, 1954, during ice reconnaissance. The office's ice program was formally transferred to the Naval Weather Service nine years later with the hopeful motto "Navy ships are where you don't find ice!" By then, Lt. Cdr. William Dehn of the Naval Weather Service was the navy's top military "ice-man."

47. James W. Winchester and Charles C. Bates, "Meteorological Conditions and the Associated Sea Ice Distribution in the Chuckchi Sea during the Summer of 1955," in *Polar Atmosphere Symposium I—Meteorology*, ed. R. C. Sutcliffe (Oxford: Pergamon Press, 1958), p. 331.

48. George J. Dufek, *Operation Deepfreeze* (New York: Harcourt, Brace, 1957), p. 47. Once a minor league baseball pitcher good enough to rate a tryout with the Brooklyn Dodgers, Mirabito could speak six languages.

49. Senter's concept derived directly from his Air War College thesis, "Organizing the Airways Communications and Weather Services" (Mar., 1949).

50. "Winds, Weather and Warships," *Naval Aviation News*, Oct. 19, 1966. Fleet weather centrals at Guam, Kodiak, and Pearl Harbor came under the Pacific Fleet command; in the east, the Port Lyautey, Morocco, central supported Commander in Chief, Northeastern Atlantic and Mediterranean. Stateside, Fleet Weather Central, Washington, came under the Atlantic Fleet command in Norfolk, Va.

51. Karl Larew, "Meteorology in the U.S. Army Signal Corps, 1870–1960" (unpublished report, Historical Division, U.S. Army Signal Corps, 1960), pp. 62–77.

52. Air Weather Service Regulation 23-16, "Organization, Field: Mission and Functions of the Weather Reconnaissance Squadron, Provisional #1," May 31, 1956. Starting in 1956, powered gliders, also known as U-2s, were equipped with the AN/AMQ-7 temperature-humidity measuring system. However, when Powers was shot down over Russia en route from Pakistan to Norway, the event blew the cover on what had been a highly valuable photo-intelligence operation. U-2s were extremely sensitive to certain meteorological elements. After the Powers incident, Allen Dulles, the director of the Central Intelligence Agency, testified before Congress that weather conditions, not political factors, were the primary determinant in scheduling U-2 flights. See " '58 Loss of Spy Jet Disclosed," *St. Louis Post-Dispatch*, Dec. 6, 1982, p. 5A.

53. Wycliffe D. Toole, "The U.S. Navy's Hurricane Hunters," *U.S. Naval Institute Proceedings* 86, no. 9 (1960): 48–56. These units were Patrol Bomber Squadron One One Four (1945), Weather Squadron Three (1945), Meteorological Squadron Three (1946), Heavy Land Based Patrol Bomber Squadron 3 (1946), Patrol Squadron 23 (1949), Weather Squadron 2 (1952), Airborne Early Warning Squadron 4 (1952), and Weather Reconnaissance Squadron 4 (1968). Operational details about

these units may be found in the last squadron's cruise book, *Once a Hunter* (Jacksonville: Allied Printing, 1975).

54. The first loss of a weather reconnaissance aircraft making low-level penetrations of tropical storms came on Oct. 26, 1952. In this instance, all ten crew members of a WB-29 from the 54th Weather Reconnaissance Squadron were killed while flying through typhoon Wilma 300 nautical miles east of Leyte, Philippine Islands. Three years later, on Sept. 26, 1955, Lt. Cdr. Grover B. Windham, plus a crew of nine and two *Toronto Star* reporters, were also lost as they entered the eye of hurricane Janet off Cuba aboard their navy P-2V reconnaissance aircraft.

55. Hurricane Hunters Reunion Committee, letter signed by R. J. Fitzsimmons, Jr. (chairman) to author Bates, Apr. 4, 1984.

56. National Hurricane Research Project Staff, "Objectives and Basic Design of the National Hurricane Research Project," *AMS Bulletin* 37, no. 6 (1956): 263–69.

57. Delmar L. Crowson, "Cloud Observations from Rockets," *AMS Bulletin* 30, no. 1 (1949): 17–22; Stanley M. Greenfield and William W. Kellogg, *Inquiry into the Feasibility of Weather Reconnaissance from a Satellite Vehicle* (Santa Monica, Cal.: RAND Report R-365, 1960, unclassified edition of RAND Report R-218 of Apr. 1951.

58. William K. Widger, Jr., *Meteorological Satellites* (New York: Holt, Rinehart and Winston, 1966), pp. 43–46.

59. Other steering group members were Dr. William K. Widger, Jr. (AFCRL), Edward M. Cortright (NACA), Dr. Sigmund Fritz (Weather Bureau), Dr. Ernst Stuhlinger (Army Ballistic Missile Agency, Huntsville, Ala.), and Dr. Charles C. Bates (Chief of Naval Operations).

Prior to Tiros, Stroud had built a "cloud cover experiment" package involving a simple image scanner; it flew unsuccessfully Mar. 17, 1958, aboard the IGY Vanguard II rocket.

60. Navy Comdr. John Mirabito and AWS Maj. James B. Jones jointly produced the first operational nephanalysis of cloud patterns derived from TIROS-1. The Mirabito-Jones display used data from the Mediterranean area scarcely four hours old, although by that time the satellite had been up for sixty hours.

61. Charles W. Dickens, and Charles A. Ravenstein, *Air Weather Service and Meteorological Satellites, 1950–1960*, AWS Historical Study No. 5 (Scott AFB, Ill.: MAC, 1973), pp. 69, 74. AWS requirements called for the satellite to provide details of daytime cloud cover, snow and ice coverage, cloud patterns at night from high-resolution infrared sensors, both direct and stored readout, global coverage, and all data from a single orbital pass to be processed within 1.5 hours after receipt at a ground station.

Peterson's sales pitch was complicated by AFCRL's Col. George A. Guy's strong argument for the joint approach, in which the Weather Bureau was to be lead agent. At the time, Guy was project officer for USAF System 433L (Weather Observing and Forecasting System), which depended heavily on Weather Bureau support. Thus, Guy's thinking undoubtedly reflected some quid pro quo.

62. John F. Kennedy, *Public Papers of the Presidents of the United States* (Washington, D.C.: GPO, 1963), p. 244.

63. A Schnapf, "The Development of the TIROS Global Environmental Satellite System," *NASA Conference Publication 2227* (1982), pp. 7–16.

CHAPTER 9

1. Gary D. Atkinson, for the U.S. Air Weather Service, *Forecaster's Guide to Tropical Meteorology*, Technical Report No. 240 (Scott AFB: MAC, 1971), 338 pp.

2. To ensure that purple-suit duty was an asset, not a liability, the secretary of defense preferred to approve promotions to flag or general officer only if the officer had performed unified command duty.

3. Prompting the report was an awareness by Congress of a dispute among AWS, the Federal Aviation Agency, and the Weather Bureau regarding jurisdiction and operation of certain aviation weather services. That dispute was one issue that brought weather operations to the attention of the highest levels in the executive branch. For the 1965 report, see U.S. Congress, House, Committee on Government Operations, *Government Weather Programs (Military and Civilian Operations and Research)*, 89th Cong., 1st sess. (Mar. 17, 1965) H. Rep. 177.

4. Once a wartime AWS lieutenant, by 1952 White was director of AFCRC's Meteorology Development Laboratory. In 1959 he became president of the Travelers (Insurance) Research Center, then came to Washington to fill Reichelderfer's shoes at the Weather Bureau. White's mentor on the nation's capital was his older brother, Theodore H. White—famous not only for his *Making of the President* books but also as a ranking reporter in the Luce newsmagazine empire (for details, see his book *In Search of History* (New York: Harper & Row, 1978).

5. Two retired colonels from AWS headquarters ultimately served in this role: during 1973, Clarence Roach, the acting coordinator; and since 1982, William S. Barney.

6. Although White continued to move upward and onward on the Washington scene, direction of the National Weather Service (the former U.S. Weather Bureau) remained in the hands of other ex-AWS officers: Dr. Cressman until 1979 and Dr. Richard E. Hallgren thereafter.

7. Joint Chiefs of Staff Memorandum 192–67, Apr. 7, 1967.

8. Of more than 35,000 people involved in environmental services within the Department of Defense (at an annual cost of more than $400 million), only approximately 18,000 employees and annual operating costs of $150 million came under the Special Assistant for Environmental Services.

9. To ensure that the air force had broad-gage environmentalists able to compete for the top DDOES slot, several AWS officers were sent each year, despite an unusually high tuition cost, to obtain advanced degrees at the Navy Postgraduate School. The most notable AWS graduate of this kind was Albert J. Kaehn, Jr., who became AWS commander in 1978.

10. When the air force hierarchy blessed Col. Best's nomination to command the AWS, they violated (probably for the first time) a rigid custom by which only flight-rated officers, preferably pilots, commanded organizations to which aircraft units were assigned.

11. Today's SESS encompasses solar and radio telescope observatories throughout the world, even receiving data from a Jesuit observatory near Manila, in the Philippine Islands, and from the National Observatory of Athens, Greece, as well as proton data acquired by the Vela nuclear-test-monitoring satellites.

12. John F. Fuller, *Air Weather Support to the United States Army—Tet and the Decade After*, Air Weather Service Historical Study No. 8 (Scott AFB: MAC, 1979), pp. 219, 220.

13. The only navy aerologist to serve as Oceanographer of the Navy was Rear Adm. Denys Knoll (1963–65), following a series of sea commands, including Service Forces, Atlantic Fleet.

14. Kotsch was the only aerologist to be promoted to rear admiral while working in meteorology. Earlier, he wrote two books, the very useful *Heavy Weather Guide* (co-authored by Capt. Edward T. Harding and published by the U.S. Naval Institute, 1965) and *Weather for the Mariner* (Annapolis: Naval Institute, 1970).

15. Secretary of the Navy, "Merger of the Geophysics (Meteorological and Oceanographic) Officer Communities," memorandum, May 5, 1975.

16. The personnel in the Navy's numerical meteorology group at Monterey grew at the following rate (four-year intervals): 1959—6; 1963—57; 1967—87; 1971—156; 1975—226; 1979—284, and 1983—283. The staffing ratio was approximately 6 : 12 : 10 for officers, enlisted personnel, and civilians, respectively.

17. Military Airlift Command, "History of the Air Weather Service, 1 July 1974–31 December 1975" (typescript, 1976), 1 : 17.

18. Despite the disbanding, the AWS continued to provide weather officers and dropsonde operators for ARRS meteorological reconnaissance aircraft. During the thirty-three years that AWS flew its own reconnaissance missions, 144 aircrew lost their lives in 23 major aircraft mishaps. Their names, plus those of other AWS weathermen killed or missing in World War II, Korea, and Vietnam, are engraved on a memorial plaque at the entrance to AWS headquarters at Scott AFB.

19. Jeanne Holm, *Women in the Military: An Unfinished Revolution* (Novato, Calif.: Presidio Press, 1982); Martin Binkin and Shirley J. Bach, *Women and the Military* (Washington, D.C.: Brookings Institution, 1977).

20. By the early 1950s, there had been two WAF weather officers of note. 1st Lt. Mary E. Scantland, a former WASP who had flown eleven types of aircraft, including the P-38, P-39, P-40, P-47, and F-51, in 1952 was on forecasting duty at Itazuke Airbase, Japan, where she briefed Korean War combat pilots, many of whom had less cockpit time than she did. The first WAF to command an AWS detachment was Maj. Jean D. Armstrong. A graduate of Chanute's officer forecaster course in 1948, she was given command of the Frankfurt, Germany, weather detachment (five male forecasters and ten WAF observers) on Aug. 22, 1951.

21. One of Somers's "wash day" forecasts was for the Rose Garden wedding of Tricia Nixon (June 12, 1971), which came extremely close to getting rained on.

22. As of late 1974, AWS was assigned 203 enlisted WAFs, or 3.4% of its entire enlisted force. Of those WAFs, 4 were forecasters, 174 were observers, and 25 were in equipment maintenance. Of the enlisted weather WAFs, 5 supervised both men and women.

23. Folze retired in September, 1970, and died less than two years later. In 1973

a WAF dormitory at Scott AFB was named after her. Remarked Brig. Gen. William Best in his dedicatory speech, "Sergeant Folze's philosophy was to not look at life to see what you could get from it, but rather what you can give it."

24. "Things were different then," Chief Master Sergeant Hill observed, recalling her first enlistment. It was "not too open race-wise; nobody pampered me but I wanted to do something different." See "A Lesson from History: Weather's First Women," *AWS Observer* 30, no. 4 (Apr., 1983): 3.

25. Quite possibly Sgt. Esposito was the first air force woman to qualify as a crew member. She observed in 1977 that she had always wanted to fly. "I asked for the job, got it, qualified for it, and was then accepted by almost everybody. In the last three years I've seen several different reactions from the guys I fly with. Some took a big brother attitude, and others just treated me as one of the guys. I have had no unfavorable reactions at all."

26. In the summer of 1983 Ivory received further good news: he would command the 2nd Weather Wing in Europe, another first for blacks in the AWS.

27. Air Weather Service, "History of Air Weather Service, 1 July 1970 – 30 June 1971" (typescript, 1971), 1: 256 – 58.

28. If the cost and speed of automobiles had changed since 1955 at the rate that computers have, a Rolls Royce in 1975 would have cost about three dollars and had a cruising speed of roughly 35,000 mph.

29. On Oct. 1, 1969, the AWN function shifted from Tinker to Carswell AFB, Tex., in order to utilize new dual Univac 1108 computers. Nine months later, Clark AFB in the Philippines became the weather intercept station for the southwest Pacific region.

30. Joint Chiefs of Staff, "Numerical Weather Central Relocation," fact sheet prepared by Brig. Gen. Robert F. Long, USAF, Special Assistant for Environmental Services, Sept. 26, 1969.

31. By 1982 the following were issued daily from Global: 425 computer-derived optimal flight plans for MAC aircraft and 190 comparable plans for other USAF components; 90 terminal forecasts; 300 weather charts for transmission by facsimile; 100 to 150 point weather warnings, and as many as 150 responses to requests for special forecast assistance.

32. Those who pushed hardest and were most influential in forecast centralization at the AFGWC were Brig. Gen. Best and Col. Ralph Steele, Col. Edwin Carmell, and Col. Hyko Gayikian. Military Airlift Command, "History of the Air Weather Service, 1 January – 31 December 1978" (typescript, 1980), 1: 167 – 76.

33. Even though AWS's pioneer numerical forecaster, Philip D. Thompson, achieved the rank of colonel in 1960, at the age of 38, he retired two years later (after twenty years) and never saw duty at Offutt AFB.

During the early 1980s AFGWC tried to overcome some of the problem by purchasing forecasting software from NOAA's National Meteorological Center. Unfortunately, by then, NOAA, too, was being surpassed in seventy-two-hour numerical forecast accuracy by the European Centre for Medium-range Weather Forecasts, a joint seventeen-member nation effort located at Shinfield Park, Reading, England. (See Frederick G. Shuman, "Numerical Weather Prediction," in *The Federal Plan for Meteorological Services and Supporting Research, Fiscal Year 1983*,

Report FCM P1-1982, released by U.S. Department of Commerce, Mar., 1982.)
Philip D. Thompson to author Bates, Aug. 28, 1983.

34. John F. Fuller, *The Yom Kippur War: A Case History of AWS Contingency Support*, Air Weather Service Historical Study No 6, rev. ed. (Scott AFB: MAC, 1975), p. 9.

35. Ibid., p. 32.

CHAPTER 10

1. Bernard B. Fall, "Hell in a Very Small Place: The Siege of Dien Bien Phu," *Great Battles of History*, ed. Hanson W. Baldwin (Philadelphia: J. B. Lippincott, 1966). During nine of the fourteen days before Dien Bien Phu fell, heavy monsoonal rains made the parachuting of personnel and supplies almost impossible. At one time, men in the bunkers were fighting in water up to their belts.

2. Theodore Draper, "Falling Dominoes," *New York Review of Literature*, Oct. 27, 1983, pp. 6–14.

3. John F. Fuller and Allan B. Milloy, *The Air Weather Service in Southeast Asia* (Scott AFB, Ill.: MAC, 1968), pp. 17–19. The controversial herbicide spray runs, which could take place only during daylight, were extremely dependent upon weather conditions: for example, air temperatures less than 85°F, surface winds under 10 knots, cloud ceilings of not less than 300 feet, and visibility of at least 3 miles. Escorting fighters needed higher ceilings—1,000 to 3,500 feet, depending upon aircraft type, tactics, and ordnance. Maximum herbicide effectiveness came during the peak growing season, which coincided with the rainy season, when rains soon after the spray would render the chemicals ineffective. The best way of verifying good conditions was to have airborne forward air controllers fly over the target area in advance of the spray aircraft. Ranch Hand aircrews also flew psychological warfare leaflet drops, for which winds were critical but difficult to predict precisely.

4. Ibid., pp. 11–12.

5. On June 20, 1964, Harkins was replaced by the much more famous Gen. William C. Westmoreland, proponent of search-and-destroy warfare. Westmoreland stayed until mid-1968, when he was replaced by Gen. Creighton W. Abrams. Until 1965 subordinate generals, such as Anthis, normally rotated annually, later biannually.

6. By Dec., 1962, the army was operating 199 aircraft in Vietnam, the air force 61. The 2nd ADVON had already been upgraded to the Thirteenth Air Force's 2nd Air Division on Oct. 8, 1962, only to be further upgraded into a separate air force (the Seventh) in Apr. 1966.

7. Robert F. Futrell, *The Advisory Years to 1965*, in *The United States Air Force in Southeast Asia*, Office of Air Force History (Washington, D.C.: GPO, 1981), pp. 267–68.

8. Margaret C. Faulbaum, *Air Weather Service in Southeast Asia, 1961–1976: A Pictorial Account* (Scott AFB, Ill.: MAC, 1979), pp. 22–43.

9. William Rust and George Jones, "Untold Story of the Road to War in Vietnam," *U.S. News and World Report*, Oct. 10, 1983, pp. 1–24.

10. Before the war ended in 1975, approximately 3 million American service men and women served in Southeast Asia. Their casualties in Vietnam came to 57,939 dead and missing, plus 303,000 wounded. The U.S. Marines were particularly hard hit, for their total casualties numbered 103,338 (14,705 dead and 88,633 wounded), or 11,620 more casualties than suffered during all the island hopping of World War II. In contrast, American service forces suffered some 157,000 dead and wounded during the Korean War.

11. U.S. Department of Defense, *Department of Defense Annual Report for Fiscal Year 1966* (Washington, D.C.: GPO, 1967), pp. 10, 21–22, and 121–24.

12. Copyright 1977, all rights reserved. Quoted with permission of the publisher, Holt, Rinehart & Winston.

13. John F. Fuller, *Air Weather Service Support to the United States Army: Tet and the Decade After*, Air Weather Service Historical Study No. 8 (Scott AFB, Ill.: MAC, 1979), 299 pp. Approximately 500 army personnel operated rawinsonde stations for the field artillery, data from which were supplied only sporadically to AWS units.

14. Forecasters who extended their duty received a thirty-day free leave with transportation anywhere in the world. Few did. However, the twenty-year veteran forecaster, M. Sgt. Dewey J. Gumaer, at Da Nang in 1969, had already been in Vietnam for three years. During the same year, S. Sgt. Dennis L. Roach, a senior weather observer supporting the army at Binh Thuy, was on his third tour in Vietnam, a total of forty-four months in a combat zone.

Air National Guard weathermen called to active duty during the USS *Pueblo* seizure in Aug., 1968, also drew duty with 30th Weather Squadron detachments.

15. Allan B. Milloy, "Text of AWS Corona Harvest Conference," Sept. 18, 1968, reprinted as supporting document No. 15 in Fuller and Milloy, *The Air Weather Service in Southeast Asia*.

16. Throughout the war Detachment 14 was variously labeled the Southeast Area Tactical Forecast Center, the Southeast Asia Forecast Center, and the Southeast Asia Weather Center.

17. Most Air Force strikes against North Vietnam and Laos were handled by F-4s and F-105s based in Thailand. Comparable strikes in South Vietnam were conducted by a variety of aircraft based within the country. Fuller and Milloy, *AWS in Southeast Asia*, p. 228.

18. Following the 1973 cease-fire, AN/MSQ-77 radars in Vietnam were no longer available to vector B-52 raids over Cambodia. Although F-4s were used as pathfinders, thunderstorms along the routes of the B-52s often gave problems. As a result, B-52 raids against primary targets in Cambodia were fouled up almost every day because of weather.

19. SAC's 3rd Air Division at Andersen AFB refused to allow either WAF meteorologists or noncommissioned officer (NCO) forecasters to provide weather briefings to the B-52 crews or to perform other staff weather officer functions. During the worst of AWS manning shortages, the SAC division commander temporarily relented, permitting NCOs to do weather briefings, but, by and large,

the doors to B-52 and KC-135 briefing rooms were closed to women and NCO weather people.

Military Airlift Command, "History of the Air Weather Service, 1 July 1972–30 June 1974," vol. 1, "Narrative" (typescript, Office of the MAC Historian), pp. 500–514. Following a long stint as an aide to Gen. LeMay, Carlton mirrored LeMay's deportment and brusque style of command. While MAC's commander, he seemed to enjoy dressing down subordinates in the presence of their peers. In contrast to LeMay, however, Carlton was no friend of weather reconnaissance as performed by the AWS. Nine days after taking over MAC's reins during Sept. 1972, he set in motion steps to mothball the AWS fleet of unique, high-altitude WB-57Fs. That was merely the beginning of a long, strained relationship with the AWS, culminating in Carlton's reassignment of the entire weather reconnaissance mission to MAC's Aerospace Rescue and Recovery Service (ARRS) two years later.

20. An air force announcement from Vietnam in 1967 that pictures from the Nimbus and ESSA satellites were being used to find holes in clouds through which to bomb caused consternation at ESSA. During the fifth WMO congress, then in session at Geneva, ESSA was pushing the world weather watch as a practical, peaceful, international program of great benefit to all nations, large and small. Communist countries could thus use the Air Force announcement to embarrass the U.S. before the WMO delegates. William W. Momyer to Headquarters, U.S. Air Force (AFRDC), Jan. 10, 1970, subject: "Transportable Weather Satellite Facility"; James W. Rivers, Jr., and Charles P. Arnold, Jr., "Defense Meteorological Satellite Program (DMSP)," *NASA Conference Publication* 2227 (1982): 31–34.

In late Nov., 1964, the Office of the Director of Defense Research and Engineering authorized establishing the Joint Meteorological Satellite Program Office (JMSPO) under AWS's Col. Peter E. Ramo, with Comdr. William S. ("Sam") Houston and Lt. Col. N. L. Durocher looking out for navy and army interests, respectively. Although JMSPO had several functions, one key task was to monitor the air force's supersecret Data Acquisition and Processing Program (DAPP), also known as Project 417. That effort launched the first RCA-built experimental defense meteorological satellite.

According to David Baker, *The Shape of Wars to Come* (New York: Stein and Day, 1981), p. 116, work on DAPP began in 1961 and resulted in the launch of a satellite into polar orbit a year later. Lt. Col. Thomas O. Haig did an outstanding job of starting up the project, which eventually became known as the Defense Meteorological Satellite Program. Credit for a well-managed system development also went to Lt. Col. Leslie W. Cowan, Maj. (later Maj. Gen.) John E. Kulpa, Jr., and Lt. Col. Wilbur B. Botzong. In fact, *Aviation Week & Space Technology* recognized Botzong in its Dec. 16, 1974, issue as one of forty persons in the world who had made that year "significant contributions" to the field of aerospace, specifically "for his skillful direction of . . . DMSP, which yielded a wealth of high-quality weather data despite unusually tight fiscal restraints."

21. U.S. Congress, House, Subcommittee on Department of Defense of the Committee on Appropriations, *Hearings, Department of Defense Appropriations for 1974*, 93rd Cong., 1st sess., pt. 6 (1973), pp. 1532–34; Ernie R. Dash and Walter D. Meyer, "The Meteorological Satellite: An Invaluable Tool for the Mili-

tary Decision Maker," *Air University Review*, 29, no. 3 (1978): 15–24; Philip J. Klass, *Secret Sentries in Space* (New York: Random House, 1971), pp. 140–41.

22. A pilot-to-forecaster contact was defined as an exchange of weather information between an AWS forecaster and an aircraft via pilot-to-forecaster radio or a telephone patch. At the peak of hostilities, such contacts in Vietnam and Thailand reached 21,155 (June, 1969).

23. Carl Berger, ed., *The United States Air Force in Southeast Asia, 1961–1973*, Office of Air Force History (Washington, D.C.: GPO, 1977).

24. In 1966, 90% of the runway settled at Phan Rang. During repair, air temperatures reached 125°F 2 feet off the matting, making new panels too hot to handle with bare hands.

25. The South Vietnam tactical air control system melded aircraft of the Seventh Air Force, the VNAF, SAC B-52s and KC-135s, the Marine Corps, and even Seventh Fleet aircraft when the latter were being used against targets in South Vietnam, Laos, and Cambodia. On a typical day 750 to 800 preplanned sorties were flown in support of ground forces, including 200 by Marine Corps aircraft in ARVN's I Corps area.

26. Weather minimums for visual bombing varied according to aircraft type, terrain, on-board ordnance, and troop situation. The slower, propeller-driven A-1s had minimums of approximately 300-foot cloud ceilings and a visibility of 2 miles. The slower jets (A-37 and B-57) needed ceilings of 1,200 feet and visibility of 4 miles; the high-performance F-4s and F-100s required 1,500-foot ceilings and 5-mile visibility.

27. Milloy, "Text of AWS Corona Harvest Conference."

28. Of the 12,864 recorded tactical photo "recce" sorties over Laos and North Vietnam from 1967 through Mar., 1968, 2,157 (approximately 16%) failed because of weather conditions.

29. Before April, 1967, some of the self-defeating engagement rules required that only "military" trucks could be hit, and then only if outside densely inhabited areas; aircraft tracking radars could not be rocketed because they might have Russian crews; and the five airfields from which nearly a hundred MIG interceptors operated could not be bombed because they were located in the heavily populated Hanoi-Haiphong area. Air Force Chief of Staff Gen. LeMay stoutly maintained that you were not going to be able to kill the barnyard flies until you were allowed to destroy the manure pile!

30. Fuller and Milloy, *Air Weather Service in Southeast Asia*, pp. 293–94.

31. During 1967, Maj. Gen. Gilbert L. Meyers, vice commander of the 7th Air Force, advised a Senate subcommittee that one reason for launching strikes despite adverse weather forecasts was the belief that "Washington" would remove the targets from the approved list if the field command stood down because of bad weather. See U.S. Congress, Senate, Preparedness Investigating Subcommittee of the Committee on Armed Services, *Hearings: Air War Against North Vietnam*, 90th Cong., 1st sesss. (1967), pp. 479, 491.

32. Milloy, "Text of AWS Corona Harvest Conference."

33. Edwin E. Carmell, interview with author Fuller, May 12, 1975.

34. William W. Momyer, *Air Power in Three Wars*, Office of Air Force History

(Washington, D.C.: GPO, 1978). In his Air War College report, "An Evaluation of Weather Service in Southeast Asia" (AWC Report 1568, Mar., 1969), Col. Morris H. Newhouse evaluated the launch forecasts made by the 1st Weather Group between Sept., 1965 and Aug., 1966. "Go" forecasts generally called for three-eighths to five-eighths cloud coverage or less, with a minimum of 5,000-foot cloud bases and 5-mile visibility. "No-go" situations were forecast correctly 91% of the time. His conclusion: the Seventh Air Force could have destroyed the assigned priority targets with a third less missions by paying attention to, rather than, ignoring, the weather forecasts.

35. Jacksel M. Broughton, *Thud Ridge* (New York: J. B. Lippincott, 1969); Maj. Isaac E. Avinger, interview with author Fuller, May 19, 1971. Col. Edwin E. Carmell investigated Broughton's complaint about bomb winds and decided that they were minimal compared with aircraft attitude and speed errors. Carmell's conclusion was that, under the stress of flying into the face of North Vietnam's formidable air defenses, if a pilot's bombs went astray, he became frustrated and looked for a scapegoat, probably the weatherman. But weatherman Avinger of Broughton's staff admitted that target winds were sometimes given cursory treatment by Detachment 14's weather central: he had once called there for such data and had been told, "Bomb winds! Do you guys really need bomb winds?"

36. Patrick J. Breitling, *Guided Bomb Operations in SEA: The Weather Dimension, 1 February–31 December 1972*, Project CHECO report (Oct. 1, 1973), pp. 30–33.

37. Military Airlift Command, "History of the Air Weather Service, 1 July 1970–30 June 1971," (typescript, 1971), 1: 230–34, 760–62. Brown soon became air force chief of staff and was appointed chairman of the Joint Chiefs by President Nixon in 1974. As chairman, he twice embarrassed the Ford administration by irresponsible remarks about Jewish influence in America and references to Israel as a military burden to the U.S.

Brown's replacement in South Vietnam, Gen. Lucius D. Clay, Jr., also noted that AWS forecasting capability had not improved much in three decades. "In Southeast Asia, there's just no way to forecast it," offered Clay; "the satellite would show the target clear, and by the time we got a FAC up, it was socked in." See Col. Alfred C. Molla, "Wall-to-Wall Briefing to ADC," memorandum for the record, Dec. 26, 1973, Headquarters MAC (XPPE).

38. U.S. Congress, House, Subcommittees on Department of Defense and on Military Construction, Committee on Appropriations, *Hearings, Department of Defense Appropriations for 1968*. 90th Cong., 1st sess., pt. 2 (1967), pp. 54–55; U.S. Congress, House, Subcommittee on Department of Defense, Committee on Appropriations, *Hearings, Department of Defense Appropriations for 1971*, 91st Cong., 2nd sess., pt. 6 (1970), pp. 796, 809, and 832.

39. Detachment 56 at Andrews AFB, Md., part of the AWS's 6th Weather Wing, provided that service until July, 1971, after which it was provided by the wing staff. Between late 1967 and 1969, Detachment 56 was commanded by Lt. Col. Katz, who had looked into the Vietnamese situation in 1961–62. Lt. Col. Joyce E. Somers, who did a very capable job as Katz's replacement at Detachment 56, still failed to make the grade of 0-6 (colonel), a fate experienced by all regular female weather officers to date in both the air force and the navy.

40. John F. Fuller, *Weather and War* (Scott AFB: MAC, 1974), p. 15.

41. William H. Best, Jr., to Gen. P. K. Carlton, USAF, July 27, 1973, copy in Headquarters AWS files.

42. During the hostilities in Southeast Asia, the air force expended 6.16 million tons of air munitions, contrasted to 2.15 million tons during World War II and only 0.46 million tons in Korea. Quotation from U.S. Congress, House, Subcommittee on Department of Defense, Committee on Appropriations, *Hearings, Department of Defense Appropriations for 1973*, 92d Cong., 2nd sess., pt. 8 (1972), pp. 31, 33, and 39.

43. For some months the actual weather briefing officer was Capt. David J. Pina, who received a Bronze Star medal plus a personal gesture of appreciation from Gen. Westmoreland.

During one of Westmoreland's regular weekly weather briefings, he was still kind enough to say that "no other U.S. military commander ever had the advantage of the outstanding weather support that I have had at my disposal." See Maj. Gen. Joseph A. McChristian, *The Role of Military Intelligence: 1965−67*, in *Vietnam Studies* (Office of the Chief of Military History, U.S. Army, 1974), p. 156.

44. Fuller, *Air Weather Service Support*, pp. 70−71.

45. Ibid., p. 71.

46. Just before the critical A Shau Valley sweep of April, 1968, Capt. Thomas E. Taylor, although staff weather officer to the 1st Cavalry Division, had to decline the divisional commander's invitation to join him on inspection flights over the area. The reason: Col. Griffin H. Wood, commander of the 1st Weather Group, forbade Taylor to make such flights. Later, Maj. Gen. Tolson advised Wood that the weather group could recall Taylor and his men immediately, for Tolson had no further use for them under such ground rules. Wood soon rescinded his edict.

47. The worst example was the AN/MMQ-2 tactical weather observing van. Although air-conditioned, it suffered from unstable power sources. In addition, its 10,000-pound weight meant it could only be moved by a C-130, a "Flying Crane," or an M-35 truck. After three years in Vietnam, most such vans, including all sixteen with the 5th Weather Squadron, were withdrawn from the theater.

48. John J. Tolson, telephone interview with author Fuller, on Aug. 2, 1979. To keep their outfit equipped with basic supplies not available through formal army channels (plus survival gear such as machines guns and hand grenades, which were not on a weather unit's authorized equipment list), Taylor and his troops developed a fecund but surreptitious bartering system. Cheap whiskey purchased during "rest and recuperation" at coastal Nha Trang was traded at upland, alcoholically dry Camp Evans for Czech AK-47 rifles taken by combat teams at the rate of roughly one bottle of "Old Granddad" for three guns. The AK-47s were then sold to air transport crews at Cam Ranh Bay for about $30 per weapon. The proceeds went for more Nha Trang whiskey, which was then bartered at Camp Evans for extra tents and plywood, boots and bullets.

49. Like many hard-boiled commanders, Maj. Gen. Tolson refused to be briefed on weather conditions by enlisted forecasters.

50. Detachment 14's weather center at Tan Son Nhut survived without casualties a determined VC mortar and rocket attack on that vast air base. In the confused

fighting of that morning, rounds of countering fire from U.S. troops whistled by Col. Carmell's head as he watched in front of the Tan Son Nhut officer's club.

51. Marine Corps weather observers were stationed at Da Nang, Dong Ha, and Chu Lai, including a rawinsonde station at Dong Ha. Three marine forecasters also worked in the AWS 30th Weather Squadron station at Da Nang. The 1st Marine Air Wing's weather unit at Phu Bai also obtained in Dec., 1968, a receiver for reading out cloud pictures from civil weather satellites. Edwin H. Simmons, "Marine Corps Operations in Vietnam, 1968," in *The Marines in Vietnam, 1954–1973: An Anthology and Annotated Bibliography* (Washington, D.C.: History and Museums Division, Headquarters U.S. Marine Corps, 1974).

52. William C. Westmoreland, "Report on Operations in South Vietnam, January, 1964–June, 1968," in *Report on the War in Vietnam* (Washington, D.C.: GPO, 1969).

53. Marine Corps weather observers at Khe Sanh transmitted hourly weather reports except when the fighting grew too intense. However, their barometer began to give erroneous altimeter settings, a critical reading for safe airdrops of cargo. After a call for volunteers, a 5th Weather Squadron observer flew to Khe Sanh with a new barometer and a AN/PMQ-7 weather observing kit, plus M-16 rifle and side arm, to help out. He more than earned his pay. In the coming days he operated with a minimum of sleep but a maximum output of much-needed, reliable barometric pressures.

54. Moyers S. Shore II, *The Battle for Khe Sanh* (Washington, D.C.: Historical Branch, Headquarters, U.S. Marine Corps, 1969); Bernard C. Nalty, *Air Power and the Fight for Khe Sanh*, Office of Air Force History (Washington, D.C.: GPO, 1973).

55. William C. Westmoreland, *A Soldier Reports* (Garden City, N.Y.: Doubleday, 1976).

56. John J. Tolson, *Airmobility, 1961–1971*, Department of the Army Vietnam Studies series (Washington, D.C.: GPO, 1973), p. 174. As the assault troops moved up Highway 9, the weather observers did, too. However, their time was mainly spent soldiering in order to stay alive. Ironically, USMACV abandoned Khe Sanh three months later on July 5, 1968.

57. Taylor's counterpart at the 101st Airborne Division, Capt. Ronald W. Clarke, had no rapport with the division commander, Maj. Gen. Olinto M. Barsanti. The general went by the book and obtained his weather information strictly through the division intelligence officer. As a result, Clarke faced a wall of indifference, occasionally even outright hostility, when he tried to get services and such supplies as radios.

58. Tolson, *Airmobility*, pp. 191–92.

59. Fuller, *Air Weather Service Support*, p. 49. Another general who liked "fighting weather men" at his side was Maj. Gen. William E. DuPuy, commander of the 1st Infantry Division. After the completion of Operation Attleboro in late 1966, northwest of Bien Hoa, DePuy approved Bronze Stars for all of his eighteen weathermen for providing "exceptionally fine" support. For details, see "Operation Attleboro, Vietnam, 1966," *AWS Observer's* "A Lesson from History," June, 1984.

60. By then, Saigon held so much American brass that COMNAVFORV, a rear admiral, sat in the third row whenever Westmoreland called a meeting of senior

USMACV officers. R. L. Schreadley, "The Naval War in Vietnam," *U.S. Naval Institute Proceedings* 97, no. 819 (1971): 190–212.

61. Milloy, "Text of AWS Corona Harvest Conference." When the war accelerated with the Proud Deep Alpha strikes into North Vietnam in Dec., 1971, Detachment 14 again began to supply weather forecasts and trends for both Vietnams to the offshore carriers.

62. Frederick K. Martin to author Bates, Nov. 7, 1983.

63. Of the navy's sixteen attack carriers (CVAs), the following served on the line during 1967: *Bon Homme Richard, Constellation, Coral Sea, Enterprise, Forrestal, Hancock, Intrepid, Kitty Hawk, Oriskany, Ranger* and the *Ticonderoga*.

A skeleton weather division consisted of a division officer, one division chief, three enlisted forecasters handling separate shifts (first-class petty officers), one office supervisor (second-class petty officer), three section leaders (third-class petty officers), and three weather observers (airmen). Weather charts were prepared every 6 hours for the South China Sea, Gulf of Tonkin, and the Asiatic mainland, supplemented by charts every twelve hours of streamlined analyses for the 5,000- and 10,000-foot levels. The latter charts were particularly useful because comparable charts out of Guam were prepared in macroscale so as to cover the entire western Pacific Ocean.

Outstanding enlisted briefers for this period included chief aerographer's mates Ronald Palmer, (*Bon Homme Richard*), Michael Kalles (*Coral Sea*), Elmer Fondern (*Kitty Hawk*), Frederick Baillie (*Forrestal*), William Lithealt (*Kersearge*), and Billy Averitte (*Oriskany*).

64. Ronald W. Palmer to author Bates, Apr. 1, 1983.

65. A shortage of jet-qualified airfields in South Vietnam between May, 1965, and Aug., 1966 caused one or two additional carriers to occupy Dixie Station to the east of Cam Ranh Bay and support army attacks on the mainland under direct orders from USMACV rather than from 7th Fleet. Malcolm W. Cagle, "Task Force 77 in Action off Vietnam," *U.S. Naval Institute Proceedings* 830 (May, 1972): 68–109.

66. Ibid., p. 95.

67. Conley R. Ward, "Recollections of Meteorological Operations during Vietnam Conflict Aboard Task Force 77" (typescript, 1983), p. 4.

68. Ibid., p. 5.

69. Ibid., p. 7.

70. Ibid., p. 9.

CHAPTER 11

1. During 1965, the 30th Weather Squadron formed small, classified forecaster cells at Da Nang and Nha Trang to support USMACV's highly secret, special operations group (the SOG effort), whose units ranged through Laos and North Vietnam on clandestine forays. Insertion, resupply, and extraction of such teams depended on the weather. For details, see William C. Westmoreland, *A Soldier Reports*; Francis J. Kelly, *U.S. Army Special Forces, 1961–1971*, Department of the

Army Vietnam Studies series (Washington, D.C.: GPO, 1973), and *The Pentagon Papers as Published by the New York Times* (New York: Bantam Books, 1971).

2. "Keith R. Grimes, Special Operations Weatherman: An Oral Autobiography," ed. John F. Fuller, filed with Office of MAC History, Scott AFB, Ill. (typescript, Mar., 1978).

3. Sullivan continued to serve in "hot spots" during his diplomatic career. The early 1970s found him in Manila, where he encouraged the Ferdinand Marcos government to assist, rather than to turn its back, on "boat-people" fleeing Vietnam. Feb. 26, 1979, found him on the cover of *Newsweek* as President Carter's embattled ambassador and temporary hostage to Iran. The same issue also showed Capt. George R. Davenport, the AWS officer commanding a solar observatory there, as a prisoner of Ayatollah Khomeini's armed rabble before barely escaping with his life.

4. "Keith R. Grimes, Special Operations Weatherman," p. 14. If not on official attaché status, all military and CIA personnel in Laos wore civilian clothes and carried identification cards stating they worked for the U.S. Agency for International Development.

5. Grimes preferred the Soviet-designed weapon over the American M-16. The former could lie for two weeks in dirt and mud and still fire; the latter would jam on the first round. In addition, American supply sergeants refused him M-16 ammunition on the grounds that weather officers never needed to shoot at anything. Ibid., pp. 164–68.

6. Other Detachment 75 personnel of note in Laos included Capt. Charles S. Smith and Capt. Robert T. Crowder, plus 1st Lt. Edward A. Town and 1st Lt. Ronald G. K. Wong. The following enlisted men, each of whom served multiple duty tours in Laos, did exemplary duty: Sgt. Frank W. West, who valiantly tried to create a written Meo language, Sgt. Wayne Fuiten, and A1c. Lloyd M. Mitchell. Most were awarded Air Medals and Bronze Stars for their work. Because such advance outposts could, unfortunately, be taken over by the North Vietnamese whenever they were willing to pay the price in human lives, at least a half-dozen Laotian observers were killed. Military Airlift Command, "History of the Air Weather Service, 1 July 1974–31 December 1975" (typescript, 1976), 1: 325–26. On Dec. 7, 1973, Capt. Warren L. Nielsen, staff weather officer to the U.S. air attaché, Vientiane, closed out the AWS effort in Laos.

7. The disagreement is mentioned in Benjamin F. Schemmer's excellent book *The Raid* (New York: Harper & Row, 1976), p. 184, a publication that prompted Zapinski to consider a libel suit against the publisher because Schemmer's account was "totally false" (see Zapinski's letter to Maj. Gen. John Collens, MAC chief of staff, Nov. 15, 1976). Zapinski considered Grimes evasive and self-centered; Grimes complained that Zapinski was cynical and ridiculed him. Grimes's side of the confrontation is found in "Keith R. Grimes, Special Operations Weatherman"; Zapinski's recollections of the affair are in his copyrighted "Ten Days in November 1970: An Incredible Story" (rev. ed.), Apr., 1984—both documents on file in the AWS historical archives and at the Air Force Historical Research Center at Maxwell AFB, Ala.

8. Commander, Joint Chiefs of Staff Joint Contingency Task Group, Report on the Son Tay Prisoner of War Rescue Operation by Brigadier General Leroy J. Manor, USAF, task force commander (typescript, ca. Dec., 1970), pt. 1, p. 29.

9. Leroy J. Manor, "Son Tay—The POW Rescue Attempt," *Aerospace Commentary* 3, no. 4 (1971): 16–37. By then, many mission elements were in motion, including the navy's diversionary force offshore, the readying of C-130 refueling tankers, and assembly of HH-53 helicopters to deposit the raiding force at the prison gates. Manor and Grimes did not go on the raid. They sweated it out at the Monkey Mountain Tactical Air Control Center, a command complex near Da Nang.

10. Air Weather Service, "History of the Air Weather Service, 1 July 1970–30 June 1971," (typescript, 1971), 1: 478. In accordance with the practice of the day, Zapinski received the Legion of Merit for his tour as the 1st Weather Group commander. In contrast, Ralston, after being selected as the group's "Airman of the Year," was nominated for the lesser Bronze Star medal. However, a blanket rule at Seventh Air Force discarded the nomination because he had not been in a supervisory role. Instead, Ralston was offered a rather meaningless Air Force Commendation Medal. Ralston respectfully declined, pointing out that about twenty-five other Detachment 14 forecasters (including Van Houdt) received Bronze Stars during his tour, and he believed he had contributed as much as they did. Spurred by Ralston's declination, Brig. Gen. Best had Zapinski and his staff members furnish justification for an appeal. In Feb., 1972, the 7th Air Force authorized Ralston the Bronze Star for his tour in Vietnam between Aug., 1970, and Aug., 1971.

Few people were aware that, soon after takeoff, the RF-4C that Frank Ross was in developed problems with its navigation aids that were serious enough to justify an abort. But the RF-4C pilot and Frank successfully completed their mission. Ross never got so much as a thank-you from anyone in AWS or on Manor's raider team.

11. Because of Udorn's lack of parking space, only two of the three WC-130A rain makers could be in Thailand at a time, with the third back home at Andersen AFB, Guam. That led to frequent shuttle flights, a situation taken advantage of by drug users, who found such contraband cheap and plentiful at Udorn. After complaints, the 54th Weather Reconnaissance Squadron began routinely shaking down each WC-130A arrival at Andersen during late 1970. Even so, the squadron was found to have thirteen drug abusers a year later, and the squadron commander was relieved after only seven months on the job. Notwithstanding, Motorpool was good duty. By Dec., 1970, twenty officers and six enlisted crewmembers had earned the coveted Distinguished Flying Cross by completing the requisite one hundred or more combat missions.

12. Westmoreland, *Soldier Reports*, p. 342.

13. During 1978 hearings, the Department of Defense witness said: "We do not believe, on the basis of demonstrated technology, that environmental modification has utility as an important weapon of war." See U.S. Congress, Senate, Committee on Foreign Relations, *Hearings, Environmental Modification Treaty*, 95th Cong., 2nd sess. (Oct. 3, 1978), p. 21. AWS was also of the opinion that the treaty's language was so vague that it did not affect its capabilities in weather modification.

14. Henry A. Chary, *A History of Air Weather Service Weather Modification,*

1965–1973, Air Weather Service Technical Report No. 74-247 (Scott AFB: AWS, 1974), pp. 10–12.

15. Air Weather Service, "History, 1 July 1970–30 June 1971," pp. 511–47.

16. Air Weather Service, "History of the Air Weather Service, 1 July 1971–30 June 1972" (typescript, 1972), 1: 394–404.

17. William H. Best, Jr., recollections recorded by author Fuller, June 12, 1972, filed in Office of the MAC Historian.

18. U.S. Congress, House, Subcommittee on Department of Defense Appropriations, *Hearings, Department of Defense Appropriations for 1973*, 92d Cong., 2d sess., pt. 8 (1972), pp. 31, 33, and 39. Gen. Lavelle and his replacement, Gen. John W. Vogt, Jr., asked Col. Berry W. Rowe, commander of the 1st Weather Group, for extra C-130 weather reconnaissance support during that frustrating period. Vogt also asked for seeding the solid stratus deck, a request rejected on the basis that it had not worked at Khe Sanh during 1968 and was not worth trying over Quang Tri Province four years later. "Transcript on Air Raids, GOP Meeting," *St. Louis Post-Dispatch*, Jan. 3, 1972, p. 1A.

19. One of Grimes's benefactors, the incoming AWS chief, Brig. Gen. (designee) John Collens had persuaded MAC commander P. K. Carlton to downgrade the squadron commander's billet from colonel to lieutenant colonel so that Grimes would have a better chance with the next promotion board.

20. The Cambodian civil weather service was also in poor shape. However, it received valiant assistance from WMO adviser Georges S. Deroo, a retired major of the Belgian Air Force who had trained at Chanute AFB.

21. U.S. Military Airlift Command, "History of the Air Weather Service, 1 July 1974–31 December, 1975" (typescript, 1976), pp. 325–26.

22. Before leaving, Grimes squeezed in a sad farewell to Heng Touch. Later, Grimes said, a hard core of Cambodian officers and men fought the Khmer Rouge to the last man at Phnom Penh and Pochentong; in all probability, Touch died in that onslaught. Subsequent reports reaching the Seventh Air Force indicated the Khmer Rouge executed all of Lon Nol's field grade officers and their families, an act of genocide later inflicted upon most of the educated city dwellers by the vicious peasant army.

23. Military Airlift Command, "History of the Air Weather Service, 1 July 1974–31 December 1975" (typescript, 1976), p. 352.

24. To support the air force fighters, KC-135 tankers logged forty-nine sorties, conducting 381 midair refuelings and offloading 3.7 million pounds of jet fuel during the process. When DMSP imagery showed too much cirrus cloud within a proposed refueling area, the fuel transfer took place further westward, over the Gulf of Thailand.

25. By the time the 10th Weather Squadron was deactivated, Lt. Col. Grimes was working in the war plans shop at Headquarters, MAC. His belated promotion to colonel was announced in Dec., 1975. Unfortunately, the unusual career of the AWS senior air commando came to a fiery end when an EC-135 he was riding to Alaska crashed into New Mexico's Manzano Mountains during takeoff in Sept., 1977.

26. Military Airlift Command, "History of the Air Weather Service, 1 July 1974–31 December 1975" (typescript, 1976), p. 419.

CHAPTER 12

1. During 1971 approximately 1% of the air force population had used or were using drugs. Even the highly technical AWS was not drug-free. For example, AWS handled 29 drug cases in 1968, 14 in 1969, 22 in 1970, 21 in 1971, 33 in 1972, and 31 in 1973, or a 0.1% to 0.3% rate relative to total personnel. Service in Vietnam was the big problem: a mere dollar per day could finance a drug habit in Southeast Asia.

Once the navy launched Project Upgrade, sailors could be separated rapidly for reasons other than proven dishonorable duty. The carrier, USS *Kitty Hawk*, for example, discharged 375 crewmen from the service during her first day in a domestic port after a long and tiring Pacific deployment. Elimination of the "dirt bags," who loafed and made frequent trouble, sharply raised the morale of the remaining ship's crew.

2. The navy's success in attracting and retaining highly competent female aerographer's mates required their male counterparts to spend most of their first enlistment at sea on combat vessels, a locale women were not permitted to invade. Because the young males thus generally preferred to get out rather than ship over for a second enlistment, there was a severe shortage of junior enlisted male forecasters during the second four-year duty tour. All reenlistment bonus money for enlisted forecasters was targeted toward those who had served less than ten years, wiping out any bonuses for senior forecasters, no matter how good they might be.

In MAC (AWS's parent command), as well as throughout the air force, the percentage of black enlistees was four times that of the AWS (i.e., 12.8% for MAC and 12.4% for the air force).

3. Melding of the services created its own personnel problems. For example, the air force general commanding the training center during 1983 was unhappy that advanced naval students could wear beards on his base. And woe betide any air force "zoomie" who called a marine private a "jar-head," because boot camp's "kill-kill" indoctrination came readily to the fore.

Chanute Technical Training Center, *Course Muster Report for 15 July 1983* (Chanute AFB, Ill., 1983). The nautical facets of advanced meteorology were taught as add-on, short-term courses by a small U.S. Navy–Marine Corps staff in residence at Chanute AFB. The Chanute school also offered supplemental courses in such topics as tropical meteorology, weather radar, weather satellite and photo interpretation, equipment maintenance, rawinsonde operation, and station chief and staff weather officer duties.

4. These schools were the universities of Arizona, California (Los Angeles), Colorado State, Michigan, North Carolina State, Oklahoma, Pennsylvania State,* Texas A&M,* Utah,* and Wisconsin (asterisk denotes schools offering beginning meteorology courses plus graduate work). The scope of the program was illustrated by the fact that Texas A&M had, since 1952, trained more than 900 AWS officers in some fifty classes. Col. George E. Chapman may well have been the star pupil: in 1982 he was the first former enlisted man and the first Texas A&M weather program graduate to command the AWS.

5. Although the Air Force Academy graduated its first female officers in 1979, none opted for a career in military meteorology. However, two of the eighteen

WAFs selected for the USAF's first women's pilot training test program during 1976 were from the AWS— 1st Lt. Ann O. Smethurst and 2nd Lt. Carol A. Scherer, the latter just having completed her studies in meteorology at Texas A&M. Scherer's classmate in meteorology, 2nd Lt. Ramona L. Roybal, was also one of six WAFs chosen for the USAF's first navigator test training program.

Following graduation from pilot training in Sept., 1977, Scherer became a WC-130 copilot at Andersen AFB, Guam, with the 54th Weather Reconnaissance Squadron (the "Typhoon Chasers"), where 1st Lt. Nancy E. Holtgard had just qualified as an aerial reconnaissance weather officer (ARWO). Scherer and Holtgard were firsts for the squadron, and Holtgard further challenged military tradition by marrying a staff sergeant assigned to the AWS detachment at Andersen AFB.

As of July, 1974, only 45 Air Force Academy graduates were among AWS' corps of 1,758 officers. Annapolis graduates were much more anxious to seek environmental careers. Thus, in 1983, when the Naval Academy's brigade totaled 4,300 midshipmen, 325 of these, including 20 women, majored in oceanography. And on May 23, 1984, Midshipman Kristine Holderied made history by being the first woman to graduate at the head of her class at any of the service academies since women were admitted in 1976. Holderied's specialty was oceanography, and her initial duty was to conduct meteorological studies at Naval Oceanography Command Center, Rota, Spain. George E. Chapman, "It Looks Good," *AWS Observer* 32, no. 4 (1984): 2.

6. Naval Oceanography Command, *Roster and Career Planning Guide for Special Duty Officers, Limited Duty Officers, and Warrant Officers* (Washington, D.C.: Oceanography Division, Office of Chief of Naval Operations, 1982). In late 1984, Capt. James E. Koehr became the newest director of the Naval Oceanography Command. A product of the Officer Candidate School, Newport, R.I., Koehr studied graduate-level meteorology at Monterey and became the first sea-ice forecaster (1964–67 at Argentia, Newfoundland) to command the navy's environmental prediction corps.

7. Charlie A. Beckwith and Donald Knox, *Delta Force* (New York: Harcourt Brace Jovanovich, 1983), 310 pp.

8. The USAF ETAC meteorologists primarily responsible for generating climatic information were Capt. Patrick L. Herod and Capt. Frank B. Holt, assisted by M. Sgt. Albert R. Meals and Dean D. Bowman.

9. Jimmy Carter, *Keeping Faith* (New York: Bantam Books, 1982).

10. As of 1980, about forty DMSP satellites had gone into orbit with an average operational life-span of one to two years (*Encyclopedia of Science and Technology* [New York: McGraw-Hill, 1982], p. 555). According to Baker's *Shape of Wars to Come*, the air force in 1976 began launching a much improved DMSP Block 5D-1 satellite. Once in orbit, such birds weighed 1,131 lbs. and could be read out in real time at field commands without using a complex processing facility. In "Defense Meteorological Satellite Program (DMSP)," by Col. James W. Rivers, Jr., and Lt. Col. Charles P. Arnold, Jr. (NASA Conference Publication no. 2227, 1982), the authors indicated that the Block 5D-1 space segment normally consisted of twin satellites in sun-synchronous polar orbits while 450 nautical miles from earth. (This permitted viewing every place on the globe at approximately 8:00 A.M., 8:00 P.M., noon, and midnight.) One of the key on-board sensors was a visible light

sensor measuring scene illumination at levels ranging from subsolar to sublunar (quarter moon), a variation of more than 10 million to 1. Linear detector resolution came in two modes: global at 1.5 nautical miles and a selected regional mode of 0.3 nautical miles.

11. Air Weather Service, "Mission Evaluation, Environmental Support," unpublished white paper, May 2, 1980, Attachment 1 to Headquarters Air Weather Service letter to Military Airlift Command (HO), Apr. 27, 1981, subject: Iranian Rescue Mission Weather Support Documents.

12. Ibid.

13. Leonard Snellman, Vincent J. Oliver, and Robert E. Beck, "Special Evaluation of Weather Support to Attempted Hostage Rescue Mission," unpublished report, May 21, 1980, Attachment 2 to ibid.

14. Ibid. During 1978 Beck worked under Barney's direction on an NOAA project to upgrade meteorological services in Iran.

15. James L. Holloway III, *Rescue Mission Report*, final report by Special Operations Review Group for Iranian Rescue Mission (sanitized) (Washington, D.C.: Joint Chiefs of Staff, Aug. 1980), pp. v–vi, 59.

16. Afterward, the deputy flight commander aboard the number-five helicopter claimed that if he had known Desert One was in the clear, he would have pushed through the last 125 miles. That would have given the additional mission-capable chopper needed to keep Eagle Claw under way.

17. By then, AWS had long since sacrificed its plans, personnel, inspector general, data automation, comptroller, history, and information functions to MĂC headquarters. In 1977, the Air Staff and MAC also forced AWS to give up 785 maintenance manpower authorizations (15% of the total AWS strength) by assigning the function to the Air Force Communications Service. Although postulated savings came to ninety-four billets, the action left AWS in a poor wartime posture if the communications people did no better with maintenance than when they met AWS's battlefield communications needs in Korea and Vietnam. See Albert J. Kaehn, Jr., interview with author Fuller, June 7, 10, and 21, 1982.

18. U.S. Army Audit Agency, "Report of Audit: Army Meteorological Activities," Audit Report EC 78-20 (Washington, D.C.: U.S. Army Audit Agency; June 12, 1978).

19. Rendered services characterized the atmosphere from the surface to 66 miles high. Among the data collected and processed were optical turbulence, electromagnetic attenuation, absorption coefficient, particulates (count and size), solar radiation, temperature, humidity, pressure, density, wind speed and direction, cloud cover, visibility, and weather forecasts.

20. Thirty-one meteorological sections and 256 associated personnel were also authorized for the National Guard and the Army Reserve. As of mid-1981, the active army had only six meteorological officer slots, all at the Atmospheric Sciences Laboratory. However, a few warrant officers, along with the representatives of the other armed forces, continued to receive weather forecaster training at Chanute AFB.

21. U.S. Army, Office of the Chief of Staff, letter signed by Gen. John W. Vessey, Jr., Vice Chief of Staff, to distribution list, July 29, 1981, subject: Meteorological

Plan for Action; U.S. Army Atmospheric Sciences Laboratory letter, signed by Sharon L. Steffey, to author Bates, Oct. 24, 1983.

22. In practice, such training was provided by the assigned AWS staff weather officer. Within TRADOC and its Combined Arms Center, a key instructional document was the joint U.S. Army–Air Force weather support regulation (1980 version). Fortunately, that all-important set of guidelines reflected the thinking of AWS Col William E. Cummins II, who spent years in the army weather support function, including a stint as 5th Weather Squadron commander in Vietnam during the hectic days of 1968–69.

23. Ronald W. Palmer, letter to author Bates, Apr. 1, 1983.

24. U.S. Coast Guard headquarters letter, signed by Capt. James A. Peebles, USCG, to author Bates, Feb. 8, 1984.

25. Sun Tzu, *The Art of War*, trans. Samuel B. Griffith (London: Oxford University Press, 1963), p. 129.

26. As far back as 1948, Cdr. Reichelderfer, in his publication, *The Weather Bureau Record of War Administration* (Part 10 of the *World War II History of the Department of Commerce*), p. 70, concluded: "Certainly when war calls for enormous expansion . . . , there are large advantages in having a quasi-independent and specialized meteorological organization in each major military branch—Army, Navy, and Air Force, in addition to the basic national weather service under the Weather Bureau. . . . It is generally agreed that American meteorological services were more highly developed and better than those found in any other country."

27. Amos R. Fields, Briefing presented to Naval Weather Service Association reunion, June 23, 1983; Chapman, "It Looks Good," p. 2. For example, the eighth (and current) chief master sergeant of the USAF is Sam E. Parish, an up-from-the-ranks weatherman. On July 1, 1973, Parish became senior enlisted adviser to the commander of AWS. In 1975 he took on that function for the commander, U.S. Air Forces, Europe and later for the commander of SAC. Then, on July 1, 1983, Parish was assigned to the top enlisted spot in the air force.

28. U.S. Army, Office of the Chief of Staff, letter of July 29, 1981, Meteorological Plan, foreword.

29. Connelly R. Ward, "Recollections of Meteorological Operations during Vietnam Conflict in Task Force 77" (unpublished paper, Aug. 15, 1983), p. 9.

30. Thomas H. Moorer, transcript of speech, Norfolk, Va., Branch, American Meteorological Society, Sept. 8, 1966.

31. John F. Lehman, Jr., "Going for the High Ground in the Deep Seas," *Marine Technology Society Journal* 16, no. 2 (1982): 3–6.

C omment on Sources

BOOKS

No secondary source has ever addressed in full the history of America's weather warriors from 1814 to the present. The closest try, although superficial and tangential, was Patrick Hughes's *A Century of Weather Service* (New York: Gordon & Breach, 1970), a public relations piece published in connection with the hundredth anniversary of the formalized United States weather program. A more useful volume is Donald R. Whitnah's scholarly but out-of-print *History of the United States Weather Bureau* (Urbana: University of Illinois Press, 1961), which, fortunately, devotes many pages to early meteorology in the Army Signal Service/Corps.

Books by heads of states and military leaders refer to weather from time to time, but it takes a lot of sifting to find the nuggets. No one of course, exceeds Winston S. Churchill for sense of history and his love and command of the English language. His detailed, six-volume series *The Second World War* (Boston: Houghton Mifflin, 1948–53) offers many comments revealing his concern for the elements. Biographies and autobiographies about or by American military leaders are many. Most reference *weather*, but only a few stand out for indicating their concerns about the environment. Chief among these was Dwight D. Eisenhower, whose *Crusade in Europe* (New York: Doubleday, 1948) contains poignant comments on the forecasts for many campaigns, particularly the famous Operation Overlord forecast for Normandy's D day. Henry H. ("Hap") Arnold's *Global Mission* (New York: Harper, 1949) includes his belief that "weather is the essence of successful air operations." Another Air Force great, Gen. Curtis E. LeMay, in his *Mission with LeMay: My Story* (with coauthor MacKinlay Kantor; Garden City, N.Y.: Doubleday, 1965), relates his dealings with Chairman Mao Tse-Tung for weather reports from northern China. Omar D. Bradley's second autobiography, *A General's Life* (New York: Simon & Schuster, 1983), notes the unique role played by AWS WB-29s in confirming Russia's detonation of its first atomic bomb in 1949 and its first hydrogen bomb in 1953.

William C. Westmoreland's *A Soldier Reports* (Garden City, N.Y.: Doubleday, 1975) notes weather effects on the conduct of the unpopular war in Vietnam, as well as the surreptitious rain-making effort of the AWS. The only Air Force general to publish on the same war is William W. Momyer. His *Air Power in Three Wars* (Washington, D.C.: Government Printing Office, 1978), published under auspices of the Office of Air Force History, is rich in observations about the weather factor in the air campaign and includes a statement about the value of military weather satellites. One of Momyer's top fighter pilots, Col. Jacksel M. Broughton, the only aviator yet to write a book on Vietnam, was very critical in *Thud Ridge* (New York: Lippincott, 1969) about the weatherman's inability to forecast winds over North Vietnamese targets for his F-105s. Lt. Gen. John J. Tolson, commander of the army's famous 1st Cavalry Division (Airmobile) in Vietnam, has a very lucid account in his *Airmobility: 1961–1971* (Washington, D.C.: Department of the Army, 1973) about weather's effects on air mobile operations spearheaded by helicopters. *Armed Forces Journal* editor Benjamin F. Schemmer's *The Raid* (New York: Harper & Row, 1976) is the best treatment by far of the daring attempt to rescue American prisoners from North Vietnam's Son Tay prison in November, 1970, and it provides a close look at the associated weather and weather support aspects.

The early history of its unique weather satellite program is still classified by the U.S. Department of Defense. However, four books available to the public offer glimpses of its beginnings and its strategic mission: Philip J. Klass's *Secret Sentries in Space* (New York: Random House, 1971); David Baker's *The Shape of Wars to Come* (New York: Stein & Day, 1981); James Canan, *War in Space* (New York: Harper & Row, 1982); and Bhupendra Jasani, ed., *Outer Space: A New Dimension of the Arms Race* (London: Taylor & Francis, 1982). A civilian air force meteorologist, William K. Widger, wrote the readable and comprehensive *Meteorological Satellites* (New York: Holt, Rinehart & Winston, 1966) concerning the parallel development of civil weather satellites.

One could not do justice to American meteorologists in, or associated with, the military without mentioning books they have written or books about them. Two such books are *Professor Abbe and the Isobars* (New York: Vantage Press, 1955) by his son, Truman Abbe; and *Autobiography* (New York: Prentice Hall, 1950) by the Nobel laureate Robert A. Millikan. Victor Boesen's *Storm: Irving Krick and the U.S. Weather Bureaucracy* (New York: G. P. Putnam's Sons, 1978), based on Krick's personal notes, is provocative but suffers from a lack of documentation, as does the book Krick coauthored with Roscoe Fleming, entitled, *Sun, Sea and Sky: Weather in Our World and in Our Lives* (New York: Lippincott, 1954), which contains a chapter labeled "Weather and War." Ivan Ray Tannehill, one of the star students at Texas A&M University's first class of military meteorologists during 1918, wrote prolifically particularly about hurricanes. His *Hurricanes, Their Nature and History* (Princeton: Princeton University Press, 1956) and *The Hurricane Hunters* (New York: Dodd, Mead, 1955) are fascinating, but they, too, lack documentation.

Books by ranking military meteorologists are relatively uncommon. Rear Adm. William J. Kotsch's *Weather for the Mariner* (Annapolis: U.S. Naval Institute, 1983) and *Heavy Weather Guide* (Annapolis: U.S. Naval Institute, 1984) have enjoyed multiple printings. Lt. Col. David M. Ludlum, made famous by *Time* and *Newsweek* magazines for his Operation Ludlum forecast, associated with the pattern bombing of Cassino, Italy, during March, 1944, formed the American Weather History Center and published several books on historical meteorology. Adm. William H. ("Bull") Halsey's aerologist, Capt. George F. Kosco, defended their joint actions in *Halsey's Typhoons—A First Hand Account* (with coauthor H. C. Adamson; New York: Crown, 1967). However, Capt. C. Raymond Calhoun, who skippered the destroyer USS *Dewey* through the first of these two destructive storms, is quite critical of the admiral and of Kosco in his *Typhoon: The Other Enemy* (Annapolis: U.S. Naval Institute, 1981). Similarly, personalities and details involved with the stop-and-go Normandy D day weather forecast may be found in the book by Eisenhower's chief weatherman, James Martin Stagg, entitled *Forecast for Overlord: June 6, 1944* (New York: W. W. Norton, 1971).

BULLETINS, PERIODICALS, AND ARTICLES

America's principal meteorological journals are those of the American Meteorological Society (*Bulletin, Monthly Weather Review, Journal of Climate and Applied Meteorology, Journal of the Atmospheric Sciences*, and *Meteorological and Geoastrophysical Abstracts*) and the independently published *Weatherwise*. Most of the articles are technical. Yet, there are enough articles of historical nature to compel any diligent researcher to peruse the indices of such periodicals. For example, do not overlook Col. Robert C. Bundgaard's warm and admiring article "Sverre Petterssen, Weather Forecaster," in the March, 1979, *Bulletin*. Nor would one want to forget Patrick Hughes's two-part series, "Francis W. Reichelderfer: Architect of Modern Meteorological Service," in *Weatherwise* 34, nos. 3 and 4 (July–Aug., 1981). Obituaries published over the years in the same journal contain much historical data, as do citations and responses to awards made by the society.

Before the *Bulletin*'s initiation in 1919, the *Monthly Weather Review* (a government periodical of the Department of Agriculture, then of the Department of Commerce, 1872–1974) served as the prime clearinghouse for information on applied meteorology. Thus in 1919 the *Review* carried a comprehensive series of articles describing activities of military weather services in Europe and the United States during World War I. Leading contributors included such famed meteorologists as Robert Millikan, Alexander G. McAdie, C. Leroy Meisinger, Oliver L. Fassig, Charles F. Brooks, and Alan T. Waterman. By then, Harvard's leading climatologist, Robert DeC. Ward, had published a four-article series with the lead phrase "Weather Controls Over the Fighting in . . ." during 1918 and 1919 in issues of the *Scientific Monthly*.

Other bulletins that bear review include the Naval Oceanography Command's quarterly *News*, which replaced the *Naval Weather Service Bulletin* in 1978. On the air force side, the AWS published either monthly or bimonthly its own *Weather Service Bulletin* between 1943 and 1950. Although many articles in these in-house bulletins are technical or administrative, others address personnel in weather support and incorporate many cameo biographies of key personnel, both officer and enlisted. Also worthy of review is the AWS monthly command newspaper, the *Observer*, published since November, 1954. Of particular value is a bylined column, "Lesson from History," by author and AWS historian John F. Fuller, which has appeared in the *Observer* continuously (except for 1980–81) since December, 1974.

Military meteorologists have also sporadically published articles pertaining to their trade in periodicals of the senior service schools, in those sponsored by such lobbyist organizations as the Air Force Association and the Naval Institute, or in trade magazines such as the *Armed Forces Journal*. Worthwhile examples include Frederick J. Nelson's "The History of Aerology in the Navy," in the *U.S. Naval Institute Proceedings* for January, 1934, and Maj. Eugene T. Blanton's "Air Operations in Vietnam: COIN Weather Support," in the *Air University Review*, May–June, 1964. Similarly, one of the few available articles on the Defense Meteorological Satellite Program appeared in the *Air University Review* for March–April, 1978, under the title "The Meteorological Satellite: An Invaluable Tool for the Military Decision Makers," written by two young but experienced satellite officers, Maj. Ernie R. Dash and Maj. Walter D. Meyer.

Interview articles also appear from time to time. For example, *Armed Forces Management* (May, 1968) carried a story, "Year-Old Group Bolsters Defense's Environmental Science Expertise," that was essentially an interview with Brig. Gen. Roy A. Nelson about the mission and role of the short-lived Special Assistant for Environmental Services within the Joint Chiefs of Staff. Similarly, Maj. Thomas L. Sack's "Air Weather Service as a Force Intensifier," in *Air Force Magazine* (November, 1980) contains an interview with the AWS commander of the period, Brig. Gen. Albert J. Kaehn.

Equally infrequent are articles about or by weathermen in official magazines of the services: *Soldiers* (army), *Shipmate* (navy), and *Airman* (air force). But there are exceptions. For instance, S. Sgt. Lorenzo D. Harris's "Where the Weather is Centered" in the March, 1981, issue of *Airman* provides an excellent overview of the Air Force Global Weather Central's importance to military operations. And Maj. Clifford H. Bernath's "Weather Wars" and "The Weather: Who's in Charge?" in the April, 1981, *Soldiers* cites historical examples in cautioning the foot soldier about the effects of the elements on military operations.

THESES AND DISSERTATIONS

Hundreds of theses and dissertations have been written over the years on meteorological subjects at graduate and senior service schools, but only a handful have significant historical content. However, there are some musts. Two of these are Paul J. Scheips's doctoral dissertation, "Albert James Myers, Founder of the Army Signal Corps: A Biographical Study" (American University, 1965), and ex-AWS historian Philip M. Flammer's master's thesis, "Meteorology in the United States Army, 1917–1935" (George Washington University, 1958). Service school theses and research reports of high value, although nontechnical, prepared at the Air War College are as follows: Col. William O. Senter, "Organizing the Airways Communications and Weather Services" (1949): Lt. Col. James B. Jones, "The National Weather Satellite Program: Its Utility as a Contribution to Military Weather Satellite Support and as a Peaceful Instrument of U.S. Foreign Policy" (1965): and Col. Morris H. Newhouse, "An Evaluation of Weather Service in Southeast Asia" (1969). Three others are worth noting: Lt. Col. Gary D. Atkinson, "Impact of Weather on Military Operations: Past, Present, and Future" (Army War College, 1973); Lt. Comdr. Sidney E. Wheeler, "Marine Fog Impact on Naval Operations" (Naval Postgraduate School, 1974); and Maj. Michael Z. Zimmerman, "The Development of Weather Reconnaissance in the European Theater during World War II" (Air Command and Staff College, 1982).

ORAL HISTORIES

A rich but limited source is made up of oral histories or taped interviews with military meteorologists. Nowhere does the colorful zest of Athelstan F. Spilhaus surface more brilliantly than during a long session with him by Robert A. Calvert during 1976 for the oral history collection at Texas A&M University Library. In the same oceanographic series, Calvert also taped (and then transcribed) interviews with former Maj. Boyd E. Olson, Capt. Dale F. Leipper, and the inimitable Army ski-trooper, Pfc. Walter H. Munk, who now holds the National Medal of Science.

The most comprehensive and penetrating interview of this type is that conducted and edited by author Fuller, the 351-page "Keith R. Grimes, Special Operations Weatherman: An Oral Autobiography" (1978). Unfortunately, the interview is classified, as is one that Fuller conducted in August, 1982, with Maj. Donald G. Buchanan, the staff weather officer during the abortive attempt of April, 1980, to rescue Americans incarcerated in Teheran, Iran.

Unclassified oral history interviews, of which copies can be obtained from the Office of MAC History, have been conducted by Fuller with the following AWS luminaries: AWS commanders Maj. Gen. Russell K. Pierce, Brig. Gen. William H. Best, Brig. Gen. Berry W. Rowe (AWS support to the army), and Brig. Gen. Albert J. Kaehn; Col. Ralph G. Suggs (AWS vice commander), Col. Arthur W. Anderson (AWS chief of staff), and Col. Edwin E. Carmell, the AWS vice commander who served as the 1st Weather Group commander, as well as staff weather officer to General Momyer, Seventh Air Force commander, in Vietnam. Oral histories by Fuller also include those with Dr. Robert D. Fletcher, longtime AWS chief scientist, and Mr. William A. Jenner, associated with and later responsible for AWS training from the late 1940s until mid-1984. The Air Force Oral History Program also published transcriptions of lengthy interviews with AWS luminaries Col. Clark L. Hosmer (1977), Lt. Gen. Lewis L. Mundell (1979), Lt. Gen. Donald N. Yates (1980), and Lt. Gen. Thomas M. Moorman (1985).

PUBLIC DOCUMENTS

The most fertile bed of information is the vast number of public documents spawned by the executive and the legislative branches. Much is "grey literature" and receives very limited circulation and library acquisition. But it is authoritative and detailed, and therefore worth the effort to locate and read.

Although environmental support per se receives scanty attention, the best source concerning weather's effects on land, sea, and air operations are the excellent, scholarly, official U.S. Army, Navy, and Air Force hardcover, unclassified histories of their participation in World War II, Korea and, just now emerging, Southeast Asia. The army's World War II history series numbered fifty-three volumes by 1960—with another twenty-five volumes in preparation for publication by the Government Printing Office. All painstakingly document the effect of weather and terrain on each battle and campaign, and each volume's index graciously tracks the entry *weather*. Volume 7 of the seven-volume series, *The Army Air Forces in World War II* (edited by Wesley F. Craven and James L. Cate, and published by the University of Chicago under contract during the 1940s and 1950s), contains a twenty-seven page chapter by Jonas A. Jonasson on the AAF Weather Service. Even if not labeled official history, the fourteen-volume *History of United States Naval Operations in World War II* (Boston: Little, Brown, 1947) by the dean of American naval historians, Rear Adm. Samuel E. Morison, contains fascinating and colorfully written stories about mariners and their brushes with Mother Nature. Not to be overlooked in the World War II period is *The Weather Bureau Record of War Administration*, Part 10 of the *World War II History of the Department of Commerce*, issued in multilithed format during 1948.

Thanks to President Franklin D. Roosevelt's initiative, each of the armed services maintains a history function manned by professional historians. Thus, Volume 15, "Aerology," by Dr. Mapheus Smith, became an unpublished part of the "World War II Administrative History, Bureau of Aeronautics," which was finally declassified in 1957. That same program sired continuing in-house weather facility historical accounts, a notable one being "History of the Fleet Weather Central, Pearl Harbor, June 1941– 15 April 1945." During January, 1941, the Joint Meteorological Committee (later designated the Joint Meteorological Group) of the Joint Chiefs of Staff was established to coordinate military and civilian weather activities and, until its demise in 1967, kept minutes, a set of which is available through the Office of the Joint Chiefs of Staff Historian. The army's history program also generated an excellent monograph. "Meteorology in the U.S. Army Signal Corps: 1870– 1960," dated August, 1960, and written by one of the Signal Corps historians, Karl Larew.

Only the air force devotes a historian full time to its weather function. Overall, weather unit histories compiled annually or semiannually since 1937 vary from excellent to useless. Command histories (typescript) of the AAF Weather Service for the World War II years, as well as the AWS command histories (1952– 60 and 1970– present), are well written, quite detailed, and superbly documented. Except for World War II and the opening years of Korea and Southeast Asia, subordinate AWS unit histories compiled as a collateral duty were generally colorless administrative chronicles. Although AWS unit histories are generally unclassified, most AWS command histories since 1950 are classified—but all are available at the Air University or at the Office of MAC History.

AWS historians over the years have published special studies and monographs from time to time. Before Fuller became historian for AWS activities, two interesting documents of this type appeared, one on the use of Women Airforce Service Pilots by the AWS during World War II and one on weather training during the same wear. Starting in 1968, Fuller generated the following publications: *AWS in Southeast Asia* (with Maj. Allan B. Milloy, 1968); *AWS and Meteorological Satellites: 1950–1960* (editor of report by Charles W. Dickens and Charles A. Ravenstein, 1973); *Weather and War* (1974); *The Yom Kippur War, 1973: A Case History of AWS Contingency Support* (1975); *Air Weather Service, 1937–1977: An Illustrated Chronology* (1977); and *AWS Support to the U.S. Army: Tet and the Decade After* (1979). In addition, Fuller's editorial assistant, Margaret C. Faulbaum, prepared *AWS in Southeast Asia, 1961–1976: A Pictorial Account* (1979).

For the early days of military meteorology until World War II, one finds authoritative information in annual reports by the secretary of war (whose reports include reports by the army surgeon general and the chief signal officer) and the secretary of the navy. The subsequent annual reports of the secretaries of army, navy, air force, and defense are worth checking but do not contain the detail of the reports before the 1940s. In 1942 Lewis J. Darter, Jr., compiled an informative multilithed monograph, *List of Climatological Records in the National Archives* (released as National Archives' Special List No. 1), which contains invaluable narrative background of material now professionally archived. Before that, the U.S. Weather Bureau published in its Bulletin No. 11 a superb overview of where meteorology stood in 1893, *Report of the International Meteorological Congress* (1894), a meeting that was part of the World's Columbian Exposition in Chicago, Illinois.

The U.S. Department of Commerce's Office of the Federal Coordinator for Meteorological Services and Supporting Research has, since its inception in 1964, published a federal meteorological plan (as well as more specific plans, such as the National Hurricane Operations Plan) each fiscal year, delineating the resources, capabilities, and budgetary hopes of each federal weather service. Another useful snapshot of the capabilities and limitations of existent military weather services may be found in the periodically published, unclassified reports (February, 1980, is the latest) of the Joint Chiefs' Deputy Director for Operations/Environmental Services entitled "Review of Military Weather Services."

Although bulky and voluminous, published testimony from the annual congressional hearings on the proposed military posture (Armed Services Commitees) and on the budget (Appropriations Committees), as well as special congressional investigations, are often invaluable to the military weather historian. For example, testimony during the Vietnam era by admirals, generals, and civilian officials provide excellent information about weather's debilitating effects on military campaigns, weapons, and personnel. Key testimony from those sources is cited in appropriate sections of this book.

Special meteorological studies have also been commissioned from time to time. Thus, the United States Strategic Bombing Survey chartered by Presidents Roosevelt and Truman resulted in, among many other reports, *Weather Factors in Combat Bombardment Operations in the European Theater* (January, 1947), which concluded that target weather forecasts furnished the Eighth Air Force by the 18th Weather Squadron between June, 1943, and April, 1945, verified with an overall accuracy of only 58 percent. Under an Army Signal Corps contract awarded in 1953, Dr. Fred W. Decker and associates at Oregon State College wrote the well-documented *Weather Effects on Army Operations*, which examined the effects of weather on more than 3,000 major army actions in World War II and the Korean conflict. The USAF contractor and think tank, the Research and Development Corporation (RAND) at Santa Monica, California, also prepared many important reports that addressed classified and unclassified meteorological issues. The names of Robert R. Rapp and Ralph E. Huscke appeared on many such RAND reports, for example, Huscke's classified RAND Report R-2100-AF, *The Military Utility of Meteorological Satellites: An Assessment for the Mid-1980s* (1978). However, one of the most useful and prophetic was Stanley M. Greenfield and William W. Kellogg's RAND Report R-365, *Inquiry into the Feasibility of Weather Reconnaissance from a Satellite Vehicle*, which, after appearing in a classified version in April, 1951, was finally declassified in 1960. Of equal interest were findings of the blue-ribbon panel of the Joint Chiefs of Staff under Adm. James H. Holloway, USN (Retired). After critiquing the aborted U.S. raid into central Iran in April, 1980, the panel's unclassified, 78-page "Rescue Mission Report" (August, 1980) spotlighted eleven major issues, of which four were related to weather or weather support.

Other "grey literature" deserves mention. Between January, 1944, and January, 1948, the Aerology Section under the Deputy Chief of Naval Operations (Air) published a series of eighteen booklets under the series titles "Aerology and Naval Warfare," "Aerology and Amphibious Warfare," "Aerology and Naval Operations," and "Aerology—Operational Analysis." These typescript documents cover many critical operations ranging from the Doolittle raid against Japan and the battle of the Coral Sea to Operations Crossroads and Nanook in 1946. Numerous weather charts make such studies particularly valuable.

In 1962 the air force launched Project CHECO (Contemporary Historical Examination of Current Operations) to document and analyze various facets of aerial operations in Southeast Asia. More than 200 CHECO reports resulted. Most are meticulously documented, and many are by historians (for an index, see *Research Guide* to the *Published Project CHECO Reports, 1964–1976*, published in 1976 by the Albert F. Simpson Historical Research Center of the Air University). Most are classified, but these three are mandatory reading for analyzing the weather factor in Vietnam operations: Col. Patrick J. Breitling's *Guided Bomb Operations in SEA: The Weather Dimension*, Feb. 1–Dec. 31, 1972, 1973; Maj. Louis Seig's *Impact of Geography on Air Operations in SEA*, 1970; and Lt. Col. Philip R. Harrison's *Impact of Darkness and Weather on Air Operations in SEA*, 1969.

Between October, 1966, and January, 1973, the 1st Weather Wing of the AWS at Hickam, AFB, Hawaii, also published a classified monthly report, each 20 to 30 pages long, entitled "Weather Evaluation, Southeast Asia Operations." Each contained a synopsis of Southeast Asia's weather for the month, plus summaries of daily weather over North Vietnam, South Vietnam, and Laos. More importantly, through the edition of September, 1969, each contained charts depicting the number of sorties, by aircraft type and service (U.S. Air Force, Navy, Marine Corps, and VNAF), that were canceled or rendered ineffective because of weather over targets in North Vietnam, South Vietnam, and Laos. The only complete set of these reports is apparently in the AWS historian's office at Scott AFB, along with more than 100 end-of-tour reports (mostly unclassified) filed between 1964 and 1973 by key AWS officers and noncommissioned officers following completion of assignments in Southeast Asia.

Index